T5-AMD-032

Forcible Rape

Forcible Rape

The Crime, the Victim, and the Offender

DUNCAN CHAPPELL,
ROBLEY GEIS,
and GILBERT GEIS
EDITORS

Columbia University Press
New York 1977

HV
6561
.F67

Library of Congress Cataloging in Publication Data
Main entry under title:
Forcible rape.
Includes bibliographies and index.
1. Rape—United States. I. Chappell, Duncan.
II. Geis, Robley, 1921– III. Geis, Gilbert.
HV6561.F67 364.1′53 77-3377

Columbia University Press
New York Guildford, Surrey
Copyright © 1977 Columbia University Press
All rights reserved
Printed in the United States of America.

FOR PAT
AND
DICK MYREN

LIBRARY
ALMA COLLEGE
ALMA, MICHIGAN

Contents

Preface

THE editors of this volume have been researching and writing on the subject of forcible rape since the late 1960s. In those seemingly distant days, forcible rape was a crime outside the spotlight of national concern. Funding sources were disinterested in sponsoring research on the topic, and criminal justice agencies myopically focused only on other "street" crimes.

All this has changed. The criminal offense of forcible rape has become, since about 1969, a rallying topic for the women's movement in the United States, transforming what until that development was a subject of parochial criminological and legal concern into one with far-reaching social importance.

Popular focus on forcible rape has brought in its wake increased scholarly attention to the issues surrounding sexual assault. Rape in the 1970s occupies almost the same prominent position in the mass media and the professional journals as racial tension and urban riots did in the past decade. When public concern and scholarly activity coalesce, the time is at hand for basic changes in social policy and social perception.

This book has been produced out of the conviction that social action and scientific inquiry and reflection must go hand in hand. We have gathered together what are, according to our judgment, many of the most important writings on the topic of forcible rape. A significant portion of the material is published here for the first time. Other chapters are republished from sources that, in many cases, are difficult to locate. The range of disciplines and interests covered by the authors is diverse, as is the perspective on forcible rape afforded by the writings. We do not agree with all of the views of our authors (indeed, we now find ourselves in disagreement with things that we ourselves wrote at an earlier time); nor do we necessarily endorse the approach or the conclusions of some of the behavioral science and legal materials. But we find what was done and what is said worth attention, discussion and, if in order, refinement or rebuttal.

The Introduction attempts to place the materials in the volume into a framework that draws a parallel to developments in the feminist movement, the behavioral sciences, and legal reform concerning forcible rape. The Bibliography represents a careful selection of further references from among the very considerable number of writings that have been published on rape.

The focus of this volume is exclusively on heterosexual forcible rape offenses. We did not want to dilute this emphasis with consideration of homosexual rape or of offenses with child victims. It is not that we regard either of these matters as of lesser importance, but only that we find them sufficiently distinctive forms of behavior to merit full-fledged treatment on their own. Homosexual rape occurs almost exclusively within institutions, and the rape or molestation of children usually is achieved not by force but by ingratiation, deceit, promise, and entreaty. These offenses intersect with forcible rape at a number of points, most notably in treatment centers, where the aim is to be of service to all persons who have been hurt or exploited by sexual aggressors. In addition, statutes often find it valuable to cover within comprehensive boundaries the broader range of sexual assaults.

Analyses that focus on the commonalities of these offenses, however, tend to lose track of the special and preeminently important distinctions that mark them.

We would like as editors to express our warm appreciation to the publishers and authors who have granted permission to incorporate material in this volume. We owe a very special debt to John Moore of the Columbia University Press for his gracious support throughout our work. Other persons who have helped us include John Monahan of the University of California, Irvine, who was of inestimable assistance, aiding us in judging the merits of articles, and clarifying conceptual issues. Harriet Spector and Ingrid McCormack of the Battelle Human Affairs Research Center, Seattle; Pat Branovan and Juanita Melgoza of the University of California, Irvine; Howard Bidna; and Lee and Bob Meier have also provided considerable assistance to us during the preparation of this book.

1 Forcible Rape: An Introduction

GILBERT GEIS

"THE struggle to understand and deal with rape is just beginning," Daniel Ben-Horin (1975:115) recently wrote in connection with his portrayal of the antics of members of the Arizona legislature as they debated amendments to the state's statute on sexual assault. The issue for the legislators, as Ben-Horin interpreted their behavior, "was sex, and in the same old terms: women 'own' it, men crave it." It would take some time, he thought, before persons in the United States came to view the crime of forcible rape as an act of violence and invasion directed by members of one sex against those of another.

The Arizona attempt at law reform forged for the moment an odd political alliance, one that often emerges in contemporary campaigns designed to deal with forcible rape. Humanists desire amendments to the law so that rape victims will be treated by the criminal justice system in a more decent and civilized manner. Retributionists join them to press for things such as reduced evidentiary requirements for conviction of rapists because they want to see more criminal offenders declared guilty and imprisoned.

Similar ironies pervade the story of forcible rape as it has been written into national consciousness in recent years. Radical or Marxist writers, for instance, who regard criminal offenders as political victims of capitalism, are at an ideological loss when they confront the issue of forcible rape. Feminists, whose cause the radicals tend to support, are in no mood for romantic notions about rapists as unfortunates, products of deprived economic circumstances. The splintering between the feminist movement and its onetime allies was put in direct terms by Susan Brownmiller, whose *Against Our Will* represents the major feminist statement on rape:

> The divisions between us and the left are going to get wider and wider over these issues. There's a lot of talk going around that radicalism is in decline, things have cooled, gone conservative. But the truth is that all the women have left for Women's Liberation, and they're not there typing and filing and running the mimeograph for Abbie and Jerry (*Time,* March 20, 1972:31).

Some feminist writers who in the past identified in almost stereotypic fashion with liberal causes now find themselves supporting positions that they once would have regarded as troglodytic. Brownmiller, for instance, responds with a biting counterattack to what she presumes will be the outrage of liberals at her insistence that pornography be censored and prostitution excised in order to control rape in the United States. Whose side are we really on, Brownmiller (1975:390) demands to know:

> The case against pornography and the case against the toleration of prostitution are central to the fight against rape, and if it angers a large part of the liberal population to be so informed, then I would question in turn the political understanding of such liberals and their true concern for the rights of women.

Statements like this merge ideological concerns with empirical questions. Does prostitution, for instance, have any impact on the rate of forcible rape? Kinsey (1948:698) thought that there was insufficient evidence to support one side or the other on the issue. (See also Bettelheim, 1974:300.) Since then, Barber (1969) has investigated the rates of forcible rape in Queensland before and after the closing of brothels in that Australian state. He found an average increase of 149 percent for rape and attempted rape for each of the eight years following the ban of brothels—a rate significantly greater than either the rise of 47 percent for convictions for offenses against the person, or 49 percent for convictions against the person by males only. A statistical test indicates that there is about one chance in a thousand that such a difference would be due to chance. Barber hedged suitably (and correctly) in noting that his figures hardly prove that the increase in rapes and attempted rapes in Queensland was a result of the closing of the brothels. But he believes (1969:174) that "the 'prostitution theory' provides a more persuasive answer . . . than do other 'theories' holding current favor." In particular, Barber was taken with the idea that "there is strong evidence to suggest that the type of person who frequents brothels is very similar to the type of person who has been responsible for the increased number of rapes and attempted rapes in Queensland."

Increases in rape rates in the United States, though not as sharp as those in Queensland, appear to be unrelated to the extent of prostitution and to correlate positively with freer heterosexual opportunities, both matters which tease the Australian findings. In addition, Barber's study is not altogether responsive to Brownmiller's fundamental thesis, which is that rape is not so much a function of available sexual outlets as it is a matter deeply rooted in misogynic male attitudes. Prostitution, she believes, even though it may (or may not) be a temporary palliative for rape, inculcates attitudes toward women that foster the rape ethos.

The relationship between rape and prostitution is but one matter in which ideological concerns and empirical information require integration and, ultimately, further investigation and later adjudication. "My purpose in this book," Brownmiller (1975:404) wrote in *Against Our Will*, "has been to give rape its history. Now we must deny it a future." It is toward this end too—to be achieved with justice for victims as well as for real and alleged offenders—that we have compiled the present volume. This Introduction considers in detail two separable, though interrelated aspects of the subject: first, the work of the feminist movement; and, second, behavioral science investigations dealing with forcible rape.

THE FEMINIST CRITIQUE

The National Organization for Women (NOW) came into being in 1966, with its early leadership drawn largely from women who had participated in the President's Conference on the Status of Women, or who had been involved in the civil rights campaigns of the early 1960s (see generally, Huber, 1976; Freeman, 1975). A fundamental focus of feminism has been on equal opportunity and equal pay for women. Drives for child-care centers, guaranteed annual incomes, and the elimination of routine volunteer work as part of the female life assignment spilled over into more generic concerns with the creation of solidarity and self-definition among women.

Early on, women's groups concerned with crime issues focused on prostitution. Susan Brownmiller, for instance, was the prime mover of a meeting sponsored by the New York Radical Feminists on prostitution. But prostitution is surrounded by treacherous ideological currents. An immediately apparent feminist thrust was for equal enforcement of the laws, which would involve arresting men soliciting prostitutes rather than taking only the woman into custody and having her client testify against her in return for a grant of immunity (see Caughey, 1974). A speaker at a feminist symposium noted that the law regarded the prostitute as a "half-person, a menace, and an outcast": "The law appraises her as being steeped in crime. The man receives no punishment, although the prostitute is only filling his desire, doing something there is a desire for" (Willens, 1971:42).

But no sure feeling came to coalesce within the feminist movement about the proper position to take in regard to the prostitute. Most often, she was viewed as a victim of male exploitation. At the same time, though, it was evident that prostitutes rarely welcomed intrusion into their business by feminists. Also, some feminists exalted the role of the prostitute. Ti-Grace Atkinson, regarded as the theoretician of the radical feminists, urged her sisters to support the prostitute as the model of the new, independent woman. "My impression is that the prostitute is the only honest woman left in America," she said. For Atkinson, the general suppression of women was equivalent to forcing them into prostitution. A liberated woman, therefore, would not succumb to male blandishments "for free" but would "up the charges." A marriage contract, Atkinson observed, forces a female to work for life without pay; prostitutes, more honest, charge for their services (Fosburgh, 1970).

With the notable and forceful exception of Kate Millett (1971), the women's movement continued to look about for targets other than prostitution in the area of crime. In 1971, the national NOW conference announced formation of a task force on the "masculine mystique," defined as the male-held conviction that violence was appropriate for the resolution of problems. Rape represented the epitomization of such a tenet. In addition, rape is a crime directed almost exclusively against women. It presents fearsome danger and devastating humiliation to its targets, and such anguish is compounded by inept and prejudicial handling of the offense by the criminal justice system. The rape victim, as Carol Bohmer and Audrey Blumberg (1975) would aptly observe, is "twice traumatized"—once by the offender, then again by the authorities.

Following the symposium she had arranged on prostitution, Susan Brownmiller set up a meeting on rape. She had only half-attentively and sometimes querulously listened to the personal testimony of rape victims at feminist speak-outs. But now she was to locate a cause. Brownmiller (1975:9) expresses the feeling of what became a moment of truth for her in the Personal Statement that introduces her book:

> I proposed a conference. Conferences are not like speak-outs. Conferences require objective information, statistics, research, and study. What will we be able to come up with, I wondered. The conference, which I had proposed out of restlessness and participated in only marginally, as a sort of senior planning consultant, proved to be my mo-

> ment of revelation. There, in a high school auditorium, I finally confronted my own fears, my own past, my own intellectual defenses. Something important and frightening to contemplate had been left out of my education—a way of looking at male-female relations, at sex, at strength, and at power. Never one to acknowledge my vulnerability, I found myself forced by my sisters in feminism to look it squarely in the eye.

Following the conference, Brownmiller began what was to be a four-year hegira toward the completion of *Against Our Will,* the volume that would push the issue of forcible rape into preeminent national prominence. In the interim, before the Brownmiller work appeared, other feminists issued studies, handbooks, tracts, and assorted additional materials about forcible rape.

Griffin and Greer

Two outstanding short statements (neither is mentioned by Brownmiller) are those of Susan Griffin (1971) and Germaine Greer (1973). Griffin's article, reprinted as the next chapter in this volume, was the precursor of the feminist literature on forcible rape. The author, who holds a master's degree in creative writing from San Francisco State University, where she studied under the novelist Kay Boyle, first wrote "Rape: The All-American Crime" for *Scanlan's* magazine. But, with the Griffin article already set in type, *Scanlan's* ceased publication, and it was almost another year before someone suggested that *Ramparts* would be interested in publishing the piece.

Griffin (1976) today believes that two major issues on forcible rape need to be carried beyond the point that she takes them in her article. She thinks that Marxist dogma insisting that rape is the product of capitalism (see, for example, Schwendinger and Schwendinger, 1974) is "nonsense," its error affirmed by the sexual ravaging of the Soviet troops during the World War II and that of the Cuban troops in Angola. "People blame outside forces for things that are within themselves," Griffin maintains. She also believes that we do not yet fully appreciate the total extent to which fears of rape affect the psychology of women.

The strongest criticism against the Griffin material is that by Lynn A. Curtis (1976a), who throws back at Griffin the ringing observation that concludes her article:

> As the symbolic expression of the white male hierarchy, rape is the quintessential act of our civilization, one which, as Valerie Solanis warns, is in danger of "humping itself to death."

What Griffin ignores, Curtis observes, is that a very considerable portion, perhaps more than half, of the rape episodes involve not white males, but rather blacks who, in this crime as in other crimes of violence, such as homicide, are greatly overrepresented among offenders in proportion to their numbers in the population. Griffin's (1976a) answer is ideological. Since whites control the American social system, she says, black rape is merely another derivative of the major sore. This kind of reasoning, however, can deteriorate into reductionism, a system with a facile explanation for everything and, often, for nothing.

Germaine Greer (1970:265) had passingly referred to rape in her classic, *The Female Eunuch:*

> It is a vain delusion that rape is an expression of uncontrollable desire or some kind of compulsive response to an overwhelming attraction. Any girl who has been bashed and raped can tell how ludicrous it is when she pleads for a reason and her assailant replies "Because I love you" or "Because you're so beautiful" or some such rubbish. The act is one of murderous aggression, spawned in self-loathing and enacted upon the hated other. Men do not themselves know the depth of their hatred. It is played upon by inflammatory articles in the magazines designed for morons with virility problems which sell for a high price in transport cafes.

Now, venturing into the pages of just such an outlet, *Playboy,* Greer elaborated on her earlier theme. She attacked the myth that women desire to be raped, arguing that it might just as well (and just as foolishly) be said that "because most men have repressed homosexual or feminine elements in their personalities, they enjoy buggery and humiliation" (Greer, 1973:164). Rape, Greer noted, devastates many women, rendering them "too terrified to leave their house by day or night or so distressed by male nearness that they cannot take a job or get into a crowded train." (See further, Burgess and Holstrom, 1974; Russell, 1975.) Female fear of rape, Greer (1973:82) thought, could best be likened to male fear of castration—an analogy that perhaps falls short because of the relative unlikelihood of castration as compared to rape. An anthropologist by training, Greer drew upon ethnographic sources to present one of the few published statements on the rape of a male by a female, an episode that has not been accorded the notice that it might warrant in feminists' attempts to convey to men the possible sequelae of forcible rape. Bronislaw Malinowski (1929:273–75) portrayed the event in *The Sexual Life of Savages in North-Western Melanesia* though, unlike Greer, he took some pain to indicate that the story might be apocryphal, "a standing myth, backed up by lively interest and a strong belief" (1929:277). Malinowski had only hearsay to go on, and he was strongly warned (and he agreed) not to venture into the region where such practices were said to occur:

> The man is the fair game of the women for all that sexual violence, obscene cruelty, filthy pollution, and rough handling can do to him. Thus first they pull off and tear up his pubic leaf, the protection of his modesty, and, to a native, the symbol of his manly dignity. Then, by masturbatory practices and exhibitionism, they try to produce an erection in their victim and, when their maneuvers have brought about the desired result, one of them squats over him and inserts his penis into her vagina. After the first ejaculation he may be treated in the same manner by another woman. Worse things are to follow. Some of the women will defecate and micturate all over his body, paying special attention to his face, which they pollute as thoroughly as they can. "A man will vomit, and vomit, and vomit," said a sympathetic informant. (Malinowski, 1929:274–75)

Greer also dwells at length on what she labels "petty rape," enunciating a theme later echoed in Medea's and Thompson's (1974:49–55) concern with what they tag as "the little rapes." Petty rape involves things such as the coercion employed by men who have the power to hire and fire women to achieve sex not spontaneously offered them. Petty rape preoccupies Greer, especially the forms in which unwitting women are taken in by spurious, practiced forms of "seduction." Available weapons against such exploitation, she maintains, might be no more than female ridicule and boycott, but such weapons could prove powerful. "Next time I write an article like this," Greer (1973:228) observes, "I'll tell you all the names."

Three Feminist Volumes

A considerable number of books followed in the wake of the essays by Griffin and Greer. A sampling of three of these major efforts conveys a sense of motifs and particular emphases; otherwise, there is a sameness about the general books regarding forcible rape that renders intensive review redundant.

The poorest of the three is that by Andra Medea and Kathleen Thompson (1974). The authors tend to push their information, which often can speak for itself with power and persuasion, into shrillness. Given their subject, an awkward analogy appears early in the volume: "Rape is not a price we must pay for our freedom, any more than lynching is the price blacks have to pay for theirs" (1974:5). The authors adopt a position similar to the one that was to bring Brownmiller criticism from many of her reviewers: that any man is a potential rapist. The difficulty inheres in a violation of fundamental rules of fairness and logic, rules which insist that a person should not be accused of meretricious actions only on the basis of the fact that he possesses the potentiality for engaging in them. Rapists, similar to other kinds of persons who perform distinctive acts, tend to be distinctive kinds of persons. That prediction is highly inexact provides no rationale for confusing potentiality with likelihood of performance. It is known, for example, that forcible rape rates vary dramatically with age. Medea and Thompson's sweeping generalization is not far different from suggesting that the woman next door is a potential perpetrator of infanticide because other women have killed their children and all mothers are capable of doing so. Medea and Thompson (1974:29) express the matter in these words:

> Most men in our country are potential rapists. But, you might ask, doesn't something have to snap in a man, doesn't something have to go dreadfully wrong with his mind for him to become a rapist? Isn't the rapist really sick, a sexual deviant whose actions are universally

condemned by other men and who rapes in spite of all the best efforts of society to stop him? Perhaps the potential for rape lies in all men in our society, but, you ask yourself, isn't it a potential that must be aggravated and exaggerated to the point of sickness before a man actually rapes. If you believe that, you are in for a shock. The rapist is the man next door.

The Medea-Thompson volume offers numerous suggestions on self-defense tactics for women trying to repel a rape attack. It is stressed that these measures should not be employed unless the woman knows that she can carry through. "Again and again," Medea and Thompson (1974:75) note, "women have explained to us that they didn't use available weapons because they were afraid to hurt [the rapist]." Considerable emphasis is placed on the fact that no defense technique is a guarantee; each represents a calculated risk.

There is a matter taken up briefly in the book that is not addressed elsewhere in the literature on rape—the victim's possible sexual response to the rape event. Most writers, understandably, find it essential to put to eternal rest the destructive and condescending clichés about women yearning to be raped. They also take inordinate care to emphasize the violent component of rape in contrast to any sexual ingredients. But, as in the instance of the Melanesian man (doubtfully) raped by the women in the vignette offered by Malinowski, Medea and Thompson (1974:105) suggest that there can be erotic female response to forcible rape:

> There are women who feel guilty because they became sexually aroused during the rape, or because they climaxed. . . . The excitement of terror can trigger a reaction so similar to sexual arousal that your body cannot distinguish between them. It's the same sort of misdirection as when children get excited and wet their pants. The body isn't always perfectly aligned with the mind.

The experience of researchers appears to contradict the Medea-Thompson observation. Judith V. Becker (1976), an assistant professor of psychology and psychiatry at the University of Tennessee Medical School, Memphis, who is investigating the nature of erotic response to rape attacks, reports that among fifty victims she interviewed none had experienced an orgasm. One victim,

Becker notes, was put into a state of sexual "confusion" by a rapist who held a gun at her head, but at the same time behaved in an extremely gentle manner and tenderly massaged her body with handcream. The research team of Ann Burgess and Lynda Holmstrom (1976), working at Boston City Hospital, report that none of the ninety-two victims they asked noted any sexual arousal. Burgess and Holmstrom suspect that fear and eroticism may be contradictory impulses. The general matter, as raised by Medea and Thompson, is significant primarily as a reflection of the need for accurate data, particularly when a book such as theirs is used as a background source for counseling information for rape victims in distress.

Sexual Assault: Confronting Rape in America (1976), by Nancy Gager and Cathleen Schurr, is an eclectic offering of fact, polemics, and advice. Unlike Brownmiller, the authors concentrate on dealing largely with contemporary issues, rather than on constructing a cohesive foundation for a particular viewpoint. There are odd pieces of information about the modus operandi of rapists, data that step gingerly in the interstices between the creation of incapacitating fear associated with the belief that one is always, everywhere at risk as a potential rape victim, and the acquisition of useful information that will serve to more adequately protect the rape victim. Rapists, the reader is informed, sometimes prepare for their victims in advance, removing inside car door handles and hiding male accomplices on the rear floor. Today's Good Samaritan, if she is female, is portrayed as "a potential rape victim" (1976:23), a point illustrated by the story of a woman who responded to a request for help on the highway and was raped by the man to whom she had proferred aid. The position of the authors (1976:280) on the underlying causes of rape is put forward near the end of the volume when they address matters of amelioration:

> Any solution to rape is complex and must involve a multifaceted approach. Basic to all reforms is a change in attitudes toward the female half of the population and in the ways in which men, ordinary citizens as well as rapists, intimidate and oppress women. Rape is not an isolated phenomenon of "sick" males, but rather an inevitable part of the

> entire social matrix which denigrates women—psychologically, physically, economically, and politically—and which still tends to regard females as male "property."

The third volume, *The Politics of Rape* (1975) by Diana E. H. Russell, a sociologist at Mills College, Oakland, California, contains interviews with rape victims, which are used by the author as a basis for generalizations about forcible rape.

Russell (1975:14) adopts the somewhat uncommon view that feminism may produce an increase in the amount of forcible rape, at least temporarily:

> There is some male backlash caused by women's growing desire to be more independent of men. This painful period of transition is a time of tremendous misunderstanding and hostility between the sexes. Rape is the way some men express their hostility to women. More threatened male egos may mean more rapes. In the short run, the more women who break out of traditional female roles and assert themselves in new ways, the more threatened male egos are.

As do virtually all writers, Russell (1975:86) stresses the violent components of forcible rape as contrasted to any sexual elements. She suggests that the insistence of some rapists on anal intercourse "may come from a need to break in a new kind of virgin." Since women often find the act particularly abhorrent and painful, it also provides the rapist with a means of expressing his contempt and hostility in regard to the victim. Russell (1975:104) captures in a quotation the nature of the response of many rape victims to their situation:

> "But the most frightening thing—as, I'd never been in a position before where it was made so clear to me that I was totally powerless, physically anyway, in the presence of another person who was going to use me. Just being put in that helpless position was really frightening. The act of rape was an enforcement of his power against my will."

To deal with rape offenders, Russell (1975:220) takes a hard line. She wavers about castration, finding it "rather extreme," but suggests that rapists should have the option of being castrated in order to gain their freedom from prison. "Many women are tired of the view that castration is a deadly sin, whereas a blind eye is turned against rape." The alternative, for Russell, is that "rapists should be indefinitely confined until there is a sound basis for believing that they will no longer be a danger to women or girls." For many persons (see, for example, Monahan, 1976), such an approach is beset with civil liberties hazards, since the art of predicting future behavior is, at best, primitive. A major difficulty resides in overprediction, so that persons (false positives) who in truth will not represent a risk are confined for unconscionably long periods on the basis of an inaccurate estimate of their dangerousness.

Russell (1975:274) offers the following ideas toward a fundamental solution of the problem of forcible rape:

> If males and females were to be liberated from their sex roles, the rape situation would change dramatically. I believe that male sexuality would become more like female sexuality, in that males would value sex within relationships more than sex for its own sake, and would respond to women more as people than as sexual objects. And female sexuality would become more similar to male sexuality, in so far as women would become more in touch with their sexual needs and less apt to obscure the real person and the true nature of the relationship with romantic fantasies. In short, I believe sex-role liberation would result in a mix of the male sexual and the female romantic elements in both males and females, so that there would no longer be a war between them. But we have a long, long way to go. And rape will be with us as long as these contradictions exist.

Brownmiller on Rape

Susan Brownmiller's *Against Our Will: Men, Women and Rape,* the major feminist statement to date on the crime of forcible rape, is something of a tour de force, particularly in regard to its skilled marshaling of historical materials to support its unswerving thesis—that "rape is the quintessential act by which a male demonstrates to a female that she is conquered—vanquished—by his superior strength and power" (1975:49). Later, Brownmiller (1975:208–9) expands on the theme in tougher language:

> Rape is a dull, blunt, ugly act committed by punk kids, their cousins and older brothers, not by charming, witty, unscrupulous, heroic, sensual rakes, or by timid souls deprived of a "normal" sexual outlet, or by *super-menschen* possessed of uncontrollable lust. And yet, on the

shoulders of these unthinking, predictable, insensitive, violence-prone young men there rests an age-old burden that amounts to an historic mission: the perpetuation of male domination over women by force.

Responses to rape, Brownmiller insists, can best be understood in terms of masculine views that women "belong" to them. Rapists are punished, if at all, because they have trespassed upon another man's possession—be he the father, husband, or another male with declared vested interests in the sexual integrity of the woman whom he raped.

In 1968, well before *Against Our Will* was planned, Brownmiller (1968), had reported in *Esquire* on the infamous Giles-Johnson case of alleged rape (see generally, Smith and Giles, 1975). Today Brownmiller is embarrassed by her own article (1975:9, 211–12); it is worth examining primarily to see how perspectives have shifted. The complainant in the Giles-Johnson case is called a prosecutrix, a term now regarded as abhorrent by feminists. Much of the Brownmiller article in *Esquire* deals with the defense's failure to bring out that the girl who claimed to have been raped apparently had a history of sexual promiscuity, and that she had been before the juvenile court three months prior to the alleged rape on a charge of being "beyond parental control." Earlier, the sixteen-year-old had been hospitalized in a psychiatric facility. At that time, her parents insisted that the police charge two other men with rape, but the girl had told officers that she would not agree to press the action, and the case was marked "unfounded."

A report with information such as this was conveyed to members of the jury that had convicted the Giles brothers and Joseph Johnson, a conviction which saw the imposition of a death sentence. Five of the eight jurors who read the report expressed to the governor their new-found reservations about their original decision. "All of the information which we didn't know at the trial," one juror wrote, "raised doubts in my mind that she was really raped." Ultimately, the three black youths were set free. The subtitle of the Brownmiller article offers the reader three choices: "It was (a) three Negroes raping a white girl; (b) two Negroes raping a white girl, or, (c) one white girl seducing three Negroes." The article leaves no doubt that explanation (c) is the most persuasive.

Perhaps it was her encounter with the Giles-Johnson case that kept Brownmiller so heavily focused on historic rather than contemporary materials. Her book provides an excellent review of the role of rape in wartime, a comprehensive discussion of rape in early America, and a probing analysis of the racial rules regarding rape in the antebellum South. The material is thorough and painstakingly collated. While it falls short (to our minds) of adequately supporting the sweeping generalizations toward which its material is directed, the source information offers vivid documentation of the cruelty and indifference with which forcible rape has been viewed historically. Occasionally, however, Brownmiller's (1975: 15) analysis gets out of control. Perhaps the best example appears in the quotation below, the last line of which sparked a flurry of rebuttal:

> Man's discovery that his genitalia could serve as a weapon to generate fear must rank as one of the most important discoveries of prehistoric times, along with the use of fire and the first crude stone axe. From prehistoric times to the present, I believe, rape has played a critical function. It is nothing more or less than a conscious process of intimidation by which *all* men keep *all* women in a state of fear (italics in original).

The dubious, off-the-cuff dictum about prehistoric times is the kind of polemical excess that brings under suspicion other of Brownmiller's opinions. Edmund Fuller (1975), in a generally sympathetic review in the *Wall Street Journal,* maintained that *Against Our Will* was "uneven," and "marred by imbalances, distortions, and convenient omissions." His major quarrel was with what he found to be a kind of "extrapolation that marks the fanatic." Brownmiller's logic about rape, Fuller maintained, at times seemed to him to be "as grotesquely exaggerated as to say that because some men murder, it keeps all mankind in a constant state of intimidation and that the murderer is the tacit agent of all those who slay." Fuller goes on in the same vein:

> It is offensive and unwarranted to assert that the rapist is the tacit agent of all men, doing their dirty work for them. It seriously weakens

> her argument; it is divisively inflammatory language at a time when deep issues between men and women need to be approached openly, honestly, and without rancor on either side—a state of mind of which the human race always fall short in the best of circumstances.

Christopher Lehmann-Haupt (1975), reviewing Brownmiller's book in the *New York Times* was, like Fuller, put off by the thematic phrase—"intimidation by which *all* men keep *all* women in a state of fear"—but was grudgingly drawn to consider that it might be appropriate, at least as a metaphor. For Lehmann-Haupt, there was one particularly nagging, unanswered question: "Raw power is the name of the masculine game, according to Miss Brownmiller," he wrote, "but why are women such a threat to that power?" Jane Wilson's (1975) review in the *Los Angeles Times* found the "central sexual conspiracy theory . . . generally fatuous intellectually," while Lionel Tiger (1976), a professor of anthropology at Rutgers University, several of whose terms, such as "male bonding," had been adopted by Brownmiller, was both critical and a bit condescending. "The idea is splendid, the moral urgency is commendable, the practical discussion of policy alternatives is necessary," Tiger wrote. But he thought that the book was "deeply scarred by dreadful and simply wrong anthropology, not to mention highly questionable assumptions about human prehistory, psychology, and the usefulness of literary materials as metaphors for empirical life." Tiger thought that the "immense clatter" that *Against Our Will* had received was a function of critics having succumbed to "formal numbness just so long as [books they review] are bristling with feminine energy and abet the cause of sociosexual change." The basis for Tiger's position, however, seems precarious. Some reviews of Brownmiller were uncritically effusive, but most reviews, as did his, praised the spadework, paid tribute to the importance of the cause, and quarreled with the book's major thesis. The only direct male retaliation was that visited by Lynn A. Curtis (1976b), who pointed out that *Against Our Will* was a special beneficiary of extremely energetic promotion "by the same male power brokers . . . who help perpetuate the inequities of sex and race and class in American society." Curtis thought that the book was being "oversold," and that the trade-off of catering to the profit motives of Madison Avenue males in order to convey a feminist message of indisputable importance was ironic.

Putting aside for the moment Tiger's objection to literary materials as sensors of social moods, mention might be made of what Edmund Fuller (1975) called the "convenient omissions" in the Brownmiller book. A case in point is Brownmiller's failure to note several highly sympathetic portrayals by male writers of the situation of the rape victim in her review of literary sources expressing male attitudes. One of the present editors had chronicled a number of fictional treatments of rape in a paper, cited by Brownmiller, which was presented in 1967 at the annual meeting of the American Sociological Association in San Francisco. Menachem Amir, an important source for Brownmiller, later employed the same material as background in *Patterns in Forcible Rape.* But while Brownmiller focuses on the chauvinistic emphases in the work of John Updike, one of the writers mentioned in our paper, she passes by works such as those by Ernest Hemingway and Nelson Algren (though she uses material from Hubert Selby, perhaps because it portrays rapist brutality at its worst). The instance of Maria, Hemingway's (1940:28) heroine in *For Whom the Bell Tolls,* is perhaps the best-known example of compassionate male literary treatment of a rape victim. "When we picked the girl up . . . she was very strange," one of the Loyalist fighters says. "She would not speak and she cried all the time and if any one touched her she would shiver like a wet dog." Nelson Algren (1941:56) portrayed the harrowing experiences of a girl raped by a streetgang in Chicago. For male writers such as these, the brutal, indifferent sadism of the gang attacking a lone female appears to represent the worst form of degeneracy.

Nonetheless, criticisms notwithstanding, Susan Brownmiller's *Against Our Will* stands as a landmark statement on the issue of forcible rape. The particular strength of *Against Our Will* lies in its historical documentation rather than in its analysis of contemporary conditions. Rather than any failing of the author, this may reflect the lack of adequate information in law and social science, for Brownmiller relies almost exclusively on secondary sources. We turn now to an assessment of the accuracy of such a possibility by reviewing law and social science materials as they deal with forcible rape.

SOCIAL SCIENCE AND RAPE

Early behavioral science work on forcible rape was confined, for the most part, to psychiatric theorizing, with clinical experience most often providing the data pool. A single rapist (see, for example, Wille, 1961) or a few victims offered fuel for far-ranging speculation about the wellsprings of the act and/or the victim's response to it. Bizarre cases and highly imaginative ideas were accorded prominent attention. Note, for instance, Devereux' (1957) "The Awarding of the Penis as Compensation for Rape: A Demonstration of the Clinical Relevance of the Psycho-Analytical Study of Cultural Data." The author, an analyst, makes much of the legendary myth of Kainis, who was raped by Poseidon and then told that any request she made would be granted. Kainis asked to be made into a man. Devereux (1957:398) interprets the myth to be justification for expansion of the psychoanalytical dogma that women may in fantasy "acquire" a penis through intercourse. Now, he observes, we also know that "a woman may [again in fantasy] acquire a penis to compensate her for having been raped, deflowered, and penetrated by a father figure; three acts which easily arouse anxiety."

In the 1960s, as Susan Brownmiller (1975:179) observes, leadership in the field of study dealing with sex offenses passed from the psychiatrists to the sociologists.* Brownmiller feels constrained to add, "And a good thing it was." That the sociologists have carried the study of forcible rape into more important realms than their predecessors is undoubted; though, at least to date, their work has neither been as extensive nor as incisive as Brownmiller's enthusiasm might suggest.

* Brownmiller (1975:179) actually says "leadership in the field of criminology." But criminology always has been concentrated in the field of sociology in the United States. It was not until the 1960s, that sociological criminologists began to do much work in the area of sex offenses and sex offenders.

The landmark sociological effort is Menachem Amir's *Patterns in Forcible Rape* (1971). Amir analyzed police reports in the city of Philadelphia for two years—1958 and 1960—and put together an elaborate set of cross-tabulations of the components of the offenses described. His study involved 1,292 offenders, of whom 845 were apprehended, and included 370 single rapes, 105 pair rapes, and 171 group rapes. Amir's (1971:xx) approach is phenomenological, aimed at "uncovering . . . recurring patterns in which particular groups of people are found to commit a particular type of crime in particular types of circumstances." Matters such as the age of offender and victim, the presence of alcohol, the ingredients and site of the offense, and a variety of other characteristics of the act and the participants are examined. In his study, Amir established categories for scrutiny that often are employed in replicative inquiries. In this volume, for instance, chapter 11, which compares Boston and Los Angeles rape statistics, and chapter 12, which details the characteristics of forcible rape in New York City, both depend upon Amir's pioneering book for structuring material and for comparative analysis.

Amir is an Israeli who now serves as director of criminological research at Hebrew University in Jerusalem. *Patterns* began as his doctoral dissertation at the University of Pennsylvania, and much of its format can best be understood by appreciating that it is carefully modeled on the structure of Marvin E. Wolfgang's *Patterns of Criminal Homicide* (1958), also the product of a doctoral dissertation.* Wolfgang's work had been a seminal contribution to criminology. The dissertation work of both Wolfgang and Amir was directed by Thorsten Sellin, a doyen of American criminology.

Amir's work evoked considerable criticism when it was reviewed. Critics' irritation with aspects of the methodology was compounded by editing and proofreading errors. At least forty spelling and typographical mistakes appear in the bibliography, figures in tables are transposed, and columns fail to add to the

* I recall asking Amir, well before his book was published, whether it would include interviews with victims of rape. "No," Amir said. "Why not?" I asked. "Well," Amir answered, with a wry grin, "Marvin didn't interview victims in his study."

sums reported. John Gagnon (1972:121) points out that one sentence, quoting another source, says in its entirety: "First offenders commit most sex crimes . . . usually for other than sex offenses." Gagnon was compelled to note that "the meaning of this must escape all but the most prescient."

There are more serious problems with Amir's work, too (Gagnon, 1972; Reiss, 1974). He fails to warn readers that police data must be handled with consummate caution. He notes that some police records were missing for the years he investigated, and he does not include episodes that were "unfounded," though it is incontrovertible that many cases thrown out by the police are actual instances of criminal rape, "unfounded" because the officers are prejudiced against the victim (or for the offender) or, probably more likely, because they do not believe a conviction or guilty plea will be forthcoming if the offender is apprehended. Amir offers no clue as to the number of cases dropped from his study cohort. Nonetheless, most reviewers were not basically negative. Amir's book was called "a major and solid contribution" by Sagarin (1972:203–4), while Gagnon (1972:70) thought the volume at least "a serious attempt to learn something new about rape." If Amir were chastened by criticisms that accompanied the praise, he could take solace from Gagnon's (1972:69) comments on another volume, *Rape Offenders and Their Victims* by John M. MacDonald, a Denver psychiatrist, reviewed at the same time:

> In addition to its lack of scientific utility, the volume is tasteless . . . in its attempts at humor. The story of a woman who is raped while circulating a petition is given comic relief by noting that the records did not show whether or not the offender signed her petition. . . . In large measure the author reinforces . . . misconceptions about rape, feeds societal fantasies through his handling of case materials, and generally obscures and distorts any understanding of sex offense behavior.

Perhaps the most controversial element in Amir's work is his adoption of Wolfgang's concept of victim-precipitation. Wolfgang (1958) had employed the term with telling analytical power in his investigation of homicide, in which he was able to report that on the basis of background material offenders often were indistinguishable from victims. In 44 percent of the killings, both persons had been drinking prior to the commission of the offense; 64 percent of the offenders and 47 percent of the victims had previous arrest records. Of the offenders with previous arrests, almost half had been arrested for aggravated assault, as had a large percentage of the victims. The lethal encounter was as often initiated by the victim as it was by the offender.

Rape victims, however, rarely aggress against the offender prior to the rape encounter, and it is only through defining rape as a sexual event with real, covert, or presumed overtures on the part of both parties that Amir was able to make headway with the idea of "victim-precipitation." Things might have been better had he chosen another term, perhaps something such as "victim vulnerability," to rate the actions and characteristics of the victim on a scale calibrated to the statistical likelihood that she might be raped. Hitchhiking, by such a standard, would be a highly vulnerable activity. In this volume we have included a study Amir coauthored on hitchhiking and rape, which elucidates his concept.

Brownmiller (1975:353) treats the idea of victim-precipitation in forcible rape with skill and perceptiveness, and her paraphrase and critique makes it look a good deal less invidious than it did in its original enunciation by Amir:

> Victim precipitation is a new concept in criminology. It does not hold the victim responsible, but it seeks to define contributory behavior. Victim precipitation says, in effect, an unlawful act has been committed but had the victim behaved in a different fashion, the crime in question *might have been avoided.* Part a priori guesswork and part armchair-detective fun and games, the study of victim precipitation is the least exact of the sociological methods, for it rests in the final analysis on a set of arbitrary standards.

Other commentaries on victim-precipitation in regard to forcible rape have been less amiable. Kurt Weis and Sandra S. Borges (1973) find a strong tendency in Amir toward what has been labeled by William Ryan (1974) as "blaming the victim." * Weis and

* Ryan (1974:3) offers a pointed illustration of how "blaming the victim" works: "Twenty years ago, Zero Mostel used to do a sketch in which he impersonated a Dixiecrat senator conducting an investigation of the origins of World War II. At the climax of the sketch, the senator boomed out, in an excruciating mixture of triumph and suspicion, 'What was Pearl Harbor *doing* in the Pacific?' "

Borges note that the assumption that a rape victim may be "responsible" for what happened to her, a widely held attitude in American society, places a heavy burden of guilt and self-doubt on the victim, often making recovery from the psychic trauma of the offense more difficult. Weis and Borges made a telling point with their observation that the concept of victim-precipitation is congruent with the existence of justifiable homicide, the legal category that includes events such as killing in self-defense. But the idea of something like justifiable rape, they point out, is clearly alien to the law, however much it may enter into folklore. All told, Weis and Borges (1973:112) find the concept of victim-precipitation to be "the personification and embodiment of the rape mythology cleverly stated in academic-scientific terms."

Patterns in Forcible Rape, much as Brownmiller's landmark effort, has serious flaws. Some are the result of the constraints under which the work was carried out; others are endemic to virtually any ground-breaking effort; and others are simply anachronisms, functions of the fact that the research was conducted before the feminist surge into the area of forcible rape, and therefore was not informed by lately emergent insights and efforts.

Matters Needing Exploration

Since Amir's work, there has been a notable increase in the amount of social science research on forcible rape, though a large number of important issues continue to be unaddressed. A particularly promising development has been the creation of the National Center for the Prevention and Control of Rape within the National Institute of Mental Health (Cimons, 1974). The center was the product of intensive lobbying by feminist groups (see Largen, 1976). It will serve as an information clearinghouse and also will allocate research and action funds for community efforts and scholarly investigations dealing with sexual assault. The new center will have to handle the delicate mission of balancing the strong desire of many of its initial supporters for money for action programs against the demand for basic and, to a lesser extent, applied research within the National Institute of Mental Health.

Seasonal Rape Rates. Dispute still exists in regard to so seemingly simple a question as the seasonal correlates of forcible rape. Early research seemed to have established beyond equivocation that forcible rape and warm weather were positively related. Havelock Ellis (1892) noted that in France, rape and "other offenses against modesty are most numerous in May, June, and July." Gustav Aschaffenburg (1913) found that sexual offenses in Germany began to increase in March and April, reached a maximum in June or July, and fell to a minimum in winter. So pervasive was the idea of outbreaks of aggression in hot weather that the novelist, Anatole France, wrote wryly that the French people never revolt in the winter: "All the great revolutionary days are in July, August, and September," France observed. "When it rains they go home, taking their flags with them. They will die for an idea, but they won't catch cold for it."

Such entrenched wisdom is challenged in this volume, however, when Chappell and Singer report that forcible rape in New York City reaches its numerical peak during the winter months. They speculate that the character of the city, its subways and apartment buildings, is probably related to this unusual finding. More generally, of course, the question of what might be the relationship of weather and sexual aggression remains largely unattended. Spring fever is known to be produced in part because the body is adjusting from cold to warm weather, but how much of the feeling is psychological and how much physical is moot. Humidity and heat overtax the 2,000-odd sweat glands in the body, upset metabolism, and cause the heart to work harder, sometimes leading to irritability. Rape rates might rise under such circumstances; but the matter needs much closer scrutiny.

General Correlates of Reported Rape. There is also a need for detailed analyses of published information on forcible rape, though such work must always be undertaken with a clear understanding of the limitations of the source materials. However much (and deservedly) maligned the *Uniform Crime Reports* are, they offer a continuing inventory for the nation of the amount of forcible rape reported to law enforcement officials. Dramatic changes in *UCR* figures probably represent real changes in criminal activity, at least until the past few years when the fraction of cases being reported seems to have increased significantly.

One recent study (Bidna et al., 1976) examined *UCR* materials in regard to six demographic variables, including items such as median family income in the jurisdiction and percentage of the population that is white; two crime variables, rate of aggravated assault and rate of other serious crimes in addition to rape; and five weather variables, including total inches of snow and average annual temperature. The study concluded that these last items accounted for only 26 percent of the variance in reported *UCR* rape rates. Crime and assault rates in a jurisdiction accounted for 53 percent of the variance, a very high relationship, to which inclusion of the demographic items and the other crime variables added only an additional 3 percent. In short, the analysis suggested that, of the things studied, the rate of assault in a jurisdiction was most closely associated with its rate of rape, though it also demonstrated that randomness and/or variables not measured are more powerful influences than those items considered. It is also possible, the authors noted, that both assault and rape rates are artifactual products of similar idiosyncratic law enforcement reporting methods.

Victim-Related Research. A particularly promising development in forcible rape research has been the combination of victim services and research inquiry. Such work is responsive to growing complaints by research subjects that they are used only for others' gain. Ann W. Burgess and Lynda L. Holmstrom (1974) entered into rape research as a part of a program designed to offer crisis and long-term counseling to victims who came to the emergency room at the Boston City Hospital. Burgess is a psychiatric nurse and Holmstrom a sociologist. Both would report to the hospital at any time, day or night, that a rape victim was admitted.

Burgess' and Holmstrom's description of what they call the "rape trauma syndrome" is included in this volume. They also have begun to delineate different forms of rape, distinguishing between "blitz" rapes (sudden attacks) and "confidence" rapes (episodes in which the assailant works his way into the confidence of the victim prior to the attack). They suggest that the response of a victim to rape tends to be related to her developmental point, that is, her age and life condition. They report that it is not guilt or shame that dominate the feelings of rape victims, but rather fear—fear of physical injury, mutilation, and death. That was true, they note, for almost all of the women.

Second, they point out that since the rape victim had recently been forced to do something without her consent, the most insensitive postrape procedures were those that took a coercive turn. Burgess and Holmstrom (1974) state that rape victims hold a profound fear that their assailant will return again. Often, they have been told by the rapist that he will injure them, their children, or other members of their family if they report the event to the police. As yet, there are no reliable statistics on the likelihood of such later retaliation, though, of course, one incident—or the possibility of such an incident—could be enough to make anyone wary.

Work such as that by Burgess and Holmstrom could prove particularly useful in responding to the important question of the long-term consequences of victimization by forcible rape. For one thing, the people they deal with include many who do not file charges with the police, which extends their sample beyond usual boundaries. Longitudinal work is essential to determine if findings of earlier studies, which deal with victims of childhood sexual violations, hold true in regard to adult rape victims. All such studies report minimal or no damage from the childhood experience.

Augusta Rasmussen (1934) examined 54 children who had sexual experiences with adult males between their ninth and thirteenth birthdays and reported that after a lapse of twenty years, 46 of them were none the worse for the experience. Lauretta Bender and Abram Blau (1937) concluded that the 11 girls and 5 boys in their sample who had been involved in sex behavior with adults showed remarkably little evidence of "fear, anxiety, guilt, or psychic trauma"; in fact, the authors found the children to have unusually attractive and charming personalities.

John H. Gagnon (1965), using materials from the original Kinsey interviews, scrutinized the records of 333 women who had reported sexual experience with an adult before the age of thirteen. Only 6 percent recalled that there had been a police report of the incident. After reviewing the women's subsequent life histories, Gagnon concluded that 5 percent of the 333 women had adult lives that could be regarded as severely damaged, for whatever reason, and that of these, only 3 women related their later situation to their early sexual experience.

The studies in the 1930s by Rasmussen and Bender and Blau can be criticized on the basis of their small and unrepresentative samples; that of Gagnon, while more comprehensive, is a secondary analysis of materials not gathered to respond to the research issue that Gagnon addressed and, therefore, at times is not satisfactorily attuned to the full range of issues related to possible harmful consequences of the childhood sexual experience. There may well be, in addition, different patterns of lasting effect attendent upon forcible rape of an adult than those found as a result of the sexual ingratiation usually employed by an older person with a child or adolescent.

The Rapist. Few studies have probed into the ideational world of the rapist. The work by Cohen and his colleagues, which appears in this volume, is the most advanced step toward a typology of rape offenders though, like an earlier study by Gebhard and his colleagues (1965), it relies exclusively on incarcerated offenders. Such persons represent a very small percentage of the total number of rapists, though they may be a better-than-average sample of rapists who inflicted severe injury on their victims.

A California study (Fisher and Rivlin, 1971) that employed standard psychological measures to study rapists found that, compared with "normal" males, they tend to be less aggressive, less independent and self-motivated, less self-assured, and less dominant. The rapists showed a greater degree of "heterosexual need" (no definition is afforded for this curious term), and a higher degree of introspection. Their findings, Fisher and Rivlin (1971:183) say, are "consonant with the theory that the act of rape is an expression of hostility by a male who feels weak, inadequate, and dependent."

This conclusion echoes a dominant theme in the feminist literature. Jean MacKellar (1975:139) has commented on the rapist's insecurity: "The man who rapes does so because he lacks a better means for making the point, 'I am a man,' " while Pauline Bart (1975:40) has stressed the anger in rape: "Psychiatrists say a gun is a substitute phallus. . . . I find the reverse to be true. When it comes to rape, a phallus is a substitute gun. Rape is a power trip, not a passion trip. The rapist is more likely to rape in cold blood, with contempt and righteousness, than with passion."

Another California study (Chappell and James, 1976), based on interviews with offenders held at the Atascadero State Hospital under the state's Mentally Disordered Sex Offender Act, probed into the manner in which rapists perceive their victims. Asked to describe the kinds of victims they "prefer," the respondents portrayed the "American dream ideal"—a nice, friendly, young, pretty, middle-class, white female. Checks were not made regarding the actual targets but, on the basis of inventories of victim characteristics, it is likely that the offenders raped in a more indiscriminant manner than their responses would indicate. A key element in the contact situation, from the rapist's perspective, was whether the woman was alone. Ninety-six percent of the Atascadero sample of 100 rape offenders said that they always checked to see if their intended prey was by herself.

A considerable majority indicated that they wanted passive acquiescence on the part of the victim once they had made their intent known. Seventy-eight percent said they desired the victim "to give up and agree to do anything." The remainder of the group said they preferred a women to plead (12 percent), to scream (6 percent), or to tell them off (4 percent). The men were asked: "How does a victim make you angry?" The largest number of responses (15 percent) indicated that negative references to masculinity most angered them. There were also references to threats to call the police (8 percent), threatened physical harm (6 percent), and sympathetic talking (5 percent).

The authors note that the "advice" proferred by these incarcerated rapists to potential victims duplicates that typically offered by police agencies. Women were warned not to go out alone by 32 percent of the respondents; not to hitchhike (36 percent); to learn self-defense (16 percent); to buy a dog (8 percent); to carry weapons (6 percent); to dress conservatively (6 percent); and not to drink alone (2 percent). Typical statements by the Atascadero rapists, falling most certainly into the "blaming the victim" area, are the following:

> I believe that women who want to be fashionable in some of the styles that are sexually stimulating to men should try to realize some of the consequences of wearing some of these styles before they wear them. . . . Men are going to look, quite naturally, but all men aren't the same. Some of them are going to make more advancements—more aggressive advancements than others in certain situations. If a woman just happens to be weak and not realize what it means, then she's in trouble. That's just the way it is.
>
> Once again, I would say again, by body language—or unconsciously they flirt—sometimes the way they dress—their minds say one thing—their bodies say another—or some come on with their seduction-type overall tone—that says one thing but could possibly mean something else. Or they put themselves in the position of being alone.

The behavior of rapists, like that of many criminal offenders, can probably be partially understood in terms of the idea of relative deprivation. The term is defined by Ted Robert Gurr (1972: 133) as the "perception of discrepancies between the goals of human action and the prospects of attaining these goals." The qualifying term, "perception of," is particularly important in the definition.

For the rapist, there is no implication that he *actually* lacks something, either in the psychic or sexual realm, but rather that on the basis of external and internal stimuli, he has come to believe that he must do something in order to achieve something that he must have. What he desires can be real or symbolic. For most property and white-collar crimes, for instance, the direct motivation seems to be a desire to obtain money, with the money representing a testament of self-worth and self-importance, as well as a vehicle for the acquisition of other valued items.

In rape, the dictates of the masculine role, as these are introjected, command that in certain situations some men must aggress against women in a manner that corresponds to the legally defined criminal offense of forcible rape. The person committing the rape is unwilling or unable to seek his goal in other ways. The goal itself appears to be the demonstration to oneself (and parenthetically to the victim) that the perpetrator is a person to be feared and, therefore, a person to be respected—the two are often joined in our society.

That outcome can be achieved by acts such as robbery or threats of bodily harm, as well as by legal acts. But methods such as robbery lack the dramatic imposition of will and demonstration of power that comes from making another person do things that you insist be done, particularly things that they particularly do not want to do. Doris Lessing (1971:53), for instance, writing of another form of criminal behavior, strikingly appreciated that the confidence man's satisfaction lies most particularly in his bending the "mark" (victim) to his will:

> His strength was—and I could feel just how powerful that strength was—his terrible, compelling anxiety that he should be able to force someone under his will. It was almost as if he were pleading, silently, in the moment when he was tricking a victim: Please let me trick you; please let me cheat you; it's essential for me.

Many American men come to believe that heterosexual conquest is a particularly significant, even a necessary, vehicle for the achievement and sustenance of status and self-worth. Perhaps, as reports almost uniformly suggest, offenders believe that their victims like being forcibly raped. The fact that some rapists request testaments of their sexual skills from their victims and that others attempt to make future appointments with them supports this idea. But we believe that for many, perhaps most, rapists there is a clear appreciation that their victims hate what is happening to them, and that this is an important element of the behavior. The transmutation of an act of force into an act of seduction is for peer consumption—there are no points to be made with other males for beating or frightening a weaker person into submission. But the perpetration of rape (and the notable chronicity of the behavior) might well stem in significant measure from its ability to dramatize the possession of power by persons who are foreclosed from achieving a condition that they have come to believe must be realized if they are to have any ease and, ironically, any self-respect.

The sexual component of rape should not be downplayed in the haste today to accentuate the violent nature of the behavior. Is rape to be judged as sexual or violent in terms of the perception of the offender, the victim, the commentator, or the society at large? For some of us, air and noise pollution and verbal sarcasm are regarded as forms of violence; for others, seemingly self-evident violent encounters, such as boxing and football, are perceived only as sports.

The matter is even more definitionally intricate in regard to sexual matters. Heroin users often describe the injection of the drug as a sexual experience, and psychiatrists are prone to find sexual ingredients in acts that most of us consider to be quite nonerotic. Rape clearly is an act of aggression—in this sense a violent act—but it also involves behavior that unquestionably fits into a category that is traditionally and reasonably regarded as sexual in American society. Studies focusing on the perceptions of rape perpetrators, particularly inquiries that strive to identify patterns of motivation and to fit these with the larger life views of the offenders, are especially needed to fill out our understanding of the dynamics of the rape event and the psychology of the rapist.

Cross-Cultural Work. That forcible rape represents to a great extent the outcome of social learning can be seen from scrutiny of cross-cultural materials. These show discrepant forcible rape rates associated with different kinds of social systems. Undoubtedly, the most widely quoted ethnographic remark on rape is that of Margaret Mead (1950:104), who observed: "Of rape the Arapesh know nothing beyond the fact that it is the unpleasant custom of the Nugum people to the southeast of them." The Arapesh concept of male nature simply does not include the possibility of rape.

Contrariwise, the Gusii of the Kenya highlands, as Robert A.

LeVine illustrates, have a very high rate of forcible rape. LeVine enumerates cultural conditions that appear to be related to the Gusii rape situation. Their common denominator is intersexual conflict, begun and buttressed by customs that may motivate men to subdue women forcibly in sexual encounters. Other characteristics of the Gusii social system, such as the women's desire for the material goods that accompany courtship, and powerful supernatural taboos against adultery, LeVine believes, also contribute to the Gusii rape rate.

An extensive review of ethnographic materials (Chappell, 1976) indicates that a number of tribal groups use rape for precisely the reasons stressed by American feminists—to punish women and to enforce property rights. E. Adamson Hoebel (1954) points out that the Cheyenne Indians employ group rape as a sanction against unfaithful wives, and D. S. Marshall and R. C. Suggs (1971:152) report a similar kind of practice among the Mangaia in Oceania: "[G]ang rape . . . is a commonly used device to bring haughty young Mangaian women to terms with their male age mates. The girl may object, but she is too ashamed for having been taken by the group to go to the police."

The attraction of ethnographic research lies, in part, in the fact that more often than with contemporary western societies there appears to be some homogeneity in cultural themes among the groups traditionally studied by anthropologists. This makes it more possible to specify relationships between values and behavior with some precision.

The sparse anthropological data on forcible rape can be supplemented by scattered information from western cultures other than the United States. Schiff (1973) reported considerable difficulty in pinpointing rape statistics in European countries, and even more in attempting to find reliable estimates of the number of unreported rapes. Most European jurisdictions, he notes, keep only judicial figures, which refer to events often far-removed from the initial event and the official response to it. Schiff's (1973) best estimates, which must be regarded as very tentative, were that the United States shows a significantly higher rape rate than most, if not all, European jurisdictions. The American rate of about 20 rapes per 100,000 population compares to rates of 1.2 per 100,000 in Spain, 1.4 in Switzerland, and only .26 in Greece.

Clinard (1976), commenting on the low rate of rape in Switzerland, notes that this occurs in a highly industrialized, heavily urbanized country, with a heterogenous population that includes about 1 million foreign workers in a total population of 6.2 million persons. In addition, virtually all Swiss men possess a weapon in their home as part of the national defense effort. In short, Switzerland manifests many of the characteristics said to be associated with high crime rates; nonetheless, its rape rate, by American standards, is very low. The Scandinavian countries also appear to have low forcible rape rates, at least as the events come to police attention. In Sweden, where, as Betty Yorburg (1974:96) notes, "enormous efforts have been made to equalize the status of men and women," there were only fifty-two cases of forcible rape in 1969 for the entire country. Malmö, the third largest city in the country, with a population of about a quarter of a million people, reported no rapes at all for the year (Swedish Ministry of Justice, 1970).

A recent, as yet unpublished study (Heiple and Jankovic, 1976), compared the rape rate in Novi Sad County in Yugoslavia, a jurisdiction with an unusually mixed population for the country, with that in Ventura County, California. The Yugoslavian rate was 15.1 per 100,000 population in comparison to 24 per 100,000 in Ventura County. Analysis of rape cases in Yugoslavia showed a much higher proportion of stranger-to-stranger offenses than in the United States and a much rarer use of weapons. Prosecutions were much more successful in Yugoslavia than in the United States, with 42 percent of the cases going to felony indictment compared to 11 percent in California. Prison sentences were also more common in Yugoslavia, being meted out to 72 percent of the cases resulting in conviction compared to 40 percent in California.

British reports indicate that while the forcible rape rate is much lower in Great Britain than in the United States—1.6 per 100,000 persons in 1973—it has been rising considerably in recent years, as have been the rates for other offenses against persons. Rape became a prominent public issue in Britain after a law lords decision (*D.P.P.* v. *Morgan,* 1975; See also Curley, 1976), that reaffirmed the traditional legal rule that a person cannot be convicted of rape if he truly acts under the belief that the victim consented. *Morgan* involved four Royal Air Force men convicted of the rape of the wife of one of the men. Their defense was that they had believed the husband when he told them that they should ignore his wife's protests, that her screams were part of the way in which she expressed her particular sexual pleasure. The law lords upheld the conviction, though they stated that had the men actually acted upon such a belief, they would not have been criminally liable, and that the judge should have so instructed the jury.

The *Morgan* decision aroused strong protest. The British National Council for Civil Liberties (Trimborn, 1975) argued that most rape cases hinge on whether the woman has consented, and that the law lords had undermined any likely successful prosecution. A member of parliament insisted that the home secretary review the ruling: "If the law really is the ass that this judgment has made it appear," he wrote, "it must be changed." A leading criminal lawyer found it difficult to believe that anyone would again be convicted of rape in Britain. He noted, with a nice cross-cultural touch: "It must be the craziest situation since Al Capone's day" (Trimborn, 1975).

The *Morgan* case prompted the appointment of an Advisory Group on the Law of Rape. The group, under the chairmanship (for so the British continue to call it) of Justice Rose Heilbron, thought that the basic question raised by *Morgan* was: "Whose mind must be guilty, the mind of the defendant or that of a hypothetical reasonable man?" and concluded (Great Britain, 1975:10) that "a man should not be found guilty of a grave offense unless he had the requisite genuine guilty mind, and that a genuine mistake negatives such *mens rea* [guilty mind]." At the same time, the advisory group offered four major recommendations for reform of the law of rape:

1. Rape should be defined in statutory terms with the emphasis on lack of consent rather than violence.

2. A woman's previous sexual experience should not be admissible as evidence in court.
3. Complainants in rape cases should not be named in the press.
4. Rape cases should be heard by a jury that has a minimum of four men and four women.

As for the recommendation that victims remain anonymous, the group stressed that to be fully effective, the protection must start from the moment the allegation is made to the police. The group refused to recommend that the defendant be cloaked with anonymity; it thought, rather, that if he is guilty, he ought not be shielded, and, if innocent, "an acquittal will give him public vindication" (Great Britain, 1975:29).

Parliament, however, in enacting the Sexual Offences (Amendment) Act late in 1976 specified that, except under unusual circumstances, *both* the accused and the rape victim were to remain anonymous in mass media reports. The British legislation also provided for the first time in the country's history a statutory definition of rape. The definition stressed the absence of consent rather than the use of force as constituting the offense. It incorporated the elements of the *Morgan* ruling, but emphasized that recklessness in presuming consent would make a defendant liable to a rape conviction. Parliament also restricted exploration of the victim's past sexual history, but it rejected the Heilbron committee's idea about stipulated numbers of men and women on rape case juries (see further, Toner, 1977).

The need for further kinds of cross-cultural examination of the detailed characteristics of laws regarding forcible rape, the ingredients of the offense, the response of the criminal justice system, and the treatment of offenders can hardly be overemphasized. The provincialism of behavioral science research on forcible rape is pronounced.

Legal Matters. Particularly intensive pressure in regard to forcible rape has been exerted in the arena of legal reform. Changes have occurred in regard to the unusual corroboration requirements attendant upon forcible rape charges. Far-ranging inquiries into the complainant's background have been eliminated in many jurisdictions. Definitions of rape have been expanded to include oral and anal penetrations rather than only vaginal entry. The notorious cautionary instruction to the jury, first enunciated in 17th Century England by Lord Hale (see Neville, 1957), has largely disappeared. It specified, in its version in California, that: "a charge such as that made against the defendant in this case is one which is easily made and once made, difficult to defend against, even if the person is innocent. Therefore, the law requires that you examine the testimony of the female person named in the information with caution."

Holdsworth (1923), in an unrelieved panegyric, finds Hale to have been a man of extraordinary learning and decency. But it should be noted that in 1664 Hale presided at the infamous witchcraft trial at Bury St. Edmunds, where two women were sentenced to death on the basis of highly implausible testimony. Their youthful accusers also failed to pass an elementary test which saw them, blindfolded, throw a fit when approached by persons they thought were the accused witches but who, actually, were women substituted for the defendants as part of the test. Many judges and laymen by this time looked skeptically at the idea of witchcraft, and Hale, as Notestein (1911:268) observes, probably set back the course of rationality in regard to demoniacal possession by at least half a century at Bury St. Edmunds.

To this can be added Hale's explanation, as recorded by North (1890:121), of his marriage to his servant after the death of his first wife: "This great man said . . . there was no wisdom below the girdle." A diatribe against young women was also recently found among Hale's unpublished papers. It notes of them (Heward, 1972:112) that, "although they cannot provide it themselves, they must have choice food prepared for them. . . . Their father's or husband's money is spent on costly clothes and entertainments." In these terms, the long-lived cautionary instruction in rape cases appears to have been more invidious than, to use the word of a recent court decision (*People* v. *Rincon-Pineda,* 1975), the "musings" of a bygone jurist.

Until recently, as Lucy Reed Harris (1976) points out, legal scholars addressing issues of forcible rape concentrated almost exclusively on minutiae, such as the proper definition of consent in rape cases that involved offenders who had impersonated husbands and doctors who had taken advantage of their profession to achieve sexual congress with patients, usually through the stratagem of defining the contact as necessary medical treatment. Now, however, an array of sophisticated legal analyses (see, for example, Cross, 1973; Giles, 1976; Maloney, 1975; Scutt, 1976) is concentrating on issues that deal with the more common forms of forcible rape, those that constitute the largest part of police blotter entries.

Research is especially needed regarding the consequences of law reforms. It has always been a shortcoming of both legislative enactments and court decisions that they are not accompanied by systematic inquiry into the consequences of the rearrangements they mandate. Only the sporadic curiosity of researchers or the dedication of protagonists is apt to unearth reliable data on whether the alterations exacerbate or calm the situation they address. Follow-up research on legal changes is a highly intricate chore but, without it, we will continue to grope about in reform efforts.

Note, for instance, the belief of a woman deputy district attorney in California (Ben-Horin, 1975:113) that the sweeping revisions of the state's rape statute will make things easier for the victim, but that "nothing will really change the number of rape convictions until we convince the public that rape is a crime of violence, not of sex." This belief is really a hypothesis, and merits some systematic testing. Similarly, it has been claimed that removal of corroboration requirements from rape statutes will serve little purpose, since prosecutors impose their own personal standards on the selection of cases with which they will go forward, and that they will not risk losing a verdict in instances in which there is no corroboration or weak corroboration of the rape.

An early examination (Reich and Chappell, 1976) of the outcome of the comprehensive revision of the sexual assault law in Michigan (Cobb and Schauer in this volume discusses the pioneering Michigan code changes) tends to support the view that these reforms are unable to affect prosecution strategies. In Detroit, the authors note "the prosecutors perceive that the new statute encourages weaker complaints which they feel bound to discourage." Prosecutors tend to believe that the flexibility of the statute provided by its designation of various degrees of rape gives them greater leverage to bargain pleas, an outcome probably not anticipated by the framers of the law. A female judge in Detroit, however, thinks that though the statute is too academic in tone and construction and philosophically too far ahead of its time, nonetheless it ultimately might have a salutary effect on rape prosecutions in the state.

A model of the kind of sociolegal research that needs to be conducted on a more extensive basis is provided by Hugo Adam Bedau (1976) in his analysis of the effects of a Massachusetts law that mandates capital punishment for persons convicted of rape-murder. Bedau set out to determine how the statute had worked so that the U.S. Supreme Court might be better informed when it considered the constitutionality of mandatory capital punishment laws. Bedau found no specific study of rape-murder, despite the preeminent importance of the subject, and he relies on Susan Brownmiller's (1975) estimate that 2 percent of all criminal homicides include rape, and that between 0.2 and 0.8 percent of all forcible rapes end in murder. Record searches by Bedau in the two largest Massachusetts counties for a twenty-five-year period located 128 cases in which men had murdered women. Of these instances, 17 appeared to involve rape-murder, and in at least 5 the evidence for a felony-murder indictment (and a mandatory death sentence on conviction) seemed very strong. The victims were helpless, the crimes brutal, and there was autopsy evidence of forcible rape. But none of the 5 cases was handled as rape-murder, though the offenders usually were sentenced to life imprisonment. Bedau concludes that mandatory capital punishment statutes, if they follow the path of the Massachusetts experience, are not likely to have any impact on the rate of the offense, for there was no change over time in the rape-murder rate in Massachusetts and these statutes will probably not be enforced.

Interest is beginning to grow as well in studies that probe citizen and juror reactions to various kinds of rape cases. More than twenty years ago, in a classic study, Kalven and Zeisel (1966) found that judges were much more prone than juries to convict accused rapists. In nonaggravated cases (where there was no physical injury), a jury would have convicted in only three cases out of forty-one, while the judges believed the suspect guilty in twenty-two. Kalven and Zeisel note that juries tend to redefine the crime of rape in terms of their own ideas about the assumption of risk on the part of the victim. In one case, a judge used the term "savage" to describe the behavior of the accused rapist (he had fractured the victim's jaw in two places), but the jury acquitted him on the basis of testimony that the complainant and the defendant had been out together before and that they had been drinking together preceding the alleged rape.

Only a few recent inquiries have mined the vein opened up by Kalven and Zeisel. A paper by Cathaleene Jones and Elliot Aronson (1974) suggests that persons will sentence an offender for a longer term for the rape of a married women than for the rape of a divorcee. It also reports that under similar circumstances, a complainant who was a virgin will be regarded as more at fault in a rape episode than will a divorcee. This seemingly paradoxical outcome is explained by the desire on the part of persons passing judgment to see the world as just, a place where people get what they deserve. Therefore, the better people (that is, the virgin) must have behaved particularly badly in order to have suffered so grievously. The explanation may be farfetched, and the study is marred by the nature of the respondent group, those ubiquitous college sophomores who form the shock troops for so many American social psychology investigations. Klemmack and Klemmack (1976) have pushed further afield, requesting the views of a random sample of persons in regard to whether they considered each of five different fact situations as rape. Not unexpectedly, the more there appeared to be an assumption of risk by the victim, the more likely a respondent was to regard the act against her as other than a true rape. The question asked, however, seems off-target, since it is not whether a respondent regards a given matter as rape that is important, but rather whether the person, having heard the facts and absorbed judicial instructions on the legal definition of rape, will vote for a conviction. The basic finding of the Klemmacks' (1976:144) investigation is noteworthy, though: that the prosecutor interested in obtaining a conviction should search for educated women who express a tolerance toward premarital sexual activities and who have adopted a nontraditional orientation toward the role of women in the family.

In sum, it is evident that research work on forcible rape is beginning to take shape. The materials in the following pages constitute source data for further investigations and provide empirical foundations, speculative ideas, and ideological fuel for such additional inquiry into forcible rape. As we noted early in this chapter, the struggle to understand and deal with rape is just beginning. We would be pleased if the materials presented in this volume move that struggle a bit further along toward a successful conclusion.

REFERENCES

Algren, Nelson. 1941. *Never Come Morning.* New York: Harper & Row.

Amir, Menachem. 1971. *Patterns in Forcible Rape.* Chicago: University of Chicago Press.

Aschaffenburg, Gustav. 1913. *Crime and Its Repression.* Trans. by Adalbert Albrecht. Boston: Little, Brown.

Barber, R. N. 1969. "Prostitution and the Increasing Number of Convictions for Rape in Queensland," *Australian and New Zealand Journal of Criminology* 2:169–74.

Bart, Pauline B. 1975. "Rape Doesn't End with a Kiss," *Viva* 2:39–42, 100–1.

Becker, Judith V. 1976. Personal communication.

Bedau, Hugo Adam. 1976. "Felony-Murder Rape and the Mandatory Death Penalty: A Study in Discretionary Justice," *Suffolk University Law Review* 10:494–520.

Ben-Horin, Daniel. 1975. "Is Rape a Sex Crime?" *The Nation* 221 (August 16): 112–15.

Bender, Lauretta and Abram Blau. 1937. "The Reaction of Children to Sexual Realtions with Adults," *American Journal of Orthopsychiatry* 7: 500–18.

Bettelheim, Bruno. 1974. "Children Should Learn About Violence." In Suzanne K. Steinmetz and Murray A. Straus, eds., *Violence in the Family,* pp. 299–303. New York: Dodd, Mead.

Bidna, Howard, William Klibinow, and Gilbert Geis. 1976. "Correlates of Rape Rates in American Cities." Unpublished.

Bohmer, Carol and Audrey Blumberg. 1975. "Twice Traumatized: The Rape Victim and the Court," *Judicature* 58:391–99.

Brownmiller, Susan. 1968. "Rashomon in Maryland," *Esquire* 69(May): 130–32.

——. 1975. *Against Our Will: Men, Women and Rape.* New York: Simon & Schuster.

Burgess, Ann Wolbert and Lynda Lytle Holmstrom. 1974. *Rape: Victims of Crisis.* Bowie, Md.: Brady.

——. 1976. Personal communication.

Caughey, Madeline S. 1974. "The Principle of Harm and Its Application to Laws Criminalizing Prostitution," *Denver Law Journal* 51:235–62.

Chappell, Duncan. 1976. "Cross-cultural Research on Forcible Rape," *International Journal of Criminology and Penology,"* 4:295–304.

Chappell, Duncan and Jennifer James. 1976. "Victim Selection and Apprehension from the Rapist's Perspective: A Preliminary Investigation." Paper presented at the 2d International Symposium on Victimology, Boston, September 8.

Cimons, Marlene. 1974. "Rape Concern Reaches the Federal Level," *Los Angeles Times,* May 9.

Clinard, Marshall. 1976. Personal communication.

Cross, Lee. 1973. Report of the District of Columbia Task Force on Rape, Prepared for the Public Safety Committee. District of Columbia City Council.

Curley, E. M. 1976. "Excusing Rape," *Philosophy & Public Affairs* 5: 325–60.

Curtis, Lynn A. 1976a. "Rape, Race, and Culture: Some Speculations in Search of a Theory." In Marcia J. Walker and Stanley L. Brodsky, eds., *Sexual Assault,* pp. 117–34. Lexington, Mass.: D. C. Heath.

——. 1976b. "Sexual combat," *Society* 13(May-June):69–72.

Devereux, George. 1957. "The Awarding of a Penis as Compensation for Rape: A Demonstration of the Clinical Relevance of the Psycho-Analytical Study of Cultural Data," *International Journal of Psycho-Analysis* 38:398–401.

Director of Public Prosecutions v. Morgan. 1975. All-England Reports 347.

Ellis, Havelock. 1892. *The Criminal.* New York: Scribners.

Fisher, Gary and Ephraim Rivlin. 1971. "Psychological Needs of Rapists," *British Journal of Criminology* 11:182–85.

Fosburgh, Lacey. 1970. "Women's Liberationist Hails the Prostitute," *New York Times,* May 29.

Freeman, Jo. 1975. *The Politics of Women's Liberation.* New York: McKay.

Fuller, Edmund. 1975. "Rape—A Tactic in the War of the Sexes," *Wall Street Journal,* October 31.

Gager, Nancy and Cathleen Schurr. 1976. *Sexual Assault: Confronting Rape in America.* New York: Grosset & Dunlap.

Gagnon, John H. 1965. "Female Child Victims of Sex Offenses," *Social Problems* 13:176–192.

——. 1972. "Two Studies of Violent Sex Crime," *Federal Probation,* Book Review 36(March):68–70.

Gebhard, Paul H., John H. Gagnon, Wardell B. Pomeroy, and Cornelia V. Christenson. 1965. *Sex Offenders: An Analysis of Types.* New York: Harper & Row.

Giles, Linda E. 1976. "The Admissibility of a Rape-Complainant's Previous Sexual Conduct: The Need for Legislative Reform," *New England Law Review* 11:497–507.

Great Britain. 1975. Advisory Group on the Law of Rape. Cmnd. 6354. London: Her Majesty's Stationery Office.

Greer, Germaine. 1970. *The Female Eunuch.* New York: Bantam.

——. 1973. "Seduction Is a Four-Letter Word," *Playboy* 20(January):80–82, 164, 178, 224–28.

Griffin, Susan. 1971. "Rape: The All-American Crime," *Ramparts* 10(September):26–36.

——. 1976. Personal communication.

Gurr, Ted Robert. 1972. "Sources of Rebellion in Western Societies: Some Quantitative Evidence." In James F. Short, Jr., and Marvin E. Wolfgang, eds., *Collective Violence,* pp. 132–48. Chicago: Aldine.

Harris, Lucy Reed. 1976. "Towards a Consent Standard in the Law of Rape," *University of Chicago Law Review* 43:613–45.

Heiple, Phil and Ivan Jankovic. 1976. Paper presented at annual meeting of the American Sociological Association, New York, September 3.

Hemingway, Ernest. 1940. *For Whom the Bell Tolls.* New York: Scribners.

Heward, Edmund. 1972. *Matthew Hale.* London: Robert Hale.

Hoebel, E. Adamson. 1954. *The Law of Primitive Man.* Cambridge, Mass.: Harvard University Press.

Holdsworth, W. S. 1923. "Sir Matthew Hale," *Law Quarterly Review* 39:402–26.

Huber, Joan. 1976. "Toward a Sociotechnological Theory of the Women's Movement," *Social Problems* 23:371–88.

Jones, Cathaleene and Elliot Aronson. 1973. "Attribution of Fault to a Rape Victim as a Function of Respectability of the Victim," *Journal of Personality and Social Psychology* 26:415–19.

Kalven, Harry and Hans Zeisel. 1966. *The American Jury.* Boston: Little, Brown.

Kinsey, Alfred C., Wardell Pomeroy, and Clyde E. Martin. 1948. *Sexual Behavior in the Human Male.* Philadelphia: Saunders.

Klemmack, Susan H. and David L. Klemmack. 1976. "The Social Definition of Rape." In Marcia J. Walker and Stanley L. Brodsky, eds., *Sexual Assault,* pp. 135–47. Lexington, Mass.: D. C. Heath.

Largen, Mary Ann. 1976. "History of Women's Movement in Changing Attitudes, Laws, and Treatment toward Rape Victims." In Marcia J. Walker and Stanley L. Brodsky, eds., *Sexual Assault.* Lexington, Mass.: D. C. Heath. pp. 69–73.

Lehmann-Haupt, Christopher. 1975. "Rape as the Combat in a War." Book review, *New York Times,* November 1.

Lessing, Doris. 1961. *In Pursuit of the English.* New York: Simon & Schuster.

MacKellar, Jean. 1975. *Rape: The Bait and the Trap.* New York: Crown.

Malinowski, Bronislaw. 1929. *The Sexual Life of Savages in North-Western Melanesia. Vol. 1. New York: Liveright.*

Maloney, Sharon. 1975. "Rape in Illinois: A Denial of Equal Protection," *John Marshall Journal of Practice and Procedure* 8:457–96.

Marshall, D. S. and R. C. Suggs, Eds. 1971. *Human Sexual Behavior: Variations in the Ethnographic Spectrum.* New York: Basic Books.

Mead, Margaret. 1935. *Sex and Temperament in Three Primitive Societies.* New York: William Morrow.

Medea, Andra and Kathleen Thompson. 1974. *Against Rape.* New York: Farrar, Straus, & Giroux.

Millett, Kate. 1971. *The Prostitution Papers: A Candid Dialogue.* New York: Basic Books.

Monahan, John. 1976. "The Prevention of Violence." In John Monahan, ed., *Community Mental Health and the Criminal Justice System,* pp. 13–14. New York: Pergamon.

Neville, D. G. 1957. "Rape in Early English Law," *Justice of the Peace and Local Government Review* 121:223–24.

North, Roger. 1890. *The Lives of Francis North, Dudley North and John North.* Edited by Augustus Jessopp. London: Bohn's.

Notestein, Wallace. 1911. *A History of Witchcraft in England from 1558 to 1718.* Washington, D.C.: American Historical Association.

People v. Rincon-Pineda. 1975. 538 P.2d 247 (California).

Rasmussen, Augusta. 1934. "Die bedeutung Sexueller attentate auf kinder unter 14 jahren für die entwicklung von geisteskrankheiten und charakteranomalien," *Acta Neurologica et Psychiatrica* 9:351–434.

Reich, Jay A. and Duncan Chappell. 1976. "The Prosecutorial Response to Michigan's Criminal Sexual Conduct Law: Business as Usual." Unpublished.

Reiss, Albert. 1974. Book Review. *American Journal of Sociology* 80:785–90.

Russell, Diana E. H. 1975. *The Politics of Rape: The Victim's Perspective.* New York: Stein & Day.

Ryan, William. 1974. *Blaming the Victim.* New York: Pantheon.

Sagarin, Edward. 1972. Book review, *Annals of the American Academy of Political and Social Science* 401:203–04.

Schiff, Arthur F. 1973. "Rape in Foreign Countries," *Medical Trial Technique Quarterly* 20:66–74.

Schwendinger, Julia R. and Herman Schwendinger. 1974. "Rape Myths: In Legal, Theoretical and Everyday Practice," *Crime and Social Justice* 1(Spring-Summer):18–25.

Scutt, Jocelynne A. 1976. "Fraud and Consent in Rape: Comprehension of the Nature and Character of the Act and Its Moral Implications," *Criminal Law Quarterly* 18:312–24.

Smith, Arthur and James V. Giles. 1975. *An Americana Rape: True Account of the Giles-Johnson Case.* New York: New Republic Press.

Swedish Ministry of Justice. 1970. Brott Som Kommit Till Polisens Kännedom. Stockholm: Statistiska Meddelander.

Tiger, Lionel. 1976. "Fearful Symmetry," *New York Times Book Review,* February 8:41.

Toner, Barbara. 1977. *The Facts of Rape.* London: Hutchinson.

Trimborn, Harry. 1975. "British Rape Law Outcry—Does 'No' Mean 'Yes'?" *Los Angeles Times,* May 2.

Weis, Kurt and Sandra S. Borges. 1973. "Victimology and Rape: The Case of the Legitimate Victim," *Issues in Criminology* 8:71-115.

Wille, Warren S. 1961. "Case Study of a Rapist: An Analysis of the Causation of Criminal Behavior," *Journal of Social Therapy* 7:10–21.

Willens, Michele. 1971. "Legal Discrimination Hit," *Los Angeles Times,* May 23.

Wilson, Jane. 1975. "Ideological View of Rape as State of War," Book review, *Los Angeles Times,* December 2.

Wolfgang, Marvin E. 1958. *Patterns of Criminal Homicide.* Philadelphia: University of Pennsylvania Press.

Yorburg, Betty. 1973. *The Changing Family.* New York: Columbia University Press.

CONTEMPORARY ISSUES

2 Rape: The All-American Crime

SUSAN GRIFFIN

I have never been free of the fear of rape. From a very early age I, like most women, have thought of rape as part of my natural environment—something to be feared and prayed against like fire or lightning. I never asked why men raped; I simply thought it one of the many mysteries of human nature.

I was, however, curious enough about the violent side of humanity to read every crime magazine I was able to ferret away from my grandfather. Each issue featured at least one sex crime, with pictures of a victim, usually in a pearl necklace, and of the ditch or the orchard where her body was found. I was never certain why the victims were always women, nor what the motives of the murderer were, but I did guess that the world was not a safe place for women. I observed that my grandmother was meticulous

Reprinted by permission from *Ramparts,* September 1971. Copyright © 1971 by Susan Griffin.

about locks, and quick to draw the shades before anyone removed so much as a shoe. I sensed that danger lurked outside.

At the age of eight, my suspicions were confirmed. My grandmother took me to the back of the house where the men wouldn't hear, and told me that strange men wanted to do harm to little girls. I learned not to walk on dark streets, not to talk to strangers, or get into strange cars, to lock doors, and to be modest. She never explained why a man would want to harm a little girl, and I never asked.

If I thought for a while that my grandmother's fears were imaginary, the illusion was brief. That year on the way home from school, a schoolmate a few years older than I tried to rape me. Later, in an obscure aisle of the local library (while I was reading *Freddy the Pig*) I turned to discover a man exposing himself. Then, the friendly man around the corner was arrested for child molesting.

My initiation to sexuality was typical. Every woman has similar stories to tell—the first man who attacked her may have been a neighbor, a family friend, an uncle, her doctor, or perhaps her own father. And women who grow up in New York City always have tales about the subway.

But though rape and the fear of rape are a daily part of every woman's consciousness, the subject is so rarely discussed by that unofficial staff of male intellectuals (who write the books which study seemingly every other form of male activity) that one begins to suspect a conspiracy of silence. And indeed, the obscurity of rape in print exists in marked contrast to the frequency of rape in reality, for forcible rape is the most frequently committed violent crime in America today. The Federal Bureau of Investigation classes three crimes as violent: murder, aggravated assault, and forcible rape. In 1968, 31,060 rapes were reported. According to the FBI and independent criminologists, however, to approach accuracy this figure must be multiplied by at least a factor of ten to compensate for the fact that most rapes are not reported; when these compensatory mathematics are used, there are more rapes committed than aggravated assaults and homicides.

When I asked Berkeley, California's police inspector in

charge of rape investigation if he knew why men rape women, he replied that he had not spoken with "these people and delved into what really makes them tick, because that really isn't my job. . . ." However, when I asked him how a woman might prevent being raped, he was not so reticent, "I wouldn't advise any female to go walking around alone at night . . . and she should lock her car at all times." The inspector illustrated his warning with a grisly story about a man who lay in wait for women in the back seats of their cars, while they were shopping in a local supermarket. This man eventually murdered one of his rape victims. "Always lock your car," the inspector repeated, and then added, without a hint of irony, "Of course, you don't have to be paranoid about this type of thing."

The inspector wondered why I wanted to write about rape. Like most men, he did not understand the urgency of the topic. But like most women, I had spent considerable time speculating on the true nature of the rapist. When I was very young, my image of the sexual offender was a nightmarish amalgamation of the bogey man and Captain Hook: he wore a black cape, and he cackled. As I matured, so did my image of the rapist. Born into the psychoanalytic age, I tried to "understand" the rapist. Rape, I came to believe, was only one of many unfortunate evils produced by sexual repression. Reasoning by tautology, I concluded that any man who would rape a woman must be out of his mind.

Yet, though the theory that rapists are insane is a popular one, this belief has no basis in fact. According to Professor Menachem Amir's study of 646 rape cases in Philadelphia, *Patterns in Forcible Rape,* men who rape are not abnormal. Amir writes: "Studies indicate that sex offenders do not constitute a unique or psychopathological type; nor are they as a group invariably more disturbed than the control groups to which they are compared." Alan Taylor, a parole officer who has worked with rapists in the prison facilities at San Luis Obispo, California, stated the question in plainer language, "Those men were the most normal men there. They had a lot of hang-ups, but they were the same hang-ups as men walking out on the street."

Another canon in the apologetics of rape is that if it were not for learned social controls, all men would rape. Rape is held to be natural behavior, and not to rape must be learned. But in truth rape is not universal to the human species. Moreover, studies of rape in our culture reveal that far from being impulsive behavior, most rape is planned. Professor Amir's study reveals that in cases of group rape (the "gangbang" of masculine slang) 90 percent of the rapes were planned; in pair rapes, 83 percent of the rapes were planned; and in single rapes, 58 percent were planned. These figures should significantly discredit the image of the rapist as a man who is suddenly overcome by sexual needs society does not allow him to fulfill.

Far from the social control of rape being learned, comparisons with other cultures lead one to suspect that, in our society, it is rape itself that is learned. (The fact that rape is against the law should not be considered proof that rape is not in fact encouraged as part of our culture.)

This culture's concept of rape as an illegal, but still understandable, form of behavior is not a universal one. In her study *Sex and Temperament,* Margaret Mead describes a society that does not share our views. The Arapesh do not "have any conception of the male nature that might make rape understandable to them." Indeed our interpretation of rape is a product of our conception of the nature of male sexuality. A common retort to the question, Why don't women rape men? is the myth that men have greater sexual needs, that their sexuality is more urgent than women's. And it is the nature of human beings to want to live up to what is expected of them.

And this same culture which expects aggression from the male expects passivity from the female. Conveniently, the companion myth about the nature of female sexuality is that all women secretly want to be raped. Lurking beneath her modest female exterior is a subconscious desire to be ravished. The following description of a stag movie, written by Brenda Starr in Los Angeles' underground paper, *Everywoman,* typifies this male fantasy. The movie "showed a woman in her underclothes reading on her bed. She is interrupted by a rapist with a knife. He immediately wins her over with his charm and they get busy sucking and fucking." An advertisement in the *Berkely Barb* reads, "Now as all women know from their daydreams, rape has a lot of advantages. Best of all it's so simple. No preparation necessary, no planning ahead of time, no wondering if you should or shouldn't; just whang! bang!" Thanks to Masters and Johnson even the scientific canon recognizes that for the female, "whang! bang!" can scarcely be described as pleasurable.

Still, the male psyche persists in believing that, protestations and struggles to the contrary, deep inside her mysterious feminine soul, the female victim has wished for her own fate. A young woman who was raped by the husband of a friend said that days after the incident the man returned to her home, pounded on the door, and screamed to her, "Jane, Jane. You loved it. You know you loved it."

The theory that women like being raped extends itself by deduction into the proposition that most or much of rape is provoked by the victim. But this too is only myth. Though provocation, considered a mitigating factor in a court of law, may consist of only "a gesture," according to the Federal Commission on Crimes of Violence, only 4 percent of reported rapes involved any precipitative behavior by the woman.

The notion that rape is enjoyed by the victim is also convenient for the man who, though he would not commit forcible rape, enjoys the idea of its existence, as if rape confirms that enormous sexual potency which he secretly knows to be his own. It is for the pleasure of the armchair rapist that detailed accounts of violent rapes exist in the media. Indeed, many men appear to take sexual pleasure from nearly all forms of violence. Whatever the motivation, male sexuality and violence in our culture seem to be inseparable. James Bond alternately whips out his revolver and his cock, and though there is no known connection between the skills of gunfighting and lovemaking, pacifism seems suspiciously effeminate.

In a recent fictional treatment of the Manson case, Frank Conroy writes of his vicarious titillation when describing the murders to his wife:

"Every single person there was killed." She didn't move.

"It sounds like there was torture," I said. As the words left my mouth, I knew there was no need to say them to frighten her into believing that she needed me for protection.

The pleasure he feels as his wife's protector is inextricably mixed with pleasure in the violence itself. Conroy writes: "I was excited by the killings, as one is excited by catastrophe on a grand scale, as one is alert to pre-echoes of unknown changes, hints of unrevealed secrets, rumblings of chaos . . ."

The attraction of the male in our culture to violence and death is a tradition Manson and his admirers are carrying on with tireless avidity (even presuming Manson's innocence, he dreams of the purification of fire and destruction). It was Malraux in his *Anti-Memoirs* who said that, for the male, facing death was the illuminating experience analogous to childbirth for the female. Certainly our culture does glorify war and shroud the agonies of the gunfighter in veils of mystery.

And in the spectrum of male behavior, rape, the perfect combination of sex and violence, is the penultimate act. Erotic pleasure cannot be separated from culture, and in our culture male eroticism is wedded to power. Not only should a man be taller and stronger than a female in the perfect love match, but he must also demonstrate his superior strength in gestures of dominance which are perceived as amorous. Though the law attempts to make a clear division between rape and sexual intercourse, in fact the courts find it difficult to distinguish between a case where the decision to copulate was mutual and one where a man forced himself upon his partner.

The scenario is even further complicated by the expectation that not only does a woman mean yes when she says no, but that a really decent woman ought to begin by saying no, and then be lead down the primrose path to acquiescence. Ovid, the author of Western civilization's most celebrated sex manual, makes this expectation perfectly clear: ". . . and when I beg you to say 'yes,' say 'no.' Then let me lie outside your bolted door. . . . So Love grows strong . . ."

That the basic elements of rape are involved in all heterosexual relationships may explain why men often identify with the offender in this crime. But to regard the rapist as the victim, a man driven by his inherent sexual needs to take what will not be given him, reveals a basic ignorance of sexual politics. For in our culture heterosexual love finds an erotic expression through male dominance and female submission. A man who derives pleasure from raping a woman clearly must enjoy force and dominance as much or more than the simple pleasures of the flesh. Coitus cannot be experienced in isolation. The weather, the state of the nation, the level of sugar in the blood—all will affect a man's ability to achieve orgasm. If a man can achieve sexual pleasure after terrorizing and humiliating the object of his passion, and in fact while inflicting pain upon her, one must assume he derives pleasure directly from terrorizing, humiliating, and harming a woman. According to Amir's study of forcible rape, on a statistical average the man who has been convicted of rape was found to have a normal sexual personality, tended to be different from the normal, well-adjusted male only in having a greater tendency to express violence and rage.

And if the professional rapist is to be separated from the average dominant heterosexual, it may be mainly a quantitative difference. For the existence of rape as an index to masculinity is not entirely metaphorical. Though this measure of masculinity seems to be more publicly exhibited among "bad boys" or aging bikers who practice sexual initiation through group rape, in fact, "good boys" engage in the same rites to prove their manhood. In Stockton, a small town in California which epitomizes silent-majority America, a bachelor party was given last summer for a young man about to be married. A woman was hired to dance topless for the amusement of the guests. At the high point of the evening the bridegroom-to-be dragged the woman into a bedroom. No move was made by any of his companions to stop what was clearly going to be an attempted rape. Far from it. As the woman described, "I tried to keep him away—told him of my Herpes Genitalis, et cetera, but he couldn't face the guys if he didn't screw me." After the bridegroom had finished raping the woman and returned with her to the party, far from chastizing him, his friends heckled the woman and covered her with wine.

It was fortunate for the dancer that the bridegroom's friends did not follow him into the bedroom for, though one might suppose that in group rape, since the victim is outnumbered, less force would be inflicted on her, in fact, Amir's studies indicate, "the most excessive degrees of violence occurred in group rape." Far from discouraging violence, the presence of other men may in fact encourage sadism, and even cause the behavior. In an unpublished study of group rape by Gilbert Geis and Duncan Chappell, the authors refer to a study by W. H. Blanchard which relates: "The leader of the male group . . . apparently precipitated and maintained the activity, despite misgivings, because of a need to fulfill the role that the other two men had assigned to him. 'I was scared when it began to happen,' he says. 'I wanted to leave but I didn't want to say it to the other guys—you know—that I was scared.' "

Thus it becomes clear that not only does our culture teach men the rudiments of rape, but society, or more specifically other men, encourages the practice of it.

> Every man I meet wants to protect me. Can't
> figure out what from
>
> —Mae West

If a male society rewards aggressive, domineering sexual behavior, it contains within itself a sexual schizophrenia. For the masculine man is also expected to prove his mettle as a protector of women. To the naïve eye, this dichotomy implies that men fall into one of two categories: those who rape and those who protect. In fact, life does not prove so simple. In a study euphemistically entitled "Sex Aggression by College Men," it was discovered that men who believe in a double standard of morality for men and women, who in fact believe most fervently in the ultimate value of virginity, are more liable to commit "this aggressive variety of sexual exploitation."

(At this point in our narrative it should come as no surprise that Sir Thomas Malory, creator of that classic tale of chivalry, *The Knights of the Round Table,* was himself arrested and found guilty for repeated incidents of rape.)

In the system of chivalry, men protect women against men.

This is not unlike the protection relationship which the Mafia established with small businesses in the early part of this century. Indeed, chivalry is an age-old protection racket which depends for its existence on rape.

According to the male mythology which defines and perpetuates rape, it is an animal instinct inherent in the male. The story goes that sometime in our prehistorical past, the male, more hirsute and burly than today's counterparts, roamed about an uncivilized landscape until he found a desirable female. (Oddly enough, this female is *not* pictured as more muscular than the modern woman.) Her mate does not bother with courtship. He simply grabs her by the hair and drags her to the closest cave. Presumably, one of the major advantages of modern civilization for the female has been the civilizing of the male. We call it chivalry.

But women do not get chivalry for free. According to the logic of sexual politics, we too have to civilize our behavior. (Enter chastity. Enter virginity. Enter monogamy.) For the female, civilized behavior means chastity before marriage and faithfulness within it. Chivalrous behavior in the male is supposed to protect that chastity from involuntary defilement. The fly in the ointment of this otherwise peaceful system is the fallen woman. She does not behave. And therefore she does not deserve protection. Or, to use another argument, a major tenet of the same value system: What has once been defiled cannot again be violated. One begins to suspect that it is the behavior of the fallen woman, and not that of the male, that civilization aims to control.

The assumption that a woman who does not respect the double standard deserves whatever she gets (or at the very least "asks for it") operates in the courts today. While in some states a man's previous rape convictions are not considered admissible evidence, the sexual reputation of the rape victim is considered a crucial element of the facts upon which the court must decide innocence or guilt.

The court's respect for the double standard manifested itself particularly clearly in the case of the *People* v. *Jerry Plotkin.* Mr. Plotkin, a 36-year-old jeweler, was tried for rape in a San Francisco Superior Court. According to the woman who brought the charges, Plotkin, along with three other men, forced her at gunpoint one night to enter a car. She was taken to Mr. Plotkin's fashionable apartment where he and the three other men first raped her and then, in the delicate language of the *San Francisco Chronicle,* "subjected her to perverted sex acts." She was, she said, set free in the morning with the warning that she would be killed if she spoke to anyone about the event. She did report the incident to the police who then searched Plotkin's apartment and discovered a long list of names of women. Her name was on the list and had been crossed out.

In addition to the woman's account of her abduction and rape, the prosecution submitted four of Plotkin's address books containing the names of hundred of women. Plotkin claimed he did not know all of the women since some of the names had been given to him by friends and he had not yet called on them. Several women, however, did testify in court that Plotkin had, to cite the *Chronicle,* "lured them up to his apartment under one pretext or another, and forced his sexual attentions on them."

Plotkin's defense rested on two premises. First, through his own testimony Plotkin established a reputation for himself as a sexual libertine who frequently picked up girls in bars and took them to his house where sexual relations often took place. He was the Playboy. He claimed that the accusation of rape, therefore, was false—this incident had simply been one of many casual sexual relationships, the victim one of many playmates. The second premise of the defense was that his accuser was also a sexual libertine. However, the picture created of the young woman (fully thirteen years younger than Plotkin) was not akin to the lighthearted, gay-bachelor image projected by the defendant. On the contrary, the day after the defense cross-examined the woman, the *Chronicle* printed a story headlined, "Grueling Day for Rape Case Victim." (A leaflet passed out by women in front of the courtroom was more succinct, "rape was committed by four men in a private apartment in October; on Thursday, it was done by a judge and a lawyer in a public courtroom.")

Through skillful questioning fraught with innuendo, Plotkin's defense attorney James Martin MacInnis portrayed the young woman as a licentious opportunist and unfit mother. MacInnis began by asking the young woman (then employed as a secretary) whether or not it was true that she was "familiar with liquor" and had worked as a "cocktail waitress." The young woman replied (the *Chronicle* wrote "admitted") that she had worked once or twice as a cocktail waitress. The attorney then asked if she had worked as a secretary in the financial district but had "left that employment after it was discovered that you had sexual intercourse on a couch in the office." The woman replied, "That is a lie. I left because I didn't like working in a one-girl office. It was too lonely." Then the defense asked if, while working as an attendant at a health club, "you were accused of having a sexual affair with a man?" Again the woman denied the story, "I was never accused of that."

Plotkin's attorney then sought to establish that his client's accuser was living with a married man. She responded that the man was separated from his wife. Finally he told the court that she has "spent the night" with another man who lived in the same building.

At this point in the testimony the woman asked Plotkin's defense attorney: "Am I on trial? . . . It is embarrassing and personal to admit these things to all these people. . . . I did not commit a crime. I am a human being." The lawyer, true to the chivalry of his class, apologized and immediately resumed questioning her, turning his attention to her children. (She is divorced, and the children at the time of the trial were in a foster home.) "Isn't it true that your two children have a sex game in which one gets on top of another and they——" "That is a lie!" the young woman interrupted him. She ended her testimony by explaining: "They are wonderful children. They are not perverted."

The jury, divided in favor of acquittal ten to two, asked the court stenographer to read the woman's testimony back to them. After this reading, the superior court acquitted the defendant of both the charges of rape and kidnapping.

According to the double standard, a woman who has had sexual intercourse out of wedlock cannot be raped. Rape is not only a crime of aggression against the body; it is a transgression against chastity as defined by men. When a woman is forced into a sexual relationship, she has, according to the male ethos, been violated. But she is also defiled if she does not behave according the double standard, by maintaining her chastity, or confining her sexual activities to a monogamous relationship.

One should not assume, however, that a woman can avoid the possibility of rape simply by behaving. Though myth would have it that mainly "bad girls" are raped, this theory has no basis in fact. Like indiscriminate terrorism, rape can happen to any woman, and few women are ever without this knowledge.

The courts and the police, both dominated by white males, continue to suspect the rape victim, *sui generis,* of provoking or asking for her own assault. According to Amir's study, the police tend to believe that a woman without a good reputation cannot be raped. The rape victim is usually submitted to countless questions about her own sexual mores and behaviors by the police investigator. This preoccupation is partially justified by the legal requirements for prosecution in a rape case. The rape victim must have been penetrated, and she must have made it clear to her assailant that she did not want penetration (unless of course she is unconscious). A refusal to accompany a man to some isolated place to allow him to touch her does not, in the eyes of the court, constitute rape. She must have said no at the crucial genital moment. And the rape victim, to qualify as such, must also have put up a physical struggle—unless she can prove that to do so would have been to endanger her life.

But the zealous interest the police frequently exhibit in the physical details of a rape case is only partially explained by the requirements of the court. A woman who was raped in Berkeley was asked to tell the story of her rape four different times "right out in the street," while her assailant was escaping. She was then required to submit to a pelvic examination to prove that penetration had taken place. Later, she was taken to the police station where she was asked the same questions again: "Were you forced? Did he penetrate? Are you sure your life was in danger and you had no other choice?" This woman had been pulled off the street by a man who held a ten-inch knife at her throat and forcibly raped her. She was raped at midnight and was not able to return to her home until five in the morning. Police contacted her twice again in the next week, once by telephone at two in the morning and once at four in the morning. In her words: "The rape was probably the least traumatic incident of the whole evening. If I'm ever raped again, . . . I wouldn't report it to the police because of all the degradation. . . ."

If white women are subjected to unnecessary and often hostile questioning after having been raped, third-world women are often not believed at all. According to the white male ethos (which is not only sexist but racist), third-world women are defined from birth as impure. Thus the white male is provided with a pool of women who are fair game for sexual imperialism. Third-world women frequently do not report rape and for good reason. When blues singer Billie Holliday was ten years old, she was taken off to a local house by a neighbor and raped. Her mother brought the police to rescue her, and she was taken to the local police station crying and bleeding:

> When we got there, instead of treating me and Mom like somebody. . . . I guess they had me figured for having enticed this old goat into the whorehouse. . . . All I know for sure is they threw me into a cell . . . a fat white matron . . . saw I was still bleeding, she felt sorry for me and gave me a couple glasses of milk. But nobody else did anything for me except give me filthy looks and snicker to themselves.
>
> After a couple of days in a cell they dragged me into a court. Mr. Dick got sentenced to five years. They sentenced me to a Catholic institution.

Clearly the white man's chivalry is aimed only to protect the chastity of "his" women.

As a final irony, that same system of sexual values from which chivalry is derived has also provided womankind with an unwritten code of behavior, called femininity, which makes a feminine women the perfect victim of sexual aggression. If being chaste does not ward off the possibility of assault, being feminine certainly increases the chances that it will succeed. To be submissive is to defer to masculine strength; is to lack muscular development or any interest in defending oneself; is to let doors be opened, to have one's arm held when crossing the street. To be feminine is to wear shoes which make it difficult to run; skirts which inhibit one's stride; underclothes which inhibit the circulation. Is it not an intriguing observation that those very clothes which are thought to be flattering to the female and attractive to the male are those which make it impossible for a woman to defend herself against aggression?

Each girl as she grows into womanhood is taught fear. Fear is the form in which the female internalizes both chivalry and the double standard. Since, biologically speaking, women in fact have the same if not greater potential for sexual expression as do men, the woman who is taught that she must behave differently from a man must also learn to distrust her own carnality. She must deny her own feelings and learn not to act from them. She fears herself. This is the essence of passivity, and of course, a woman's passivity is not simply sexual, but functions to cripple her from self-expression in every area of her life.

Passivity itself prevents a woman from ever considering her own potential for self-defense and forces her to look to men for protection. The woman is taught fear, but this time fear of the other; and yet her only relief from this fear is to seek out the other. Moreover, the passive woman is taught to regard herself as impotent, unable to act, unable even to perceive, in no way self-sufficient, and, finally, as the object and not the subject of human behavior. It is in this sense that a woman is deprived of the status of a human being. She is not free to be.

In the *Elementary Structures of Kinship,* Claude Levi-Strauss gives to marriage this universal description, "It is always a system of exchange that we find at the origin of the rules of marriage." In this system of exchange, a woman is the "most precious possession." Levi-Strauss continues that the custom of including women as booty in the marketplace is still so general that "a whole volume would not be sufficient to enumerate instances of it." Levi-Strauss makes it clear that he does not exclude Western civilization from his definition of universal and cites examples from modern wedding ceremonies. (The marriage ceremony is still one in which the husband and wife become one, and "that one is the husband.")

The legal proscription against rape reflects this possessory view of women. An article in the 1952–53 *Yale Law Journal* describes the legal rationale behind laws against rape: "In our society sexual taboos, often enacted into law, buttress a system of monogamy based upon the law of 'free bargaining' of the potential spouses. Within this process the woman's power to withhold or grant sexual access is an important bargaining weapon." Presumably then, laws against rape are intended to protect the right of a woman, not for physical self-determination, but for physical "bargaining." The article goes on to explain explicitly why the preservation of the bodies of women is important to men:

> The consent standard in our society does more than protect a significant item of social currency for women; it fosters, and is in turn bolstered by, a masculine pride in the exclusive possession of a sexual object. The consent of a woman to sexual intercourse awards the man a privilege of bodily access, a personal "prize" whose value is enhanced by sole ownership. An additional reason for the man's condemnation of rape may be found in the threat to his status from a decrease in the "value" of his sexual possession which would result from forcible violation.

The passage concludes by making clear whose interest the law is designed to protect. "The man responds to this undercutting of his status as *possessor* of the girl with hostility toward the rapist; no other restitution device is available. The law of rape provides an orderly outlet for his vengeance." Presumably the female victim in any case will have been sufficiently socialized so as not to consciously feel any strong need for vengeance. If she does feel this need, society does not speak to it.

The laws against rape exist to protect rights of the male as possessor of the female body, and not the right of the female over her own body. Even without this enlightening passage from the *Yale Law Journal,* the laws themselves are clear: In no state can a man be accused of raping his wife. How can any man steal what already belongs to him? It is in the sense of rape as theft of another man's property that Kate Millett writes: "Traditionally rape has been viewed as an offense one male commits against another—a matter of abusing his woman." In raping another man's woman, a man may aggrandize his own manhood and concurrently reduce that of another man. Thus a man's honor is not subject directly to rape, but only indirectly through "his" woman.

If the basic social unit is the family, in which the woman is a possession of her husband, the superstructure of society is a male hierarchy in which men dominate other men (or patriarchal families dominate other patriarchal families). And it is no small irony that while the very social fabric of our male-dominated culture denies women equal access to political, economic, and legal power, the literature, myth, and humor of our culture depicts women not only as the power behind the throne, but the real source of the oppression of men. The religious version of this fairy tale blames Eve for both carnality and eating of the tree of knowledge, at the same time making her gullible to the obvious devices of a serpent. Adam, of course, is merely the trusting victim of love. Certainly this is a biased story. But no more biased than the one television audiences receive today from the latest slick comedians. Through a media which is owned by men, censored by a state dominated by men, all the evils of this social system which make a man's life unpleasant are blamed upon "the wife." The theory is: Were it not for the female who waits and plots to trap the male into marriage, modern man would be able to achieve Olympian freedom. She is made the scapegoat for a system which is in fact run by men.

Nowhere is this more clear than in the white racist use of the concept of white womanhood. The white male's open rape of black women, coupled with his overweening concern for the chastity and protection of his wife and daughters, represents an extreme of sexist and racist hypocrisy. While on the one hand she was held up as the standard for purity and virtue, on the other the Southern white woman was never asked if she wanted to be on a pedestal, and in fact any deviance from the male-defined standards for white womanhood was treated severely. (It is a powerful commentary on American racism that the historical role of blacks as slaves, and thus possessions without power has robbed black women of legal and economic protection through marriage. Thus black women in Southern society and in the ghettos of the North have long been easy game for white rapists.) The fear that black men would rape white women was, and is, classic paranoia. Quoting from Ann Breen's unpublished study of racism and sexism in the South, "The New South: White Man's Country," Frederick Douglass legitimately points out that had the black man wished to rape white women, he had ample opportunity to do so during the Civil War when white women, the wives, sisters, daughters, and mothers of the rebels, were left in the care of blacks. But yet not a single act of rape was committed during this time. The Ku Klux Klan, who tarred and feathered black men and lynched them in the honor of the purity of white womanhood, also applied tar and feathers to a Southern white woman accused of bigamy, which leads one to suspect that Southern white men were not so much outraged at the violation of the woman as a person, in the few instances where rape was actually committed by black men, but at the violation of his property rights. In the situation where a black man was found to be having sexual relations with a white woman, the white woman could exercise skin-privilege, and claim that she had been raped, in which case the black man was lynched. But if she did not claim rape, she herself was subject to lynching.

In constructing the myth of white womanhood so as to justify the lynching and oppression of black men and women, the white male has created a convenient symbol of his own power which has resulted in black hostility toward the white "bitch," accompanied by an unreasonable fear on the part of many white women of the black rapist. Moreover, it is not surprising that after being told for two centuries that he wants to rape white women, occasionally a black man does actually commit that act. But it is crucial to note that the frequency of this is outrageously exaggerated in the white mythos. Ninety percent of reported rape is intra- not interracial.

In *Soul on Ice,* Eldridge Cleaver has described the mixing of a rage against white power with the internalized sexism of a black man raping a white woman: "Somehow I arrived at the conclusion that, as a matter of principle, it was of paramount importance for me to have an antagonistic, ruthless attitude toward white women. . . . Rape was an insurrectionary act. It delighted me that I was defying and trampling upon the white man's law, upon his system of values and that I was defiling his women—and this point, I believe, was the most satisfying to me because I was very resentful over the historical fact of how the white man has used the black woman." Thus a black man uses white women to take out his rage against white men. But in fact, whenever a rape of a white woman by a black man does take place, it is again the white man who benefits. First, the act itself terrorizes the white woman and makes her more dependent on the white male for protection. Then, if the woman prosecutes her attacker, the white man is afforded legal opportunity to exercise overt racism. Of course, the knowledge of the rape helps to perpetuate two myths which are beneficial to white male rule—the bestiality of the black man and the desirability of white women. Finally, the white man surely benefits because he himself is not the object of attack—he has been allowed to stay in power.

Indeed, the existence of rape in any form is beneficial to the ruling class of white males. For rape is a kind of terrorism which severely limits the freedom of women and makes women dependent on men. Moreover, in the act of rape, the rage that one man may harbor toward another higher in the male hierarchy can be deflected toward a female scapegoat. For every man there is always someone lower on the social scale on whom he can take out his aggressions. And that is any woman alive.

The notion of power is the key to the male ego in this culture, for the two acceptable measures of masculinity are a man's power over women and his power over other men. A man may boast to his friends that "I have twenty men working for me." It is also aggrandizement of his ego if he has the financial power to clothe his wife in furs and jewels. And, if a man lacks the wherewithal to acquire such power, he can always express his rage through equally masculine activities—rape and theft. Since male society defines the female as a possession, it is not surprising that the felony most often committed together with rape is theft. As the following classic tale of rape points out, the elements of theft, violence, and forced sexual relations merge into an indistinguishable whole.

The woman who told this story was acquainted with the man who tried to rape her. When the man learned that she was going to be staying alone for the weekend, he began early in the day a polite campaign to get her to go out with him. When she continued to refuse his request, his chivalrous mask dropped away:

> I had locked all the doors because I was afraid, and I don't know how he got in; it was probably through the screen door. When I woke up, he was shaking my leg. His eyes were red, and I knew he had been drinking or smoking. I thought I would try to talk my way out of it. He started by saying that he wanted to sleep with me, and then he got angrier and angrier, until he started to say, "I want pussy," "I want pussy." Then, I got scared and tried to push him away. That's when he started to force himself on me. It was awful. It was the most humiliating, terrible feeling. He was forcing my legs apart and ripping my clothes off. And it was painful. I did fight him—he was slightly drunk and I was able to keep him away. I had taken judo a few years back, but I was afraid to throw a chop for fear that he'd kill me. I could see he was getting more and more violent. I was thinking wildly of some way to get out of this alive, and then I said to him, "Do you want money. I'll give you money." We had money but I was also thinking that if I got to the back room I could telephone the police—as if the police would have even helped. It was a stupid thing to think of because obviously he would follow me. And he did. When he saw me pick up the phone, he tried to tie the cord around my neck. I screamed at him that I did have the money in another room, that I was going to call the police because I was scared, but that I would never tell anybody what happened. It would be an absolute secret. He said, okay, and I went to get the money. But when he got it, all of a sudden he got this crazy look in his eye and he said to me, "Now I'm going to kill you." Then I started saying my prayers. I knew there was nothing I could do. He started to hit me—I still wasn't sure if he wanted to rape me at this point—or just to kill me. He was hurting me, but hadn't yet gotten me into a strangle-hold because he was still drunk and off balance. Somehow we pushed into the kitchen where I kept looking at this big knife. But I didn't pick it up. Somehow, no matter how much I hated him at that moment, I still couldn't imagine putting the knife in his flesh, and then I was afraid he would grab it and stick it into me. Then he was hitting me again and somehow we pushed through the back door of the kitchen and onto the porch steps. We fell down the steps and that's when he started to strangle me. He was on top of me. He just went on and on until finally I lost consciousness. I did scream, though my screams sounded like whispers to me. But what happened

was that a cab driver happened by and frightened him away. The cab driver revived me—I was out only a minute at the most. And then I ran across the street and I grabbed the woman who was our neighbor and screamed at her, "Am I alive? Am I still alive?"

Rape is an act of aggression in which the victim is denied her self-determination. It is an act of violence which, if not actually followed by beatings or murder, nevertheless always carries with it the threat of death. And finally, rape is a form of mass terrorism, for the victims of rape are chosen indiscriminately, but the propagandists for male supremacy broadcast that it is women who cause rape by being unchaste or in the wrong place at the wrong time—in essence, by behaving as though they were free.

The threat of rape is used to deny women employment. (In California, the Berkeley Public Library, until pushed by the Federal Employment Practices Commission, refused to hire female shelvers because of perverted men in the stacks.) The fear of rape keeps women off the streets at night. Keeps women at home. Keeps women passive and modest for fear that they be thought provocative.

It is part of human dignity to be able to defend oneself, and women are learning. Some women have learned karate; some to shoot guns. And yet we will not be free until the threat of rape and the atmosphere of violence is ended, and to end that the nature of male behavior must change.

But rape is not an isolated act that can be rooted out from patriarchy without ending patriarchy itself. The same men and power structure who victimize women are engaged in the act of raping Vietnam, raping black people, and the very earth we live upon. Rape is a classic act of domination where, in the words of Kate Millett, "the emotions of hatred, contempt, and the desire to break or violate personality," takes place. This breaking of the personality characterizes modern life itself. No simple reforms can eliminate rape. As the symbolic expression of the white male hierarchy, rape is the quintessential act of our civilization, one which, Valerie Solanis warns, is in danger of "humping itself to death."

3 Rape and Rape Laws: Sexism in Society and Law

CAMILLE E. LeGRAND

IN hundreds of ways, large and small, a woman's life is shaped by the persistent threat of rape: women hesitate to venture out at night without male escorts, to live alone, to hitchhike, to stay late at the office to work alone, to take certain jobs. Men in prison who live with the threat of homosexual rape are probably the only men in our society who experience fear comparable to that felt by all women. The fear of rape . . . also exaggerates the dependency of women upon men. The law concerning forcible rape and the way it functions both influences and is influenced by the relationship between men and women in our society. Yet the legal commentators who have written on the subject have not analyzed rape laws with any sensitivity to this phenomenon. And they have ignored the possibility that rape laws as they are presently conceived, rather than protecting women, might actually work to

Reprinted by permission from the *California Law Review* (May 1973), vol. 61. Copyright © 1973 California Law Review, Inc.

their disadvantage by hindering prosecution of rapists and by exacerbating the inequality between men and women.

This article argues that rape laws are largely based on traditional attitudes about social roles and sexual mores. The structure of the laws, enforcement, and prosecution are all based on untested assumptions about the incidence of the crime, the motivation of the criminal, and the psychology of the victim. The laws do not effectively deter rape: Police enforcement of complaints is inadequate, and judicial treatment of defendants is oversolicitous. Rape laws are not designed, nor do they function, to protect a woman's interest in physical integrity. Indeed, rather than protecting women, the rape laws might actually be a disability for them, since they reinforce traditional attitudes about social and sexual roles. . . . If the laws were changed to relate more rationally to the reality of the crime and to the goal of sexual equality, attitudes about the crime might also change.

This article is concerned only with forcible rape, which generally refers to sexual intercourse accomplished without the consent of the female. Since consent is the crucial element in rape, forcible rape may include many kinds of conduct that do not involve physical force. California, for instance, defines forcible rape as including situations in which: (1) the victim is legally incapable of giving consent due to her mental condition; (2) her resistance is overcome by force; (3) she is prevented from resisting by threats or drugs; (4) she is unconscious; or (5) she is deceived into believing the perpetrator is her husband. Thus it is possible to commit rape without putting the victim in fear. The available data show, however, that nearly all reported rapes involve either verbal threats, the use of a weapon, or physical force. Therefore, forcible rape as used here generally means rape committed by means of physical force or threats, either actual or implied. . . .

INDIVIDUAL AND SOCIAL INTERESTS PROTECTED BY RAPE LAWS

In order to place the phenomenon of rape in its legal context, it is necessary to understand the conceptual framework in which rape laws exist. Here the focal question is: Who or what do rape laws protect? Legal writers analyzing rape laws have concluded that rape laws protect male interests: Rape laws bolster, and in turn are bolstered by, "a masculine pride in the exclusive possession of a sexual object" (Comment, 1952:72); they focus a male's aggression, based on fear of losing his sexual partner, against rapists rather than against innocent competitors (Dworkin, 1966: 684); rape laws help protect the male from any "decrease in the 'value' of his sexual 'possession'," which results from forcible violation (Comment, 1952:73). It is pointed out that using words like "ravaged" and "despoiled" to describe the rape victim reflects the idea of a stain attaching to the woman's body and the subsequent loss of her value to her male possessor. However accurate these conclusions are, it is interesting that these analyses have not focused on a woman's physical integrity, peace of mind, or freedom of movement without fear of sexual attack as fundamental values to be protected by rape laws. The male values that are protected by rape laws are easily translated into societal values. This may explain why so many countries and some states classify rape as a crime against society, not as a crime against the person. California, for instance, categorizes rape along with gambling, indecent exposure, horse racing, and abortion as crimes against the person *and* against public decency and good morals.

The statutory rape laws offer a further indication that rape laws seek to protect male interests. Statutory rape laws ostensibly protect girls too young to make an intelligent decision when hazards such as pregnancy and venereal disease are involved. This justification might be convincing if laws protected only the very young, but applied to a seventeen-year-old woman they appear more likely to reflect moral value judgments. Because only the sexual activity of young women, not young men, is regulated, it may be argued that the value served by statutory rape laws is the preservation of the market value of virginal young women as potential brides, rather than the protection of the naïve from sexual exploitation. A young woman's right to choose whether to be chaste or sexually active appears to have been given little consideration in the formulation of statutory rape laws. Her consent to sexual intercourse is, by law, irrelevant to whether that intercourse is or is not rape.

The legal impossibility of rape of a wife by her husband is another indication that rape laws are not aimed at protecting women from sexual assault. If the laws were designed to protect women, this exception would make no sense. There are, of course, conceptual difficulties involved in making rape a crime between husband and wife.[1] But if a woman suffers no less pain, humiliation, or fear from forcible sexual penetration by her husband than by a relative, a boyfriend, or a stranger, the difference is not great enough to warrant the total insulation of the former but not the latter from legal sanction. One writer (Comment, 1954: 724–25) has recognized that women need protection from forcible sexual encounters with their husbands. He concludes, however, that only the law of battery lends itself to that use—and even its use presents difficulties. Rather than suggesting a means to protect the interests of wives against forcible sex with their husbands, this commentator concludes that only after an absolute and final divorce decree should a husband be prosecuted for rape of his wife. Such a rule, he argues, is necessary to encourage reconciliation between the spouses during the interim waiting period.

Rape laws, and legal discussions of those laws, are also shaped by the fear of the stereotypical maniac rapist who leaps from the bush with knife in hand. The fear of the psychopathic rapist, and the high value of the male interests threatened by rape (for example, the "despoiling of his goods") have no doubt combined to produce the severe sentences that the laws stand ready to impose for rape. A number of states provide . . . for sentences up to life imprisonment. Comparisons with crimes of comparable magnitude show that rape carries very high penalties. Conviction for assault with a deadly weapon or with force likely to produce great bodily injury carries a minimum sentence of six months in California. Yet rape under the same circumstances carries a minimum sentence of three years. Furthermore, in California, sodomy is punished by a one-year to life sentence, whether or not force is used.

INVESTIGATION AND PROSECUTION: THE IMPEDIMENTS TO CONVICTION

Although rapes tend to be both violent and planned, very few apprehended rapists are ever charged with and convicted of rape; fewer yet are committed to institutions. In California, there is a higher acquittal rate for rape than for any other felony. Regional studies (e.g., Dunham, 1951:73) show that about 10 percent of those originally charged with rape go to prison. The reasons for this failure to charge and convict are clear: Legal and social attitudes about rape have produced a network of formal and informal restraints on the actions of police, prosecutors, judges, and juries that hinder prosecutions for forcible rape.

Investigation of Rape Complaints

Unfounding of Rape Complaints. About one-fifth of the rape complaints received by police are "unfounded" after they are made (Comment, 1968:280; Federal Bureau of Investigation, 1971:14; Schiff, 1969:108). This term is a technical one, meaning only that police, for various reasons, have decided not to advise prosecution. It does not imply that the woman's report of the rape is inaccurate. The unfortunate ambiguity of the term and the high rate of "unfounding" have perhaps contributed to the myth that women make many false rape complaints.

Most complaints subsequently "unfounded" by police involve at least one of the following factors: (1) evidence that the victim was intoxicated, (2) delay in reporting by the victim, (3) lack of physical condition supporting the allegation, (4) refusal to submit to a medical examination, (5) the previous relationship of the victim and the offender, and (6) the use of a weapon without accompanying battery. Police also "unfound" complaints because victims fail to preserve necessary physical evidence (for instance, they may douche before reporting the crime) or because victims are too emotionally upset, too young, too afraid, or too embarrassed to cooperate with the ordeal of the police investigation. Most of these factors are not relevant to whether or not a rape has been committed. They are, however, relevant to the chances of obtaining a conviction in court. For that reason, complaints presenting these prosecutorial disadvantages are "unfounded."

Victim precipitation (Amir, 1971:266) may weaken an otherwise strong case against a rapist and lead police to "unfound" the complaint. Victim precipitation is a conclusory label applied to cases where the victim either retracts from an initial agreement to have sexual relations or enters into a vulnerable situation. Police commonly refuse to proceed with a complaint involving victim precipitation since such a complaint has little chance of leading to a conviction. As a post facto conclusion, however, a finding of victim precipitation depends upon the perspective of the largely male police, prosecutors, and judges who appraise the case. The concept of victim precipitation hinges primarily on male definitions of expressed or implied consent to engage in sexual relations, and is shaped by traditional restrictive stereotypes of women. Thus, hitchhiking and walking alone at night in a rough neighborhood may be considered behavior encouraging a sexual attack. This view of what a *man* can assume to be a sexual invitation is unreasonable, but is so well engrained in society that women often accept it as well. As a result, a woman may react to being raped with considerable guilt and refuse to report the attack. A woman hitchhiker may later feel that she encouraged the rape simply by accepting a ride. Yet, when the female hitchhiker first sets out to get a ride, she normally is not expecting—or hoping for—a sexual encounter. A woman should not be made to feel guilty for acts that do not involve express sexual invitation; nor should she be denied the right to change her mind. In its failure to accord any consideration to the woman victim's intentions, victim precipitation becomes nothing more than a male view of the circumstances leading up to the incident.

Certainly many complaints "unfounded" by police would, as a practical matter, result in acquittals were they brought to court. This is not to say, however, that most "unfounded" complaints are false or that they involve victim precipitation, although this may be the contention of the police. Rather the high rate of "unfounding" may instead indicate that the rape laws as they are now structured are overly solicitous to the defendant and overly suspicious of the complainant. If laws were structured so as to facilitate rather than prevent the conviction of rapists, the "unfounding" rate by police would almost certainly diminish.

Failure to Use Scientific Investigation. A recent study (Comment, 1968:310–11) found that although medical examinations were obtained from 60 percent of the rape victims, the examination results were actually used in only 18 percent of the complaints to help determine whether or not to "unfound." The police insisted that a medical examination be performed, discrediting the woman's veracity if she refused, yet they made little use of the evidence derived from the examination when determining whether or not to press charges.

Thirty years ago a police medical examiner (Rife, 1940) stated that it was possible to reconstruct most rapes by means of scientific evidence, and since then investigative techniques have been greatly refined. Neutron activation analysis, by establishing with a high degree of probability that hairs or other materials found in separate places have a common origin, can help exonerate a defendant or establish his presence at the scene of the rape (Karjala, 1971). The victim's clothing can be examined microscopically and under fluorescent light to establish facts about the scene of the offense. Teeth marks, scratches, and bruises can be located; lesions on or about the introitus and the condition of the hymen can be noted. Tests for venereal disease can be performed. Washings taken from the vulva, perineum, and vaginal vault can give rise to strong evidence of recent intercourse. Similarly, the accused's clothing and person can be examined. Washings taken from the accused's penis can determine that he has recently engaged in intercourse (Thomas and Van Hecke, 1963). Fingernail scrapings from both parties are extremely valuable in establishing the identity of the rapist and the degree of the victim's resistance (Bornstein, 1958). Similarly to blood groups, semen can be typed in order to prove whether a particular suspect could have committed the rape.

Although these tests cannot always prove that a rape occurred, and although women sometimes delay reporting a rape so that this type of investigation cannot be performed, a thorough investigation by a medical examiner often can prove not only that intercourse has occurred but also the probability that there has been a rape and the probability that the accused is the rapist. Yet these scientific tests are seldom employed. In view of the prevalent concern about false rape reports, it is curious that practical methods of combating such false reports are not used more frequently.

Obstacles to Rape Convictions

The rape laws and the literature concerning them have been dominated by fears that false rape charges might result in the convictions of innocent men. The false complaint is feared more in rape cases than in other crimes because of the basic assumptions that many women are either amoral or hostile to men (Note, 1972: 1373), and that women can induce rape convictions solely by virtue of fabricated reports. The motives seen as prompting false accusations of rape are: shame, protection of an innocent party, blackmail purposes, hatred, revenge, and notoriety. The writer points out that to whatever extent these motives exist, they are outweighed by the disincentives to report rapes and by the ease with which modern criminal investigation and traditional legal rules can uncover them. The commentators, however, consistently have failed to document or closely analyze these assumptions. Nevertheless, these fears have produced and sustained laws and attitudes that seek to protect the innocent from an unjust rape conviction, rather than to protect women from rape.

Concomitant with the assumption that women make false rape charges is the belief that it is difficult to defend against a charge of rape. Lord Chief Justice Hale's (1778:635) old saw that rape is a charge "easily to be made and hard to be proved, and harder to be defended" expresses that partnership of fears and has been quoted by virtually every legal writer who has discussed rape. It is further preserved in California jury instructions. The notion that it is difficult to defend against a rape charge originates in the belief that, since there is seldom any corroborative evidence in rape cases (Comment, 1958:651), the outcome hinges on oath against oath. Also, it is believed that juries are inordinately sympathetic with rape victims (Comment, 1970:460; Puttkammer, 1925:422). Actually, jury sympathy often may be with the defendant.[2]

Another attitude affecting the conviction rate is the pervasive belief that women like to be raped (Dworkin, 1966:682). Psychological literature is a prime source of this myth. Concurrently, there is a feeling that men who rape are not responsible for their acts since they are victims of "uncontrollable emotions and passions, unexplainable urges, and fierce desires which can be considered impossible to control once they have been aroused" (McLaughlin, 1962:28). Once a man is aroused, the belief goes, rape is the natural result if the woman is not willing to satisfy the appetite she has created. Notions that women enjoy assaults and that men are subject to uncontrollable sexual passions aroused by women diminish the amount of blameworthiness society is willing to ascribe to rapists. As a result, rape is redefined as an act that is viewed as scarcely criminal. Thus, it is not surprising that psychologists, generally men, declare rapists to be normal (Amir, 1971:314).

Psychiatric Examination of Victims. Some commentators press for a psychiatric examination of the victim as a means of identifying the fabricated complaint. One writer (Note, 1950:102) stated that false accusations often are made by mentally disturbed women; thus, if the state offers neither corroborating evidence nor a psychiatric report, "it would not be assumed that the witness is a normal individual, notwithstanding the persuasiveness of her testimony." Another writer (Comment, 1958:651) stated that sex complaints are easily made, therefore psychiatric examination of alleged victims is recommended. Neither offered evidence either for the proposition that unsubstantiated or false charges are frequently brought or for the assumption that psychiatric examinations can determine the facts of the case or the veracity of the victim's testimony. A third writer (Jarrett, 1966:238–40) recognized that such an examination will not produce reliable results if the victim submits to it unwillingly, yet he still concluded that she should be forced to submit to one if the issue of her mental condition is raised. An English writer (Williams, 1962:664) conceding the unreliability of psychiatric examinations, suggested that lie detector tests for victims be required, since sex cases are prone to deliberately false charges resulting from neurosis, fantasy, jealousy, spite, or the woman's refusal to admit that she consented to the sexual relations. Yet no evidence supporting these underlying assumptions was provided.

In California, the supreme court has held to a middle course on the issue of psychiatric examination of victims (*Ballard* v. *Superior Court,* 1966) vesting discretion in the trial judge to order such an examination if little corroboration supports the charge and if the defense raises the issue of the victim's mental condition affecting her veracity. The judge may comment to the jury on the victim's refusal to undergo examination. Although a psychiatrist can tell if his patient is subject to sexual delusions, he cannot thereby prove she has not been raped (Note, 1967:1143; Slovenko, 1966:20). Apparently no firm legal definition of delusion exists since legal writers interchange fantasy and delusion. Certainly most women and most men have sexual fantasies, but that is unrelated to a person's veracity. Even if delusion is carefully restricted to describe only persons with serious mental disorders, a grave problem remains. If a psychiatrist's statement that a woman is subject to delusions creates a presumption that she has not been raped, then the law will, in effect, license the rape of mentally disordered women. Women patients in mental hospitals, for example, would have little protection from sexual assaults.

Mandatory psychiatric examination of victims would inflict additional trauma upon the complaining victim, would further discourage women from reporting sexual assaults, and would increase the tendency to place the victim rather than the accused on trial—while failing to achieve its intended purpose of establishing the victim's veracity.

The Consent Standard and Credibility of the Victim. Attacks on the consent standard, which defines rape in terms of the woman's frame of mind, have also been based on the fear of convicting innocent men of rape. Psychological theorizing, states one writer (Dworkin, 1966:683), indicates the unreliability of a woman's account of a rape, so "nothing should be left to the conceivably unreasonable opinion of the alleged victim," the woman's opinion is often distorted. He suggests that a "resistance" standard replace the consent standard. Another writer (Puttkammer, 1925: 421–2) also suspicious of the consent standard, believes that the complaining witness is "compelled by many motives of self-interest" to assert that the sexual act was rape. He believes that false charges can be constructed with exceptional ease and are "extremely likely to succeed." Yet virtually no evidence is offered in support of any of these beliefs.

One precaution taken on behalf of the accused is the well settled rule that evidence of another sex crime committed by the defendant at a different time and against another person, having no connection with the crime charged, is not admissible unless to show, for instance, the identification of the accused (*People* v. *Paxton,* 1967). Although evidence of past sexual acts cannot be used to impeach the male, however, it is a general rule that evidence of the "unchastity" of the female is admissible for the purpose of showing the probability of her consent to the act of intercourse. It is considered more probable that an "unchaste" woman will consent more readily to intercourse than a chaste woman. "Unchastity" simply means, of course, that the woman, if unmarried, is not a virgin. California incorporates this presumption into a mandatory cautionary instruction which states that the jury may infer that a woman who has once consented to sexual intercourse would be more likely to consent again, and that the evidence of her "unchastity" goes both to the issue of her consent and to her credibility. Moreover, defendant may show (*Lewis*

v. *State,* 1953) that the prosecutrix has engaged in intercourse with him before, thus raising a presumption of her consent to the sexual act charged. Thus, legally, a man's previous sexual attacks, even if criminal, are of no relevance to his credibility, but once a woman has had sexual relations with one man, a legal presumption exists that she has consented to sexual relations with all men. And if a woman once submits willingly to a man, the presumption raised by her prior consent means that that man is quite safe in forcing her submission later. The law further insists that if the victim delays in reporting the rape, the delay will be considered a circumstance tending to show she consented to the intercourse (*State* v. *Risen,* 1951).

Because of the fear of false rape complaints, other legal writers (Note, 1972:1367) have defended corroborative evidence rules, which require some evidence other than the victim's testimony to convict for rape. A judge (Ploscowe, 1960:223), defending the necessity for the New York corroborative evidence rule, which had virtually eliminated conviction for rape, commented that prosecuting attorneys must continually guard against charges of rape brought by spurned females seeking revenge or blackmail. He categorically stated that "far too many men have been railroaded on sex offense charges." Another writer (Note, 1967:1137–38) found that the corroborative evidence rule owes its existence to the inordinate danger that innocent men will be convicted of rape. He further stated that the word of the complaining witness is "very often false . . . since stories of rape are frequently lies or fantasies." He cited as evidence for this conclusion one Michigan case in which the court found a possible motive for a false rape complaint. Only two writers (Ludwig, 1970; Note, 1972) have found no rational basis for inherent suspicion of the victim's testimony.

Sentencing

The belief that rape is really an uncontrollable urge and that women are basically to blame for rape arises in case law, and it may well be responsible for the imposition of very light sentences by some judges. The disproportionately high percentage of rapists who receive probation is indicative of peculiar judicial attitudes toward rape. *State* v. *Chaney* (1970:446–47), an Alaska supreme court case, exemplifies how these attitudes can affect the sentencing process. The evidence of this case revealed that after the accused and a companion invited the victim into a car, they beat her and raped her four times. The accused forced her to perform fellatio with his companion, took all her money, and threatened her with reprisals if she told the police. The facts apparently were not disputed, and the important question was the severity of the sentence. A military spokesman (the accused was in the Armed Services) told the sentencing court: "An occurrence such as the one concerned here is very common and happens many times each night in Anchorage. Needless to say, Donald Chaney was the unlucky 'G.I.' that picked a young lady who told." Despite the undisputed evidence of the brutality of this rape and the unusual severity of the local problem, the trial judge sentenced the accused to two concurrent one-year terms and urged immediate parole.

As the supreme court pointed out in reviewing this sentence, the record was devoid of any trace of remorse by the defendant. The supreme court, feeling that the trial court treated the defendant as though "he was only technically guilty and minimally blameworthy," was sufficiently outraged to order imposition of a stiffer sentence. Nevertheless, the supreme court stated that the judge properly considered that the victim's voluntary entrance into the defendant's car was a mitigating circumstance, which would properly go to reduce the sentence.

The problem raised by *Chaney* is not so much the light sentence imposed by the trial judge, but the judge's attitude that rape is not really a crime deserving punishment. Where attitudes about rape, based on misconceptions, lead judges to believe that the victims are always to blame, the sentencing of defendants is apt to be arbitrarily light. Although light sentences may be generally sufficient in terms of deterrence and rehabilitation, each case should be decided on its facts and not under the prejudice that rape is acceptable behavior.

Summary

The fear of the maniac and the genuine desire to protect chaste, totally innocent women from sexual assault clash mightily with the fear of convicting innocent men. As a result, we have on one hand harsh penalties for rape; on the other, however, we have few convictions and a myriad of laws and attitudes that tend to protect men from conviction except when the complainant is a chaste, mentally healthy woman who reports the attack promptly, and who is willing and able to undergo the horrors of a rape trial.

Furthermore, rape laws regard the nonmarital sexual activity of men as irrelevant to the rapist's veracity, yet the nonmarital sexual activity of the woman condemns her. The sexually active woman is not only regarded as a liar, she is considered fair game. Such a double standard, which considers male sexuality normal and female sexuality abnormal, serves to enhance the dichotomy between the "good" woman, who is the sole sexual possession of one male, and the "bad" woman who, lacking status as a sole possession, functions as the outlet for normal male promiscuity and therefore cannot be raped.

SUGGESTIONS FOR REFORM

Rape laws are structured so as to frighten would-be rapists by potentially heavy sentences and at the same time to prevent the conviction of rapists except in rare instances where the offense is so outrageous that sentiment of the police, prosecutors, judge, and jury, overpowers the mechanisms that impede conviction. Jury antagonism to rape victims ("she was asking for it"; "she could have resisted") is blamed by prosecutors for the low conviction rate, but the cumulative effect of the cautionary instructions probably gives the jury little choice but to acquit in a great many cases. The jury is told that a charge of rape is easily made and difficult to defend against and that the victim's testimony must be examined with caution. Even if the jury is told that corroborative evidence is not necessary, they are generally bombarded with evidence of the "unchastity" of the victim, which, they are told, discredits her testimony. If she has delayed reporting the rape or if she has refused to submit to a medical examination, her testimony is partially discredited. If she refuses to submit to a court-ordered psychiatric examination or if she is found to be mentally unbalanced, her testimony is further discredited. If evidence is presented that she previously consented to intercourse with the accused, her testimony is almost entirely discredited.

Nothing comparable to these restrictions exists elsewhere in criminal law. If, for example, a woman brings a charge of kidnapping, and the question of her consent to be moved depends upon whether the testimony of the accused or the victim is more credible, no set of laws comparable to rape laws comes into play to protect the accused. As far as the jury's ability to resolve the issues is concerned, however, there seems to be no substantial difference between an uncorroborated charge of kidnapping and an uncorroborated charge of rape. Juries exist, after all, to decide whose testimony is the most credible, and they are instructed to convict only if satisfied of the accused's guilt. There should be no special rules for rape.

The most unrealistic aspect of rape law is the treatment of the victim's chastity in court. The concept of chastity is apparently based upon the nineteenth century view that there are two kinds of women: "good" and "bad." Those who are either faithful wives or virgins deserve the law's protection; women outside these groups are deemed unworthy of protection. The sharp differentiation between the faithful wife or virgin on one hand and the "loose" woman on the other has long since disappeared, and its central role in rape law is, at best, anachronistic. The courts should take judicial notice of the fact that a great many women in our society have sexual relations outside of the marriage relationship (Luckey and Nass, 1969; Vener et al., 1972). The chastity requirement today places significant numbers of women, rather than a few outcasts, beyond the protection of the law. Attempts to introduce evidence of unchastity into rape trials should be rejected altogether. The relationship between a woman's chastity and whether or not she has been raped is simply too attenuated to warrant consideration as relevant evidence.

The reluctance of police and prosecutors to proceed with complaints involving an accused previously known to the victim suggests the difficulty in securing convictions in such cases. In view of the large number of rapes committed by men known to their victims, however, it is essential that juries not be permitted to assume that such previous acquaintance undercuts the victim's credibility. Evidence concerning the prior relationship of victim and accused should be admissible only for the purpose of showing a bad faith motive by the complainant in making the charge or in verifying the identification of the accused. Instructions should carefully caution the jury against assuming that the bare existence of a prior relationship is otherwise relevant to the victim's credibility.

Much of the fear of convicting innocent men could be overcome if scientific techniques for reconstructing the sexual acts charged were fully exploited. Prosecutorial discretion is minimally regulated, but it would not be unreasonable for the law to require that this discretion be based upon an examination of all facts potentially available to the prosecutor—including such scientific data.

Punishment of the rapist also should be reevaluated. Procedures for mentally disordered sex offenders may help control the psychopathic rapist, but little has been done to discourage the more frequently encountered "normal" rapist. Potentially high sentences probably serve more to deter victims from complaining and juries from convicting than they serve to deter rapists from raping. It seems clear that increased penalties for rape do not give increased protection to women (Schwartz, 1968). Lower maximum sentences, along with mandatory psychiatric evaluation, would probably be more effective in securing convictions. Serious consideration might be given to castration as a rehabilitative technique as used in European countries where it is generally performed with the rapist's consent and is accompanied by intensive psychotherapy (Stürup, 1960). Castration instead of prison may well be a choice that the convicted rapist should be permitted to make. There is precedent for the castration of criminals in this country. In the past, California provided for the compulsory asexualization (castration) of the recidivist in state prison who had given evidence while in prison that he was a "moral or sexual degenerate or pervert." Those serving life sentences could be castrated even if they were not recidivists. The statute was never tested in court. A major defect in this proposal, however, is that castration of rapists would tend to reinforce the myth that rapists are abnormal men seized by uncontrollable urges and that the problem is physical and psychological rather than societal.

Consideration should also be given to whether it makes sense to limit rape to cases of penetration of the vagina by a penis. Since the offense actually consists of a sexual outrage to the person, that outrage should probably include a broader range of sexual contact. In any case, there is no sound reason for restricting rape to male offenders and female victims. Men who are sexually assaulted should have the same protection as female victims, and women who sexually assault men or other women should be liable for conviction as conventional rapists. Considering rape as a sexual assault rather than as a special crime against women might do much to place rape law in a healthier perspective and to reduce the mythical elements that have tended to make rape laws a means of reinforcing the status of women as sexual possessions.

CONCLUSIONS

Available statistics indicate that rapes not only are heavily underreported, but are also increasing very rapidly. Contrary to popular belief, rapes are generally planned, involve physical force, and are committed by normal young men who are often acquainted with their victims. There are few false rape complaints, and these are easily disposed of by the police. Apprehended rapists are rarely convicted of rape. Scientific investigation, although of great value, is seldom conducted or, if conducted, is seldom used by the police.

On the other hand, there exists a great network of laws and attitudes based on the assumptions that false rape complaints are plentiful and that innocent men can easily be convicted of rape. As the facts show, both these assumptions are generally unfounded. An entire legal framework of myths and stereotyped preconceptions unrelated to reality has been constructed. This gulf between myth and reality necessitates reevaluation of rape laws. A reconstruction of these laws with careful attention to the reality of rape could not only make the disposition of rape charges and convictions more efficient and more fair, but it could also serve to promote a much needed change in society's attitude toward rape.

NOTES

1. The primary conceptual barrier to making forcible sexual intercourse between husband and wife rape is the consent standard. This doctrine is based on the premises that consent to sexual relations is inseparable from the marriage relation itself and that consent is a total defense to a charge of rape. Since a woman is, theoretically, consenting to all sexual intercourse with her husband as long as she remains married, rape is not possible between marital partners. The other barriers to defining an offense by a husband against his wife as rape are largely administrative—problems of proof and evidence as well as opportunity for malicious prosecution.

2. A deputy district attorney for Los Angeles County related a recent case in which a nineteen-year-old secretary was raped in a parking lot in daylight. A witness to the rape made a positive identification. The district attorney commented that "all rape cases are hard to prosecute, of course, but this one was so solid." Yet the jury acquitted the accused. One juror stated: "I just couldn't believe that a boy whose girlfriend was as pretty as the one who came into court to testify would have even wanted to rape such a plain-looking girl." The juror's inability to imagine the possibility of such a rape is hardly warranted: although the evidence could not be admitted into court, the defendant had been acquitted, just nine days before the victim was raped, on a charge of assault with intent to rape. That time he had a gun (Stumbo, 1972).

REFERENCES

Amir, Menachem. 1971. *Patterns in Forcible Rape.* Chicago: University of Chicago Press.

Ballard v. *Superior Court.* 1966. 410 P.2d 838.

Bornstein, F. P. 1958. "The El Paso County Program for the Medical Investigation of Sexual Offenses," *Journal of Forensic Science* 3:123–30.

Comment. 1970. "The Corroboration Rule and Crimes Accompanying a Rape," *University of Pennsylvania Law Review* 118:458–72.

Comment. 1958. "Evidence, Sex Offenses, and Credibility of Complaining Witness," *Iowa Law Review* 43:650–54.

Comment. 1952. "Forcible and Statutory Rape: An Exploration of the Operation and Objectives of the Consent Standard," *Yale Law Journal* 62:55–83.

Comment. 1968. "Police Discretion and the Judgment That a Crime Has Been Committed—Rape in Philadelphia," *University of Pennsylvania Law Review* 117:277–321.

Comment. 1954. "Rape and Battery between Husband and Wife," *Stanford Law Review* 6:719–34.

Dunham, H. Warren. 1951. *Crucial Issues in the Treatment and Control of Sexual Deviation in the Community.* Lansing: Michigan Department of Mental Health.

Dworkin, Roger B. 1966. "The Resistance Standard in Rape Legislation," *Stanford Law Review* 18:680–89.

Federal Bureau of Investigation. 1971. *Uniform Crime Reports 1970.* Vol. 1. Washington, D.C.: United States Government Printing Office.

Hale, Matthew. 1778. *The History of the Pleas of the Crown.* London: Richard Tonson.

Jarrett, Tommy W. 1966. "Criminal Law—Psychiatric Examination of the Prosecutrix in Rape Cases," *North Carolina Law Review* 45:234–40.

Karjala, Dennis S. 1971. "The Evidentiary Uses of Neutron Activation Analysis," *California Law Review* 59:997–1080.

Lewis v. *State.* 1953. 64 So. 2d 634 (Mississippi).

Luckey, Eleanore B. and Gilbert D. Nass. 1969. "A Comparison of Sexual Attitudes and Behaviors in an International Sample," *Journal of Marriage and the Family* 31:364–79.

Ludwig, Frederick J. 1970. "The Case for the Repeal of the Sex Corroboration Requirement in New York," *Brooklyn Law Review* 36:378–86.

McLaughlin, Walter V. 1962. "The Sex Offender," *Police Chief* (December), 29:26–29.

Note. 1967. "Corroborating Charges of Rape," *Columbia Law Review* 67: 1137–48.

Note. 1950. "Psychiatric Aid in Evaluating the Credibility of a Prosecuting Witness Charging Rape," *Indiana Law Journal* 26:98–103.

Note. 1972. "The Rape Corroboration Requirement: Repeal not Reform," *Yale Law Journal* 81:1365–91.

People v. *Paxton.* 1967. 255 Cal. App. 2d 62 (2d Dist.)

Ploscowe, Morris. 1960. "Sex Offenses: The American Legal Context," *Law and Contemporary Problems* 25:217–25.

Puttkammer, Ernst W. 1925. "Consent in Rape," *Illinois Law Review* 19: 410–28.

Rife, Dwight W. 1940. "Scientific Evidence in Rape Cases," *Journal of Criminal Law, Criminology and Police Science* 31:232–35.

Schiff, Arthur Frederick. 1969. "Statistical Features of Rape," *Journal of Forensic Science* 14:102–9.

Schwartz, Barry. 1968. "The Effect in Philadelphia of Pennsylvania's Increased Penalties for Rape and Attempted Rape," *Journal of Criminal Law, Criminology and Police Science* 59:509–15.

Slovenko, Ralph. 1966. "Witnesses, Psychiatry and the Credibility of Testimony," *University of Florida Law Review* 19:1–22.

State v. *Chaney.* 1970. 477 P.2d 441 (Alaska).

State v. *Risen.* 1951. 235 P.2d 764 (Oregon).

Stumbo, Bella. 1972. "Rape: Does Justice Turn Its Head?" *Los Angeles Times,* March 12, Section E at 1.

Stürup, Georg K. 1960. "Sex Offenses: The Scandinavian Experience," *Law and Contemporary Problems* 25:361–75.

Thomas, F. and W. Van Hecke. 1963. "The Demonstration of Recent Sexual Intercourse in the Male by the Lugol Method," *Medical Science and Law* 3:169–70.

Vener, Arthur M., Cyrus Stewart, and David L. Hager. 1972. "The Sexual Behavior of Adolescents in Middle America: Generational and American-British Comparisons," *Journal of Marriage and the Family* 34:696–705.

Williams, Glanville. 1962. "Corroboration—Sexual Cases," *Criminal Law Review,* pp. 662–71, October.

4 Forcible Rape in the United States: A Statistical Profile

MICHAEL J. HINDELANG
AND BRUCE J. DAVIS

MORE than four decades ago, Thorsten Sellin (1931:346) wrote that "the value of a crime rate for index purposes decreases as the distance from the crime itself in terms of procedure increases." Biases resulting from "a selective process into which enter the willingness to report a crime, the desire to record it, the ability on the part of the police to detect and arrest the criminal, the policy which guides the prosecutor in deciding whether to bring the offender to trial . . . on the crime charged; the desire on the part of the jury or judge to convict, and, finally, the sentencing policy of the judge, which is in itself governed to a large extent by legislative policies (Sellin, 1931:341)" color or pollute inferences about the initiating act. The more proximate the source, in terms of process, the more accurate the description of the criminal act will tend to be.

For all practical purposes, no body of information, from which generalizations might be made, has been produced from any source except rape victims themselves. Large-scale victimization surveys conducted in recent years by the Law Enforcement Assistance Administration in cooperation with the United States Bureau of the Census are a valuable source for such information. Police statistics on offenses known are one step removed from victimization survey statistics in that the event must be observed by the police or reported to them to be recorded. Offenses known, as well as arrest statistics, are published annually in the FBI's *Uniform Crime Reports.* Recorded arrests are influenced to some unknown extent by variables such as the ability of the police to arrest and the ability of the offender to elude their grasp; and, therefore, those arrested may not be representative of those who engage in rape. As Sellin has suggested, inferences made about the criminal act on the basis of postarrest data—court records, prisoner statistics, and parole statistics—are even more problematic because of the increasing distance from the crime. In spite of the limitations of such data, when statistics from all these sources are simultaneously examined, they can provide a useful composite picture of the nature of forcible rape and the nature of the criminal justice system's reaction to it.

A SURVEY OF VICTIMIZATION

In 1966, the President's Commission on Law Enforcement and Administration of Justice contracted with the National Opinion Research Center (NORC) to conduct the first nationwide victimization survey. In this survey, a probability sample of 10,000 households was selected and within each a household respondent was asked about victimizations that may have been suffered by household members 16 years of age or older in the preceding twelve months. When such a victimization was reported by the household respondent to the interviewer, the victim was interviewed about its details (Ennis, 1967).

More recently, the Law Enforcement Assistance Administration has contracted with the Bureau of the Census to conduct a series of victimization surveys known generically as the National Crime Panel. As part of this effort interviews have been conducted with probability samples of respondents in 10,000 households in each of twenty-six American cities.

In both the NORC and the LEAA/Census surveys, rape was one of the victimizations that the interviewees could have reported. In considering these data, several caveats are in order. (1) The NORC sample was sufficiently small so that the incidence and characteristic of rape—a statistically rare event—were not measured with great precision: It must be recalled in viewing the NORC rape estimates that data on rape are statistically less precise than the data for all other index offenses except homicide, which is even rarer than rape. In fact, few people realize that all data on rape in the NORC report (Ennis, 1967) are based on only fifteen rapes reported to interviewers in the national survey. (2) Since the NORC interviewers only interviewed other members of the household if the respondent reported that a household member had suffered a victimization, a rape victim who was not the household respondent could not have been interviewed unless the household respondent was aware of the rape and willing to report it. (3) In contrast to inquiries made of NORC survey respondents, National Crime Panel respondents were not asked directly whether they had been raped. Instead, they were asked a series of questions about having been beaten, attacked, or threatened. After these questions, they were asked whether anyone had tried to attack them in any other way. (4) The San Jose Methods Test of Known Crime Victims (LEAA, 1972) revealed that in a reverse record check, in which victims selected from police files are interviewed to ascertain whether they will report the victimization to interviewers, one-third of the rapes that had been reported to the police were not reported to the survey interviewer: Although only 16 percent of the rapes known to the police that had been committed by strangers were not reported to the survey interviewer, 46 percent of the rapes known to the police that were committed by someone known to the victim were not reported to the survey interviewer. (5) Although some of the rapes reported to the survey interviewers were, according to the respondents, not reported to the police, it is currently unknown what proportion of rapes that victims do not report to the police are also not reported by them to survey interviewers. (6) In the victim surveys the respondents themselves are left to decide, without any guidance from the interviewer or substantiation from third parties, whether they have been victims of rape.[1]

The LEAA/Census survey data reported in this section were obtained from interviews conducted in 1972 with about one-quarter of a million persons. The data were collected in Chicago, Detroit, Los Angeles, New York, Philadelphia, Atlanta, Baltimore, Cleveland, Dallas, Denver, Newark, Portland, and St. Louis. In each city a probability sample of 10,000 households was selected and interviewed by the Bureau of the Census. Within each household interviews were conducted with each person 12 years of age or older.[2] The response rate was high: About 95 percent of the occupied housing units selected were interviewed, and within households more than 95 percent of the eligible respondents were interviewed. Respondents were asked about victimizations that they may have suffered during the preceding twelve months. When a victimization was reported, a series of questions was asked to elicit further details.

In the results that follow, rates of victimization are reported per 100,000 females 12 years of age and older. In comparing the victimization survey rates with the *Uniform Crime Report* (UCR) rates, the following should be kept in mind: (1) the UCR rape rates are reported per 100,000 males and females in the general population; (2) the UCR rates include persons of all ages while the victim survey rates include only females 12 years of age and older; (3) the victim survey rate is based on survey results from thirteen cities, which are *not* representative of the entire U.S. population; (4) the victim survey results include rapes reported to the police and rapes not reported to the police; and (5) rapes reported to the police, unlike rapes reported in the survey, are subjected to an "unfounding" procedure.

Race of Victim

There were 315 reported rapes for every 100,000 females age 12 years and older [3] in the thirteen cities. Nearly one-quarter of these rapes were completed; the remaining three-quarters were attempts.[4] The reported rape rate for black/others [5] (385) was more than one-third greater than the reported rate for whites (286). The proportion of completed rapes to total reported rapes was also higher for black/others; 32 percent of the rape rate for black/others, but only 20 percent of the rape rate for whites represented completed rapes. The joint effect of these relationships is evident in that the rates of attempted rape for black/other (261) and whites (229) differ little, while the rate of completed rape for black/others (124) is more than twice that for whites (57).

Race and Age of Victim

Although the overall rate of reported rape for black/others was more than one-third greater than the rate for whites, table 4.1 shows that there exists substantial variation in this relationship according to the age of the victim: the rates for black/others were higher than the corresponding rates for whites in the two youngest (12–15, 16–19) and two oldest (50–64, 65 and older) age categories, identical to the rate for whites in the 35–49 age category, and less than the rates for whites in the 20–24 and 25–34 age groups. This relationship is generally consistent for completed and attempted rates considered individually.

The rate of reported rape was highest in the 16–19 age group, regardless of the race of the victim. The rate for this age group is nearly three times the aggregate rate.

As was noted, the rate of completed rape for black/others was more than twice the rate for whites. The highest rates of completed rape for black/others were for victims under 20 years of age (12–15, 16–19), while for whites the highest rates were found in the 20-34 age range. The lowest rate of completed rape for black/others was in the 35–49 age category (47), with somewhat higher rates reported in the older categories (50–64, 54; 65 and

Table 4.1. Estimated Rates of Completed and Attempted Rape, by Race and Age of Victim.[a]

	Thirteen Cities: Aggregate							
	12–15	*16–19*	*20–24*	*25–34*	*35–49*	*50–64*	*65 & Older*	*Total*
Population base (female only)								
White	435,886	467,045	620,431	996,753	1,207,920	1,348,075	1,074,138	6,150,248
Black/Other	297,123	263,876	307,659	530,577	596,056	400,002	219,809	2,615,102
Completed Rape								
White rate	91	111	138	124	30	7	3	57
number	(395)	(519)	(854)	(1,231)	(363)	(98)	(31)	(3,491)
Black/Other rate	308	316	74	100	47	54	112	124
number	(914)	(835)	(227)	(528)	(279)	(217)	(246)	(3,247)
Attempted rape								
White rate	375	745	635	284	100	56	22	229
number	(1,635)	(3,477)	(3,937)	(2,827)	(1,203)	(753)	(232)	(14,065)
Black/Other rate	452	831	427	211	83	90	0	261
number	(1,344)	(2,193)	(1,313)	(1,118)	(493)	(358)	(0)	(6,820)
Total								
White rate	466	856	772	407	130	63	24	286
number	(2,030)	(3,996)	(4,791)	(4,059)	(1,566)	(851)	(263)	(17,556)
Black/Other rate	760	1,148	501	310	130	144	112	385
number	(2,258)	(3,029)	(1,540)	(1,646)	(773)	(575)	(246)	(10,067)

[a]The data in this table are estimates of population parameters based on the sample results. Estimated rates are per 100,000 female population, 12 years of age or over.

older) (112)—while for whites the rate was nearly zero (7 and 3, respectively) in the two oldest age categories.

Analysis of rates of attempted rape shows the relationship between race categories at different age levels to be similar to that observed for completed rape rates, although the differences are generally smaller. As was the case for completed rape, rates of attempted rape rise some from the youngest age group to the 16–19 group, and fall thereafter quite drastically (by more than one-half) from the 20–24 group to the 25–34 group, and again to the 35–49 group. For whites, the rate continues decreasing by one-half in each of the remaining categories; while for black/others, the rate increases slightly in the 50–64 age group then drops to zero in the 65 and older age group.

Major Activity of Victim

A general inverse relationship between rates of reported rape and age of victim has been shown. One would expect, then, that the categories of major activities in which younger persons are more likely to be involved—"going to school," "looking for work," and "under 16"—would show the highest rates. The expectation is founded: those looking for work have the highest rate (797), those going to school the second highest (644), and females under 16 years of age rank third (585). The rates of reported rape in these categories are approximately twice the rates found in any of the remaining categories. The importance of age, again, seems to be evidenced in that the lowest rate is found in the "retired" group (57). Women keeping house had a rate of reported rape (216) that was lower than the aggregate (315), while rates for the remaining categories (employed, 300; other, 331) approximated the aggregate rate for the thirteen cities.

Marital Status of Victim

Women who had never married or who were divorced or separated from their husbands showed the highest rates of rape (650 and 486, respectively); the rate for married women (141) was less than one-fourth the rate for women who had never married, while the rate for widows (97) was less than one-sixth the rate for women who had never married. The proportion of the total rate representing completed rapes varied from 29 percent for women who were divorced or separated to 16 percent for widows, with intermediate proportions for women who had never married (24 percent) or were presently married (24 percent). The net effect is that the rate of completed rape for women who had never married (157) was nearly ten times the rate for widows (16) and five times the rate for married women (35).

Time and Place of Occurrence

More than one-third of the rapes occurred during the daytime (6 A.M. to 6 P.M.). About one-half of the rapes occurred during evening hours (6 P.M. to midnight) and one-sixth between midnight and 6 A.M. It is clear, then, that on an hourly risk basis, rape in these thirteen cities is much more likely to have occurred during the evening hours than during any other period.

About one-fifth of all reported rapes occurred in the victim's home or apartment, and an additional 14 percent took place nearby (that is, in a yard or carport, or on a sidewalk or driveway near the victim's home). Nearly one-half of all reported rapes took place on the street, in a park, field, playground, school grounds, or parking lot. More than 6 out of 10 (65 percent) rapes in the thirteen cities occurred in open, outdoor places.

Number of Victims and Number of Offenders

In completed rapes 95 percent, and in attempted rapes 91 percent, of the victims reported that they were alone at the time of the attack. About 60 percent of the completed rapes and 80 percent of the attempted rapes were perpetrated by lone offenders.[6] A greater proportion of attempted rapes (72 percent) than completed rapes (60 percent) involved lone-victim–lone-offender encounters. The majority of rapes, therefore, involved only one victim and one offender.

Victim-Offender Relationship

Of the completed and attempted rapes reported to the survey interviewers, 4 out of 5 involved offenders who were not known to the victim. There was a smaller percentage of stranger victimizations for completed rapes (71 percent) than for attempted rapes (82 percent); only very slight differences were observed when the data were further subdivided by race of victim.

Virtually all of the black/other victims of lone offenders in completed (98 percent) and attempted (97 percent) rapes were attacked by offenders thought to be of the same race. The intraracial nature of rapes of black/other victims does not characterize rapes of white victims, however: about 3 out of 10 white victims of lone offenders in completed and attempted rapes were attacked by offenders who were thought to be black/other. Similar findings emerged for victims of multiple offenders. All of the black/other victims of completed rape and 94 percent of the black/other victims of attempted rape were attacked by multiple offenders all of whom were perceived to be black/other. Also, more than 3 out of 5 of the white victims of completed and attempted rape were attacked by multiple offenders, all of whom were thought to be of black or other races. Although it is extremely rare for black/other victims to be attacked by whites, it is not rare for white victims to be attacked by lone black/other offenders, and in fact, it is typical for white victims in multiple offender rapes to be attacked by black/other offenders.

For offenses involving a single offender, 7 out of 10 of the completed rapes and 8 out of 10 of the attempted rapes were committed by offenders perceived to be 21 years of age or older. For offenses involving multiple offenders, all or some of the offenders involved in any one incident were estimated to be 21 years of age or older in 60 percent of the completed rapes and 40 percent of the attempted rapes. Overall, these data suggest that offenders involved in attempted rapes and in rapes involving multiple offenders are disproportionately younger than those involved in completed rapes and lone-offender rapes.

Use of Weapons

About one-third of the completed and attempted rapes reported to survey interviewers involved weapons and about one-half involved no weapons; for the remaining victimizations, the victim was uncertain whether the offender had a weapon. For white victims, completed rapes more often involved weapons than attempted rapes (44 percent vs. 32 percent); for black/other victims, weapons were involved in attempted rapes slightly more often than in completed rapes (36 percent vs. 31 percent). For completed rapes in which weapons were used, 71 percent of the white victims were faced with a knife and 33 percent were faced with a gun.[7] For black/other victims of completed rape in which weapons were used, 60 percent were faced with a gun and 40 percent with a knife. Thus, the typical weapon used against a white victim of completed rape was a knife, while the typical weapon used against a black/other victim was a gun; this tendency, although weaker, holds for attempted rapes as well.

Use of Self-Protective Measures

In completed rapes, half of the victims took some measure to protect themselves from, or to ward off, the attacker; in attempted rapes, more than four out of five of the victims took self-protective measures. Of those victims of completed rape who used self-protective measures, 60 percent hit, kicked, or scratched the offender; 44 percent screamed or yelled for help; and 37 percent tried to reason with the offender.[8] In attempted rapes, hitting, kicking, or scratching (44 percent); screaming or yelling for help (42 percent); and reasoning with the offender (20 percent) were also commonly used. Running away was much more common in attempted than completed rapes (29 percent vs. 4 percent). When the self-protective measures taken are examined by race of the victim, it is seen that white and black/other victims of attempted rape took similar self-protective measures. However, for completed rapes whites were more likely than black/others to have hit, kicked, or scratched the offender (71 percent vs. 48 percent) and black/others were more likely than whites to have reasoned with the offender (46 percent vs. 29 percent). In toto these data on self-protective measures suggest that rape victims are generally active in resisting attack and use a variety of measures at their disposal to protect themselves and ward off their attackers.

Injury

More than one-half of those victims who reported completed rapes and one-eighth of those who reported attempted rapes were injured to the extent that they required medical attention. About three-fifths of those requiring medical attention received emergency room treatment only; about one out of ten rape victims who required medical attention were hospitalized overnight or longer. If all of the rape victims in the survey are included, 7 percent of the completed rape victims and 3 percent of the attempted rape victims received hospital medical care overnight or longer.

Failure to Report Victimizations to the Police

Most researchers who have used police statistics in their investigations of rape have noted that, for a variety of reasons, many rape victims do not report their victimizations to the police. Table 4.2 shows that in completed rapes 84 percent of the black/other victims, and 65 percent of the white victims, reported their victimizations to the police; for attempted rapes about half of the white and black/other victims reported the attempt to the police. For those victims not reporting the crime to the police, the reasons given differ dramatically by race of the victim and by the nature of the criminal attack.[9] For example, three-fourths of the black/other victims of completed rape, but only one-eighth of the white victims of completed rape, gave "fear of reprisal" as a reason; further, only 5 percent of the former, but 75 percent of the latter reasoned that the rape was a "private matter." Among both black/others and whites "lack of proof/nothing could be done" and "not important" were reasons most often given for not reporting

Table 4.2. Reasons Given For Not Reporting Attempted or Completed Rape Victimizations to Police, by Race of Victim.

		Reported to Police			Thirteen Cities: Aggregate — Reasons for Not Reporting Victimization[a]								
		Yes	Don't Know	No	Lack of proof; nothing could be done	Did not think it important enough	Did not want to bother police	Did not want to take time	Private matter	Did not want to get involved	Fear of reprisal	Reported to someone else	Other
White													
Completed													
rate		65%	0%	35%	7%	0%	5%	0%	75%	17%	12%	1%	19%
number	(3,491)	(2,264)	(0)	(1,227)	(86)	(0)	(59)	(0)	(916)	(212)	(145)	(14)	(229)
Attempted													
rate		46%	1%	53%	38%	27%	12%	7%	22%	3%	10%	9%	22%
number	(14,065)	(6,567)	(137)	(7,498)	(2,812)	(2,025)	(902)	(517)	(1,669)	(229)	(738)	(645)	(1,660)
Black/Other													
Completed													
rate		84%	1%	15%	31%	0%	16%	0%	5%	0%	74%	3%	28%
number	(3,247)	(2,757)	(22)	(490)	(152)	(0)	(79)	(0)	(24)	(0)	(361)	(17)	(139)
Attempted													
rate		53%	0%	47%	35%	13%	4%	0%	11%	7%	10%	10%	20%
number	(6,820)	(3,626)	(0)	(3,194)	(1,128)	(428)	(125)	(0)	(339)	(236)	(319)	(324)	(637)

[a]Subcategories within rows will sum to greater than total because data are taken from a multiple response question.

attempted rapes. However, in completed rapes, none of the white or black/other victims gave "not important" as the reason for failing to report the victimization to the police. The finding that some victims of completed rape and many victims of attempted rape fail to report their victimizations to the police is critical to bear in mind as the data in the next section on police statistics are discussed.

POLICE STATISTICS ON OFFENSES KNOWN

Police statistics are one step removed from victim survey statistics in that the event must somehow come to the attention of the police if it is to become an official statistic. Although the Federal Bureau of Investigation's *Uniform Crime Reports* have been criticized on many grounds [10]—most notably that many offenses, particularly rapes, are never reported to the police—these data are the best available for some types of analyses, especially time series.

Table 4.3 shows the rates of reported violent index offenses (criminal homicide, forcible rape, aggravated assault, and robbery) compiled by the Federal Bureau of Investigation for the past four decades. In the forty-year period from 1933 to 1973, the reported violent index crime rate increased 170 percent while the reported rape rate increased 557 percent—an increase for reported rape more than three times the overall increase for reported violent index offenses. This table also shows that the reported rape rate [11] of 3.7 in 1933 doubled to 7.4 by 1943, and had more than doubled again to 15.4 by 1968; by 1973 the reported rape rate was 24.3. Not only did the reported rape rate increase more rapidly than the rate for any other violent offense in the 1933–1973 period, but it increased more rapidly than the rate for any other violent offense in the 1970–1973 period as well; [12] while the reported violent index crime rate increased 14.8 percent in that three-year period, the reported rape rate increased 30.6 percent.

Table 4.3. Variation in Reported *UCR* Violent Index Offense Rates (per 100,000 persons): 1933–1973.

Year	*Combined Rate 4 Major Violent Crimes*	*Criminal Homicide*	*Forcible Rape*	*Robbery*	*Aggravated Assault*
1933	153.6	7.6	3.7	93.9	48.4
1934	131.3	6.1	4.0	74.3	46.9
1935	116.7	7.0	4.4	61.1	44.2
1936	106.5	7.1	5.1	49.9	44.4
1937	107.9	7.0	5.3	53.3	42.3
1938	104.6	6.6	4.5	52.4	41.1
1939	103.0	6.6	5.3	48.5	42.6
1940	100.3	6.5	5.2	46.4	42.2
1941	98.0	6.5	5.3	42.8	43.4
1942	113.0	6.4	6.1	46.6	53.9
1943	108.8	5.5	7.4	44.6	51.3
1944	114.2	5.6	7.9	43.6	57.1
1945	131.5	5.9	8.9	54.2	62.5
1946	142.0	6.9	8.7	59.4	67.0
1947	139.8	6.2	8.5	55.8	69.3
1948	135.9	5.9	7.6	51.9	70.5
1949	138.0	5.3	7.2	54.8	70.7
1950	132.9	5.3	7.3	48.7	71.6
1951	127.7	5.1	7.5	46.8	68.3
1952	139.1	5.3	7.1	51.5	75.2
1953	145.2	5.1	7.3	54.9	77.9
1954	146.5	4.8	6.8	57.6	77.3
1955	136.6	4.7	8.0	48.2	75.1
1956	136.0	4.7	8.5	46.7	76.7
1957	140.7	4.6	8.4	49.6	78.1
1958	147.6	4.6	9.3	54.9	78.8
1959	146.8	4.8	9.3	51.2	81.5
1960	159.0	5.0	9.4	59.9	84.7
1961	156.4	4.7	9.2	58.1	84.4
1962	160.5	4.5	9.3	59.4	87.3
1963	166.2	4.5	9.2	61.5	91.0
1964	188.2	4.8	11.0	67.9	104.5
1965	197.8	5.1	11.9	71.3	109.5
1966	217.2	5.6	12.9	80.3	118.4
1967	249.9	6.1	13.7	102.1	128.0
1968	294.6	6.8	15.5	131.0	141.3
1969	325.4	7.3	18.3	147.4	152.5
1970	361.0	7.8	18.6	171.5	163.1
1971	393.0	8.6	20.3	187.2	176.9
1972	398.0	8.9	22.3	180.0	186.8
1973	414.3	9.3	24.3	182.4	198.4

Table 4.3. *Continued*

Percent change					
1933–73	+169.7	+22.4	+556.8	+ 94.2	+309.9
1960–73	+159.6	+86.0	+155.8	+204.5	+132.9
1970–73	+ 14.8	+19.2	+ 30.6	+ 6.4	+ 21.6

SOURCES: D. J. Mulvihill, M. Tumin and L. Curtis, *Crimes of Violence; A Staff Report Submitted to the National Commission on the Causes and Prevention of Violence,"* Vol. 11. Washington, D.C.: U.S. Government Printing Office, 1969, p. 54. U.S. Department of Justice, Federal Bureau of Investigation, *Uniform Crime Reports*. Washington, D.C.: U.S. Government Printing Office, 1933–73.

NOTE: It should be noted that in this table, pre-1959 rape rates have been adjusted to exclude statutory rapes. For details regarding additional adjustments see Mulvihill et al., *A Staff Report,* Vol. 11, Appendix 2, 1969.

Another method of examining the changing rates of reported rape is to examine them in relation to rates of reported homicide and aggravated assault. In 1933 for example, there were more than two criminal homicides reported for each forcible rape reported; by 1973 there were more than five reported rapes for every two reported homicides.[13] Thus, in this forty-year period there was a substantial *reversal* in the relative rates of reported criminal homicide and forcible rape. The same examination can be made for reported forcible rape and reported aggravated assault. In 1933 the ratio of the latter to the former was thirteen, but in 1973 the ratio had fallen to only eight. Therefore, reported forcible rape is not only increasing in relation to its 1933 level, but it is also increasing in relation to reported criminal homicide and reported aggravated assault as well.

An important question to address is whether these very substantial increases in rates of reported rape are uniform across cities of varying sizes. Table 4.4 provides the relevant data. In 1940, the rate of reported forcible rape in cities of 250,000 or more population was 6.0, but by 1973, the rate was 51.4—a rate increase of 771 percent. As phenomenal as this rise in the rate of reported forcible rape is for the largest cities, it is even more dramatic for cities of 100,000 to 250,000 in population (845 percent). In recent years, smaller cities have been experiencing sharper *rises* in rates of reported forcible rape than have larger cities. In the 1960–1970 period and the 1970–1973 period the larg-

Table 4.4. Rates (per 100,000 persons) of Reported Forcible Rape for Cities with Population of 25,000 and over, by Size of City: 1940, 1950, 1960, 1970, 1973.

	I *250,000 & Over*	*II* *100,000–250,000*	*III* *50,000–100,000*	*IV* *25,000–50,000*
1940				
Rate[a]	6.0 (11.4)	3.3 (7.1)	3.8 (6.7)	2.6 (5.9)
No. of cities	36	55	100	191
Population	28,894,166	7,792,650	6,929,998	6,666,956
1950				
Rate[a]	8.8 (16.8)	4.0 (8.8)	4.1 (7.3)	2.6 (5.8)
No. of cities	37	67	123	238
Population	25,936,568	9,882,796	8,697,121	8,360,623
1960				
Rate	15.2	7.6	5.5	4.7
No. of cities	49	80	189	379
Population	35,337,512	11,548,156	13,003,030	13,242,472
1970				
Rate	39.7	23.7	15.3	11.2
No. of cities	56	98	252	504
Population	42,181,000	14,051,000	17,425,000	17,398,000
1973				
Rate	51.4	31.2	22.8	16.2
No. of cities	58	101	264	505
Population	43,336,000	14,629,000	18,477,000	17,760,000

SOURCE: U.S. Department of Justice, Federal Bureau of Investigation, *Uniform Crime Reports,* Washington, D.C.: U.S. Government Printing Office, 1940, 1950, 1960, 1970, 1973.

[a]1940 and 1950 rates in this table are estimates of the rates of forcible rape. The actual rates reported in the *UCR* are printed in parentheses; these rates include statutory rape. Estimates are based on the proportion of forcible and statutory rape offenses by city size from the Federal Bureau of Investigation, *Uniform Crime Reports.* Washington, D.C.: U.S. Government Printing Office, 1940, Table 87.

est increase in the rate of reported forcible rape was in cities with 50,000 to 100,000 population. Even so, it should also be pointed out that the *rate* of reported forcible rape declines monotonically with city size; in 1973 (table 4.4) the rates from the largest to the smallest city size groups were 51.4, 31.2, 22.8, and 16.2, respectively.[14] This positive relationship between city size and rate of reported forcible rape is also apparent for all other years shown in the table.

The dramatic increase in the rates of reported forcible rape holds generally for the various geographic areas of the country—

Northeast, North Central, South, and West. From 1960 to 1973, the Northeast and the South showed increases of almost 200 percent, while the North Central and the West showed increases of nearly 150 percent. In very recent years (1970–1973) the Northeast showed a rate increase (50 percent) that was larger than that of any of the other areas of the country.

In every year since 1960 the West has had, by far, the highest rate of reported forcible rape. In fact, the rate for the West has generally been at least half again as great as the rate for the geographic area with the second highest rate (which since 1970 has been the South and in prior years was the Northeast).

Can this geographic variation be accounted for by differences among the geographic areas in the extent of urbanization? The *Statistical Abstract of the United States: 1974* shows that in the West three-fourths of the 1970 population lived in metropolitan areas, while in the Northeast—the geographic areas of the country that from 1960–1970 consistently showed the lowest rape rate—almost four-fifths of the 1970 population lived in metropolitan areas. Further, the areas of the country in which the smallest percentage of the 1970 population lived in metropolitan areas (the South) has had in recent years, the second highest rape rate. Therefore, the difference in the rates of reported forcible rape across geographic areas does not appear to be accounted for by the percentage of persons living in metropolitan areas in the various geographic sections of the country.

In sum, the police statistics on offenses known indicate that rates of forcible rape have been increasing over time and that these rates are especially high in large urban areas and in the West. The magnitude of these differences is probably larger than could be accounted for by differential reporting alone.

ARREST

As noted in our discussion of victimization survey results, a high proportion of rapes about which victims told interviewers were not reported to the police. In such a case, of course, an arrest for that specific offense would, in all likelihood, not occur. Therefore, clearance rates (the number of offenses of a particular type for which an arrest has been made and the person has been charged and turned over to the court for prosecution, divided by the number of offenses of that type known to the police) will be artificially high because the demoninator on which clearance rates are calculated is a marked underestimate of the number of offenses actually occurring. This problem aside, trends in clearance rates provide some very disturbing information:

1. Clearance rates for three major crimes of violence (criminal homicide, aggravated assault, and forcible rape) have been steadily decreasing since 1960.
2. The percent change in the clearance rate for forcible rape in the 1960 to 1973 period was −29 percent, about double the decline for criminal homicide (−14 percent) and aggravated assault (−16 percent).
3. In 1973 the clearance rate for rape (51 percent) was substantially lower than that for aggravated assault (64 percent) and criminal homicide (79 percent).
4. The decrease in the clearance rates from 1972 to 1973 for all three offenses was much larger than the decrease for almost all other one-year periods.[15]

Because the clearance rate for rape is so low, those arrested for the offense may be a select (that is, nonrandom) sample of those engaging in rape. This possibility is compounded by the fact that a high proportion of rapes are not reported to the police. Thus, data on arrestees must be viewed with extreme caution, and it must be kept firmly in mind that these data *are* about arrestees and are not necessarily reflective of the offender population.

An examination of *UCR* arrest data for criminal homicide, forcible rape, and aggravated assault for the years from 1963 through 1973 reveals that forcible rape arrestees were younger than those arrested for criminal homicide or aggravated assault. In 1963, for example, more than three out of five of those arrested for rape, but fewer than one out of two of those arrested for homicide and aggravated assault, were under 25 years of age. It is interesting to note that while there has been a steadily increasing proportion of homicide and aggravated assault arrestees who are under 25 years of age, this has not been the case for rape, for which the percentage has hovered within the 61 to 65 percent range during the 1963–1973 period. When one considers the fact that those under 14 years of age account for fewer than three percent of the 1973 rape arrests, and that in 1970 fewer than 20 percent of the general population was between the ages of 14 and 25, the fact that more than 60 percent of the rape arrestees were under 25 years of age is very significant; rape clearly appears to be a young man's offense.

Comparable information about the percentage of white arrestees for criminal homicide, forcible rape, and aggravated assault indicates that from 1963 to 1973 there was a generally decreasing tendency for whites to be arrested for criminal homicide and forcible rape, but an increasing tendency for them to be arrested for aggravated assault. In 1973, 44 percent of those arrested for forcible rape were white; while for aggravated assault and criminal homicide, the figures are 53 percent and 35 percent, respectively. Nonwhites constituted a substantially greater percentage of arrestees for forcible rape than for aggravated assault. When one considers that in 1970 86 percent of the general population was white, it is clear that white arrestees for aggravated assault, forcible rape, and criminal homicide are very substantially *under*represented in relation to their proportion in the general population.

JUDICIAL PROCESSING OF OFFENDERS

One of the perennial problems faced by those using crime statistics is that generally there is no means for linking data from one part of the criminal justice system to data from other parts of the system. While data on arrests are available from the police, the disposition of those arrested generally is not. It has not been feasible, given the way in which most data systems have been designed, to track a person as he proceeds from arrest to charging to trial to disposition to release from prison, jail, or probation.

Project SEARCH was established with LEAA funds, in part, to

test the feasibility of implementing offender-based transaction statistics (OBTS). Under the OBTS concept the offender serves as the unit of count as he proceeds from one criminal justice system decision point to the next; in this scheme the offender links one part of the criminal justice system to the next. Although the OBTS concept is simple in design, it has proved extremely difficult to implement, primarily because its successful operation requires the cooperation of all segments of the criminal justice system; this has proven to be a formidable task. While several states and cities have begun to implement OBTS data collection, very few such systems are operational.

Data from a pilot OBTS system that was designed by the Bureau of Criminal Statistics in California are available. The data include all adult felony arrests in twelve counties from 1969 through 1971. The flow of felony arrestees for two crimes in addition to rape will be examined. The first is felonious assault, a crime against the person that has *some* similarity to rape, and the second is a crime against property, burglary, which, in many respects, is very different from rape and assault.

Nearly 30 percent of the persons arrested for rape or assault were dismissed either by the police or the prosecutor prior to any appearance in court; only 20 percent of the burglary arrestees were similarly freed. Of those cases retained for court action, a much greater percentage of assault than rape cases were handled by the lower court. In fact, of those cases held for court action, nearly twice the percentage of assault cases (56 percent) as rape cases (29 percent) were handled by a lower court. Only *felony* arrestees are included in the California OBTS data. Because the California lower courts handle only misdemeanors, this means that the prosecutor reduced the charge from a felony to a misdemeanor—probably as a result of plea bargaining. The fact that virtually all of the rape (99 percent), assault (99 percent), and burglary (100 percent) cases handled at the lower court resulted in a conviction (though it may have been overruled in a higher court) gives substantial credence to the hypothesis that these cases involved substantial plea bargaining. At the lower court level, about the same percentage of rape (46 percent) and assault (43 percent) convictees were sentenced to jail, and their respective sentence lengths were comparable.

Of those cases that were handled in superior court, about four out of five of the rape and assault cases, and nine out of ten of the burglary cases, resulted in a conviction. In superior court cases, convicted rapists were about twice as likely as convicted assault offenders to be sentenced to prison (29 percent vs. 15 percent); a slightly higher percentage of assault than rape convictees (49 percent vs. 43 percent) received jail sentences. Lengths of jail sentences for rape and assault defendants convicted at the superior court level were comparable. Unfortunately, because of the California indeterminate sentence law, the length of sentences for imprisoned rape and assault offenders is unavailable from these OBTS data.

Differences among the selected offenses in the nature of the sentence imposed can also be investigated by aggregating convictions for lower and superior court cases, then computing the proportion of offenders, for each of the offenses, who received prison sentences, jail terms, etc.; these data are shown in table 4.5.

In these twelve California counties, convictions for rape were more than three times as likely as convictions for assault to result in a sentence to prison (19.4 percent vs. 5.9 percent). On the other hand, a burglary conviction was almost twice as likely as an assault conviction, but only about half as likely as a rape conviction to result in a sentence to prison. When sentences to jail are also taken into account, more than three out of five rape and burglary

Table 4.5. Percentage of Those Convicted at Either Lower or Superior Court Receiving Probation, Jail, and Prison Sentences.

	Rape		*Assault*		*Burglary*	
	Number	*Percent*	*Number*	*Percent*	*Number*	*Percent*
Convicted	206	100.0	1,820	100.0	3,463	100.0
Probation	57	27.6	672	36.9	974	28.1
Jail	91	44.2	824	45.2	1,772	51.1
Prison	40	19.4	109	5.9	360	10.4
Other[a]	18	8.7	215	11.8	357	10.3

[a]Fines, suspended sentence, etc.

offenders, and about half of the assault offenders were sentenced to incarceration. Unfortunately, system flow data do not give us satisfactory information regarding time actually served. However, *Uniform Parole Reports* (UPR) do provide such information.

PRISONER STATISTICS

National data about prison populations have been periodically published by the U.S. Bureau of the Census since 1850. Many substantive procedural changes were undertaken in succeeding years which make longitudinal analyses suspect. A decision, made in the late fifties, to discontinue the practice of reporting data about imprisoned rapists and to subsume the offenders under the generic category of sex offenses,[16] has disallowed any national analysis of the characteristics of rape offenders in contemporary prison populations. Recent data are available, however, about convicted rape offenders paroled from prison.

THE UNIFORM PAROLE REPORTS

In a recent study using Uniform Parole Report (UPR) data, Gottfredson et al. (1973) have examined the length of time served by more than 100,000 male felons. The study included inmates in institutions in all fifty states and the District of Columbia who were paroled from their prison sentences for the first time between 1965 and 1970. The amount of time served by the offender on the charge for which he was confined at the time the parole board made the decision to release him was analyzed.

The Gottfredson et al. report shows the median time served by parolees. As would be expected, persons paroled from homicide sentences served the longest average time in prison, 58.6 months. Those paroled from sentences for forcible rape served an average of only nine months less time—49.5 months. Rape parolees in the study served an average of 50 percent longer than armed robbery parolees (33.1 months), 100 percent longer than unarmed robbery parolees (24.8 months), and more than 200 percent longer than aggravated assault parolees (15.4 months). These differences were generally maintained even when prior record was controlled.[17] In fact, rape parolees with prior records served an average of only four months less than homicide parolees with prior records (52.5 months vs. 56.9 months).

An analysis of success rates—defined as the percentage of parolees continued on parole with no adverse action taken by the parole board during the one year follow-up period after parole from prison[18]—for each offense grouping of parolees revealed that: "All of the offenses associated with the highest success rates are crimes against the person. This fact is noteworthy in view of what is generally considered to be the more serious nature of a crime involving violence or threatened violence rather than the taking of the property of another" (Gottfredson et al., 1973:11). In this connection, the violent offense groups are rather homogenous. Aggravated assault parolees showed the lowest level of success (80 percent), followed by forcible rape (84 percent) and statutory rape parolees (84 percent), other sex offense parolees (87 percent), manslaughter parolees (89 percent), and homicide parolees (90 percent).

In a three-year national follow-up study of male parolees released from prisons in 1969,[19] the *major new convictions* of these parolees were examined (National Council on Crime and Delinquency, 1974). This study found that during the follow-up period, 12 percent of the 18,000 parolees were returned to prison as a result of new major convictions or in lieu of prosecution for new major offenses.[20] For forcible rape and aggravated assault, the rate was 7 percent; this compares with 4 percent for willful homicide and 14 percent for burglary. Of the twenty-nine forcible rape parolees in the study who were returned to prison for major new convictions (or in lieu of prosecution for major offenses), the offenses for which they were most frequently returned were forcible rape (five) and aggravated assault (five). Thus, although only a small minority of forcible rape parolees were returned to prison for a new major offense, one-third were returned for forcible rape or aggravated assault.

SUMMARY

The LEAA/Census victimization survey data provide more detail about rape victimization than is generally available from any other large-scale body of data. Victimization surveys, however, are not without their shortcomings in the measurement of the incidence of rape and the circumstances surrounding its occurrence. In spite of such shortcomings, the victimization survey data provide an abundance of information that is nowhere else available in standardized form for so many geographic areas.

The victimization survey results show that attempted rapes reported to the interviewers outnumbered completed rapes by about three to one. Black/others and younger persons were found to have disproportionately high rates of reported rape victimizations. Rape victims were often attacked either by offenders who outnumbered them or by offenders who brandished weapons of one sort or another; the victim survey rapes typically occurred in open, public places. Most of the women who were attacked actively resisted or attacked the offender, or ran away in order to protect themselves. Only a very small minority of rape victims were injured to the extent that they required hospitalization overnight or longer.

Although only one out of two attempted rapes was reported to the police, nearly three out of four completed rapes were reported. For completed rapes, the reason most often given for not reporting the victimization to the police was, for white victims, that the incident was a "private or personal matter" and for black/others that there was "fear of reprisal." In attempted rapes, "lack of proof/nothing could be done" was the reason most often cited by both white and black/other victims for not reporting the victimization to the police.

The *UCR* data on offenses known show a rate of increase in reported forcible rape over the past forty years of such a magnitude that it would be extremely difficult to argue that this rate increase is artifactual. The rates of increase are extremely large for all city size groups and the four geographic areas of the country.

The data on flow of rape arrestees through the criminal justice system show that although a relatively large proportion of offenders are dismissed from the system before court processing, those convicted of rape are likely to be sentenced to jail or prison. Further, the Uniform Parole Report data show that in the United States only homicide parolees serve longer terms than rape parolees.

The data on rape examined herein have been drawn from diverse sources of varying quality. The types of data themselves are fragments, each of which has its own limitations and shortcomings. However, when considered in toto, these data constitute a mosaic that is quite informative regarding the nature of forcible rape, characteristics of rapists, and societal reaction to the crime of rape. It is unfortunate that the data currently available are such a patchwork—data from thirteen cities on victimization; OBTS data from twelve California counties; and national offense, arrest, and parole data. National victimization data will soon be available and OBTS systems are slowly becoming operational in various cities and states around the country. As these data sources mature, it will be possible to construct a more complete statistical profile not only of forcible rape, but also of other major crimes.

NOTES

1. While this is essentially true for all crimes covered in the survey, more detailed questions are asked for crimes other than rape in order to ascertain whether the event described meets the legal requirements for that particular crime.

2. For respondents who were 12 to 13 years of age, interviews were through proxy respondent.

3. Hereafter rates of rape will be presented without necessarily repeating "per 100,000 females 12 years of age and older."

4. A small minority of the completed rapes and attempted rapes also involved an actual or an attempted theft. In about 1 out of 5 of the rape victimizations reported, a theft or an attempted theft was also reported to have occurred.

5. In these cities, persons of "other" races made up a very small proportion of the total population; they have been combined with blacks to form "black/other." Black respondents constitute more than 95 percent of the black/other.

6. These same proportions apply regardless of whether there was only one victim or several.

7. The offender(s) may have had more than one weapon, hence the types of weapon total is more than 100 percent.

8. Percentages cited in the remainder of the discussion on self-protective measures are based only on those victims who reported using some self-protective measure.

9. Respondents were permitted to give as many reasons for not reporting as they liked.

10. See Hindelang (1974) for a summary.

11. All rates will be reported per 100,000 persons unless otherwise noted; for economy, "per 100,000 persons" will not generally be stated but will be implied.

12. In the 1960 to 1973 period, the reported robbery rate increased more than the reported rape rate.

13. For ease in discussion we have referred here to the number of homicides and rapes. Because in any given year the population count on which rates are calculated will be the same for all offenses, what we say about the ratio of the reported number of offenses will hold true for the ratio of their reported rates as well, and vice-versa.

14. Although not shown in tabular form, the rates for cities with 10,000–25,000 populations, under 10,000 population, and rural areas, are somewhat consistent with this trend. Their 1973 rates of reported forcible rape are 13.1, 11.0, and 11.9, respectively. These rates are not shown in Table 4.4 because rates for rural areas are not available for 1940–1960, and adjusted rates for the two smallest city size groups are not available for 1940–1950.

15. Some caution should attend the interpretation of these findings since the percent of the U.S. population covered by jurisidictions reporting *arrest* data to the FBI increased from 64 percent in 1960 to 74 percent in 1973. However, because this increase is largely accounted for by cities outside of SMSA's—where clearance rates tend to be as good as or better than in SMSA's—this increase in coverage is likely to have worked against the decline in clearance rates.

16. This category includes: forcible rape, statutory rape, indecent assault, carnal abuse, sodomy, adultery, cohabitation, incest, indecent lib-

erties, indecent exposure, lewdness, peeping Tom, seduction, soliciting, prostitution, commercialized vice, pandering, obscenity, and pornography.

17. Prior record was defined as a conviction and sentence (although not necessarily to prison) prior to the sentence from which the offender was paroled.

18. See Gottfredson et al., 1973:8–12, for further details.

19. Not all states are included in these data. See National Council on Crime and Delinquency, 1974, for details.

20. It should be noted that this 12 percent does not include absconders and technical violators who were returned to prison without new convictions or allegations. See National Council on Crime and Delinquency, 1974:Table 1, for other excluded groups.

REFERENCES

Ennis, Philip. 1967. "Criminal Victimization in the United States. A Report of a National Survey," *Field Surveys 2.* Washington, D.C.: U.S. Government Printing Office.

Federal Bureau of Investigation. 1940, 1950, 1960, 1970, 1973. *Uniform Crime Report.* Washington, D.C.: U.S. Government Printing Office.

Hindelang, Michael. 1974. "The *Uniform Crime Reports* Revisited," *Journal of Criminal Justice* 2:1–18.

Gottfredson, Don, Marcus Neithercutt, Joan Nuffield, and Vincent O'Leary. 1973. *Four Thousand Lifetimes: A Study of Time Served and Parole Outcome.* East Hackensack, New Jersey: National Council on Crime and Delinquency.

Law Enforcement Assistance Administration, United States Department of Justice. 1972. *San Jose Methods Test of Known Crime Victims.* Washington, D.C.: U.S. Government Printing Office.

Mulvihill, Donald, Melvin Tumin, and Lynn Curtis. 1969. *Crimes of Violence. A Staff Report Submitted to the National Commission on the Causes and Prevention of Violence.* Vol. 11. Washington, D.C.: U.S. Government Printing Office.

National Council on Crime and Delinquency. 1974. *Uniform Parole Reports Newsletter.* East Hackensack, New Jersey: National Council on Crime and Delinquency.

Sellin, Thorsten. 1931. "The Basis of a Crime Index," *Journal of Criminal Law and Criminology* 22:335–56.

U.S. Bureau of the Census. 1974. *Statistical Abstract of the United States: 1974 (95th Edition).* Washington, D.C.: U.S. Government Printing Office.

5 Race, Rape, and the Death Penalty

MARVIN E. WOLFGANG AND MARC RIEDEL

THE effects of the race of the offender, as well as racial combinations of offender and victim, on the imposition of the death penalty become particularly clear when studies on rape offenses are examined. Among persons sentenced to death for rape in North Carolina from 1909 to 1954, Elmer Johnson (1957) found that 56 percent of blacks compared to 43 percent of whites were executed. A Florida study (Florida Civil Liberties Union, 1964) of sentences for rape between 1940 and 1964 noted that only six cases, or 5 percent, of white males who raped white females received the death penalty. But of the eighty-four black males who raped

Reprinted by permission from *Annals of the American Academy of Political and Social Science,* vol. 407, titled "Race, Judicial Discretion, and the Death Penalty."
Originally copyrighted © by the American Academy of Political and Social Science.

white women, forty-five, or 54 percent, received the death penalty, while none of the eight white offenders who raped black females received the death penalty.

Data from the Federal Bureau of Prisons (1969) suggest that racial differentials are most clear among death sentences for rape. Of the 455 persons executed for rape since 1930, 405 were black; only 2 were from other racial minorities. All of the executions for rape were in southern or border states or the District of Columbia. In Louisiana, Mississippi, Oklahoma, Virginia, West Virginia, and the District of Columbia not a single white man was executed for rape over the forty-two-year period from 1930 to 1972. Together, these jurisdictions executed sixty-six blacks; Arkansas, Delaware, Florida, Kentucky, and Missouri each executed one white man for rape since 1930, but together they have executed seventy-one blacks.

Findings of racial discrimination in previous studies, as well as suspicions of racial discrimination raised by the data from the Bureau of Prisons, have been reinforced recently by more conclusive findings based on refined and detailed analyses of rape convictions in several states where rape has been a statutory capital crime. Differential sentencing has required further examination to determine whether racial discrimination exists.

THE DEATH PENALTY FOR RAPE IN THE SOUTH, 1945–1965

During the summer of 1965, research was initiated to examine in detail the relationship between race and sentencing for rape in eleven southern and border states in which rape was a capital offense. The study was sponsored by the NAACP Legal Defense Fund and conducted by the Center for Studies in Criminology and Criminal Law at the University of Pennsylvania by Professors Anthony Amsterdam and Marvin E. Wolfgang.

At each step in the development and implementation of the research design, from selection of the sample to analysis of the data, the emphasis was on the use of research criteria that would increase the reliability and objectivity of the data while minimizing sources of bias and subjectivity. Interfacing with scientific demands was the selection of dimensions of inquiry that would increase understanding of racial discrimination, if it existed, in a judicial system and that would also be of possible use in subsequent litigation.

The research findings were presented as evidence in six states to support petitioners' claims of racial discrimination in the administration of the death penalty. They were part of the brief in the *Maxwell* case (1970) argued before the U.S. Supreme Court and part of the testimony offered before a subcommittee of the House of Representatives considering bills to suspend the death penalty for two years or to abolish it.

Although eighteen American jurisdictions allowed the imposition of the death penalty for rape, substantial numbers of persons have been executed for this crime during the past thirty years in only twelve: Alabama, Arkansas, Florida, Georgia, Louisiana, Maryland, Mississippi, North Carolina, South Carolina, Tennessee, Texas, and Virginia. It was decided that the study could be profitably confined to these twelve states.

In order to form an empirical basis for conclusions about the effect of racial factors on capital sentencing for rape, it was necessary to gather data about a substantial number of rape cases in each state. Moreover, a sufficiently long period of time covered by the research was necessary in order to satisfy the notion of custom, or of an institutionalized, systematic judicial norm of sentencing behavior; hence the twenty-year period used in this study.

To meet the demands of proper statistical analysis, cases could have been obtained by seeking every rape conviction in each state for a decade, or by selecting counties by standard statistical sampling techniques over a twenty-year period. This latter process was used. For each of the twelve states, a sample of counties was chosen to represent the urban-rural and black-white demographic distributions of each state. The counties chosen comprised more than 50 percent of the total population of the twelve states. For the counties included in each state sample, every case of conviction for rape from January 1, 1945 to the summer of 1965 was recorded. Maryland was initially included in the survey, but time limitations precluded full data collection in that state. Therefore, data was gathered for a twenty-year period for over three thousand rape convictions in 230 counties in eleven states.

The states included in the study were not only those that most often executed persons for rape; they also displayed an apparent racial disparity, for black offenders were more frequently executed than were white offenders. In seeking to explore the meaning of this apparent racial disparity in capital sentencing, only rape *convictions* were considered. It might be asserted that blacks more frequently than whites commit rape, are more frequently arrested, or are more frequently charged with that offense. Whether these or any combination of these assertions were true was not questioned in this study. Instead, the focus was on the reliable and objectively ascertainable fact that defendants had been convicted for the crime of rape. Using this point of departure meant that the effect of racial factors on the criminal process prior to conviction could not be explored. There would be no way of knowing—if blacks were disproportionately sentenced to death for rape—whether the pattern could be accounted for by a disproportionate frequency in the commission of rapes by blacks or by a disproportionate frequency in the conviction of blacks for rape. However, *among convicted defendants,* it was possible to determine whether black defendants were disproportionately frequently sentenced to death and, if so, whether the disproportion would be explained by nonracial variables.

In order to explore the effect of racial as well as nonracial variables on the imposition of the death penalty, it was necessary to determine which variables could be obtained from the county records of rape convictions. In addition to collecting information on the race of the defendant and the victim on the type of sentence, information was gathered about many nonracial variables that could be construed as mitigating or aggravating circumstances. If standards were sought for sentencing in capital cases, some of the nonracial variables listed below might be seriously considered. These were the variables included in the study reported here.

1. 1. Offender characteristics
   a. age
   b. marital status
   c. prior criminal record
   d. previous imprisonment
   e. employment status
2. Victim characteristics
   a. age
   b. marital status
   c. dependent children
   d. prior criminal record
   e. reputation for chastity
3. Nature of relations between victim and offender
   a. offender known to victim
   b. prior sexual relations
4. Circumstances of offense
   a. contemporaneous offense
   b. type of entry—authorized or unauthorized
   c. location of offense—indoor or outdoor
   d. display of weapon
   e. carrying of weapon
   f. amount of injury to victim
   g. threatened victim
   h. degree of force employed
   i. victim made pregnant by offense
   j. one or multiple offenders
   k. date of offense
5. Circumstances of the trial
   a. plea
   b. defense of insanity
   c. appointed or retained counsel
   d. length of time of trial
   e. defense of consent
   f. whether defendant testified

An elaborate 28-page research schedule was constructed to obtain reliable and uniform data from records of widely varying quality in geographically dispersed locations. To reduce the amount of subjective or judgmental variation recorded by field investigators, each variable was described in a manner that focused the investigators' attention on objective facts or quantities that could be recorded on a check list.

There is little difficulty in establishing accurate schedule categories when the information to be obtained, like race or plea, is unambiguous. More difficulty occurs in obtaining reliable and objective data for items like "injury sustained by victim, companion victim, or other persons." To make reliable comparisons from case to case, a checklist of categories of predescribed injuries was developed, using brief phrases that focused the recorders' attention on specific, significant, objective details and the consequences of injuries. For example, categories for the latter item included recording whether the victim suffered "minor injury requiring no medical treatment," suffered "physical injuries requiring medical treatment, but not requiring hospitalization," or suffered "physical injuries requiring hospitalization." These particular categories were developed in an earlier study where a system of standardized descriptions and evaluation of the degrees of injury was constructed (Sellin and Wolfgang, 1964).

Thirty law students were recruited from different parts of the country to serve as field investigators. Before going into the field, the students were given a two-day orientation by the two principal investigators. The instruction process outlined in detail the research design and the legal components of the task. Emphasis was placed on the importance of providing reliable data which depended upon uniformity in the observation and recording. It was particularly emphasized that the investigators should not let their personal assumptions about the probable results of the study influence the manner in which they recorded the data. The field investigators were instructed to call central personnel for advice if instances arose in which they had trouble classifying their observations while in the field. After completion in the field, the schedules were forwarded to the Center for Studies in Criminology and Criminal Law for coding and statistical analysis.

The method of analysis used to determine whether the death penalty is given disproportionately frequently to blacks employed the null hypothesis and the chi-square (χ^2) statistical test, for which $p < 0.05$ was chosen as the level of significance. One major null hypothesis stated that among all defendents convicted of rape there is no significant association between the race of the defendant and the type of sentence imposed. The second major null hypothesis stated that among all defendants convicted of rape there are no significant differences between the proportions of black defendants with white victims and all other classes of rape defendants sentenced to death. Both of these hypotheses were rejected in each state analyzed.

The data were compiled and analyzed in seven states—Alabama, Arkansas, Florida, Georgia, Louisiana, South Carolina, and Tennessee—for purposes of submitting testimony in litigation conducted by the Legal Defense Fund. Each state was separately reviewed with its own set of tables and conclusions. The findings were uniformly similar for each state and the conclusions the same. In future analyses planned by the Center for Studies in Criminology and Criminal Law, all states for which data are available will be comprehensively reviewed. In the present article, only a brief summary with an illustration of the procedure can be presented. In the tables that follow, the total number of cases varies by the particular factor analyzed because of differences in the availability of information over the twenty-year period in each of the states.

Among 1,265 cases in which the race of the defendant and the sentence are known, nearly seven times as many blacks were sentenced to death as were whites. Among the 823 blacks convicted of rape, 110, or 13 percent, were sentenced to death; among the 442 whites convicted of rape, only 9, or 2 percent, were sentenced to death. The statistical probability that such a disproportionate number of blacks could be sentenced to death by chance alone is less than one out of a thousand. More particularly, a statistically significantly higher proportion of black defendants whose victims were white were sentenced to death. From a total of 1,238 convicted rape defendants, 317 were black defendants with white victims, and 921 were all other racial combinations of defendant and victim—including black/black, white/white, and white/black. Of the 317 black defendants whose victims were white, 113, or approximately 36 percent, were sentenced to death. Of the 921 defendants involved in all other racial combinations of defendant and victim, only 19, or 2 percent were sentenced to death. In short, black defendants whose victims were white were sentenced to death approximately eighteen times more frequently than defendants in any other racial combination of defendant and victim. Again, the probability of such a distribution, or such a relationship between the sentence of death and black defendants with white victims is, by chance alone, less than one out of a thousand.

But the obvious fact that there is differential sentencing by race, as shown in table 5.1, does not alone permit a conclusion of racial discrimination in sentencing. We may hypothesize, for

Table 5.1. Race of Defendant, Racial Combinations of Defendant/Victim, and Presence/Absence of Contemporaneous Offense by Type of Sentence.

	Death		*Other*		*Total*	
	Number	*Percent*	*Number*	*Percent*	*Number*	*Percent*
Race of Defendant[a]						
Black	110	13	713	87	823	100
White	9	2	433	98	442	100
Total	119		1,146		1,265	
Racial Combinations of Defendant and Victim[b]						
Black defendant/ white victim	113	36	204	64	317	100
All other combinations	19	2	902	98	921	100
Total	132		1,106		1,238	
Presence/Absence of Contemporaneous Offense[c]						
Contemporaneous offense	53	22	133	78	186	100
No contemporaneous offense	92	8	840	92	932	100
Total	145		973		1,118	

[a]States included are Florida, Georgia, Louisiana, South Carolina, and Tennessee. $\chi^2 = 41.9924; p < 0.001$.

[b]States included are Arkansas, Florida, Georgia, Louisiana, South Carolina, and Tennessee. $\chi^2 = 275.7192; p < 0.001$.

[c]States included are Arkansas, Florida, Georgia, Louisiana, South Carolina, and Tennessee. $\chi^2 = 39.4915; p < 0.001$.

example, that, as a group, black rape defendants more often than white defendants commit another offense along with the commission of the rape offense. It could generally be asserted that the commission of a contemporaneous offense, like burglary or robbery, is an aggravating circumstance and could account for the disproportionate frequency with which black defendants receive the death penalty.

Because of these considerations, all the nonracial variables previously listed were introduced in a further examination of the associations between race and the imposition of the death penalty.

First, each nonracial variable was examined relative to type of sentence. If no significant relationship existed between the nonracial variable and type of sentence, further analysis of that variable was not undertaken, for it could at that point be concluded that no significant difference in type of sentence occurred because of that variable. Table 5.1, however, also illustrates that there is a significant association between offenses committed contemporaneously with the rape offense and type of sentence.

If there was a significant association between the nonracial variable and sentence, the nonracial variable was then cross-tabulated with the race of the defendant. If the resulting chi-square was not significant, no further analysis was performed. There could be, however, a significant association between the nonracial variable and race, as is shown in table 5.2. This table indicates that among 572 black defendants, 150, or 26 percent, had committed contemporaneous offenses, while among white defendants 45, or 15 percent, had committed contemporaneous offenses.

Table 5.2. Contemporaneous Offense by Race of Defendant.

	Black		*White*		*Total*
	Number	*Percent*	*Number*	*Percent*	*Number*
Contemporaneous offense	150	26	45	15	195
No contemporaneous offense	422	74	264	85	686
Total	572	100	309	100	881

NOTE: States included are Arkansas, Florida, Georgia, Louisiana, Tennessee. $\chi^2 = 15.1583; p < 0.001$.

Table 5.3. Contemporaneous Offense by Racial Combinations of Defendant/Victim.

	Black Defendant/ White Victim		*All Other Combinations*		*Total*
	Number	*Percent*	*Number*	*Percent*	*Number*
Contemporaneous offense	58	40	81	14	139
No contemporaneous offense	88	60	480	86	568
Total	146	100	561	100	707

NOTE: States included are Florida, Georgia, Tennessee.
$\chi^2 = 45.3139$; $p < 0.001$.

Table 5.3 would seem to add one more piece of evidence that the nonracial variable of contemporaneous offenses is a contributory factor producing a more frequent imposition of the death penalty for blacks, particularly those with white victims. Data from this table indicate a significant association between the presence or absence of contemporaneous offenses and racial combinations of defendant and victim. Among the 146 black defendants with white victims, 40 percent had committed contemporaneous offenses, whereas only 14 percent of the 561 cases making up all other racial combinations involved contemporaneous offenses.

Although it might appear that the presence or absence of contemporaneous offenses is a contributory factor, more refined procedure shows that it does not play a significant part in explaining the association between black defendants and the imposition of the death penalty. To perform this further analysis, the nonracial variable of contemporaneous offenses was split into two subgroups. The first subgroup included all cases in which the defendant had committed a contemporaneous offense—table 5.4. Within this subgroup, chi-square analysis shows a significant association between racial combinations of defendant and victim and imposition of the death penalty. More specifically, among the 58 black defendants with white victims, 39 percent received the death penalty, but among all other racial combinations of defendant and victim, only 3 percent of the 81 defendants received the death penalty.

For the other subgroup in which no contemporaneous offenses were committed, there is also a significant association between racial combinations of defendant and victim and the impo-

Table 5.4. Racial Combination of Defendant/Victim and Presence/Absence of Contemporaneous Offense by Type of Sentence.

	Death		*Other*		*Total*	
	Number	*Percent*	*Number*	*Percent*	*Number*	*Percent*
Presence of Contemporaneous Offense						
Black defendant/ white victim	22	39	36	61	58	100
All other	2	3	79	97	81	100
Total	24		115		139	
Absence of Contemporaneous Offense						
Black defendant/ white victim	34	39	54	61	88	100
All other	9	2	471	98	480	100
Total	43		525		568	

NOTE: States included are Florida, Georgia, and Tennessee. $\chi^2 = 27.3231$; $p < 0.001$.

sition of the death penalty. Table 5.4 also indicates that among the 88 black defendants with white victims, 39 percent received the death penalty, whereas among 480 cases of other racial combinations, only 2 percent received the death penalty.

It is important to repeat the final descriptive assertion derived from these data: It is not the presence of the nonracial factor of a contemporaneous offense that affects the decision to impose the death penalty more frequently on blacks. Rather, it is the racial factor of the relationship between the defendant and victim that results in the use of the death penalty. Whether or not a contemporaneous offense has been committed, if the defendant is black and the victim is white, the defendant is about eighteen times more likely to receive the death penalty than when the defendant is in any other racial combination of defendant and victim.

Over two dozen possibly aggravating nonracial variables that might have accounted for the higher proportion of blacks than whites sentenced to death upon conviction of rape have been analyzed. Not one of these nonracial factors has withstood the tests of statistical significance. That is, in none of the seven states carefully analyzed can it be said that any of the nonracial factors account for the statistically significant and disproportionate number of blacks sentenced to death for rape. This is a striking conclusion. It cannot be said that blacks are more frequently sentenced to death because they have a longer prior criminal record than whites, because they used more force on the victim, because they committed a robbery or burglary, because they entered premises without authorization, because they used a weapon or threatened the victim with a weapon, because they had an accomplice in the commission of the rape, because they impregnated the victim, because they more frequently attacked persons under age sixteen, and so forth. All the nonracial factors in each of the states analyzed wash out, that is, they have no bearing on the imposition of the death penalty in disproportionate numbers upon blacks. The only variable of statistical significance that remains is race.

CONCLUSION

In *Furman* v. *Georgia,* the U.S. Supreme Court declared the death penalty unconstitutional because it is a "cruel and unusual" punishment. That the history of this penalty has been marked by elements of racial discrimination was alluded to by at least two justices, but the Court has not directly ruled out the death penalty on this basis, which could be grounded in the Fourteenth Amendment and the due process dictum.

That blacks have been disproportionately sentenced to death and executed in the United States has long been noted. But general social differentials in sentencing may not alone denote racial discrimination, or failure of blacks to be given all due process in the administration of criminal justice. An elaborate research scheme, reported here, which collected data on capital rape convictions over a twenty-year period from 1945 to 1965 has now provided material on many nonracial variables to determine whether they, rather than race, could account for the disproportionately and significantly high frequency of blacks sentenced to death compared to whites.

Based upon a refined statistical analysis of rape convictions in states where rape has been a capital crime, this study shows that there has been a patterned, systematic, and customary imposition of the death penalty. Far from being freakish or capricious, sentences of death have been imposed on blacks, compared to whites, in a way that exceeds any statistical notion of chance or fortuity. Moreover, the systems of criminal justice in the jurisdictions studied have inflicted the death penalty on blacks in such disproportions without statutory or other legally acceptable bases. Thus, with the benefit of a carefully designed and objectively analyzed study of these conditions, it can be concluded that the significant racial differentials found in the imposition of the death penalty are indeed produced by racial discrimination.

The study has shown that racial discrimination has long existed and exists with currency above the conviction stage of the judicial process. That there may be more systematic features of racial differentials, from which discrimination may be inferred, remains for future and further research to determine. Discretion at earlier stages in the administration of justice could also carry elements of racial discrimination: arrest, hearing, plea bargaining, decisions to prosecute or drop charges, and many others, when death is a permissible penalty. Neither mandatory sanctions nor the reduction of racial discrimination at the sentencing stage would eliminate the untoward systemic effects of racial discrimination elsewhere in the processing of defendants. By declaring the death penalty unconstitutional, and reaffirming this declaration if necessary, the Supreme Court at least and at last could remove the consequence of finality which differential justice has produced.

REFERENCES

Federal Bureau of Prisons. 1969. "Capital Punishment 1930-1968," *National Prisoner Statistics* Bulletin 45. Washington, D.C.: U.S. Government Printing Office.

Florida Civil Liberties Union. 1964. *Rape: Selective Electrocution Based on Race.* Miami: Florida Civil Liberties Union.

Johnson, Elmer H. 1957. "Selective Factors in Capital Punishment," *Social Forces* 36 (December):165–169.

Maxwell v. *Bishop.* 1970. 398 U.S. 262.

Sellin, Thorsten and Marvin E. Wolfgang. 1964. *The Measurement of Delinquency.* New York: Wiley.

6 Black Offender and White Victim: A Study of Forcible Rape in Oakland, California

MICHAEL W. AGOPIAN,
DUNCAN CHAPPELL,
AND GILBERT GEIS

THE rape of white women by black men may be regarded at times by the offender (see Cleaver, 1968:28) as a particularly satisfying fracturing of a fundamental element of the mythology of American racial etiquette, one which placed high value on protecting white women from the presumed lust of black men (Cash, 1941: 84–89). As Jessie Bernard (1966:75) has written: "[T]he white world's insistence on keeping Negro men walled up in the concentration camp (of the ghetto) was motivated in large part by its fear of their sexuality." The use of capital punishment, particu-

Reprinted, with revisions, by permission of the publisher from *Victimology,* Israel Drapkin and Emilio Viano, eds. (Lexington, Massachusetts: Lexington Books, D.C. Heath, 1974).

larly in southern states, for black-white rape but not for its counterpart (Koeninger, 1969:141; Partington, 1965:43), further defined both terror and temptation into the behavior, and undergirded an extensive lore among blacks about sexually compliant white females who, faced with discovery, maintained that they had been taken by force (for instances, see Baker, 1908:8–9; Rowan, 1952:26–33).

White male rape of black females has its own distinctive attributes. Historically, black females were regarded as notably accessible to white men, if not by the submission of the female [for there were advantages to be gained from such liasions (Myrdal, 1944:127)], then by use of force which involved little, if any, likelihood of subsequent penalty (Smith, 1961:103; Wolfgang and Cohen, 1970:49).

Today, such historical conditioning is overlaid with elements of the contemporary interracial ethos in the United States. There has been an increase in social interaction between black men and white women, especially among the young in the more cosmopolitan American cities. Black women reportedly resent attention that black males sometimes give to white females (Staples, 1972). Traditional male initiative in such matters, among other things, inhibits similar overtures to white males by black females, and also removes potential masculine partners from the realm of the black female—and often men who are especially desirable. These, and similar social conditions, all probably play a role in establishing and giving meaning to interracial forcible rape rates (see generally, Savitz, 1973).

THE NUMERICAL PERSPECTIVE

Our original study sample consisted of 66 instances of interracial forcible rape reported to the police during 1971 in the city of Oakland, California. The total number of reported rapes for the year was 192. We had intended to analyze and to compare the white male–black female cases with those involving black offenders and white females, but the small number of the former cases—only three—necessitated our concentrating on the 63 instances of black male–white female. We know of no other work which has examined in detail the characteristics of cases of interracial rape, though there are several studies which provide information on its relative occurrence. In table 6.1, we have compared our findings to the results reported in these other investigations.

The varying distributions of intraracial and interracial rape indicated by the table may be a function of phenomena such as the location of the jurisdictions surveyed, the racial demography of the sites, and the study populations involved. The work of Hayman and his colleagues (1971), for instance, was concerned only with persons who appeared at a hospital for treatment, a sample that represented about half of the reported cases in the District of Columbia. Our study found the largest percentage of black male–white female forcible rapes among the reported inquiries. It also represents the only investigation listed in the table in which white women constitute more than half of the total of rape victims. Another contribution to the literature on forcible rape, that by MacDonald (1971:51), has noted that 60 percent of some two hundred rape cases reported to the Denver Police Department in the late 1960s involved black offenders and white victims, while only one case in twenty-nine had a white offender and black victim.

Perhaps the most interesting speculation deriving from table 6.1 is that which suggests that the striking difference between the black offender–white victim forcible rape rate found by us and that reported by Amir (1971:44) from Philadelphia in the late

Table 6.1. Reported Percentage of Forcible Rape by Race of Offenders and Victims in Four Studies.

Type of Case	*Hayman (1971:6)*	*Amir (1971:44)*	*NCCPV (1971)*	*Our Results*
Number	1,243	646	465	192
Black male–black female	76%	77%	60%	40%
White male–black female	.4	4	.3	2
Black male–white female	21	3	10.5	33
White male–white female	3	18	30	19
American Indian–Chicano				7
Total	100.4%[a]	102%[a]	100.8%[a]	101%[a]

[a]Errors due to rounding.

1950s is a function not of the sites and the characteristics of their populations (for both Oakland and Philadelphia have relatively similar reported proportions of black residents—34 percent in the former, and 41 percent in the latter), but rather represents a true increase in the amount of the behavior over time, and an index perhaps of a changing climate of race relations. The intermediate numbers reported by Hayman (1971) for the District of Columbia (with a black population of more than 70 percent) and by the Violence Commission (1969), based on a nationwide sampling, would tend to provide support for such a hypothesis.

FURTHER FINDINGS

In terms of the age of perpetrators and victims, our results contradict the result reported from Philadelphia by Amir (1971:56–57). He found that white offenders in interracial rape followed the usual pattern of selecting victims either of the same age bracket or one younger than themselves. Black offenders, to the contrary, in 44 percent of the cases chose victims who were ten or more years older than themselves. It was this finding in particular which led Amir (1971:57) to suggest that the dynamics of interracial rape might vary significantly from those of the intraracial offense. We found, however, that in about two-thirds of our cases the offender chose as his victim someone in the same ten-year age bracket as himself or someone younger. More than half of the cases of victims who were ten or more years older than offenders involved blacks 19 years of age or younger choosing victims in the 20-to-29 bracket. Only two rapes by blacks involved white victims above the age of 40. Most offenders (62 percent) and most victims (71 percent) fell in the 20-to-29 age grouping.

Our study once more confirmed the finding of earlier published research (cf., Falk, 1950) that warm weather months are the high season for the offense of rape. Fifty-nine percent of the cases occurred in spring and summer, with the highest percentage for the four seasons—33 percent—taking place during the summer. Especially interesting, though, was an analysis, the re-

Table 6.2. Season of Year Rape Committed and Age of Offender.

		Season of Year Rape Committed			
Age of Offender		*Fall*	*Winter*	*Spring*	*Summer*
19 or less		4	5	0	12
		(20.0%)	(27.8%)	—	(54.5%)
20–29 years		6	9	16	10
		(30.0%)	(50.0%)	(100.0%)	(45.5%)
30–39 years		10	2	0	0
		(50.0)	(11.1%)	—	—
40–49 years		0	2	0	0
		—	(11.1%)	—	—
Total	Number	20	18	16	22
	Percent	(100.0)	(100.0)	(100.0)	(100.0)

$\chi^2 = 46.89$; $p < .001$.
Lambda (asymmetric) .171 with age dependent; .333 with season dependent.

sults of which are presented in table 6.2, which took into account the relationship between the offender's age and the season in which the offense was committed. The results showed that 50 percent of the offenders were in the 30-to-39 age group during the fall season. For winter, the modal age dropped to 20–29. In the spring, all cases (N = 16) were in the 20–29 bracket, while in the summer the modal offender age dropped to 19 or less. School vacations and youthful sexuality associated with recess freedom, plus seasonal employment patterns, might partly account for this finding.

The Oakland interracial rape data differed from that in other general studies of crimes of violence, both of rape (Amir, 1971: 81–82) and of homicide (Wolfgang, 1958:106–13), which report that peak activity takes place during the weekends. The mid-week period showed the largest amount of interracial forcible rape. Wednesday was the day with the greatest number of offenses (24.5 percent), and the combination of Monday, Tuesday, and Wednesday included 62 percent of the cases. The weekend days—Friday, Saturday, and Sunday—accounted for only one-quarter of the number of interracial rapes.

The location of the rape event provides some initial indication of the dynamics of the situation which led to its occurrence. Intraracial rape, studies have indicated (Amir, 1971:87–95), tends to take place indoors, quite often in the residence of one of the participants. These findings do not hold up, however, for the Oakland interracial sample. Rather, most of the offenses—some 40 percent—took place in nonresidential settings, not including automobiles, which were the locus of an additional 22 percent of the cases.

While anger and hatred may underlie many of the interracial rapes, these emotions do not manifest themselves generally in severe beatings of victims by offenders. Only two of the victims, according to the police reports, suffered what could be classified as "brutal beatings," though 11 of the 63 victims were reported to have been beaten by their assailants in the course of the offense.

The victims' degree of submissiveness was closely related to the use of physical violence against her. Most of the victims—57 percent—reported themselves submissive to the rape. Only 4 of these—out of a total of 36—were beaten, and only one was beaten severely. Of the women who fought back, more than half—7 of 13—were physically beaten. The interactive chronological nature of these events cannot be determined from the reports, however. Victim belief that use of force was imminent may have led to heavy resistance, which in its turn could have triggered the violence of the offender.

In regard to the response to rape by the victim in terms of her age, we found that the younger the woman, the greater the likelihood that she would be submissive. Young women may have been frightened into submission, or reacted in a more acquiescent manner because they possessed fewer racial and sexual fears.

The suggestion has been offered by Amir (1971:158–61) that rape offenses might be examined in terms of what he labels "sexual humiliation." This term embraces, rather indiscriminately (as well as in part invidiously and moralistically), repeated intercourse, fellatio, and cunnilingus. Such events might better be regarded for what they are in fact, without guessing at the motive of the offender or the feelings of the victim. In Philadelphia, Amir (1971:158–61) found that 44 percent of the black male–white female rapes involved repeated intercourse [i.e., more than one act of intercourse, separated either by time or orgasmic response by the offender(s)]. Cunnilingus took place in 22 percent of the cases, and fellatio in the same proportion. In our sample, repeated intercourse was reported in only two cases. Fellatio occurred in nine instances, while there were no reports of cunnilingus. The last finding is consistent with observations that black men are more reluctant than whites to engage in cunnilingus (Staples, 1972:11).

Multiple offender or group rapes were considerably rarer in the Oakland sample than they have been found to be elsewhere (Amir, 1971:182–226; Chappell et al., 1971; Geis and Chappell, 1971). Fifteen percent of the offenses involving black men and white women were multiple offender cases, a figure that contrasts to more than half of the interracial rapes involving black men in Amir's Philadelphia study. We also found that in at least a third of the cases the rape was combined with another felony, usually robbery, which is approximately similar to the result reported by Amir (1971:178–81) for interracial rape.

The prior relationship, if any, between the offender(s) and the victim in the Oakland sample proved to be at most slight. In a majority of instances, the victim and offender were unknown to each other until events very closely related to the rape began to unfold (such as the offering of a ride to a woman waiting for a bus). This finding is strikingly different from that reported elsewhere in regard to intraracial rape. Thus Amir (1971:259–76), for instance, noted that in 53 percent of the intraracial cases the victim and the offender were at least acquaintances. Using the same classifatory schema as Amir employed, we found that in 90 percent of our interracial cases the victim and offender were strangers, and that for 97 percent the relationship was no more than that of acquaintanceship.

We had only one case in which something possibly resembling ideological rape found its way into the police reports. These reports, of course, tend toward the skeletal in terms of the information supplied, though there is some effort to establish a modus operandi which might aid in solving other offenses.

The single ideological offense was marked by particular hostility toward the victim as well as a flurry of activity whose meaning is not at all clear to us. The victim was intercepted on her way to do her marketing at about five o'clock in the evening. She was first accosted in the street and was beaten and kicked. Then, when she escaped momentarily, she reported that her assailants followed her into the supermarket and dragged her out. She said that she had been forced to walk to the apartment of one alleged offender, who repeated over and over again, "I want a white woman." She was, she maintained, subjected for three and a half hours by two men to a variety of sexual attacks involving, the police report notes, "numerous positions." The most puzzling item in the report is the observation that the suspect told the complainant that "she was going to steal for him because he needed money," indicating perhaps a known status of the woman or a fantasy of the offender.[1]

Another case history provides a flavor of the events that cannot be as readily transmitted by numerical summaries. The case is a felony-rape, in which the sexual assault appears almost as an afterthought, the consequence of a sudden catalytic realization that a potential object of rape is at the offender's mercy. The victim in this case was a 24-year-old student; the offender a 16-year-old:

> Complainant states she was riding her bicycle when she noticed another bicycle rider riding very close behind her and to her left side. She did not turn around and therefore did not see who it was. He turned off to her right. About half a block further up the complainant hit a bump causing her to fall. She then noticed that her purse was missing from the basket mounted on the rear of her bike. She went back to where the other bike rider had turned off behind her and found suspect #1 with his bike. She asked him if he had seen her purse and he told her it was on the side of a hill which was part of the freeway foundation. She climbed up the hill and found her purse with its contents scattered. While she was picking it up, suspect attacked her and told her he wanted to screw her. She resisted but he overpowered her and succeeded in making penetration into her vagina with his penis. When he was finished, she asked him for her money back, he gave her back the four one-dollar bills she had had in her purse. He then grabbed three of them from her hand, ran to his bicycle and rode out of sight on a side street.

The ambivalence of the offender, returning her money momentarily to the victim before grabbing most of it back, is somewhat indicative of a phenomenon which seemed to occur with unusual regularity in the series of police reports we examined. It involved the offender attempting to redefine the encounter into a more commonplace or even romantic event after his use of force. We found similar kinds of behavior in intraracial rapes in Boston and Los Angeles (Chappell et al., 1971), but such redefinition seemed particularly common in the Oakland cases, being noted in about 20 percent of the reports. Offenders often made attempts to meet their victims at a further date, and went to some trouble to take the victim to her home rather than dropping her near the offense site. One report notes, for instance: "Complainant states that when suspect was finished, suspect dressed himself, being very nonchalant about what had just happened, making small talk as he dressed. Suspect then drove from scene to bus stop, gave complainant a dollar for bus fare, and left complainant there."

If, indeed, this kind of behavior is more common among black offenders dealing with white victims than in other offender-victim combinations, we would hypothesize that it represents in part a response by the offender to the acquiescent (translated by him into approving) behavior of the victim,[2] as well as an understandable effort to transmute force into seduction, to shore up his self-esteem.

DISCUSSION

Interracial rape in Oakland, according to our data, is overwhelmingly a stranger-to-stranger crime. Unlike intraracial relations, where the rape offender and his victim frequently make initial contact in a social context, such as drinking at a bar together, the access of black offenders to white women is obviously restricted. The crossing of interracial boundaries takes place at those points at which the white victim is most readily available and vulnerable. The dominant scene of interracial rape in Oakland is of victims being seized in public places, as they await transportation or walk in a street or park. That the majority of offenses occur on weekdays suggests that victims are more likely to be engaged in work-oriented tasks, involving unescorted movement in open urban areas. The victim may be a student on the way home from class, a housewife out shopping, a secretary leaving the office for home, and similar targets of opportunity.

Amir (1971) advanced the thesis that intraracial rape is primarily the culmination of a misfired attempt at seduction. In Amir's intraracial sample, many victims and offenders were acquaintances, Saturday evenings accounted for the highest frequency of rapes, and the majority of rapes took place indoors. While Amir (1971:96–108) reported that about one-third of the intraracial cases in Philadelphia involved alcohol, our reports show that not a single victim and only one offender was reported to have been drinking.

Our data indicate, then, that the social interaction data does not apply for interracial rape. The Oakland material also suggests that important elements of interracial rape reported by Amir and other investigators do not necessarily apply to other urban settings. We have noted earlier that in Oakland, unlike Philadelphia, for instance, we did not find a high incidence of multiple-offender interracial rape, did not show black offenders selecting victims significantly older than themselves, and did not support the view that blacks are more often the victims of rape than whites.

Such variations, however, may not reflect actual differences in the phenomenon of rape but the manner in which it is dealt with. Police reporting and recording, and police-community relations, for instance, may distort the data that becomes available (Gagnon, 1972). For example, one informant we questioned about the very small number of white offender–black victim rapes in our sample remarked: "No black woman would report being raped by a white man to the police in Oakland. They might report it to the Panthers, but never the police."

Demographic factors and the race relations may also condition findings. Racial tensions between police and citizens are believed to be higher in Oakland than in most cities (compare,

Turner, 1968:169–83), with Oakland having a militant black population seeking greater access to power in the city. Under these conditions, cooperation with the police by the blacks may be minimal, while white victims may more often than in other places take their reports of victimization to law enforcement officials. Similarly, the police may respond differentially—in terms of recording and investigating events—when the victim is white rather than black.

There are other factors, too, that bear upon the accuracy of any crime statistics, and which also influence the number of criminal events in one place compared to another. The ecological distribution of ethnic groups, the age structure of the population, transportation networks, and similar variables are apt to bear upon criminal behavior and its explanation. Before any firm conclusions can be drawn about national patterns of interracial rape, we require more extensive research using uniform definitions of the offense, and involving homogeneous reporting forms and procedures. Such research may throw light on the "dark figure" of interracial rape, and upon variables which tend to elevate or lower its rate.

NOTES

1. An interesting hypothesis, more notable for its feeling content than for its testable accuracy, has been advanced by Hernton (1965:67–68). "I am well aware, like murder, rape has many motives. But when the motive for rape, however psychotic, is basically racial, that is a different matter. I think now that, at one time or another, in every Negro that grows up in the South, there is a rapist, no matter how hidden. And that rapist has been conceived in the Negro by a system of morals based on guilt, hatred, and human denial."

2. Gebhard et al., (1965:195) noted a similar kind of interpretative behavior among rapists he interviewed in prison: "The rapist . . . often looks upon grudging and reluctant cooperation as evidence of enthusiasm. Often we heard the plaint, 'It wasn't rape—she took her clothes off!'" Gebhard says that in only 4 percent of the offenses that he investigated did there seem to have been initial encouragement by the female followed by a change of heart.

REFERENCES

Amir, Menachem. 1971. *Patterns in Forcible Rape.* Chicago: University of Chicago Press.

Baker, Roy S. 1908. *Following the Color Line.* New York: Macmillan.

Bernard, Jessie. 1966. *Marriage and Family among Negroes.* Englewood Cliffs, N.J.: Prentice-Hall.

Cash, W. J. 1941. *The Mind of the South.* New York: Knopf.

Chappell, Duncan, Gilbert Geis, Stephen Schafer, and Larry Siegel. 1971. "Forcible Rape: A Comparative Study of Offenses Known to the Police in Boston and Los Angeles." In J. Henslin, ed., *Studies in the Sociology of Sex,* pp. 169–90. New York: Appleton Century Crofts.

Chappell, Duncan and Susan Singer. 1973. "Rape in New York City: A study of the data in police files and its meaning." Unpublished.

Cleaver, Eldridge. 1968. *Soul on Ice.* New York: Dell.

Falk, Gerald J. 1950. "The Influence of the Season on the Crime Rate," *Journal of Criminal Law, Criminology, and Police Science* 43:199–213.

Gagnon, John N. 1972. Book review, *Federal Probation* 36 (March):69–71.

Gebhard, Paul H., John H. Gagnon, Wardell B. Pomeroy, and Cornelia Christenson. 1965. *Sex Offenders.* New York: Harper & Row.

Hayman, Charles, Charlene Lanza, Roberto Fuentes, and Kathe Algor. 1971. "Rape in the District of Columbia." Paper presented to the American Public Health Association, October 12.

Hernton, Calvin. 1965. *Sex and Racism in America.* New York: Grove Press.

Koeninger, R. C. 1969. "Capital Punishment in Texas," *Crime and Delinquency* 15:132–41.

MacDonald, John. 1971. *Rape Offenders and Their Victims.* Springfield, Ill.: Charles C. Thomas.

Myrdal, Gunnar. 1944. *An American Dilemma.* New York: Harper & Row.

National Commission on the Causes and Prevention of Violence. 1969. *Crimes of Violence.* Washington, D.C.: U.S. Government Printing Office.

Partington, Donald H. 1965. "The Incidence of the Death Penalty for Rape in Virginia," *Washington and Lee Law Review* 22(Spring):43–75.

Rowan, Carl. 1952. *South of Freedom.* New York: Knopf.

Savitz, Leonard. 1973. "Black Crime." In Kent S. Miller, ed., *Comparative Studies of Blacks and Whites in the United States,* pp. 467–516. New York: Seminar Press.

Smith, Lillian. 1961. *Killers of the Dream.* New York: Doubleday, Anchor Books.

Staples, Robert. 1972. "The Sexuality of Black Women," *Sexual Behavior* 2(June):4–15.

Turner, Wallace. 1968. *The Police Establishment.* New York: Putnam.

Wolfgang, Marvin C. 1958. *Patterns in Criminal Homicide.* Philadelphia: University of Pennsylvania Press.

Wolfgang, Marvin C. and Bernard Cohen. 1970. *Crime and Race.* New York: Institute of Human Relations, American Jewish Committee.

7 Forcible Rape and the Problem of the Rights of the Accused

EDWARD SAGARIN

FORCIBLE rape is without question one of the most terrifying crimes in which the victim survives. The fright has an enduring quality; its consequences remain with the victim for many years or perhaps a lifetime, accounting for deep psychological problems. While the act is occurring, the fear of being seriously injured, even killed, may be similar to that felt while one is being robbed at gunpoint, with the possibility that a wrong move or an interpretation of a flicker may cause the gun to be shot. Further, in rape the stigma falls upon the most innocent victim, who is hence perceived as marred or unchaste, someone impure, as if she were more a collaborator than she claims. A relic from the era of the cult of virginity, this last absurdity may be disappearing in the Western world.

Rape is a crime for which convictions have not been easy to obtain, even when the evidence against the accused was quite

Reprinted by permission from *Intellect,* May/June 1975.

strong. It is no wonder, then, that the new militant women's movement, weary of waiting for the male-dominated police, courts, and legislative bodies to put their house in order, have demanded better protection against rapists and more vigorous prosecution of the perpetrators of this heinous offense.

Successful prosecutions of rape have been difficult for several reasons:

1. A defendant will sometimes admit that there was sexual intercourse, but will claim that it was voluntary; although his claim is untrue, the woman has no evidence to establish this.
2. A woman is discouraged from prosecuting in a situation of this sort, for fear that a verdict of not guilty will stigmatize her.
3. A woman is further discouraged because, as complaining witness, she frequently has been subjected to embarrassing cross-examination about her prior sex life by counsel for the defense, particularly if the defense sought to establish that she was not an unwilling partner.

Rape, however, is unique in some other respects that warrant careful attention. A charge of rape has sometimes been made when there has been no sexual encounter (a few examples are cited below); probably more than any other crime in which the perpetrator is actually seen at close range by the victim and even by others, the conditions make identification rather suspect; and finally, the crime of rape is probably the only illegal act that has been so inextricably interwoven with the deliberate effort to oppress the black people.

THE ACCUSATION WITHOUT THE CRIME

The accusation of a crime where there has been none at all is not entirely unknown in other legal areas. To reverse the well-known phrase of Edwin Schur (1965), one might look into a category of victims without crimes. People have been accused of murder, when further investigation revealed that the deceased had died a natural death or had died by his own hand (that is, there was no murder) or even when the "deceased" was still alive (because of improper identification of a body or an assumption of death without the *corpus delicti*). Accusations of robbery have been made for various reasons by persons who knew that they had not been robbed (for revenge or to obtain an insurance claim); and of larceny by those who mistakenly thought that something had been taken when actually it had been misplaced.

The charge of rape may occur falsely under essentially three conditions, each of which deserves separate consideration. The first two involve instances in which there was no rape, and the third in which the crime did occur but the person accused was not the perpetrator. In sum:

1. No sexual act has taken place between the accuser and the accused, and the alleged victim has not been subjected to rape at the hands of the accused or anyone else.
2. Sexual intercourse between the complaining witness and the defendant has occurred,[1] perhaps once or on several occasions, but it has been consensual; however, the woman decides to make an accusation of rape against the man.
3. The female has indeed been raped, and the perpetrator is someone previously unknown to her; in good faith, she makes an identification, but the person accused has not been the offender.

THE RAPE THAT WASN'T

It would appear that the first of the three categories can be disposed of with the least amount of difficulty. A recent newspaper story (*New York Post,* May 9, 1973) carried the headline, "Raped Girl Wasn't." A 16-year-old girl claimed that she had been raped repeatedly in New York's Central Park. When hospital tests showed that she had not been raped, the girl thereupon changed her story, saying that "she had skipped school to go to the park with a girl friend." The police and medical authorities can usually detect a lie of this sort.

There has been almost no research on this type of false claim (a sort of corollary to what is in all likelihood the much more frequent case of the girl who has been victimized in what was indisputably a forcible rape and has suppressed information about it). With little data available, it would appear that a statement that one has been raped when there has been no sexual encounter is probably rare.

However, the most blatant and frequent experience of a false accusation of rape, in the complete absence of sexual contact, forcible or consensual, involves racial matters and the entire sexual-racial mythology that has grown up in America. It is impossible to read the history of the American South, the terrible story of lynching and of courtroom travesties, without concluding that the cry of rape was a systematic and deliberate invention of white males who made accusations against black males and who then compelled the white females to echo and support the charges. It was a cry raised for the sole and exclusive purpose of perpetrating the caste oppression of the blacks that followed the ascendancy of the Klan and the defeat of Reconstruction. Historical studies show that nothing remotely resembling forcible sexual attack had occurred in the overwhelming majority of cases for which black males were lynched, legally or extralegally.[2]

SCOTTSBORO AND AFTER

In the 1930s, the truth about the cry of rape against pure, white womanhood was brought dramatically to the attention of the entire world in what came to be known as the *Scottsboro* case (cf. Carter, 1969; *Powell* v. *Alabama,* 1932). In the midst of the depression, nine black youths, the youngest only thirteen years of age and the oldest twenty, were riding the freights in Alabama, and on a train they became embroiled in a fight with two white youths. Blacks and whites, all were what was known as hobos. The whites, outnumbered, overpowered, and defeated, were thrown off the train, picked up by local authorities, and allegedly said there were two white girls on the freight who had been raped by the blacks. At the next stop, the latter were rounded up, arrested, and in a one-day trial, without representation by counsel, in an atmosphere that the Supreme Court described as "tense, hostile, and excited public sentiment,'' were found guilty of rape by an all-white jury. The youngest boy was sentenced to life imprisonment, the others to death.

Northern radicals entered the case, and a new defense brought forth evidence that the girls were prostitutes. One of the girls vehemently denied, through an entire series of later trials and interrogations, that she had been attacked, molested, or in any way had had sexual contact with any of the youths. A worldwide outcry, led or exploited (the words really mean the same thing, and the choice of language depends on political preferences) by the international Communist movement, joined by Negro reformist groups, liberals, and civil libertarians, stopped the hand of the legal lynchers. The result was the gradual release of the youths, the last in 1950, after nineteen years in prison and after America had entered and emerged victorious from a war to save the world from racism.

The important thing about *Scottsboro* is that it was not unique, except in that it came to the attention of the entire world. The cry that black men were raping white women was an integral and deliberate effort of the white ruling group in the South to continue to stir up fear and hatred against blacks so that the movement of the latter toward enfranchisement, legal rights, trial by juries on which their peers were sitting, and other liberties granted to white American citizens (and noncitizens too) would be effectively combatted. It was an anti-union battle cry (unionism was extremely weak in the South, and wages were far lower than elsewhere in the United States) to keep the hostility between white and black workers at a feverish height.

Of the approximately three thousand extralegal mob lynchings that took place in America from the Emancipation Proclamation to World War II, more than 90 percent of the victims were black, more than 90 percent occurred in the Deep South, approximately 20 percent of the victims were accused (if one can dignify a lynching by referring to the victims as accused) of committing rape. Investigation has led observers to state that in the great majority of instances, there was no sexual encounter (consensual

sexual conduct. There are only two exceptions: evidence of prior sexual activity with the actor and evidence of specific instances of sexual activity to show the origin of pregnancy, disease, or semen. However, this evidence will only be admitted after the defense has filed a written motion and offer of proof within ten days after arraignment, and the judge has determined that the evidence is material and that its probative value outweighs its inflammatory nature.

In the past, such evidence was allowed either to impeach the victim's credibility or to show the probability that she consented. These two purposes are quite separate, although their effects may merge. Where the premise is accepted that women who have consented in the past will probably consent in the future, the defense can cross-examine the victim on her past sexual history and present witnesses to show the probability that she consented. Similarly, impeachment is used to suggest that the victim is lying, and not to be believed. With regard to that hypothesis, general evidence of a bad reputation or specific sexual activities have been allowed, but evidence of specific acts with third parties have not been admissible except to show the origin of a pregnancy.

The new act attempts to focus the attention of the court on the criminal act and its circumstances. In the past it was believed that the protection of the defendant from untrue accusations required that all means be put at his disposal to determine the veracity of the accusations, including evidence of the prosecutrix's past history (Landau, 1974). However, this evidence served as a deterrent to reporting and prosecuting rapes, victims being reluctant to submit to a harrowing trial. Since this deterrent effect could pose a large problem, an exception was created, limited by the judge's discretion, to allow the admission of evidence of prior relations between the actor and the victim. The exception, while more limited than in the past, is still open to abuse. The court must protect the defendant from false accusations and simultaneously protect the victim from having mere acquaintanceship or physical proximity construed as consent to sexual conduct. The second exception, allowing evidence of specific instances of sexual activity to show the source of semen, pregnancy, or disease, also appears vulnerable to abuse, but it is designed to protect the defendant's rights. If the identity of the actor is at issue, the defendant must be permitted to admit evidence showing that a third party was the source of the semen. Likewise, since pregnancy and venereal disease are types of personal injury that would elevate a simple offense to the aggravated level, the defendant must be allowed to admit such evidence to show his innocence as to the pregnancy or disease.

It has been argued that the evidentiary limitations provided for in the new law (that is, total exclusion of any testimony of prior sexual relations between the victim and third parties) abridge the defendant's constitutional right to due process and to confrontation. Admitting such evidence may be *logically* relevant, (that is, that the existence of A makes it more likely that B has occurred), the legislature has, in the new law, determined that this testimony is not *legally* relevant.

Courts have in numerous circumstances, where overriding policy considerations were at stake, totally excluded evidence which may be logically relevant but which is held as a matter of law not to be legally relevant. An example is the case of subsequent repairs made to a facility which may have caused an injury (see Falknor, 1956). Presently, in many jurisdictions, it is clear error for a trial court judge to admit such evidence. The analogy of this example to the statutory rule excluding evidence of a victim's prior sexual conduct with third parties is compelling. In cases involving evidence of subsequent repair, the court evolved a fixed rule of law through policy-balancing in individual cases: In the Sexual Assault Act, the legislature enacted a fixed rule of law after it balanced the countervailing policies for and against admission of such evidence. The distinction between the two law-making processes is probably too slight to support a finding that one is constitutionally valid and the other is not.

Corroboration

Although some states (Note, 1967) require that the victim's testimony be corroborated by other evidence of one or more of the elements of nonconsent, penetration, or identity of the assailant, neither the Michigan common law nor the existing statutes have required corroboration of the victim's testimony. The law relies completely on the jury to weigh the credibility of each witness and this rule is continued under the new law.

However, even in Michigan, where corroboration never has been officially required, few defendants have been convicted without some corroborative evidence. An unofficial corroboration rule may exist in practice where overloaded police departments and prosecutor's offices refuse to press a case without some independent evidentiary support for the victim's testimony (Note, 1972). In doubtful cases the complaining party is often required to take a polygraph test (Note, 1967:1139).

There are several reasons advanced in favor of the corroboration requirement. One is the theory that rape is more likely to be falsely charged than other crimes. Coupled with this are the beliefs that juries are prejudiced in favor of the victim and that defendants need extra protection in rape cases because there is seldom an eyewitness available to refute the victim's testimony.

Empirical evidence on the relative veracity of rape reports, as opposed to reports of other crimes, has not been compiled (LeGrand, 1973:921), but there is evidence (LeGrand, 1973:921) that only a small percentage of rapes are reported. The many disincentives for reporting a rape tend to discourage frivolous reports. Complainants face an often embarrassing police interrogation, grueling cross-examination from defense counsel, and poor odds for a conviction. Also, the studies conducted by Kalven and Zeisel (1966:253) indicated that juries are not prejudiced against the defendant; indeed, there is great reluctance on their part to convict if the parties had previously known each other.

There is some validity to the argument that identification should be corroborated, but the identification problem exists in all facets of criminal law and arguably can best be handled by the traditional "beyond a reasonable doubt" standard. There is reason to believe that modern criminal investigation techniques, traditional legal rules, and disincentives to reporting are sufficient in weeding out false complaints (Note, 1972:1375), whereas strict corroboration requirements allow many guilty parties to go free.

The rule also presents a constitutional problem of equal protection for women, since corroboration is required only in rape cases (Note, 1972:1371).

For these reasons, the Michigan legislature quite properly excluded any corroboration requirement from the statute. It remains to be seen whether the bill will have any effect on law enforcement agencies which tend to require independent supporting evidence before proceeding with a case.

Other Reform Features

Suppression of Names and Evidence

Under the new law, the names of the victim and the actor as well as details of the offense can be suppressed at the request of counsel, the actor, or the victim until the actor is arraigned on information, the charge is dismissed, or the case is otherwise concluded. Similar protection is afforded to juveniles; the juvenile court in Michigan cannot disclose court records unless there is a "legitimate interest" (*People* v. *Smallwood,* 1943). Although newspapers are not prohibited from publishing the names of juvenile offenders if they can obtain the names through other sources such as police records, they generally do not do so. Newspapers have also established a policy of not publishing the names of rape victims. These policies suggest the obvious; that there is a stigma attached to juvenile offenders and to rape victims as well, since they are treated in a similar manner. Consistent with these policies, the Sexual Assault Act appears to be a preliminary device to protect the parties from unnecessary distress through the publishing or broadcasting of their identities.

However, "suppression" may imply that no one, not even the defendant will have access to information prior to the arraignment. If this is the legislative intent, this section may face constitutional challenges for depriving defendents of their constitutional rights. A similar Georgia statute, presently under attack, only prohibits the name of the victim from being published or broadcast but does not withhold the evidence from the defendant.[4] Under the first interpretation where only publishing or broadcasting is prohibited, the new Michigan law is apt to be viewed uncritically, but the latter interpretation involving suppression of names and evidence may face serious challenge.

Husband and Wife

The common law definition of rape required unlawful carnal knowledge. A husband could not be guilty of raping his wife, since the marital relationship was sanctioned by the law. This still would be true under the Sexual Assault Act unless the spouses were living apart and one had filed for separate maintenance or divorce.

A person has always been protected against murder and manslaughter by his or her spouse, and the new Act seeks to extend the protection of the law to a limited group of married but separated people. The new law, however, still does not protect spouses with continuing marriages, thus presenting a possible denial of equal protection in that only married couples who are living apart are protected.

There are several considerations that led to the limitation of the Act's coverage to couples living apart. Acts between a married couple may provide difficult evidentiary problems (Comment, 1954:725). It may be argued, however, that difficult evidentiary problems do not justify withholding the protection of the law from married persons. There is a belief that the situation of spouses living together is susceptible to misinterpretation and likely to allow either spouse to use the law to obtain a better property settlement or child custody. It also might act as an obstacle to reconciliation. In balance, therefore, the legislature decided to avoid bringing this difficult evidentiary and social problem within the scope of the Act. . . .

CONCLUSION

The Michigan Sexual Assault Act reflects a major rethinking of the common assumptions about rape. Legislation cannot eliminate the various myths that are apparently held by many jurors, but the Act properly directs the court's attention to the level of violence used, rather than to the victim's prior sexual activity. The legislation reflects the fact that the motives of the rapist are not primarily sexual and, therefore, traditional ideas about sex do not apply to the rape situation.

Hopefully, the new Act will encourage the reporting of rapes since women will no longer be required to testify about past relationships. Prosecutors may be less reluctant to handle rape cases. Also, convictions for nonaggravated rape may increase because there are now lesser offenses which are matched to less violent acts. An added advantage of the bill is that rape of a separated spouse is now a crime, although it could be argued that spouses should not have to be living apart in order to be covered by the Act.

The bill may be criticized because it does not limit the felony status of the aggravated offenses to forcible felonies. The absence of minimum sentences and the ambiguity concerning the terms mental anguish and bodily injury may tend to undercut the degree structure of the statute. These and other difficulties must await judicial interpretation before it will be possible to determine the ultimate effects of the Sexual Assault Act.

NOTES

1. Some aspects of the existing unrepealed law and the new sexual assault act remain irreconcilable. Under sections which were not repealed, a marriage is void if the couple has enough consanguinity for the relationship to amount to incest. Yet, if the marriage is solemnized outside the state, the marriage will be recognized when the couple returns. However, under the new Sexual Assault Act, sexual intercourse between people with the requisite degree of consanguinity is prohibited only if one or both parties is less than sixteen years old. In that case, the act is punished as an aggravated offense, even if no force or coercion is used. One might question the wisdom of legislation which decriminalizes the sexual act in an "incestuous relationship" but which invalidates the marriages of such couples.

2. The treatment of statutory age relationships under the new law may be inconsistent with the concept of grading each offense according to the blameworthiness of the actor's conduct. For example, a 15-year-old female who represents that she is older will expose her unknowing 18-year-old companion to a possible fifteen-year prison sentence if they have intercourse, but a 30-year-old man who has intercourse with a 16-year-old is guilty of no crime under the statute.

3. Nonconsent would not accompany force in the exceptionally aberrant case of a sado-masochistic relationship.

4. Editor's Note: The Georgia statute was deemed unconstitutional in *Cox Broadcasting* v. *Cohn* (1975).

REFERENCES

Amir, Menachem. 1971. *Patterns in Forcible Rape.* Chicago: University of Chicago Press.

Comment. 1954. "Rape and Battery between Husband and Wife," *Stanford Law Review* 6:719–34.

Cox Broadcasting v. *Cohn.* 1975. 420 U.S. 469.

Curtis, Lynn A. 1974. "Victim Precipitation and Violent Crime," *Social Problems* 21:594–605.

Dworkin, Roger B. 1966. "The Resistance Standard in Rape Legislation," *Stanford Law Review* 18:680–89.

Falknor, Judson D. 1956. "Extrinsic Policies Affecting Admissibility," *Rutgers Law Review* 10:574–600.

Federal Bureau of Investigation. 1974. *Uniform Crime Reports 1973.* Washington, D.C.: U.S. Government Printing Office.

Freud, Sigmund 1933. *New Introductory Lectures on Psychoanalysis.* Trans. by W. J. H. Sprott. New York: Norton.

Hirdes v. *Ottawa Circuit Judge.* 1914. 146 N. W. 646 (Michigan).

Kalven, Harry, Jr. and Hans Zeisel. 1966. *The American Jury.* Boston: Little, Brown.

Landau, Sybil. 1974. "Rape: Victim as Defendant," *Trial,* 10(July/August): 19–22.

LeGrand, Camille E. 1973. "Rape and Rape Laws: Sexism in Society and Law," *California Law Review* 61:919–41.

Masters, William. 1960. "The Sexual Response of the Human Female," *Western Journal of Surgery, Obstetrics and Gynecology* 68:57–72.

Note. 1972. "The Rape Corroboration Requirement: Repeal Not Reform," *Yale Law Journal* 81:1365–91.

——. 1967. "Corroborating Charges of Rape," *Columbia Law Review* 67: 1137–48.

People v. *Ayres.* 1917. 161 N. W. 870 (Michigan).

People v. *Burrell.* 1931. 235 N. W. 170 (Michigan).

People v. *Crosswell.* 1865. 13 Michigan 427.

People v. *Dockery.* 1969. 173 N. W. 2d 726. (Michigan).

People v. *Geddes.* 1942. 3 N. W. 2d 266,267 (Michigan).

People v. *Jackson.* 1972. 202 N. W. 463 (Michigan).

People v. *Don Moran.* 1872. 25 Michigan 356,363.

People v. *Murphy.* 1906. 108 N. W. 1009 (Michigan).

People v. *Myers.* 1943. 10 N. W. 2d 323 (Michigan).

People v. *Palmer.* 1973. 209 N. W. 2d 710 (Michigan).

People v. *Smallwood.* 1943. 10 N. W. 2d 303 (Michigan).

Strang v. *People.* 1871. 24 Michigan 1.

BEHAVIORAL SCIENCE STUDIES

10 Gusii Sex Offenses: A Study in Social Control

ROBERT A. LeVINE

AMONG the Gusii of southwestern Kenya, the high frequency of rape is a major social problem and has been a source of concern to British administrators and Gusii chiefs for over twenty years. In this paper I shall inquire into the causes of that situation and attempt to formulate some general hypotheses concerning the control of sexual behavior in human societies.

Before proceeding with the inquiry, it is necessary to define "rape." In the contemporary legal system of South Nyanza District, where the Gusii live, a heterosexual assault is classified as rape (or defilement of a girl under sixteen years of age) only when an examination by the district medical officer indicates that the hymen of the alleged victim was recently penetrated by the use of painful force. Such cases are heard by the resident magistrate of the district, a European judge. When medical evidence is unob-

Reprinted by permission of the American Anthropological Association, from the *American Anthropologist* (1959), 61(6).

tainable due to the lateness of the examination or the fact that the alleged victim was not a virgin, the case is classified as indecent assault and is usually heard by one of the African tribunal courts presided over by Gusii judges. Most cases are of the latter kind. The Gusii themselves do not distinguish between rape and indecent assault. They use the following expressions to refer to heterosexual assault: *okorwania*—"to fight" (a girl or woman), a euphemistic expression; *ogotachira inse*—"to stamp on" (a girl or woman); *ogosaria*—"to spoil" (a girl or woman); *ogotomana*—"to engage in illicit intercourse," inclusive of adultery and incest. Any of these expressions could be accurately applied to a case legally classified as rape or indecent assault; the act they refer to is universally considered illicit by the Gusii. I shall use the term "rape" to mean the culturally disvalued use of coercion by a male to achieve the submission of a female to sexual intercourse; this includes both of the legal categories.

Evidence for the high frequency of rape among the Gusii is not entirely impressionistic. An extremely conservative estimate of the annual rate of rape (including indecent assault) indictments based on court records for 1955 and 1956 yields the figure of 47.2 per 100,000 population.[1] During the same period the annual rate in urban areas of the United States was 13.85 per 100,000 (rural areas, 13.1). On the basis of the relatively few serious rape and defilement indictments entered at the resident magistrate's court, it is possible to make a limited comparison of the Gusii with the major adjacent tribal groups, the South Nyanza Luo and the Kipsigis. During 1955–1956 the Gusii (1948 population: 237,542) accounted for thirteen such indictments, the South Nyanza Luo (1948 population: 270,379) for six, and the Kipsigis (1948 population: 152,391) for four. Though the figures are small, they clearly indicate the Gusii lead over the other two groups in number of rape indictments relative to population size. Thus on a comparative basis it is possible to state that the contemporary rate of reported rape among the Gussii is extraordinarily high. It should be noted that the years chosen for comparison, 1955 and 1956, were locally recognized as being high years but by no means the worst on record. In 1937 a mass outbreak of rape created a law enforcement emergency and induced the district commissioner to threaten a punitive expedition. In 1950 the number of rapists convicted was so great that the district prison facilities were not adequate to hold them. The great amount of rape, then, is a problem of unusual persistence in Gusiiland.

In the following sections I shall attempt to explain the prevalence of rape in Gusiiland by presenting and analyzing data on institutionalized forms of sex antagonism, traditional and contemporary limitations on premarital sexuality, the differing motivations of rapists, and the role of bridewealth rates in delaying marriage.

SEX ANTAGONISMS IN GUSII SOCIETY

The Gusii are a Bantu-speaking people practicing agriculture and animal husbandry in the Kenya highlands just east of Lake Victoria. They are strongly patrilineal and have a segmentary lineage system with a high degree of congruence between lineages and territorial groups. Before the onset of British administration in 1907, clans were the most significant political units and carried on blood feuds (cf., Mayer, 1949). Each of the seven Gusii tribes consisted of one or more large, dominant clans and a number of smaller clans and clan fragments. Clans of the same tribe united for war efforts against other tribes, but feuded among themselves at other times.

Each clan, although an independent military and territorial unit, was exogamous and patrilocal, so that wives had to be imported from clans against which feuds had been conducted. The Gusii recognize this in their proverb, "Those whom we marry are those whom we fight." Marriages did not mitigate the hostilities between clans on a permanent basis; in fact, women were used by their husbands' clans to aid in military operations against their natal clans. A captive from an enemy clan might be tortured in a pillory-like device while a married woman originally from his clan would be sent to relate tearfully to her kinsmen, "Our brother is being killed!" and to urge them to save his life by a ransom in cattle. Marriage among the Gusii was thus a relationship between hostile groups and it continues to be nowadays although blood feuds are prohibited. Clan territories in some areas have been broken up into discontinuous fragments, but local communities are homogeneous with respect to clan membership. Social relations between adjacent communities of different clans are minimal, whereas neighboring communities of the same clan have a considerable common social life. Marriages are still contracted with the aid of an intermediary *(esigani)* between members of alien and unfriendly groups.

The clearest expression of the interclan hostility involved in marriage can be found in the *enyangi* ceremonial. Enyangi is the final ceremony in a Gusii marriage and can be performed either shortly after the start of cohabitation or any number of years later, even after the children have grown up. During the ceremony, iron rings (*ebitinge*) are attached to the wife's ankles and are never removed until the death of her husband or her willful desertion of him. The practice of enyangi is rapidly disappearing in many areas of Gusiiland, partly because of its expense and partly because many girls become nominal Christians to escape the indignities described below. However, the attitudes and emotions expressed in the traditional rite persist in the contemporary situation.

On the following day the groom in his finery returns to the bride's family where he is stopped by a crowd of women who deprecate his physical appearance. Once he is in the house of the bride's mother and a sacrifice has been performed by the marriage priest, the women begin again, accusing the groom of impotence on the wedding night and claiming that his penis is too small to be effective. He attempts to refute their insults. The next day bride and groom go to the latter's home. The groom enters the door of his mother's house but when the bride attempts to follow, she is met by a bellicose crowd of women who keep her at the door for a long time. They scream insults at her, mock her, pinch her, sometimes even smear dung on her lips. Throughout it all she must remain silent. Some brides have been kept at the door for so many hours that they have given up and returned home. Usually, however, the bride is allowed in and treated with kindness thereafter. Other examples of hostile interaction between affines at enyangi could be given, but Mayer (1950a) has described them in great detail.

The enyangi ceremony allows the expression of hostility which in-laws must never give vent to under ordinary circumstances and is indicative of the interclan tensions which are involved in every Gusii marriage. Inevitably, it is the bride who experiences this tension in its most acute form. She must move from her childhood home into the enemy camp; she must sever allegiance to her native group and develop loyalty to an opposing group.[2] It is not surprising, then, that girls are ambivalent toward marriage. On the one hand, they yearn for it because women can only achieve security and prestige in Gusii society through legitimate motherhood and especially through bearing numerous sons. On the other hand, they have heard the folk tale in which the innocent bride discovers her parents-in-law to be cannibalistic ogres, and other similar tales; they all know of girls who have returned to their parents claiming that their in-laws were witches who tried to lure them into witchcraft. They are thus as frightened by the prospect of marriage as they are attracted to it.

The fears of the bride are institutionalized in her traditional resistance to being taken to the home of the groom. Among the adjacent Luo and other East African tribes, it is customary for kinsmen of the bride to fight with kinsmen of the groom and attempt to prevent her departure. With the Gusii, however, it is the bride herself who resists, or who hides herself in a nearby house, and her father, having received the bridewealth cattle by this time, may even help persuade her to go if her reluctance appears to be sincere. Five young clansmen of the groom come to take the bride; two immediately find the girl and post themselves at her side to prevent escape, while the others receive the final permission of her parents. When it has been granted, the bride holds onto the house posts and must be dragged outside. Finally she goes, crying and with her hands on her head. Her resistance is token and not really intended to break off the marriage, but it expresses the real fears of every Gusii bride.

When the reluctant bride arrives at the groom's house, the matter of first importance is the wedding night sexual performance. This is a trial for both parties, in that the impotence of the groom may cause the bride to break off the marriage, and the discovery of scars or deformities on the bride's body (including vaginal obstruction) may induce the groom to send her home and request a return of the bridewealth. The bride is determined to put her new husband's sexual competence to the most severe test possible. She may take magical measures which are believed to result in his failure in intercourse. These include chewing a piece of charcoal or phallic pod commonly found in pastures, putting either of these or a knotted piece of grass under the marriage bed, and twisting the phallic flower of the banana tree. The groom is determined to be successful in the face of her expected resistance; he fortifies himself by being well fed, which is believed to favor potency, by eating bitter herbs, and nowadays by eating large quantities of coffee beans, valued as an aphrodisiac. His brothers and paternal male cousins give him encouragement and take a great interest in his prospects for success. Numerous young clansmen of the groom gather at the homestead in a festive mood; chickens are killed for them to eat and they entertain themselves by singing and dancing while waiting for the major events of the wedding night.

The bride usually refuses to get onto the bed; if she did not resist the groom's advances, she would be thought sexually promiscuous. At this point, some of the young men may forcibly disrobe her and put her on the bed. The groom examines the bride's mouth for pods or other magical devices designed to render him impotent. As he proceeds toward sexual intercourse she continues to resist and he must force her into position. Ordinarily she performs the practice known as *ogotega,* allowing him between her thighs but keeping the vaginal muscles so tense that penetration is impossible. If the groom is young (by traditional standards, under twenty-five), the young men intervene, reprimand the bride, and hold her in position so that penetration can be achieved on the first night. An older groom, however, is considered strong enough to take care of himself, and the young men wait outside the door of the house, looking in occasionally to check on his progress. It is said that in such cases a "fierce" girl in the old days could prevent the groom from achieving full penetration as long as a week. Brides are said to take pride in the length of time they can hold off their mates. In 1957, a girl succeeded in resisting the initial attempts of her bridegroom. His brothers threatened and manhandled her until she confessed to having knotted her pubic hair across the vaginal orifice. They cut the knot with a razor blade and stayed to watch the first performance of marital coitus by the light of a kerosene pressure lamp.

Once penetration has been achieved, the young men sing in jubilation and retire from the house to allow the groom to complete the nuptial sexual relations. They are keenly interested in how many times he will be able to perform coitus on the first night, as this is a matter of prestige and invidious comparison. He will be asked about it by all male relatives of his generation, and the bride will also be questioned on this score when she returns to visit her own family. It is said that the groom's clansmen also question the bride, in order to check on the groom's account of his attainment. Six is considered a minimally respectable number of times and twelve is the maximum of which informants had heard. They claimed that it was traditional to achieve orgasm twelve times but that performances were lower in recent years.

The explicit object of such prodigious feats is to hurt the bride. When a bride is unable to walk on the day following the wedding night, the young men consider the groom "a real man" and he is able to boast of his exploits, particularly the fact that he made her cry. One informant quoted some relevant conversation from the *enyangi* ceremony which is performed at a later time. At the bride's home the insulting women say to the groom: "You are not strong, you can't do anything to our daughter. When you slept with her, you didn't do it like a man. You have a small penis which can do nothing. You should grab our daughter and she should be hurt and scream—then you're a man." He answers boastfully: "I am a man! If you were to see my penis you would run away. When I grabbed her, she screamed. I am not a man to be joked with. Didn't she tell you? She cried—ask her!"

The conception of coitus as an act in which a man overcomes the resistance of a woman and causes her pain is not limited to the wedding night; it continues to be important in marital relations. Wives in monogamous homesteads never initiate sexual intercourse with their husbands, and they customarily make a token objection before yielding to their husbands. The wife does not take an active role in the foreplay or coitus and will not remove her clothes herself if she has not already done so for sleeping. Most importantly, it is universally reported that wives cry during coitus, moaning quietly, "You're hurting me, you bad man," and other such admonitions. Gusii men find this practice sexually arousing. The following statement by a 36-year-old husband epitomizes the attitude of the Gusii male toward his wife's sexuality.

> During coitus the husband asks her, "What do you feel? Don't you think it's good?" The wife says, "Don't ask me that." She will never say yes. When the woman cries and protests during intercourse you are very excited. . . . We are always mystified as to whether women enjoy it. But the wives in polygymous homesteads complain when their husbands neglect them, so they must like it.

There is good reason to believe that the reluctant sexual pose of Gusii wives is not feigned in all cases. Young husbands claim to desire coitus at least twice a night, once early and once toward dawn. In a number of monogamous marriages, however, this rate is not achieved, primarily due to the stubborn resistance of wives. Every community contains some married women with reputations for refusing to have intercourse with their husbands for up to a week at a time. Such husbands are eventually moved to beat their wives and even send them back to their parents. I knew of one case of this kind in which the wife's distaste for coitus was the only major source of conflict between husband and wife. Among monogamous wives who do not have antisexual reputations, refusal to have intercourse with their husbands usually occurs when they have quarreled over something else. Since family modesty prescribes the performance of intercourse in the dark after the children have fallen asleep, wives enforce their refusal by pinching a child awake if the husband is insistent. Such evidence suggests that for some Gusii wives the resistant and pained behavior in marital intercourse does not represent a conventional pose or an attempt to arouse their husbands, but a sincere desire to avoid coitus.

On the basis of the Gusii case alone, it is difficult to arrive at a satisfactory solution to the problem of whether the sado-masochistic aspect of Gusii nuptial and marital sexuality is inexorably connected with, and a reflection of, the antagonism of intermarrying clans. Many of the above facts point to such a connection, but it is noteworthy that there is at least one culturally patterned form of expressing heterosexual antagonism within the clan. This is the practice of "arousing desire" (*ogosonia*) which Mayer (1953: 22–23) has described in some detail. When Gusii boys undergoing initiation are recuperating from their circumcision operation, adolescent girls of the same clan come to the seclusion huts, disrobe, dance around the novices in provocative attitudes, challenge them to have intercourse, and make disparaging remarks about the genitals of the boys. The latter are of course incapable of coitus, and the girls are well aware of this. According to Mayer (1953:23), "Most Gusii think that the purpose of *ogosonia* is to cause pain. The girls have their triumph if a resulting erection causes the partly healed wound to burst open, with acute pain to the novice." Here, then, is the use of sexuality to inflict pain occurring between girls and boys of the same exogamous clan. It could be argued that the adolescent girls have already developed the attitudes appropriate to the wedding night and apply them to the nearest males whom they know to be in a uniquely vulnerable sexual condition. In any event, the practice of ogosonia indicates that the antagonism of Gusii females toward male sexuality and their view of sexual intercourse in aggressive terms are components of a general pattern of behavior not limited to the marital relationship.

Regardless of what other conclusions can be drawn from the foregoing descriptions of institutionalized forms of sex antagonism, one major point has been established: Legitimate heterosexual encounters among the Gusii are aggressive contests, involving force and pain-inflicting behavior which under circumstances that are not legitimate could be termed rape. In the following sections I shall discuss the conditions which lead to the performance of such behavior under illegitimate circumstances.

SEX RESTRICTIONS WITHIN THE CLAN

Since males are almost by definition the active participants in rape and are held responsible when its occurrence is made public, it is appropriate to examine the circumstances leading to rape from the point of view of the typical male, the potential rapist. This examination will begin with the intraclan restrictions on premarital sexual behavior which face the Gusii youth and will proceed in the next section to the situation he faces when attempting to make his way sexually with females of other clans.

Gusii parents do not tolerate the sex play of their children; they beat both boys and girls for indulging in it. Children have opportunities to escape parental supervision and engage in heterosexuality, and adults are aware that children in general do such things, though they become upset upon learning that a particular child of their own has done so. After initiation, at ages 8 to 9 for girls and 10 to 12 for boys, the situation becomes somewhat different. The boy or young *omomura* ("warrior") lives in a separate hut near that of his parents and is allowed considerable privacy in his sexual conduct, since a rule of intergenerational sex avoidance prohibits parents from paying attention to the sexual affairs of their initiated sons. It is just the opposite for girls, however, since their reaching puberty makes parents fearful of sexual scandal (described below) and leads to stronger parental attempts at sexual control.

Although parents generally ignore the sexual behavior of their initiated sons, the latter find their choice of sexual objects limited by restrictions operating in the community. In many East African societies young men are allowed sexual privileges with brothers' wives, fathers' young widows, or other married women, but among the Gusii such practices are prohibited and viewed with utmost horror. No provision is made for a young man to receive sexual education from an experienced woman. Furthermore, he is barred from having intercourse with any of the married women in his clan; wives are expected to be faithful to their own husbands, with no deviations allowed. This rules out as sex objects all the married women in the local community, since they are all married to his clansmen.

The rules concerning marital fidelity are enforced by three types of sanctions. One is a supernatural sanction known as *amasangia* which can be incurred at any time after the transfer of bridewealth to the bride's parents. *Amasangia* literally means "sharing," and refers to the consequences of illicit sharing of a married woman's sexual attentions. Amasangia is caused by the adulterous behavior of a woman, but it directly affects her husband and children rather than herself. The Gusii believe that if a woman has sexual intercourse with a man other than her husband and continues to cohabit with her husband, then when the latter becomes ill, her presence in the same room may cause his death. It is said that the sick husband begins to sweat profusely when approached by his adulterous wife; if he has cut himself, her attempt to bandage the wound will promote bleeding rather than arrest it. Some of the older polygamists will not allow their wives to visit them when they (the husbands) are ill, since they jealously suspect their wives of adultery. The shared wife may also unintentionally kill her child by her proximity to him when he is ill, and miscarriages are regularly attributed to adultery. Belief in amasangia appears universal among Gusii women, including Christians. They see it as punishment directed against themselves, since no woman wants to be a widow or to lose children. When a woman has committed clandestine adultery, she can avoid the evil consequences either by confessing to her husband and having a purifying sacrifice performed or by running away with her lover.

The second type of sanction enforcing marital fidelity is also part of the amasangia complex but is directed at men rather than women. When two men of the same clan have had intercourse with the same married woman, regardless of whether or not she is married to either of them, it is believed that a visit by one to the sickbed of the other will result in the death of the sick one. This enters significantly into the relations of brothers, half-brothers, and first cousins. If one of them has an affair with a married woman, he must concern himself with whether any of the male clansmen whom he often visits has also had intercourse with her. Sometimes suspicion of adultery with a wife is aroused when a man becomes ill and finds that a particular half-brother or paternal cousin has not visited him. I knew of two young married men who were constantly seeking extramarital affairs and who would tell each other of the married women they had had intercourse with so as to avoid sickbed visits if any of them were the same. Such collaboration to prevent supernatural punishment is rare; ordinarily amasangia acts as a check on male access to the wives of others.

The third sanction is the discovery and disapproval of the elders. Each Gusii clan is divided according to generation with respect to any individual, so that every clansman is his "brother," "father," "grandfather," "child," or "grandchild." With his "brother," "grandfather," and "grandchild," he may make sexual jokes and discuss sexual matters, but with members of adjacent generations he must avoid all mention of sex. Persons of the latter group are said to be *abansoni,* in whose presence one experiences *ensoni,* "sexual shame." It is particularly shameful to have one's sexual behavior come to the attention of members of one's father's generation. Furthermore, in the case of a young man, his paternal generation contains many of the lineage elders who sit as an informal judicial body with traditional power to place curses on serious offenders. A man convicted of raping a married woman in his own clan would be punished by a fine in livestock. If he refused to pay, the elders would turn their drinking tubes upside down in a pot of beer and utter a curse that is believed to result in his death. If a man repeatedly sought the wives of his clansmen, the elders might decide to slaughter his cattle as a punishment. Even apart from these formal sanctions, however, the mere disapproval of the elders is a force which cows many a young man. In engaging in sexual affairs with local married women, every effort is made to achieve the utmost secrecy. The anxiety attendant upon such affairs is too much for most unmarried men, who consider the risk not worth taking.

These three sanctions together operate to keep the amount of adultery among the Gusii at what seems a low level. The women are genuinely afraid of supernatural punishment, and the men fear supernatural punishment to some extent and discovery by the elders within the clan to an even greater extent. Widows in stable leviratic unions are bound by the same rules and sanctions as ordinary married women, although a neglected widow is likely to be sexually promiscuous until a clansman of the dead husband decides to cohabit with her regularly. Even women whose husbands are working far from home usually remain faithful, aided by the fact that their husbands return home or send for them frequently enough to impregnate them at regular intervals. Several cases were reported in which women whose husbands were away loudly rebuffed adulterous advances, accusing the embarrassed males of desiring to kill (through amasangia) the husbands they intended to cuckold. All in all, the opportunities for the average young Gusii male to have sexual relations with married women are few and far between.

Another possible category of sex objects for the unmarried Gusii male is that of unmarried girls in his own clan and local group. The desire of youths for these girls whom they are forbidden to marry is recognized in the annual institution of *ogochabera,* "taking by stealth" (Mayer, 1953:31). During the initiation seclusion of a girl, the older girls sleep with her in her mother's house. It is customary for the younger unmarried men to sneak in and attempt to have intercourse with the girls on such a night. The boys hope that the girls will pretend to continue sleeping, so that coitus may be performed without interruption. Some girls acquiesce, but in some cases the boys are rebuffed by the intervention of a married woman sleeping there who decides to be scandalized or by one of the girls herself who may throw things at the boys and try to drive them out. Nowadays some girls are said to knot their petticoats to prevent sexual access. Frequently even the more successful boys have premature ejaculations due to the excitement and anxiety of the occasion. Since "taking by stealth" occurs in the dark, it sometimes happens that kin as close as full brother and sister are sexually united (Mayer 1953:31), although some informants deny this possibility. Such a union would be condoned during the time of girls' initiation so long as pregnancy did not result. The initiation period covers a maximum of two months toward the end of the year in any given locality, so that the practice of "taking by stealth," especially with its inherent limitations, does not provide a substantial outlet for the sexual impulses of young men.

At other times of the year adolescent boys and girls of the same clan and even the same community do carry on sexual liaisons. It was not always so easy to do as it is nowadays, for in the past the young men lived in cattle-villages apart from the ordinary homesteads and were concerned with defending and grazing their own cattle as well as raiding the herds of other clans. Females were not allowed to enter the cattle-villages. This segregation was a barrier to sexual contact between young men and the girls of their own home communities. The cattle-villages were abolished by governmental decree in 1912, bringing the young men back to the family settlements and giving them more opportunity to develop relationships with girls of their own communities. Nowadays boys of fourteen to seventeen years of age have sexual intercourse with girls of twelve to fifteen in their own communities, following many patterns of premarital seduction described in the following section. As they get older, however, they become increasingly fearful of impregnating these girls whom they may not marry.[3] A clandestine affair with a related girl is a matter of little import to the community, but should it become public, both boy and girl suffer some measure of disgrace. Pregnancy insures public notice of the incestuous adventure and may bring punishment in its wake. In one case a young man impregnated his classificatory daughter and she confessed it during childbirth. He was rebuked and criticized in the community on so many occasions that he did not visit other homesteads for a long time. Eventually he had to make a public confession and apology to the elders. With such consequences awaiting an unfortunate youthful violator of the incest regulations, it is not surprising that boys of eighteen begin looking for sexual partners beyond the confines of the exogamous clan.

Before proceeding to premarital sexuality of an interclan nature, we must consider three other outlets for males possible within the local group, i.e., masturbation, homosexuality, and bestiality. Masturbation is punished by parents and, according to all reports, never practiced by Gusii boys except the ones in boarding schools who have learned it from members of other cultural groups. Gusii men consider homosexuality almost inconceivable and could not recall cases of it. If the practice occurs at all, it is extremely rare and certainly not socially condoned. Bestiality, on the other hand, is familiar to Gusii men. It is impossible to estimate its incidence, but everyone interviewed could recall cases of it from different localities, and one case of it appears in the records of the resident magistrate's court. When a boy of early adolescence, up to sixteen, is discovered having intercourse with a goat or cow, punishment is light, as it is assumed that the youth is attempting to find out if he is potent in a rather harmless way. The animal is considered defiled and is either killed or traded to an alien cultural group. If the animal belonged to someone other than the boy's father, it must be replaced. The son is warned against such activity by his father and sometimes by other elders as well. Nevertheless, it is probably performed clandestinely by many boys who are never caught at it. When a boy older than about sixteen is found having intercourse with an animal, it is taken more seriously and treated in the same manner as incest within the nuclear family, or as mental disorder. The assumption in such cases is that the ancestor spirits forced the individual to commit the act by way of retaliation for some ritual misdeed such as omitting a funeral sacrifice. He is taken to a diviner who usually prescribes a sacrifice. Despite the formal assumption of supernatural responsibility, if the individual has had any history of sexual misconduct, he will become the subject of hostile gossip. Furthermore, the necessity of replacing the defiled cow adds to the punishment, for cows are valuable and expensive. Thus a youth whose bestiality has been revealed on one occasion is unlikely to repeat it unless he has developed a strong preference for animals as sexual objects.

The evidence presented in this section points to the conclusion that the sexual activity of the Gusii youth within his own community and even in other communities of the same clan is drastically limited. Married women are barred to him by the rules of marital fidelity and the sanctions supporting them; unmarried girls are available when he is unsure of his virility, but as he grows older, he turns from them in fear of the consequences of incest. Animals are also available to him in his earlier years but are prohibited as continual sexual objects. All of these restrictions within the clan are enforced by the moral sanctions and legal penalties which the clan as an extended kin unit, and its component communities as groups of closely related kin, can use to effect conformity to group norms.

CHANGING PATTERNS OF PREMARITAL SEXUAL BEHAVIOR

With so many restrictions and sanctions operating to limit his sexual behavior within his own community and other communities whose members belong to the same clan, the unmarried Gusii male turns his attention to females of other clans. In the past, when interclan feuding was a reality, there were relatively few occasions for meeting girls of other clans. Marriage ceremonies provided almost the only legitimate situation for premarital contact. Twice during the arrangement of a marriage, a party of young men would accompany the groom to the bride's home and would sing and dance with girls there. On the second occasion the unsupervised indoor dancing would go on for most of the night and the young men and women would sleep in the same house. Informants claim that sex play such as kissing and fondling of breasts was practiced but that intercourse was forbidden and did not occur.[4] The individuals who participated in these sessions were of marriageable age and were consciously scrutinizing each other's looks, dancing ability, and behavior in terms of mate selection. Since there is considerable feeling among Gusii young men even nowadays against prenuptial intercourse with one's mate, it may be that this consideration, coupled with female resistance, acted to restrain sexuality at these marriage dances. In light of the fact that contemporary marriage dances often result in sexual intercourse, however, the allegation of their past chastity must be held in question.

It is difficult though necessary to reconstruct the premarital situation of the Gusii male prior to British administration of Gusiiland. My own findings concur with those of Mayer (1953:10–11) in placing the age at which males were circumcised and initiated in the past at sixteen to eighteen in contrast to the ten-to-twelve-year-old age of initiates today. The uninitiated boys spent most of their time at the homes of their parents, while their elder brothers were out in the cattle-villages. The boys at home received no instruction in sexual matters from their parents or other elders and had relatively little contact with the initiated youths who might have given them sexual information. Consequently, it is said, adolescent boys were sexually innocent until a later age than they are today. After initiation, they became involved in the active life of the cattle-village, herding, raiding and conducting skirmishes against hostile clans. For the youths of the cattle-villages, "taking by stealth" provided an annual period of sexual activity within the clan, and the marriage dances of their friends involved them in some sexual contact with girls of other clans. For the most part, however, their interests were in cattle-raiding, not only for its own sake but because the cattle acquired could be used in bridewealth and thus help speed the day of obtaining a legitimate and steady sexual partner.

An outstanding aspect of traditional premarital relations in Gusiiland was the social and physical distance between exogamous clans. Each clan was a territorial unit separated from neighboring clans by a strip of uninhabited bush. The people of a clan did not tolerate trespassing by males of other clans except in connection with marriage arrangements and ceremonies. Blood feuds could begin when a trespasser was slain or injured and when cattle were raided and women abducted or raped by men of hostile clans. Warriors were inevitably attracted to the territories of neighboring clans by good grazing land, herds of cattle, and women. Sometimes they would take their herds to graze on a good pasture of another clan in the middle of the night, hoping to return before morning and before detection by the warriors of the trespassed territory. If they were detected, however, spear-fighting would ensue. The abduction or rape of a girl belonging to another clan was a more serious offense, and some prolonged feuds are traced to such a cause. Elders tried to prevail upon warriors not to commit reckless acts which would endanger the lives of all the clan members, though they were not always successful. Inter-clan rape and abduction were definitely kept in check, however, by the threat of violent retaliation and the distinct physical boundaries between clans.

The British administration eliminated the traditional system of controlling interclan sexual behavior by military deterrence and territorial separation. Under the Pax Britannica, clans were effectively prohibited from feuding, regardless of provocation. This meant that they could no longer enforce their prohibition on the trespassing of male outsiders, and they could no longer take up arms to avenge their ravished clanswomen. The judicial system introduced by the government did not substitute sanctions of equivalent force. Whereas previously a prospective rapist could anticipate the possibility of annihilation of himself and his fellows by the clansmen of his victim, nowadays he faces an indecent assault charge with maximum prison sentence of one year and a fine of $70.[5] Furthermore, two-thirds of indecent assault indictments are dismissed, mostly because the enforcement agencies cannot prevent the escape of rapists to European plantations in Kericho District where they stay and work until the charges are dropped. Thus in the present situation a rapist has only one chance in three of being punished at all, and if he is, the punishment is a light one by his standards. It is not surprising that young men do not find this as discouraging to interclan sexual activity as their grandfathers found the real threat of a blood feud.

The Pax Britannica also created many new opportunities for contact between unmarried people of different clans. With peace established and population growing rapidly, settlements filled up the previously uninhabited strips between clans. Many Gusii migrated to adjacent areas that had been no-man's-lands between the Gusii and the Kipsigis and Masai. In these new areas clans became territorially fragmented, having no military need for territorial integrity. Each community has a single clan identity which it shares with some adjacent communities as well as with many others farther away. But nowadays boundaries between adjacent communities of hostile clans are indiscernible to the untutored eye. The members of such groups use the same streams and have common paths. Boys who are watering cattle or fishing at the stream can easily meet girls from a nearby community of another clan who are fetching water or washing their clothes. They may also encounter these girls along paths running between the communities. Finally and most importantly, the government established markets, usually at or near clan boundaries, where young people of numerous clans can meet in an atmosphere free of the supervision of elders.

Since most of the negative sanctions limiting premarital sexual activity within the clan are still in force while the traditional barriers to interclan activity have disappeared, young men naturally turn to girls outside their own clan for premarital sexual gratification. That they do not do so in younger adolescence is apparently due to the availability within the community of sexual partners whose adolescent sterility prevents conception and to the inexperience of the boys in approaching strange girls. When the boy reaches seventeen or eighteen, his presence in a community of differing clan affiliation is accepted as that of a young man looking for a wife, although in fact his aim may be seduction. At this age a boy ordinarily has a confidence which allows him to approach strange girls, though he would not have done so before.

Nowadays most Gusii young people of both sexes have sexual intercourse before marriage. They may meet under a variety of circumstances, some of which have already been mentioned.

When a girl visits her father's sister, it is expected that a half-brother or paternal cousin of her father's sister's son will attempt to seduce her. She may refuse, and in any case the act must be kept secret from members of the parental generation, but apparently such liaisons do occur. At marriage dances, too, youths establish contacts with girls whom they try to seduce. Both situations are only occasional, however; the boy must go to the marketplace for the more frequent social mixing which leads to sexual adventures.

Each marketplace has its day of the week when activity is greatest and trading goes on; this is when girls dress up and go in groups to sell some family produce and be seen by boys. The boys and young men also attend, singly and in groups, looking for attractive girls. In the 1930s the young people used to perform traditional dances in the marketplace on market days but this was banned after the 1937 outbreak of mass rape and has never been resumed. Youths approach strange girls, often through girls they already know or through male friends who know them. There is an initial period of small talk in which the girl may immediately reject the boy by claiming that she is married or by assuming a cold and aloof attitude. If she is friendly and laughs, however, the boy is encouraged and may begin some sexual joking. If the girl is favorably inclined to him, she will respond in kind, usually using terms of obscene abuse. The boy may grab her arm and attempt to pull her away from the group but she will refuse, at least until he buys her a present in one of the market shops or treats her to some food. Even then he may not succeed in detaching her from the other girls, and he will let her go after arranging a rendezvous and possibly promising a phonograph party. She may agree to the assignation but not show up, in which case the youth will try to woo her later with more gifts and provocative exhortations. Eventually she meets him at a small party in his house or in a secluded part of the bush or forest. The following is a story completion by a Gusii schoolboy writing in English; it is a typical account of a Gusii seduction.

> Before they go into the forest Moraa [the girl] will be pretending not to be pleased with this boy for he is talking to her matters concerning

> sex. But as Gesimba [the boy] is very serious about it, he will force her and even try to pull her into the forest. When Moraa is being pulled, she will fall down, just pretending, and Gesimba having high sex now will lie with her. She will pretend to cry and Gesimba will be trying hard to get the one thing he only wants. He will just catch one of her thighs and lift it, and as a result he will get between the two thighs and push his male organ into the vagina. At this time she will be quiet and all the work will be going on smoothly. After he has spermed several times he will now be satisfied and leave her to dress properly, also himself dress, and thank her many thanks.

In this as in other accounts, it is assumed that the girl will resist and have to be forced even if she desires intercourse. The Gusii girl avoids looking into the eye of her seducer during coitus, and some go so far as to cover their faces with their dresses. Some Gusii girls cry out of shame and revulsion after intercourse and, unlike Moraa of the fantasy, may refuse to repeat the act on the same occasion. They often become panicky about the discovery of the illicit act and the possibility of a premarital pregnancy.

With respect to premarital sexual activity, three types of Gusii girls may be distinguished. The first type is stigmatized as a slut because she has achieved a reputation for promiscuity. This type of girl engages in intercourse with men and boys she knows very slightly, and after relatively little persuasion. With her, resistance in coitus is probably conscious role-playing designed to please her lover. Some girls of this type occasionally take on a number of young men in succession. Although she is in demand as a sexual partner, a girl with this sort of reputation is considered highly undesirable as a wife and is ordinarily not married with bridewealth unless her marriage takes place at an early age before her reputation has spread. She is likely to elope from the home of her father or legitimate husband and live as the concubine of one man after another.

The second, and probably modal, type is that of the girl with real ambivalence about engaging in premarital intercourse. She desires it but is careful not to be taken advantage of. Thus she will not meet privately with a boy until after he has bestowed numerous gifts upon her from the market; these may be headscarves, bananas, and candy. She rejects the advances of some boys whom she finds unattractive. Her accessibility for sexual liaisons also depends on her moods and the skill of her would-be seducer. Sometimes she is unapproachable; on other occasions, such as a marriage dance, her resistance may be easily broken down, especially by a dashing young man who serenades her on the guitar. She engages in provocative behavior, mostly of a hostile sort such as sexual joking, but is determined not to be publicly compromised and not to give away her sexual favors until she has received tangible rewards and flattering attention from her prospective lover. With her, resistance in coitus is partly conscious role-playing and partly an expression of real fears and hostility. This type of girl, if her sexual activity is not discovered and does not result in premarital pregnancy, is considered desirable as a wife, for the marriage intermediary will have no scandal to report to the groom. The prospective husband and his family do not want the intermediary to pry so deeply into the girl's affairs that he reports her casual liaisons; if she has been discreet enough not to acquire a reputation as a "slut," then he ordinarily informs them that she is chaste. There is no inspection of the hymen, for the husband does not desire knowledge of his wife's premarital experience so long as she is considered a proper girl.

The third type of Gusii girl is the one in whom sex anxiety and hostility toward men outweigh heterosexual desires. Such a girl may acquire a reputation for rejecting sexual advances and eventually be avoided by boys in the marketplace, though her desirability as a wife is in no way diminished. Ordinarily, a girl of this type continues going to the market with the other girls and meets numerous boys who know neither her nor her reputation. Despite her fear of sexuality she enjoys the gifts, the flattery, the attention from the boys, and thus tends to exploit her suitors without giving them the sexual satisfaction they desire in exchange. Though she may even refuse sexual overtures at wedding dances and scold the young men who make them, it appears that most girls of this type do occasionally have intercourse before marriage. When they do, their resistance and crying is probably commensurate with their real feelings, and they are more likely to cover their faces during coitus and be overcome with remorse or other) between the lynched individual and any white woman (Myrdal, 1944; Raper, 1933).

One might say that all that is in the past, but is it? A group calling itself the Prisoners Solidarity Committee of Norfolk, Virginia, made the following statement, published in the letters column of a radical newspaper, *The Militant,* in 1974:

> James Carrington is a young black man who has served four years of a 75-year sentence on a frameup rape charge. He is attempting to win a new trial on the basis of racist discrimination in the selection of the jury. The jury that sentenced him was composed entirely of elderly men, all white.
>
> During the trial, a doctor testified that there was no evidence of a sexual act, much less rape, and even the FBI said there was no evidence of abduction. All that the evidence showed was that Carrington had been found sitting in a car with a white woman friend on the night of April 10, 1970.
>
> The true purpose of the "trial" was revealed by the prosecutor who stated, "We're going to make an example of this boy, so that no colored man will ever lay hands on a white girl again."

The facts, as presented in this letter, have not been checked, and there may well be something that would substantiate the case of the prosecution. However, the all-white jury, the verdict of guilt in the light of the testimony of a doctor (even if there were other doctors who testified to the contrary), the barbaric sentence, and the inflammatory remarks of a local prosecutor are entirely consistent with American history. "There has been an enormous danger of injustice," wrote Judge David Bazelon in the *Wiley* case (*U.S.* v. *Wiley,* 1974), "when a black man accused of raping a white woman is tried before a white jury. Of the 455 men executed for rape since 1930, 405 (89 percent) were black. In the vast majority of these cases the complainant was white."

This is not to deny that interracial rape (and specifically black against white) exists, and perhaps is not as uncommon as the statistics of Menachem Amir (1971) would suggest. Eldridge Cleaver (1968) has even written of rape of a white woman as having been, at one time, a political act for him. Whether the act occurs because it was fostered by the atmosphere of racial tensions or for reasons similar to those prevailing for intraracial rape, the victim has the right to protection, and the offender should be required to face prosecution. But one must never overlook the circumstances surrounding the event in order to be certain that it is not racial persecution for a rape that never occurred.

CONSENSUAL INTERCOURSE AND THE CHARGE OF RAPE

There are many instances in which an accused admits having had sexual relations with a woman, but denies that he did so without her consent. In the crime of rape there is a broad spectrum of variation from the instance where a girl or woman is grabbed from behind by someone who does not know her, brought into an alleyway entirely against her will, held down by one person while the other mounts her, or is clubbed or submits because of threat and fear: This is forcible rape, and there can be no question about the enormity of the crime, the nature of the sexual assault, and the lack of consent. On the other end of this spectrum, one finds a man and a woman (or boy and girl) having regular, consensual amorous sexual relations, she allegedly as eager as he, until some point at which she decides to say that he has raped her.

Between these polar extremes, there are infinite variations. A man may meet a woman in a bar and end up in a situation in which the girl says no when she is already half undressed, and the man either fails to control himself, decides that the girl does not have the right to deny him at that point, or believes that she merely wants more persuasion. Or it may be that a man goes out on several occasions with a woman who has already had intercourse with him, and she decides to discontinue the sexual part of their relationship; disbelieving, he uses more than persuasion—he resorts to force. Between the male's view of an act as voluntary, and the female's view as forcible, a court faces problems fraught with tragedy.

Perhaps one of the most interesting examples of injustice

was the Giles-Johnson case (see MacDonald, 1971) in which three black youths were accused of rape, convicted, and sentenced to death in Maryland in 1961.[3] The men did not deny that they had had intercourse with the white complainant; they claimed that she had told them that she had had sex with sixteen or seventeen boys that week, and a few more wouldn't matter. The girl denied the statements, testifying that she had submitted out of fear. Investigation turned up a history of what a commentator called "almost incredible promiscuity." The girl had told the police that she had no idea how many men she had had sex with, including oral and group sex with six or eight men at a time (information the police did not pass on to the court). Although she was on probation at the time of the alleged rape, she denied this on the witness stand. Only after the U.S. Supreme Court granted an appeal were two men freed (in 1967, after spending six years in prison), and the third was released by gubernatorial pardon soon thereafter.

This is the sort of case that cries out for the right of a defendant to examine a complainant on her prior sexual history; on the other hand, it has been these fishing expeditions in open court of prior sexual history that have discouraged raped women from vigorous prosecution. The American Civil Liberties Union in 1976 adopted the following proposed guidelines, which appear to come as close to defending the sexual privacy of the woman *and* the rights of a defendant to a fair trial as any other legal or social document on the subject:

> There is in many rape cases a potential conflict between the right of the defendant to a fair trial and the complainant's right to have his or her claim to protection of the law vindicated without undue invasion of sexual privacy. In many cases this conflict may be irresolvable, and when that is the case the right to a fair trial should not be qualified, no matter how compelling the countervailing concerns. However, careful application by trial judges of the proper standards of relevance of testimony, control of cross-examination and argument, and elimination of prejudicial instructions unique to rape and similar cases could do much to preserve rape complainants from unnecessary imposition upon their rights to sexual privacy, without detracting from the fairness of the trial. Closed hearings should be used to ascertain the relevance of any proposed line of testimony or cross-examination that

may involve a witness' prior sexual history. The determination of relevance or irrelevance should be stated by the court on the record along with its reasons for so holding.

A determination as to the relevance of the prior sexual history of either the complainant or the defendant in rape * cases is acceptable only if it is administered fairly and free from sexist assumptions. Subject to special evidentiary rules designed to protect defendants for reasons other than relevance, the criteria for admitting evidence of prior sexual history employed in rape cases must apply equally to the prosecution and the defense. Similarly, any pre-trial screening process must apply equally to the prosecution and the defense.

Some aspects of some current rape laws clearly do not meet minimum standards of acceptability. Even where the defense is consent, the prosecution should not be permitted, as a matter of course, to introduce evidence of the complainant's prior chastity; neither should the defense, without more, be permitted to prove the complainant's prior unchastity. Unchaste witness instructions which permit an inference of lessened credibility from the fact of prior sexual activity are based on no rational inference and violate a complainant's right to sexual privacy—just as a 'chaste witness' instruction would violate a defendant's right to a fair trial if invoked by the prosecution. A statute, for example, which makes admissible evidence tending to prove that the complainant has been convicted of a prostitution offense, or even evidence concerning prior consensual sexual relations between the complainant and the defendant, without the necessity of showing a particular relevance, unconstitutionally infringes on the right to sexual privacy of such complainants.

MISTAKEN IDENTIFICATIONS

In many rape cases, the victim was not previously known to the perpetrator, and she must identify him on the basis of her memory of his face, imprinted in her mind at the time of the offense. Most rape victims do see their attackers, though sometimes not

* While sexist assumptions and practices cause harm most often to victims of rape or attempted rape, their rights can be protected if rape is treated as but one form of sexual assault by statutes and courts. We therefore urge that standards and procedures be developed to apply to all forms of sexual assault and that the phrase "sexual assault" be used instead of "rape" in policy statements, law, etc., in order to remove special legal disabilities from rape complainants.

very well, particularly if the entire action takes place in the dark. Sometimes there is another witness: the rape occurs in the presence of a friend or members of the family, usually bound and gagged but able to watch the scene.

For a variety of reasons, eyewitness identifications are notoriously unreliable, almost never acceptable without corroboration; a simple denial, if buttressed by a credible alibi, should be sufficient when such corroboration is lacking. The history of criminal justice is replete with honest errors, made in good faith, by people who were positive that their identification of the perpetrator could not be incorrect (MacNamara, 1969; see also Buckhout, 1974). While some persons might suggest that a rape victim usually obtains an excellent look at the face of the rapist, and from close by, this is often under conditions of extreme fright. Furthermore, in the case of interracial rape, the inability of people to distinguish members of other racial groups, and the tendency to confuse them with one another, is not a myth.

In New York City, during the period of late 1972 to early 1973, two men, on entirely different occasions and in unrelated matters, were arrested for rape, and each was positively identified in a police lineup. Each was accused independently by more than one victim. After several harrowing weeks, another arrest took place, and it was noted that there was some similarity in appearance of the persons being charged. In each instance, the old suspect was dismissed (*New York Times,* November 11, 1972, and May 18, 1973). Had the later arrests not taken place, and had there been no requirement for corroboration, it is unlikely that the defendants could have established their innocence in the face of more than one positive identification. Against this, they could have offered only their denials, some character witnesses, and perhaps alibis which are not usually airtight because for the ordinary person it is difficult to reconstruct his activities at a given hour some weeks or months later (perhaps he was at home watching television, or was with his family—although not unlikely, these are hardly unassailable alibis). It is entirely possible that one or both of the incorrectly accused men may have faced such a compelling array of evidence that the case would have ended with plea bargaining, resulting in a suspended sentence, a lifetime record, and a ruined career.

In a famous compilation of cases in which innocent people have been convicted, Yale law professor Edwin M. Borchard (1932:367) came to the following conclusion:

> Perhaps the major source of these tragic errors is an identification of the accused by the victim of a crime of violence. . . . Juries seem disposed more readily to credit the veracity and reliability of the victims of an outrage than any amount of contrary evidence by or on behalf of the accused, whether by way of alibi, character witnesses, or other testimony. These cases illustrate the fact that the emotional balance of the victim or eyewitness is so disturbed by his extraordinary experience that his powers of perception became distorted and his identification is frequently most untrustworthy. Into the identification enter other motives, not necessarily stimulated originally by the accused personally—the desire to requite a crime, to exact vengeance upon the person believed guilty, to find a scapegoat, to support, consciously or unconsciously, an identification made by another. . . . In eight of these cases the wrongfully accused person and the really guilty criminal bore not the slightest resemblance to each other, whereas in twelve other cases, the resemblance, while fair, was still not at all close.

An instance of false identification is recounted by a defender of the women's liberation thrust on rape. According to this writer (Lichtenstein, 1974), a woman was forcibly raped by two men who were complete strangers to her. At police headquarters, she was shown photographs of many men, and finally came to one. This was the younger of the two perpetrators, she said. The detectives had hit paydirt! Was she sure? She was 95 percent positive. All one had to do was find the culprit. Not a difficult task, for he was in prison, where he had been on the day of the offense.

Let us suppose that he was no longer in prison, but was an ex-convict, and she picked him out of a lineup. She would be told that 95 percent positive was insufficient, and having to make a decision, she might very well have decided that there was not a scintilla of doubt in her mind (it is not certain that she would have resolved the doubt against the man in the lineup, for many victims insist under such circumstances that they still retain doubt). What chance would he have against her accusation? As an ex-con, the supporters of his alibi might well have been less than model witnesses; and his lawyer could not call character witnesses without exposing his criminal record on prosecutorial cross-examination. An innocent man would be found guilty, one more case would be marked as closed, while the actual rapist would be free to continue to terrorize women.

FEMINIST CAMPAIGNS AND CRIMINAL JUSTICE

The feminist campaign against rape is justified and overdue, and such a campaign cannot be conducted without insisting on vigorous prosecution. The impediments for such prosecution are formidable, and they include the harassment of the complaining witness, the delving into private and irrelevant aspects of the lives of the victim, and the stigmatization of the victim, sometimes accompanied by the exoneration of an offender. Remedies are necessary, but some of those proposed—not all, I emphasize—would challenge fundamental concepts of the administration of justice. In certain instances, writers have described situations in which no contemporary court of justice could find a defendant guilty, but the feminists nevertheless express their indignation and disgust. For example, Martha Lear (1972:55), noting that rape is seldom subject to impartial witness, states: "Thus, if two suspects were to be picked up and positively identified by the victim in a police lineup, and if they were to deny her charges, the case would be dropped for lack of evidence."

This is written as if it were a cry of anguish, clearly carrying an implication of injustice in dropping the charges. Of course, a case is never quite so simple. Suspects are asked questions concerning their whereabouts at the time of the offense. The woman's original description is compared with the men being detained, and other factors are taken into account. But if a case were as simple as Lear makes out, and consisted of nothing more than the positive identification by one victim and the denial by two accused, what is open for the prosecution but to drop the case "for lack of evidence"? Would conviction meet the standards of guilt having been established beyond reasonable doubt?

A New York detective is quoted by Lear (1972) as saying that

> "when the woman never saw the guy before in her life, and she tells you he raped her in the park or in the hallways, and she identifies him . . . what more corroboration should a judge need? Why isn't this woman's word good enough?" (Ellipses in original)

What more corroboration should a judge need? It is a rhetorical question, and the answer is supposed to be, resoundingly, none. But such an answer makes no sense, for if he denies the charge, why isn't his word as good as hers? Because he is a man? Or because he is black? Further, if the testimony of the complainant and the defendant is equally believable, then the case must be adjudicated in favor of the accused, because of presumption of innocence and the requirement that guilt be established beyond a reasonable doubt.

However, there is always more to a case than an accusation and a denial. Was he caught on the spot? Did he have a hammer with him when apprehended that matched a weapon she had described? Did she tear part of his clothes off and did the sample match what he was wearing when caught? Did she describe a scar on his thigh which she could not have seen in the lineup, but which he actually did have? Failing all these and any other corroboration, can anyone demand a conviction on the basis of a believable accusation and identification and an equally believable and unequivocal denial?

Another story is related by Lear (1972:63) which was told to her by the girl involved. The latter claims that she invited a man to her apartment for coffee after a date, and when there, he proposed sex. She rejected the idea; he pushed, threatened, and held his fist in front of her face until she gave in. Later, she went to the police, who brought the man in for questioning, and he said, "She was perfectly willing," which ended the matter.

"Now, what do you call that?" the girl asked Lear, who replies, "I call it rape, and share her outrage that the bloody bastard got away with it."

This is an instance of a girl who had sexual intercourse in her own apartment, with a man that she was dating and who was in the apartment at her invitation. The girl comes to the police with no bruises, says it was rape, and the man says she was a willing partner. For the purposes of parlor games, you can believe whomever you wish, but the court does not have such a choice. It should not even hold a man for trial under these circumstances. Unless the country is ready to institutionalize the use of truth serums, lie detectors, and examination under hypnosis (which I am not advocating), a court must have something to balance the scale strongly against an accused in order to find him guilty.

There is another incident, narrated by Gail Sheehy (1971:66), in which a charge of force was made explicit: The young woman who was raped by a gynecologist—"my mother arranged the date"—went willingly to his room in the hospital residence. He forced her to the floor, raped her, washed his hands, and apologized. No one had responded to her screams. She gave up and let the gynecologist take her to dinner.[4]

The anecdote as told by Sheehy is quoted in full above; it is all the information available to me, and perhaps all that Sheehy had when she used the word "raped" without hedging with a description that it was a claim or an allegation. I find the story less than believable. I am intrigued by the girl who describes a meeting with a gynecologist in his office as a "date" rather than an appointment. Supposing, however, that it occurred as Sheehy relates it, passing on second-hand information as if it were gospel truth; could a court of law convict in the face of his denial? Is a jury expected to believe the woman and throw out the denial of the physician, in an instance in which she accompanied him to dinner afterward?

A militant feminist (Margolin, 1975:20) points out an "accurate figure of false accusations [of rape] is 20 percent, and most of these are detected right away." The statement is made without a citation and without a modicum of research, evidence, data, or proof. Nevertheless, if as many as one out of five accusations should prove to be false, and if "most" but not all these are easily detected, then is it not reasonable to consider that the charge leveled against the gynecologist is among the false accusations, detected or undetected?

Judge Bazelon, in the concurring opinion in the *Wiley* (1974) case, quotes the statement of Lord Chief Justice Hale (1778), that rape "is an accusation easily to be made and hard to be proved, and harder to be defended by the party accused, tho never so innocent." The U.S. Supreme Court, in discussing a case in which a man had been accused of making a solicitation to another man in a park, overheard by no one but the person to whom the invitation was made and in no way corroborated (*Kelly* v. *U.S.*, 1951; Sagarin and MacNamara, 1970), upheld the appeal of the defendant, on the grounds that an accusation of this sort is so easily made and so difficult to refute that it should not be accepted lightly without corroboration. Would not the same words be applicable to the gynecologist?

GUIDELINES

Some guidelines on rape prosecutions and defenses, particularly as they apply to previous sexual history, have been suggested by the American Civil Liberties Union, quoted earlier. It should be the aim of those who are concerned with law, order, and justice to work out mechanisms leading to greater protection of the victim, more vigorous prosecution of the guilty, with extreme probability (approaching but never attaining certainty) of exoneration of the guiltless, and at the same time to protect the constitutional guarantees of a fair trial and the protection of the rights of the accused.

Toward such ends, a sharp line of demarcation can be drawn between cases in which the accuser and the accused knew each other in the past and those in which they had hitherto been strangers. If known to each other, the nature of their previous relationship should be explored. A man may be in a woman's apartment, or she in his, with no intention or willingness on her part to participate in sexual activity. However, with lack of signs of a physical battle, and with no witness, her word cannot be taken against his.

If he claims that they had met that evening for the first time but that she had been a willing sex partner, then pretrial *in camera* testimony can determine whether examination on her past sexual history is relevant and admissible. That an investigation of her prior sexual life may indeed lead to harassment under cross-examination cannot be a reason for barring such evidence if it is deemed relevant. Ordinarily, the same would be true of the man's psychiatric and sexual history, except that an investigation of this aspect of his life cannot violate his rights as a defendant (which are greater than the rights of the complainant), and should in no way abrogate the Fifth Amendment which protects him from being compelled to testify against himself.

The complainant in a rape case might be afforded the protection of anonymity, similar to that offered to complainants in cases of blackmail. If this can be accomplished by the voluntary consent of the press and other media, it would be preferable; if it must be done by judicial decree or legislative act, it might be desirable, but that is a matter of public policy that goes beyond the question of rape; and if it involves a closed court and the denial of the right to a public trial for the defendant, it might require a constitutional amendment, and most persons concerned with justice, I would speculate, would oppose such a move as having greater potential for harm than for good.

On the question of corroboration, the testimony of a complainant, when it is denied by the accused, should always require corroboration, but this ought not to mean that each and every contention that she makes must be corroborated, nor that she should be required to bring to court a witness to the rape. Fundamentally, rape should be handled like any other crime in that the uncorroborated testimony of a complainant, in the face of a denial by a defendant, should be insufficient to convict.

A woman claiming to have been sexually assaulted should not be required to establish proof of penetration or the presence of ejaculate, but if she claims penetration, then medical evidence ought to be required. However, an assault may be indubitably sexual without resulting in either penetration or ejaculation, but to establish its sexual nature, the woman must be subject to examination and cross-examination on intimate physical details of the nature of the contact. The woman should be protected from unsympathetic police officers, and if female officers are better equipped for that purpose, then a logical argument is that they should be favored in the hiring for a rape investigation squad.

When the complainant asserts that the accused was unknown to her until the time of the attack, and he does not deny such a claim, but defends himself on the grounds of mistaken identity, then her previous sexual life is immaterial and irrelevant, and she should be protected from embarrassment of examination on that issue. However, in the absence of corroboration or confession, an identification of a stranger is suspect, and all the more so if he is not of the same race as the accuser. His alibi becomes important, although most persons cannot establish their whereabouts at a given time after a lapse of more than a few days.

What, then, can be done to reduce the incidence of rape and obtain more convictions of rapists? Greater and more vigorous work on the part of the police, careful studies of patterns of individual offenders, surveillance of their expected places of criminal offense, investigation of alibis: in other words, hard work, not the shortcuts of abrogation of civil liberties for the accused. And, above all, a massive effort to remove the sources of violence in society.

To combat the plague of rape, one manifestation of the violence so rampant in recent decades, every effort should be made to convict an offender short of denying the accused the right to a fair trial. In such a trial, he enters the courtroom an innocent man, which means clothed in the presumption of innocence, and the burden of proof is on the prosecution to establish beyond a reasonable doubt that a forcible rape was committed and that the defendant was indeed the perpetrator. The burden is never upon an accused to disprove these assertions.

It is tragic that there are so many rapes and other crimes of violence, but it is likewise tragic that the elementary principles of criminal justice governing all criminal trials should need restating.

NOTES

1. In this article, I refer to the victim as the complaining witness or complainant, not the prosecutrix. It appears to me that a clear delineation should be made between the officers of the state, including the prosecutor (if female, a prosecutrix), and witnesses for the state.

2. There is a very rich fiction that offers remarkable insights into this phenomenon. Particularly pertinent is a short story by William Faulkner, "Dry September."

3. This case was reported in a tone of moral indignation about the fate of the alleged offender by Susan Brownmiller (1968). Ms. Brownmiller (1975:7–8), however, had later second thoughts about her position.

4. What apparently is the same episode, though the source is not identified, appears in Brownmiller (1975:355–60). In this version, the woman is reported as saying "we went out to have dinner. We proceeded along with the dinner as if nothing had happened. I was in such a state of shock I just went along with the rest of the date."

REFERENCES

American Civil Liberties Union. "Policy on Prior Sexual History," No. 311, April 1976.

Amir, Menachem. 1971. *Patterns in Forcible Rape.* Chicago: University of Chicago Press.

Borchard, Edwin M. 1932. *Convicting the Innocent.* Garden City, N.Y.: Garden City Publishing Co.

Brownmiller, Susan. 1968. "Rashomon in Maryland," *Esquire* 69 (May): 130–32, 145–47.

——. 1975. *Against Our Will.* New York: Simon & Schuster.

Buckhout, Robert. 1974. "Eyewitness Testimony," *Scientific American* 231 (December) :23–31.

Carter, Dan T. 1969. *Scottsboro: A Tragedy of the American South.* Baton Rouge: Louisiana State University Press.

Cleaver, Eldridge. 1969. *Soul on Ice.* New York: McGraw-Hill.

Hale, Matthew. 1778. *Pleas of the Crown.* London: Richard Tonson.

Kelly v. *U.S.* 1951. 194 F.2d 150 (District of Columbia Circuit).

Lear, Martha. 1972. "Q. If You Rape a Woman and Steal Her TV, What Can They Get You For in New York? A. Stealing Her TV." *New York Times Magazine,* January 30, pp. 10–11.

Lichtenstein, Grace. 1974. "Rape Squad," *New York Times Magazine,* March 3, pp. 10.

MacDonald, John M. 1971. *Rape Offenders and Their Victims.* Springfield, Ill.: Charles C. Thomas.

MacNamara, Donal E. J. 1969. "Convicting the Innocent," *Crime and Delinquency* 15:57–61.

Margolin, Debbi. 1975. "Rape: The Facts," *Women: A Journal of Liberation* 3:20–21.

Myrdal, Gunnar. 1944. *An American Dilemma.* New York: Harper & Row.

New York Post. 1973. "Raped Girl Wasn't." *New York Post,* May 9.

Powell v. *Alabama.* 1932. 287 U.S. 45.

Raper, Arthur F. 1933. *The Tragedy of Lynching.* Chapel Hill:University of North Carolina Press.

Sagarin, Edward and Donal E. J. MacNamara. 1970. "The Problem of Entrapment," *Crime and Delinquency* 16:363–78.

Schur, Edwin M. 1965. *Crimes without Victims.* Englewood Cliffs, N.J.: Prentice-Hall.

Sheehy, Gail. 1971. "Nice Girls Don't Get into Trouble," *New York Magazine* 4 (15 February):26.

U.S. v. *Wiley.* 1974. 492 F2d 257.

8 Judicial Attitudes Toward Rape Victims

CAROL BOHMER

IN criminal proceedings against suspected rapists, there is a tendency to regard the rape victim as just another piece of evidence. The victim's role is to establish a legal case against the offender; little concern is shown for her efforts to adjust to the alleged rape, for the responses of her family and peers, or for the attitudes she encounters in interacting with the criminal justice system. Victims frequently report that their encounters with the police, district attorneys, and courtroom personnel were more traumatic than the rape incident itself.

Most observers seem to accept the biases evidenced by police and defense attorneys toward rape victims as inevitable, but feel that the judge will balance any inequities. There is a common assumption that the judge is the objective source of authority and control in courtroom procedures and that his presence assures a

Reprinted by permission from *Judicature* (February 1974), vol. 57. Copyright © American Judicature Society.

balance between these highly charged, goal-oriented factions. His function is presumed to guarantee that an evenhanded justice which serves the best interests of society in punishing offenders and protecting victims will prevail.

In recent interviews with thirty-eight Philadelphia judges who have handled rape cases, I found that judicial attitudes toward rape victims are far less impartial than is frequently supposed. The judges' comments supported the allegation of courtroom victimization of some rape victims and established the need for further inquiry into judicial attitudes.

The basic assumption of this research is that judicial attitudes are correlated with judicial behavior and that the first are the key factor in determining the effects of courtroom experience on rape victims.* It is for this reason that the research focused on an investigation of judicial attitudes toward rape victims (see generally, Blumberg, 1967; Hogarth, 1971).

The thirty-eight judges chosen for study were all judges of the Philadelphia court system (municipal court and common pleas division) who had been involved in trying rape cases. Several of the judges were not interviewed because their experiences in this area were either nonexistent or too limited to be of benefit in responding to inquiries.

The approach of personal interview based on a standardized set of questions was selected for two reasons: (1) since the judges operate under heavy schedules, it seemed more likely that they would grant time for an interview than for responding to a questionnaire; and (2) since the topic of judicial attitudes toward rape victims is a sensitive area of inquiry, the spontaneous remarks and responses of the judges in an interview situation

* There is social psychological material which provides a theoretical background for this relationship between attitudes and behaviors, making it theoretically acceptable to question judges about their attitudes and from their responses to infer how they would behave in court situations. "An attitude represents both an orientation toward or away from object, concept, or situation and a readiness to respond in a predetermined manner to these or related objects, concepts, or situations." See Hilgard and Atkinson, (1967:538). Additionally, the research on cognitive dissonance provides data which show the need in individuals to bring their attitudes and behavior as close as possible to each other, for example, Festinger and Carlsmith (1959).

would yield useful information which might not be elicited without personal contact. The interviews were conducted from June to September 1971.

POSSIBLE DEFENSES

The defenses available in a rape case are limited to three: that the alleged event did not take place, that sexual intercourse between the complainant and the defendant did take place but that intercourse was consensual, or that a rape may have occurred but the defendant is not the rapist, i.e., the defense of identity.

The kinds of evidence judges accept have a bearing on the proof of any of these defenses. For example, the scene of the rape may be relevant to the existence of consent. The fact that the alleged rape took place in a dark alley or a parking lot has very different implications for the judge than if it took place in an apartment or a car. In the latter situations, the judge will want to know how the complainant and defendant arrived at the scene. If the complainant went willingly to the apartment or car in question, she is likely to receive a less sympathetic hearing than if the defendant had broken into her apartment. In these types of situations, the existence and degree of a prior offender-victim relationship become important in determining the likelihood of a consensual situation.

The interviews with the judges revealed that their central orientation in trying rape cases is to evaluate the credibility of the victim's allegation that forcible rape (as defined by the law) occurred. As several of the judges stated: "Rape is the easiest crime to allege, and the hardest to prove." Their recognition of the complexity of legal issues involved in rape cases, coupled with the belief that the worst error the criminal justice system can commit is to convict an innocent man, results in a fairly high level of judicial skepticism toward those who allege rape. Despite these attitudes, the judges' responses also indicated their awareness of the rights of the defendant and the sensitivities of the victim as they face the trauma of testifying in court.

THE VICTIM

Genuine Victim

The judges interviewed appear to divide rape cases into three basic types, giving each category a different degree of credibility. The first type includes those women they consider genuine victims. They give these women sympathetic hearings and react very punitively toward the men who raped them. An evaluation of this sort occurs when the situation is such that the judges have no problem defining the circumstances as those of forcible rape. The suitable paradigm for this category might be the "stranger leaping out of the shadows in the dark alley situation." In such cases, the judges apparently agree with the graphic description of an articulate victim who said, "Who would consent to lying flat on her back in a dark alley in January?" The judges feel that in this type of situation the effects on the woman can be traumatic, and they make an effort to buffer her court experience. As one of them said: "The effect on the average girl is devastating, she will never get over it, the indignities, the knowledge on the part of her associates; rarely do they ever adjust to a full, happy life."

Consensual Victims

However, judicial attitudes can be very different in cases which may be rape according to law, but which they classify as consensual intercourse. In these situations they see the complainant as "asking for it." An example would be when a woman meets a man in a bar, agrees to let him drive her home, and then alleges he raped her. Judges have several graphic ways of describing this situation: "friendly rape," "felonious gallantry," "assault with failure to please," and "breach of contract."

Vindictive Female

The third type of situation occurs when they see the accusation as marked by "female vindictiveness." In these cases, the judges believe either that the event that occurred was totally consensual or that the alleged event did not in fact occur. Therefore, they judge the allegations as reflections of a woman's desire to get even with a man. Several judges described the typical situation in this category as that of a woman who is tired of her husband or boyfriend, wants to get rid of him, and so convinces her daughter to allege the defendant raped her.

The kinds of evidence which a judge allows to be admitted into the trial record and which he weighs in assessing the merits of a rape case can have an important bearing on the atmosphere in the court and on the victim's reactions to her court experiences. For example, the judge controls the amount of evidence the defense attorney can submit as testimony of a female's reputation, which is an area of inquiry that can produce strong emotional and psychological repercussions for the victim.

Table 8.1 outlines the kinds of evidence the judges indicated they weighed in their evaluations. As can be seen from the table, the most important kind of evidence is circumstantial since that is usually the only way to prove the complainant's charge. (The term circumstantial evidence includes all evidence of an indirect nature. It means that the existence of certain facts is only inferred from circumstances rather than deduced by a process in which tangible facts are utilized.) Circumstantial factors which are con-

Table 8.1. What Kind of Evidence Do You Place Weight on in Rape Trials?

Type of Evidence	*Number*
Demeanor of complainant	4
Medical	11
Circumstantial[a]	23
Don't know	3
No information	10
Total	51[b]

[a]Circumstantial evidence can include the following: enticement; prior history of promiscuity; torn or disheveled clothing; bruises or physical marks; prior relationship; where, how, and when it occurred; drinking in a bar; resistance; immediate outcry; presence of a weapon; time between incident and filing of complaint; whether complaint made without intervening circumstances; confession; flight of defendant; cooperation with identification; age differential (big gap more likely to be rape).

[b]Some of the judges gave more than one response.

sidered indicators of the good faith of the complainant include the speed with which she filed the complaint, the reasons she decided to file the complaint, and the amount of cooperation she offers legal authorities for the prosecution. Judges often feel that a complainant's indecision about her willingness to testify indicates that she has started to doubt her allegation of rape. According to this view, a complainant who does not cooperate in judicial proceedings (usually because she feels that the officials are insensitive or skeptical), must be lying.

Although medical findings can indicate whether intercourse occurred if the examination takes place immediately following the incident, they cannot provide evidence concerning the presence or absence of consent. Indication of physical trauma, however, can provide support to substantiate nonconsent. Similarly, testimony of witnesses who saw the victim in a state of physical disarray or injury soon after the incident lends credence to the allegation of rape.

In the interviews the judges revealed a high level of concern for the effects of the courtroom experience on child victims of rape. In assessing the rape allegations of children, the judges feel protective toward the complainant and to a large extent abandon their category of the vindictive female. Although the judge may feel antagonistic toward the child victim who alleges rape to assist her mother in getting even with a man, he also tends to view the child as a pawn in an adult world. Several of the judges indicated that in such situations the child is frequently incapable of knowing that she is lying.

The Child Witness

Since the admissibility of a child's testimony depends on her ability to distinguish truth and falsehood and to comprehend the significance of swearing an oath on the Bible, the judge is responsible for assessing the child's understanding of her role as a witness. In Pennsylvania, the determination of a child's ability to testify is the sole responsibility of the judge since there is no minimum age set for the legality of a witness' testimony. Although judges are aware that lengthy questioning about her alleged sexual experience may be traumatic for a child, they are also aware of their responsibility for deciding whether the child qualifies as a witness. Judges feel a great sense of conflict in these situations since they are concerned for the well-being of the child and yet are also charged with the legal responsibility of determining that the child fully understands the seriousness of the proceedings, and with the further responsibility of assuring that the defendent is given a fair trial in open court with the right to cross-examine all witnesses for the prosecution.

Although most judges agree that it can be a very difficult experience for a young child to give evidence, many of them also maintain that there is no way to eliminate the trauma without sacrificing the current system of adversary justice in the U.S. These judges feel that the United States could never adopt the system used in Denmark and Israel in which a court official questions the child privately for both the prosecution and defense, eliminating the need for her public appearance in an open court. Although several judges expressed a wish to deviate from the adversary procedure, they felt such a change would violate the defendant's essential constitutional rights. Therefore, those judges who did offer suggestions for alternative methods of introducing the testimony of children, formulated their ideas so they could be implemented without any radical changes to the present judicial system. Suggestions for making a child's experience less traumatic included: Let the child sit on her father's lap while giving evidence; treatment by a psychiatrist; clear courtroom, take over questioning; try to keep them out of court (i.e., guilty pleas); tape record first interview to avoid trauma of repetition; try to get confession; have child in court the shortest possible time; have defense counsel talk to parents to indicate the importance of child's testimony; control defense attorney; try certain cases less rigidly; bring child to side bar.

Judges apparently do try to lessen the frightening aspects of court appearances for children. The effectiveness of the measures they use obviously depends on the sensitivities of the judges and attorneys and the emotional and mental receptiveness of the children to these procedures.

RACIAL OVERTONES

An attempt was made to determine the racial attitudes of the judges interviewed by asking the judges whether any particular types of people make better witnesses than others. Although most responses indicated a differentiation in terms of age (older women being seen as better witnesses than children), several responses definitely reflected racial attitudes which may be presumed to affect judicial behavior. Some judges alluded to the chaotic life styles and attitudes of ghetto dwellers—by which they meant blacks. Several judges indicated that they correlate the category of "vindictive women" with females of the black ghetto. One actually stated: "With the Negro community, you really have to redefine the term rape. You never know about them." (Another possible indication of racial overtones in judicial attitudes might be found in the fact that none of the judges ever used the term "black." Instead, they referred to the black population with words such as "Negro," "nigra," or "colored.")

In contrast to responses such as these were those which indicated judicial sensitivity for black rape victims. One judge referred to a specific case involving a black woman who had been raised in a strict religious atmosphere and was therefore experiencing great difficulties in adjusting to her rape experience. Others referred to the prejudices they witnessed in white victims toward black offenders. They pointed out that many white females have difficulty identifying black offenders because all black men look alike to them. Some of the judges also indicated their belief that many interracial rapes may go unreported because some white women find it abhorrent to admit that they were touched by a black man.

The responses given by the judges which reflected social biases and sensitivities illustrate the need for further inquiry into this area of judicial attitudes and their effects on courtroom proceedings.

The process of interviewing judges in Philadelphia to ascertain their attitudes toward the adjudication of rape cases has provided sufficient information to warrant further inquiry into the effects these attitudes might have on the outcome of the trial over which the judge is presiding. A judge can affect the proceedings both directly by his rulings on the evidence presented and indirectly by his demeanor toward the participants in the trial. Furthermore, his attitude toward the victim and her testimony can play a role in determining her adjustment to the effects of the rape.

An important aspect of my further research will be to observe the courtroom interactions experienced by the alleged rape victims and to analyze both the differential attitudes and behaviors of courtroom personnel and the differential responses of the victims. I hope to use this information to devise ways to assist rape victims to prepare for and adjust to their experiences in court. I am also hopeful that my findings will increase the sensitivity and awareness of personnel in the criminal justice system to the difficulties rape victims experience in taking their cases to court.

REFERENCES

Blumberg, Abraham S. 1967. *Criminal Justice.* Chicago: Quadrangle Books.

Festinger, Leon and James Carlsmith. 1959. "Cognitive Consequences of Forced Compliance," *Journal of Abnormal and Social Psycology* 58: 203–10.

Hilgard, Ernest R. and Richard C. Atkinson. 1967. *Introduction to Psychology,* 4th ed. New York: Harcourt.

Hogarth, John. 1971. *Sentencing as a Human Process.* Toronto: University of Toronto Press.

9 Michigan's Criminal Sexual Assault Law

KENNETH A. COBB AND NANCY R. SCHAUER

UNDER increasing pressure from women's rights groups and other reform organizations, the Michigan legislature has re-evaluated its centenarian rape statute, found it inadequate for the realities of the mid-twentieth century, and enacted a new sexual assault act. While people may refer to the act as the new rape law, it should be noted at the outset that the statute is intended to prohibit a variety of sexual acts which involve criminal assault.

Michigan's new criminal sexual assault law was formulated to distinguish among degrees of violence as motivated by hostility rather than passion; rape, like other crimes, is more heinous in certain contexts than others. The new law acknowledges that criminal sexual conduct is generally a premeditated crime of violence rather than a crime provoked by the victim's behavior. The

Reprinted by permission from *Journal of Law Reform* (Fall 1974), vol. 8.

victim is no longer required to resist. Where force is used, it is now presumed that the victim did not consent. Similarly, evidence is limited to that which applies to the specific crime rather than evidence concerning the victim's past sexual behavior.

LEGISLATIVE HISTORY

The new law could almost be described as victim-initiated. In the last two or three years several rape counseling centers have been founded throughout the state. Their primary purpose is to provide psychological counseling, back-up, and reassurance for the ever-increasing number of rape victims. However, at a conference attended by counselors of rape victims in 1973, attention was drawn to the fact that their efforts to help rape victims were seriously hampered by the rape laws then in effect. The conference organizer observed that, "The rape counselors would counsel a victim only to see her 'raped' again in court." After a subsequent meeting with the Michigan House Judiciary Committee, it was evident that any drive for new rape legislation would have to be catalyzed by outside interest groups. This prompted efforts to enlist the aid of the legal community of Ann Arbor, Michigan. These groups assisted in drafting the bill which its initial sponsors introduced in the Michigan Senate on February 28, 1974. Despite objections to the evidentiary provisions in the bill, a new statute closely resembling the submitted bill was signed into law on August 12, 1974.

ANALYSIS OF THE LAW

Clarification of Terms

The new law for the first time has codified definitions which may be determinative of the defendant's guilt or innocence—such as what constitutes "intimate parts" of the body, when a person is "mentally defective," or "physically helpless," what type of "personal injury" may be grounds for a higher charge under the statute, and what "sexual conduct" and "sexual penetration" entail.

Some of these terms were alluded to under prior statutes, but it was left to the courts to construe them. It is not clear that the courts have interpreted them consistently over the years (compare, for example, *People* v. *Crosswell,* 1865 with *Hirdes* v. *Ottawa Circuit Judge,* 1914). While the newly codified definitions may be open to charges of ambiguity under certain circumstances, the definitions are nonetheless needed to delineate the contours and fringe areas of the prohibited acts. Certainly they are a preferable alternative to the vague concept of "carnal knowledge," which was the prevailing standard under the old law.

Consolidation

In passing the Sexual Assault Act, the legislature has incidentally effected a much needed consolidation and simplification of widely dispersed statutory provisions covering the problem. A number of existing statutes have been repealed and substantially incorporated in the new Act: the statutory formulations of common law rape ("unlawful carnal knowledge"), assault with intent to commit rape or sodomy or gross indecency (though consensual sodomy remains a crime), attempted rape, indecent liberties, carnal knowledge of a female ward by guardian, incest, debauchery of youth, and ravishment of a female patient in an institution for the insane. Many of the latter provisions have been removed from the statutory section on indecency and immorality,[1] and, in recognition of the fact that they are more closely linked to acts of assault than to acts of public indecency, are now covered by the new criminal provisions. Left intact are those activities more aptly described as acts of public immorality or indecency such as self-exposure or the vending of obscene materials.

It should also be noted that the new law can be described as sex-neutral—extending protection to men as well as to women. If the Equal Rights Amendment becomes part of the Constitution, the Sexual Assault Act should not be affected.

Degrees of Offenses

The new statute includes a hierarchy of degrees which relate to the severity of the criminal act involved. The advantage of this hierarchy is that it allows a jury to find a defendant guilty of an appropriate lesser offense in nonaggravated rape or sexual contact cases (Dworkin, 1966). Under prior Michigan law, the minor rape offenses included assault, assault and battery, and assault with intent to commit rape. Only the latter was a felony. This framework left large gaps between the highest charge and the less severe offenses. Thus, where a prosecutor plea-bargained or a jury declined to convict a defendant of rape, the less severe offenses often bore little relationship to the crime committed. The result was that juries often refused to convict a defendant of rape unless aggravating circumstances were present (compare, Kalven and Zeisel, 1966:253).

The new degree structure offers the courts objective guidelines for matching the crime with the offensiveness of the actor's conduct; the lower level offenses in the new law constitute an appropriate midpoint between the old extremes of rape and mere assault.

Penetration-Contact Distinction. The four degrees of criminal sexual conduct set out in the new law are distinguished on two general grounds: (1) whether sexual penetration, as opposed to contact, occurred; and (2) whether certain forceful elements were present in the commission of the crime. Penetration is required for first- and third-degree criminal sexual conduct, whereas second- and fourth-degree provisions apply only to sexual contact. The new statute reflects traditional notions of blameworthiness; sexual penetration is deemed to be a more serious crime than sexual contact. The statute applies to an actor who engages in penetration and therefore would include situations in which the victim was forced to penetrate the actor in some manner. Sexual penetration is defined as sexual intercourse, cunnilingus, fellatio, anal intercourse, or any other intrusion, however slight, of any part of a person's body or of any object into the genital or anal openings of another person's body, but emission of semen is not required.

Aggravating Circumstances. The statute further separates penetration and sexual contact into higher and lower offenses, depending upon whether certain aggravating circumstances are present.

The fourth degree of offense, the only misdemeanor classification, includes engaging in sexual contact with any person through the use of force or coercion or where the actor has reason to know that the victim is mentally or physically incapable of refusing consent. Force is defined to include: (1) the application of physical force, (2) coercion of the victim by threats of violence, (3) coercion by threats of future retaliation, (4) fraudulent medical treatment or examination of the victim, or (5) overcoming the victim through concealment or surprise. An offense is categorized as third-degree criminal sexual conduct if the actor engages in penetration and either force is used or the victim is helpless. It is also third-degree conduct to engage in penetration with a victim who is between the ages of 13 and 16, whether force is used or not.[2]

It is the existence of certain aggravating circumstances that will raise an offensive sexual act—otherwise a third-degree offense—to first degree and which can raise the fourth-degree misdemeanor to a second-degree felony. For purposes of discussion these first- and second-degree provisions will be referred to as "aggravated offenses." The actor is guilty of the charged aggravated offense if any of the following listed elements is present.

Statutory age or relationship. There are two situations in which the age of the victim is the aggravating circumstance. The first is any circumstance in which the victim was under the age of 13 years, and the second is the case in which the actor either lives with, is related to, or is in a position of authority over a victim who is between the ages of 13 and 16 years.

Other felonies. If the actor commits any other felony in connection with the sexual conduct or shortly before or after the sexual act, the offense is of a higher degree. Thus, an armed robber who commits rape is subject to first-degree penalties. More questionable might be the situation where an unrelated felony is committed shortly before a rape.

Use of weapons. The attendant use of a weapon likewise raises the charge to the aggravated offense. It is important to note that the assailant does not have to employ an actual weapon; it is sufficient if the victim reasonably believes it to be a dangerous weapon.

Aiders and abetters. The presence of aiders or abetters will also result in the higher penalty. Absent any indication to the contrary, aiders and abetters will be defined in light of prior common law decisions (*People* v. *Burrell* (1931); *Strang* v. *People* (1871)). Evidently this category includes all gang-rape situations.

Personal injury. The further aggravating factor is the infliction of personal injury during the sexual act. This term is defined in the statute as "bodily injury, disfigurement, mental anguish, chronic pain, pregnancy, disease, or loss or impairment of a sexual or reproductive organ."

Penalties

The penalties in the new law were intended to match the gravity of the offense committed. First-degree conduct carries a maximum of life in prison, second- and third-degree offenses are punishable with a maximum of fifteen years, and fourth-degree conduct is a misdemeanor carrying a maximum two-year sentence or a fine not exeeding $500.

However, because the law specifies no graded minimum sentences, it will be possible for some lesser offenders to receive longer sentences than some higher degree offenders. While this arguably undermines the intent of the new degree structure, it might be justified in certain cases. For example, sexual conduct by a third-time offender might warrant a longer sentence than penetration by a first-time offender. And a case of sexual contact with infliction of injury might be deemed more heinous in some contexts than a case of penetration at gunpoint with no injury.

THE EVIDENTIARY PROVISIONS

Perhaps the most significant aspect of the Sexual Assault Act will be the new evidentiary provisions and the shifted burdens of proof therein. The new law does not require the victim to resist the actor, nor does it require the victim's testimony to be corroborated. The prosecution is required to prove that force was used, but it does not have to prove the victim's nonconsent. Consent is now an affirmative defense in certain situations, but the use of the victim's past sexual conduct to prove consent is severely limited.

Evidentiary Policy and the Mythology of Rape

The manner in which burdens of proof are allocated between the prosecution and the defense in criminal trials is based largely on generally accepted policy considerations. Likewise, the need for a creation of presumptions is also based on policy choices. These policy choices are, in turn, based on the perception, both of the judiciary and the public at large, of what is fair, what is expected, what is normal, or what is likely. These machinations established the presumptions and allocated the burdens of proof under the old rape laws.

Unfortunately, it now appears that the perceptions of the judiciary and the public on which these presumptions were based were themselves grounded to some extent on the mythology rather than the reality of rape.

Rape as Crime of Passion or Lust. Recent studies make it clear that rape is a crime of violence (Federal Bureau of Investigation, 1974: 13). It is committed by actors who are *not* primarily moved by passion or even lust; rather, the actors are primarily motivated by hostility and the urge to brutalize and humiliate their victims. A major study of forcible rape (Amir, 1971:152–53) showed that in 85 percent of all reported rapes there was some form of overt violence such as beating or choking.

Rape as a Provoked Reaction to Victim's Behavior. Rape is not a crime in which a person's passion is provoked uncontrollably by a woman who subtly consents to intercourse through her manner (body language) or dress: 82 percent of all rapes are planned or partly planned in advance with regard to either the intended victim or the intent to perpetrate a rape (Amir, 1971:141–42); 43 percent of all rapes are gang rapes involving two or more attackers with a single victim (Amir, 1971:193). The National Commission on Crimes of Violence reports that only a low percentage of rapes involve any precipitative behavior on the part of the woman, such as gestures or style of dress (Curtis, 1974). Yet studies indicated that juries are strongly influenced by the behavior of the victim. Despite instructions by the judge, juries often respond as though they were applying the legal theory of assumption of risk (Kalven and Zeisel, 1966:249–57).

Rape as a Pleasurable Experience. That such an assertion (Freud, 1933:158) could be believed is incredible; however, such a representation or belief may be a key part of the defense strategy. That there is a vast physiological difference between the concept of normal intercourse and rape is perhaps best understood by the studies of Masters (1960). Certainly, in light of the percentages of cases involving beating or choking, the belief that rape is pleasurable is unreasonable.

As medical, sociological, and psychological studies progressed, the foundation of the presumptions in the old rape laws became less firm. The following sections explore four particular provisions in detail.

Force and Resistance

Under the old statute a defendant could be convicted of rape only if the prosecution proved the use of force by the assailant and the unwillingness of the victim. This requirement was construed by Michigan courts to mean that the victim had to resist the actor "from the inception to the close" (*People* v. *Murphy,* 1906), and such resistance had "to be to the utmost" (*People* v. *Geddes,* 1942). The resistance standard was developed as an objective test of whether the carnal knowledge was "against the will" of the victim (Dworkin, 1966:682), but the standard has been attacked on several grounds. Rape has been the only violent crime which required any level of resistance by the victim. Thus, the victim was called upon to risk his or her life in order to make conviction possible. This requirement contradicts the advice of police, who counsel victims of sexual assault to avoid resisting the actors where such resistance would not be to the victim's advantage in attempting to escape.

Perhaps the most compelling argument is that nonconsent usually accompanies the use of force;[3] therefore, nonconsent should be presumed in cases of forcible sexual conduct.

The new statute codifies this view—resistance by the victim is not an element of the prosecutor's case. Rather, the new law regards the coercion used by the actor, not the victim's state of mind, as determinative. While consent may be raised as an affirmative defense in certain situations, under the new law it is clearly no longer necessary for the prosecution to prove nonconsent.

The new law also presumes nonconsent in the absence of force when the victim is under the age of 16 or when the victim is physically or mentally helpless. The helpless victim cases had presented a problem under the prior statute, which required proof of both force and nonconsent, but Michigan courts evolved tests that achieved roughly the same result as the new law (*People* v. *Don Moran,* 1872), holding the actor liable if he knew or had reason to know of the victim's condition.

In recent years the Michigan courts have relaxed the resistance requirement. The early judicial stance was that there could be no conviction for rape if the prosecutrix ceased to resist at any point before consummation of intercourse (*People* v. *Ayers,* 1917). However, more recent cases have excused nonresistance if the victim "was overcome by fear of the defendant" (*People* v. *Myers,* 1943). This rationale has been used most often in cases of gang rapes (*People* v. *Dockery,* 1969; *People* v. *Jackson,* 1972), and rapes at gunpoint (*People* v. *Myers,* 1943) but has also been applied recently where the actor had no weapon and was acting alone (*People* v. *Palmer,* 1973). Thus, the new provision regarding resistance may reflect the current judicial view.

The Victim's Sexual Conduct

The Sexual Assault Act now limits the admissibility of evidence to the specific circumstances of the charged criminal act and excludes evidence of the victim's chastity, sexual reputation, and

afterwards. It seems likely, though I have no definite evidence on this point, that such girls become the difficult wives who restrict marital sexual activity and who quarrel over it with their husbands.

Although Gusii girls vary in their reactions to the premarital situation, there are common features which characterize a majority of them. They enjoy the initial phase of the relationship with a young man in which they are given gifts and fervently wooed, and many of them attempt to prolong this phase in order to obtain more goods and attention, regardless of whether or not they seem to enjoy inflicting frustration on a male or at least putting him in a position of subordination, and this is also indicated by their provocative and hostile sexual abuse of the young men they meet in the marketplace. Premarital sexual affairs are extremely brittle, being terminated after a boy and girl have had intercourse once or twice, so the girls have opportunities to go through the early stages of seduction over and over again. Another behavior pattern common to all young Gusii females, except the most extreme girls of type one, is sexual inhibition and some degree of distaste for the act of coitus. While this is variable from one individual to another, Gusii girls as a group exhibit a greater degree of inhibition and anxiety about sexual intercourse than do girls of surrounding tribes. To understand the premarital behavior exhibited by Gusii girls in their sexual relationships it is necessary to examine briefly their childhood experiences and the pressures acting upon them before they marry at an average age of 15 to 16.

Are the childhood experiences of Gusii females substantially different from those of Gusii males whose adult heterosexual attitudes are so different? On the basis of an Oedipal hypothesis we would consider the relation of the child to the parent of opposite sex as the model for later heterosexual relationships. In exploring the implications of this hypothesis for the Gusii family, intergenerational avoidance relationships are of primary importance. Both parents practice sexual avoidance of their children, in the sense that they attempt to prevent the children from seeing their nude bodies, in coitus or at any other time. There are clearly recognized degrees of avoidance: father-daughter avoidance is most strict, father-son next, then mother-son, and finally mother-daughter. The father usually insists that any of his daughters over three or four years of age sleep in a different hut in the homestead (with the grandmother or mother's co-wife) when he is sleeping with the mother. This is not required of a son until he is about seven years old. The son has a close and dependent relationship with his mother until he is circumcised and initiated into manhood at 10 to 12 years of age. The daughter never has such a relationship with her father, who is aloof from all the children in the family, but more especially his daughters. Furthermore, the father has a greater role in punishing the children and is used by the mother as a bogey man with which to threaten misbehaving children of both sexes. Using an Oedipal hypothesis, we could say that the father-daughter relationship in the Gusii family provides the girl with training in avoiding and fearing men, while the mother-son relationship promotes in males a positive attraction toward women.

There are other specific differences in the life histories of males and females in Gusii society. Girls are required to wear dresses and to sit so that their genitals are not exposed from the age of three or four onward. Sometimes this training is begun earlier, but it is never put off beyond the age of five. A girl of six who runs naked in the morning or who does not sit properly in mixed company is curtly reprimanded by one of her parents. A boy may go naked until he is circumcised. This earlier modesty training of girls may well have an impact on their adult sexual attitudes. Another difference is that the girl is under the domination and supervision of her mother and a few other women from birth until marriage, while the boy is freer of maternal supervision from the time he first goes out to herd cattle (which may be as early as the age of three), and is completely free of it after circumcision. The effect of this supervision on the Gusii girl is to isolate her from intensive contact with men and to make her accountable to her mother for her expenditure of time during the day. After the girl is initiated at age eight or nine, she begins spending time washing herself and her clothes at the stream and making little expeditions to the marketplace. Girls of this age are aware that they are destined to leave the parental home for that of their husband, and they are preparing for their role in courtship. This causes friction with the mother, who expects the girl to attend to cooking, fetching water, and other domestic chores more than ever since her competence at these tasks is well developed. Disobedient girls as young as nine years old are told by their mothers, "You'll probably elope and cheat your parents of the bridewealth cattle!" This aspect of child rearing is probably more pronounced now than it was in the past, when the possibility of elopement was not as great.

As the girl approaches marriageable age, her mother becomes increasingly suspicious that the time she spends away from the homestead (or from agricultural work) will involve her in sexual affairs detrimental to her reputation and desirability as a wife, and which may also result in her elopement (without the payment of bridewealth). At this point the father also steps in to use his authority to discipline the daughter and prevent her from seeing boys. A girl who returns home late at night can expect to be scolded and harangued by both parents, particularly her father if he is at home, and there are Gusii fathers who beat their daughters on such occasions. Whatever fear of sexual involvement a girl has developed in the course of her early life is strongly augmented by parental punishment during adolescence. Thus when a girl is tempted to have sexual intercourse with a young man, she is anxious about whether her parents will notice her absence, whether someone will see her going off with a male and report it to her parents, and whether she will become pregnant and be disgraced. Her premarital behavior, then, can be seen as compounded by attitudes carried over from childhood experience (some of which may not have been covered in this analysis) and feelings resulting from her contemporaneous position in the family of orientation.

To recapitulate; the spatial and military barriers to interclan premarital sexual activity in Gusiiland have disappeared as the result of British pacification of the area and rapid population growth. The barriers that now exist reside not so much in the structure of the situation as in the behavior of Gusii females, whose sexual inhibitions and antagonism to males (learned in childhood and enforced in adolescence) present young men with a different set of obstacles to premarital sexual outlet. It is possible to seduce girls, but seduction requires social and musical skills as well as money. Even the most adept seducers are rarely able to obtain sexual partners more than twice during a week, and youths who are less attractive, skillful, and wealthy may go for several weeks at a time without heterosexual intercourse. When premarital intercourse occurs, it has many behavioral similarities to rape, but so long as the eventual acquiescence of the female is won, the act will not be considered rape by Gusii cultural standards. In the following section the several conditions are described which can result in the female refusing to acquiesce.

TYPES OF SEX OFFENSES

The typical Gusii rape, so far as I can determine from anecdotal evidence (court records being deficient in this respect), is committed by an unmarried young man on an unmarried female of a different clan. There are some cases in which married men and married women are involved in rape, and also those in which both rapist and victim have the same clan affiliation, but these appear to be relatively infrequent. Furthermore, rapes of married women or of girls in the same clan as the rapist are more likely to be settled locally without resort to the courts, so that they probably form a very small proportion of the high rate of rape indictments which is in question here. Thus I shall concentrate on explaining interclan rape involving unmarried persons. On the basis of the conscious intent of the rapist, three types of Gusii rape may be distinguished: rape resulting from seduction, premeditated sexual assault, and abduction.

Rape Resulting from Seduction

Since the typical Gusii seduction bears a strong behavioral similarity to rape, it is only necessary to understand the conditions under which Gusii females who are being seduced decide to bring the act to the attention of the public and eventually to the authorities. First of all, the standard reluctant pose of the Gusii girl provides many opportunities for a young man to misunderstand her motives. Although she may sincerely want to reject his advances because she finds him unattractive or because of her own current fears, the young man may confidently assume she is pretending and proceed to use physical force to achieve his aim. If her revulsion or fear is great enough she may cry for help and initiate a rape case. Such misunderstandings can be due to the eagerness of the youth and his consequent inability to perceive her subtle cues of genuine rejection, or to the girl's failure to make the signs of refusal in unequivocal fashion.

Second, fear of discovery is ubiquitous in Gusii seduction. Opportunities for privacy exist, but a couple may be seen going off together. If they are engaging in intercourse out-of-doors, someone may pass nearby and either actually observe them or arouse their fears of being seen. When this happens, a girl who was originally willing may decide to save her reputation by crying out (or reporting it later), pretending that she was being raped. Although this may be considered pseudorape, such cases appear to be common in societies in which rape is considered a crime and probably inflate the rates of rape indictments in all of them. There is no way of determining what proportion of rape cases in Gusiiland or anywhere else are of this kind.

Finally, as mentioned above, Gusii girls who have no desire for sexual relations deliberately encourage young men in the preliminaries of courtship because they enjoy the gifts and attention they receive. Some of them act provocative, thinking they will be able to obtain desired articles and then escape the sexual advances of the young man. Having lavished expense and effort on the seduction of an apparently friendly girl, the youth is not willing to withdraw from the relationship without attempting to obtain sexual favors. If the girl is of the third type described above, rape may easily result. An aggressive conclusion is particularly likely if the girl is actually married. In the early stages of marriage brides spend a good deal of time in their home communities visiting their parents. Such a girl may accompany a group of unmarried females going to the marketplace and may pretend to be unmarried in order to be bribed and flattered by the men there. No matter how emotionally and financially involved in her a young man becomes, the bride is too afraid of supernatural sanctions against adultery to yield to him sexually. After she fails to appear at several appointments in the forest or at his hut, he may rape her in desperation the next time they meet, and she will report the deed.

Thus, the similarity of Gusii seduction to rape, the communication difficulties arising out of this similarity, the girls' anxiety about their reputations and consequent fear of discovery, and the provocative behavior by girls whose motivations are not primarily sexual—all of these contribute to turning the would-be seducer into a rapist.

Premeditated Sexual Assault

In some cases Gusii youths decide to obtain sexual gratification from girls by force with no semblance of a friendly approach. One or more boys may be involved in an attack on a single girl. Usually the object is to frighten her first so that she will not cry or resist; for this reason young (eleven to thirteen years old) and easily frightened girls are more likely to be chosen as victims. The boys disguise themselves by draping cloaks or skins over their heads, hide at a place out of hearing distance of the nearest homesteads, and dart out from behind bushes when the girl comes walking by collecting firewood or carrying a pot of water. Sometimes they beat her badly and tear her clothing. Girls are brought into court with lacerations and bites inflicted by sexual attackers. They may drag her off to the hut of one of them, and there force her into coitus. They intend to let her go eventually, but they may hold her for a couple of days. By this time her father has gone to the chief for the services of tribal policemen in finding the attackers. If the policemen track them down in time, the case is more likely to be brought to the resident magistrate's court, since rupture of the hymen and other signs of attack are common in this type of rape.

Abduction

When a Gusii man lacks the economic means for a legitimate bridewealth marriage and does not have the personal attractiveness or seductive skill needed to persuade a girl to elope with him, he may resort to desperate measures. Determined to obtain a mate, he enlists the aid of some clansmen in an attempt to abduct a girl from a different clan. Sometimes the girl is one he knows fairly well but who has refused to live in concubinage with him. The young men act for him as they would in a legitimate marriage, accosting the girl and taking her away by force. Under these conditions, however, they take pains not to be seen by the girl's parents or anyone else of her community. Another difference is that the girl's resistance is sincere, since she desires a legitimate marriage or concubinage with a man she finds unusually attractive. The young men frequently are rough on her, beating her and tearing her clothes. When she arrives at the home of her would-be lover, he exhorts her in peaceful terms to remain with him until bridewealth can be raised to legitimize their union. Her refusal is ignored in the hope that she will eventually acquiesce, and the wedding night sexual contest is performed, with the clansmen helping overcome her resistance. If she does not escape and report the offense to her father, the latter will eventually come with tribal policemen and arrest the abductor.

The type of abduction described is not to be confused with elopement in which the girl is willing to go despite her father's ire at being deprived of bridewealth. Such cases are entered in the tribunal courts under a customary law offense, "removing a girl without the consent of her parents." In the abductive rape which is of interest here, the girl is not a willing accomplice and must be forced into sexual relations not only on the first night but subsequently as well. This type of case results in an indecent assault indictment.

Of the three types of rape described above, two are unlawful versions of patterns which are normally law-abiding and socially acceptable by Gusii standards. The first type develops out of seduction, which has gained acceptance as a culture pattern when kept within the bounds of discretion; the third type is an imitation of traditional wedding procedures, but lacking the legitimizing bridewealth and the consent of the bride and her parents. In both cases there is a close parallel between the criminal act and the law-abiding culture pattern to which it is related. The question arises, Why does an individual commit the criminal version of the act rather than its law-abiding counterpart? I have attempted to show how various limitations on the premarital sexual behavior of Gusii males tend to make them sexually frustrated and hence inclined to a less discriminate use of the aggressive aspects of accepted sexual patterns. The occurrence of the abductive type of rape, however, poses an important question: If difficulty of premarital access to females is what frustrates Gusii males, what prevents them from marrying at an earlier age and thus solving their problem in a law-abiding way? In the following section I shall describe the barriers to marriage in contemporary Gusii society and what effect they have on the incidence of all types of rape.

THE BRIDEWEALTH FACTOR IN SEX OFFENSES

A legitimate Gusii marriage requires the transfer of cattle (and goats) from the father of the groom to the father of the bride (Mayer 1950b; 1951). The number of animals transferred is a matter of individual agreement between the fathers, but it is influenced by the prevailing bridewealth rate in Gusiiland. The rate has fluctuated throughout the years from as many as twenty cows to as little as one cow. Reduction in the rate resulted from a severe cattle epidemic, in one case, and from actions taken by traditional and British authorities, in other cases. Despite attempts by authorities to control it, the Gusii bridewealth rate has a tendency to rise which can only be understood in terms of the uses to which bridewealth is put.

The father of the bride receives in one lot most of the bridewealth animals before he allows his daughter to live with her prospective mate; installment payments are not ordinarily permitted.

Bridewealth given in marriage for a girl is most often used to procure a wife for her uterine brother (or in some instances for her half-brother or father), and her father is concerned lest the number of animals he accepts for her marriage will prove insufficient to obtain a wife for her brother at a later time. Fearing that the bridewealth rate will rise between the two marriages, the father of the bride demands more cattle than the current rate and thereby helps to bring about a rise.

One consequence of the inflation in bridewealth rates and the reduced availability of cattle because of pasturage overcrowding and British prohibitions against intertribal cattle raids is that young men who come from cattle-poor families and who do not have uterine sisters old enough to be married must postpone their own marriages. They can wait until their sisters grow up (if they have sisters), secure a loan from close patrilineal kinsmen, or attempt to raise money to buy cattle through wage labor. (The minimal bridewealth rate in 1957 was equivalent to the total wages a Gusii plantation worker would receive in forty months.) Meanwhile, fathers attempt to marry off their daughters as secondary wives to wealthy old men. Among the poorer young men, the enforced postponement of marriage creates a group who reach their late twenties or early thirties before they can afford marriage. A majority of Gusii males marry between eighteen and twenty-five, but there are numerous men who are unmarried at later ages and even some who never have legitimate wives. Some of these unfortunates persuade girls to elope without the payment of bridewealth, and such concubinage has been increasing despite efforts by girls' fathers and the courts. Inevitably, however, there are men who lack the economic means for a legitimate marriage as well as the attractiveness and seductive arts needed to convince a girl to elope. In desperation a man of this type may resort to abductive rape as described in the preceding section.

The relationship between excessive bridewealth demands and rape is not a conjectural one. In 1936–1937, the bridewealth rates were up to eight to twelve head of cattle, one to three bulls, and eight to twelve goats. This was the highest they had been since before the great cattle plague of the 1890s. Many young men could find no legitimate way of getting married, and they resorted to cattle theft and all types of rape. On one market day in Kisii township, a large group of young men gathered and decided to procure mates for themselves by abduction. They grabbed girls in the marketplace and carried them off. Many of the girls returned after being raped. The incident precipitated action by the administration. The district records report the following for November 29, 1937:

> A large general baraza [assembly] was held to deal with (1) indecent assaults on girls and defilements of girls under 16 years of age, (2) increased stock theft. The district commissioner pointed out the bestial nature of practice (1), comparing it to that of dogs and condemned the young men. He also held the elders responsible for demanding a prohibitive marriage price.

Under the orders of the district commissioner, the Gusii elders present at the meeting swore an oath to reduce the amount of bridewealth demanded to 6 cows, 1 bull, and 10 goats. The reduction was effective until 1942, when the rate resumed its upward trend. By 1950 high bridewealth rates resulted in a serious outbreak of rape again, though without the dramatic or organized qualities of the earlier one. Further efforts at control of bridewealth have been made by the African District Council, but with ephemeral success. In 1956, one of the years covered in the figures on rate of rape indictments presented earlier, bridewealth rates averaged 10 head of cattle in the area studied, but wealthy, older men were given considerably more. All in all, it is likely that the high rate of rape indictments in Gusiiland is in part a function of the economic barrier to the marriage of young men created by excessive bridewealth demands.

DISCUSSION

The foregoing analysis of the etiology of rape in Gusiiland may be summarized as follows: Normal forms of sexual intercourse among the Gusii involve male force and female resistance with an emphasis on the pain inflicted by the male on the female. This general heterosexual aggression appears to be related to the hostility of exogamous clans, since marriage is the prototype of a heterosexual relationship in Gusii culture. Regardless of its origin, the aggressive pattern of sexuality is not entirely pretense but shows clear signs of involving sadistic and masochistic impulses on the part of some Gusii individuals. Rape committed by Gusii men can be seen as an extension of this legitimate pattern to illegitimate contexts under the pressure of sexual frustration. The sexual frustration of Gusii young men is due to effectively enforced restrictions on intraclan sexual activity, the sexual inhibitions and provocative behavior of Gusii girls, and high bridewealth rates which force postponement of marriage. Prior to British administration of Gusiiland, rape was not such a problem because interclan controls were as effective as intraclan controls. Pacification of the district, however, has eliminated the threat of force and the spatial distances between clan settlements, increasing opportunities for interclan heterosexual contact in the face of greatly diminished penalties for interclan rape. Had Gusii girls proved uninhibited, promiscuity rather than rape would have been the consequence of pacification. However, Gusii values favor restriction of premarital sexuality and the burden of enforcing this restriction now falls upon the girls themselves rather than upon their clansmen. Thus the contemporary system of sanctions operating in Gusii society is not adequate to control the effects of the factors motivating men to commit rape.

If the above analysis is valid, there are four factors in the Gusii situation which should be found in any society with a high frequency of rape: (1) severe formal restrictions on the nonmarital sexual relations of females, (2) moderately strong sexual inhibitions on the part of females, (3) economic or other barriers to marriage which prolong the bachelorhood of some males into their late twenties, (4) the absence of physical segregation of the sexes. This last condition distinguishes high rape societies from societies in which women are secluded and guarded, where rape is not feasible and homosexuality may be practiced instead. These four factors should be regarded as necessary but not sufficient conditions for a high frequency of rape, as they may also be found in societies having prostitution or other functional alternatives.

The Gusii case raises some general points about the control of sexual behavior in human societies. Not all societies have restrictive sexual rules; in many groups nonmarital sexual relations are permitted and carried on relatively unhampered by cultural restrictions. In societies which do have severe formal limitations on heterosexual gratification, the problem of control, in the sense of enforcing conformity to ideal rules, is a great one. How can such control be achieved? Students of social organization have emphasized the role of structural arrangements and social sanctions in social control; psychoanalytic theorists have emphasized the role of repression and superego (acquired in childhood) in the individual's inhibition of culturally unacceptable impulses. Assuming that both types of variables play a part in the control of sexual behavior, I shall discuss their respective contributions to the control process, referring to them as *structural barriers* and *socialized inhibitions.*

A *structural barrier,* as I define it for sexual control processes, is a physical or social arrangement in the contemporary environment of the individual which prevents him from obtaining the sexual object he seeks. A *socialized inhibition* is a learned tendency to avoid performing sexual acts under certain conditions. Structural barriers are part of the settlement pattern and group structure; socialized inhibitions are the products of the socialization process which the individual undergoes in his early years. I do not assume that these two are concretely separate factors in social control but that their relative weight in a particular situation may be analytically assessed. Societies with restrictive sexual rules vary in the extent to which they depend on structural barriers or socialized inhibitions to achieve conformity to these rules.

The purest forms of structural barriers to heterosexual gratification involve spatial segregation of the sexes. There is the royal harem with high walls, barred windows, and armed guards and, less elaborately, the veiled seclusion of ordinary married women in some Near Eastern and Indian societies. Where the regulation of premarital sexual activity is the aim, it can be partly achieved by keeping males and females in separate schools until late adolescence, as among higher class groups in some European societies. These physical types of structural barriers have the effect of preventing opportunities for social contact between potential sexual partners. A somewhat less extreme form of structural barrier is chaperonage. Where it is practiced, potential sexual partners may be physically proximate and perhaps even have social contact, but only under the surveillance of one or more persons whose special duty it is to see that no sexual act occurs. Punishments for transgressions of sexual rules are likely to be severe, particularly if there are any opportunities for unsupervised contact. The social rather than purely physical type of structural barrier is also found in those societies in which the entire community or neighborhood acts as chaperone. While possible violators of sexual rules may be in frequent contact, the ubiquity of the cohesive social group with its power to punish is assumed to act as a strong deterrent to misbehavior. The effectiveness of such a system is probably inversely related to the amount of opportunity for privacy which potential sex offenders have.

In a sense there is no structural barrier which does not depend on the willingness of individuals to cooperate with it, and in that sense a certain amount of socialized inhibition is involved in all of the above-mentioned structural barriers. Insofar as harem walls fail to prevent adultery, it is because the guards and inmates are not inhibited in their sexual behavior. For a structural barrier to be effective in enforcing a restrictive sexual rule, it must be supported by socialized inhibitions; individuals must at least anticipate the penalties to be incurred by transgressing the barriers, and inhibit their responses on that account. While recognizing the universal necessity for a minimum of socialized inhibition, we may distinguish those societies which depend less on it for control from those which use it more. Where there is physical segregation of the sexes, the socialized inhibition required to restrict heterosexuality is less than where the sexes are in continual contact. In the former case, simple difficulty of access is a deterrent; in the latter, impulses are aroused which must be inhibited by the individual if conformity is to be achieved. When temptation is removed, it is not difficult to be an ascetic, but when the temptation is present, only the individual trained to asceticism can resist it. In societies where community chaperonage acts to restrict sexual behavior, individuals are ordinarily socialized to avoid public sexual performance, and in some cases their fear of discovery is so great that they inhibit sexual responses even when the opportunity for transgression arises. In societies where socialized inhibition is even stronger, individuals control their own impulses in the absence of any structural barriers to violation of sexual rules. Thus Gusii wives are trusted not to commit adultery when their husbands are working far away from home, although they have opportunities for clandestine intercourse. The question of whether sexual inhibition in the absence of structural barriers results from child training, as I have assumed, or from later socialization, is an empirical question which can be tested cross-culturally.

The analysis presented above has implications for the study of contemporary culture change and the breakdown of traditional controls of sexual behavior in many parts of the world. When, as among the Gusii, structural barriers to premarital sexual activity are removed without being replaced by other structural barriers of equal effectiveness, the socialized inhibitions of individuals are put to the test. If both sexes are highly inhibited, premarital activity may be only slightly greater than before. If females are highly inhibited but males are not, rape is likely to occur. If both sexes are low on inhibition, promiscuity will result. Since socialized inhibitions are probably more resistant to change in acculturative situations than are structural barriers,[6] it may be necessary to pay more attention to such individual factors in order to predict the direction of cultural change and the future incidence of sex offenses.

NOTES

1. I have chosen to underestimate grossly the Gusii rape rate rather than make dubious extrapolations from available figures. There are three Afri-

can tribal courts in Gusiiland, with somewhat overlapping jurisdictions: Manga, Kuja, Gesima. The annual rate reported above is based entirely on the indecent assault indictments entered at Manga, combined with the very few rape (and indecent assault) indictments entered at the resident magistrate's court. Manga handles more cases than the others but not more than half of the total cases heard by tribunals. By letting the Manga figures plus the resident magistrate's figures stand for the entire Gusii people, I may have reduced the actual rate of rape indictments by half or more. The figure for Gusii population which was used in the computation was 270,000, which is higher than the Agricultural Department's formula of 1948 census figures plus 10 percent. The use of the higher figure also serves to depress the number of indictments per 100,000.

2. This can be considered a special case of a general phenomenon which has been noted by Murdock (1949:18): "Where marriages are exogamous with respect to the community . . . spouses of one sex find themselves living among comparative strangers, to whom they must make new personal adjustments and upon whom they must depend for the support, protection, and social satisfactions which they have previously received from relatives and old friends. They thus find themselves at a considerable psychological and social disadvantage in comparison with the sex which remains at home."

3. Although Gusii informants claimed that the fear is based on the greater ability of eighteen-year-old boys to impregnate, it seems probable that the realistic basis of the fear is that older boys choose as sexual partners older girls who are outgrowing their "adolescent sterility." For a general discussion of the adolescent sterility of women and its implications for anthropological accounts of premarital sexuality, see Ford and Beach (1952:172–173).

4. Unlike other Kenya groups, such as the Luo, Kipsigis, and Kikuyu, the Gusii did not practice partial (interfemural) intercourse before marriage, or at least the practice was not institutionalized. This is consistent with the fact that these other groups are specifically concerned with the physical virginity of brides, while the Gusii are not.

5. In the resident magistrate's court, prison sentences up to fourteen years can be given for rape, but such a small proportion of the rape cases are taken there that it is unlikely that its sentences have an effect on prospective offenders. African tribunal courts, which hear most of the rape cases (as "indecent assault") are not empowered to give sentences of more than one year in jail and 500 shillings fine. Even the fourteen-year sentence does not compare in severity with the traditional sanction.

6. This statement is based on the plausible hypothesis of Bruner (1956: 194), "That which was traditionally learned and internalized in infancy

and early childhood tends to be most resistant to change in contact situations."

REFERENCES

Bruner, Edward M. 1956. "Cultural Transmission and Cultural Change," *Southwestern Journal of Anthropology* 12:191–99.

Ford, Clellan S. and Frank Beach. 1952. *Patterns of Sexual Behavior.* New York: Harper & Row.

Mayer, Philip. 1949. *The Lineage Principle in Gusii Society.* London: International African Institute.

——. 1950a. "Privileged Obstruction of Marriage Rites among the Gusii," *Africa* 20:113–25.

——. 1950b. *Gusii Bridewealth, Law and Custom.* London: Oxford University Press.

——. 1951. "Bridewealth Limitation among the Gusii." In *Two Studies in Applied Anthropology in Kenya,* Colonial Research Studies, No. 3, pp. 16–123. London: His Majesty's Stationery Office.

——. 1953. "Gusii Initiation Ceremonies," *Journal of the Royal Anthropological Institute* 83:9–36.

Murdock, George Peter. 1949. *Social Structure.* New York: Macmillan.

11 A Comparative Study of Forcible Rape Offenses Known to the Police in Boston and Los Angeles

DUNCAN CHAPPELL,
GILBERT GEIS,
STEPHEN SCHAFER,
AND LARRY SIEGEL

THIS essay examines a random sample of cases of forcible rape known to the police in Boston and Los Angeles, two cities that generally are regarded as supporting quite distinct styles of life. John Gunther (1951:518) notes of Boston that "there is nothing in the country to rival it for a kind of lazy dignity, intellectual affluence and spaciousness, and above all a wonderful acquired sense of responsibility for its own past. Of course, it suggests rather

Revised version of paper from *Studies in the Sociology of Sex,* James M. Henslin, ed. (Englewood Cliffs, N.J.: Prentice-Hall, 1971). Reprinted by permission of Prentice-Hall.

than overstates. Indeed, the quality of understatement characterizes much in Boston life."

Los Angeles, on the other hand, appeared to Gunther (1951: 4) to be an area of "petroleum, crazy religious cults, the citrus industry, towns based on rich *rentiers,* the movies, the weirdest architecture in the United States, refugees from Iowa, a steeply growing Negro population, and devotees of funny money." In Los Angeles, according to the anthropologist Ashley Montagu (1966: 190) "the very fact that the sun shines continuously, that the air is warm, comfortable, and only occasionally cold, attracts individuals who are interested primarily in creature comforts." Montagu remarks, in a piece of rhetoric not unrelated to alleged precursors of the criminal offense of forcible rape, that "a high positive correlation is likely to exist between a devotion to physical comforts and a lack of interest in the spirit, the essential qualities of humanity." *

The comparative focus of the present essay is designed to circumvent the more elementary pitfalls inherent in investigations confined to a localized geographic area. The comparative approach offers a method for avoiding ethnocentric conclusions and unicultural, idiosyncratic interpretations of such conclusions. It is responsive, in this respect, to the fundamentally scientific inquiry of the statistician who, when asked by a colleague, "How are you?" wanted to know, "Compared to what?"

The use of comparative material, however, has many pitfalls. For one thing, procedural and definitional variations between jurisdictions regarding the behavior to be examined must be controlled. For another, it is very difficult to determine which elements of a culture can be said to account for variations in the examined behavior. It also may be true that the alleged variations in the cities' cultural climates are no more than a collection of

* Further notation of the point is readily available. For instance: "Though no one has really done a thorough investigation of the matter, the casualness about sex . . . is said to permeate large segments of Los Angeles society" (Becker, 1965:119). And observe the free associational antithesis between Boston and Los Angeles by a psychiatrist (Gaylin, 1970:5) discussing draft evasion: "Life in Canada cannot be that different from life in the United States. While Toronto is different from Boston, it is probably less different than Los Angeles is."

stereotypes, or perhaps a statement only of the way of life of the more visible or more powerful segments of the populations of the two areas. These items—and others that we shall note below—make cross-cultural conclusions inordinately hazardous. Nonetheless, possible gains from such a procedure—first in terms of speculative insights and later in terms of the refinement of such insights—make it an attractive scientific enterprise.

THE SEARCH FOR HYPOTHESES

A reasonably satisfactory explanation for variant rape rates ought to be deduced from consideration of the sexual climate of a given setting. Published research sheds some light on discrete items that appear to be related to rape rates. Sociological studies (for example, Amir, 1971), for instance, agree that rapists tend to be young, unmarried and, at least in terms of those imprisoned (Gillin, 1946:129), to suffer unusually from physical handicaps. The psychiatric material (e.g., Guttmacher, 1951:50) concentrates on the view that rape is fundamentally an act of aggression and that its sexual component is primarily sadistic.

Most published material regarding forcible rape concentrates upon the dynamics of the situation between offender and victim and their personal characteristics rather than upon social and cultural circumstances and their possible connection with the rate at which the offense occurs. Rape is often seen as a tribute to the virility and aggressiveness of the perpetrator, a theme notable in Greek mythology (Licht, 1969), where rape tends to be an explicable, although somewhat unfortunate, event in the lives of heroic figures and gods, such as Paris and Zeus. In Western societies, rape also tends to be viewed as an omnipresent latent impulse in male nature. It is on the basis of his sudden awareness of his own drive toward rape, for instance, that Levin (1956:492–94) claims to have at last understood Nathan Leopold's urge toward murder.

Anthropological evidence is most persuasive in support of the view that the number of rapes committed, the manner in which rape is carried out, and the persons involved in it are tied to the social and sexual climate of an area. There are some societies, for instance, in which rape is virtually unknown. The Arapesh of New Guinea, according to Margaret Mead (1950:80–81), know nothing of rape beyond the fact that it is the unpleasant custom of the Nugum people to the southeast of them. Arapesh people, Mead reports, do not have any conception of male nature that would make rape understandable to them. On the other hand, the Gusii, a tribe located in the Kenya highlands, show a rape rate that is conservatively estimated to be four to five times that in the United States, with the dynamics of rape among the Gusii providing insight into the manner in which a culture can elicit an aggressive sex offense (LeVine, 1959).

In regard to the United States, at least two related hypotheses might be employed to explain the relationship between sexual mores and rape rates. The first would suggest that the more restricted and rare are opportunities for cooperative heterosexual performance (given a reasonably intense stress on such performance and some chance to engage in it), the higher the rape rate is apt to be. In such terms, forcible rape represents an almost classic response along the lines of Merton's (1957) paradigmatic representative of deviation, standing as a behavior emerging in the face of compelling pressures toward a kind of action combined with the absence of legitimatized opportunities for such action. The Merton-derived view, stated simply, would maintain that the more sexually permissive a society, the lower its forcible rape rate.

We did not find this position persuasive, however, and came to our data with an hypothesis which maintains that the forcible rape rate should be higher in a social setting in which there exists a relatively permissive sexual ethos than in one in which heterosexual contacts are less readily available because of cultural prohibitions—assuming, of course, that all other relevant items were equivalent in the two settings. It is believed that the relative "frustration" of the male is significantly higher in the more permissive setting than in the less permissive situation. Such frustration need have no relationship to objective conditions; it largely stems, we believe, from the discrepancy between what the person perceives to be "desirable," even demanded, behavior and the opportunities for such behavior. The hypothesis argues that a rejected male in a nonpermissive setting is more able to sustain his self-image by allegating that it is the setting itself that is responsible for any sexual setback he suffers. Women are inhibited, church rules are too oppressive, parents too strict, or laws too stringent—any of these conditions may be used to explain an inability to achieve a desired sexual goal, or more generally, recognition, power, or whatever it is that he believes to be his right. In the permissive setting, the rejected male becomes more hard-pressed to interpret his rejection. We would argue that forcible rape represents a response arising out of the chaos of a beleaguered self-image.

It may be suggested, of course, that in the permissive settings there are apt to be fewer potential rapists because there will be by the nature of things fewer rejected males. It is our belief, however, that in its present stage, despite growing sexual permissiveness, the culture of the United States keeps a significantly large number of men from achieving desired heterosexual relations of the type they desire both in its permissive and nonpermissive regions. In addition, we believe that cultural prohibitions reduce irritation in many instances by inhibiting a certain number of ideas about sexual conquest. It needs noting, perhaps, that rapists reasonably ought not desire what they do, or ought to control such desires. The attempt to explain the discrepant appearance of the rape impulse can find it a natural consequence of certain social arrangements, however, without deeming the behavior any the less meretricious.

An explication of our view appears from the behavior of men in the homosexual bars in San Francisco. Contrary to popular belief, they do not engage in a spontaneous round of pick-ups, despite the fact that almost all have gathered to form sexual liaisons. Rather there is a great deal of reticence and holding back with very tentative approaches. Hoffman (1969:55–66) explains the behavior in terms of the exclusive value homosexuals place on physical attractiveness, downgrading in the process other criteria that have some suasion in heterosexual relationships, criteria such as wealth, humor, education, and occupation:

> If they are rejected in making a conversational opening, this is interpreted (probably correctly) to mean a rejection of that crucial part of themselves, namely, their desirability as a sexual partner. Hence, their self-esteem is very much at stake and they have a great deal to lose by being rejected . . . a rejection by a desired partner is a rejection of the only valued part of one's identity in that world.

It is well known, of course, that homosexuals have a high homicide rate, growing out of sexual quarrels between partners (Guttmacher, 1960:83). We would interpret this, in terms of our hypothesis, as an indication of the relative unavailability to homosexuals of rationalizations to account for rejection. We would rely on the same reasoning to anticipate a high rate of forcible rape in a permissive city, such as Los Angeles is said to be, compared to a nonpermissive city, such as Boston is said to be.

THE REPORTED TOTALS OF RAPE

The differences between the reported forcible rape rates in Boston and Los Angeles are striking. In 1967, the *Uniform Crime Reports* of the Federal Bureau of Investigation (1968) indicated that the forcible rape rate for the Los Angeles-Long Beach Standard Metropolitan Statistical Area was 35.4 per 100,000 population. This was the highest rate in the United States. It was almost two and a half times the rate for the nation as a whole, and compares in that year with rates of 24.2 in Chicago and 17.6 in New York. The comparable rate for Boston was 7.7 per 100,000—almost one-half the overall rate for the United States and one-fifth that of Los Angeles.

The figures in the *Uniform Crime Reports* also show that forcible rape makes up a quite different proportion of the so-called index (i.e., serious) crimes in the two cities. In Boston, forcible rape (126 cases in 1967) constitutes about 0.5 percent of the index crimes (homicide, forcible rape, robbery, aggravated assault, burglary, larceny of $50 or more, and auto theft). In Los Angeles (1,421 rape cases) the offense accounts for slightly more than 1 percent of the total number of index crimes. The discrepant forcible rape rates, therefore, are not a function of different prevailing rates of crime in the two jurisdictions, but are specific to the offense itself. The 1967 figures, in addition, are not idiosyncratic manifestations of a single year, but rather reflect long-standing differences between the forcible rape rates reported from Boston and Los Angeles.

RAW MATERIAL: THE POLICE REPORTS

In the search for an explanation of the discrepancies in the forcible rape rates of Los Angeles and Boston, the writers examined in some detail a random sample of police reports on forcible rape cases in the two cities during 1967. This sample—136 cases from Los Angeles and 46 from Boston—was made available to us by the National Commission on the Causes and Prevention of Violence. These were the cases upon which the tallies of forcible rape forwarded to the FBI were founded.

Our first concern centered upon the accuracy of the reports themselves and, most importantly, upon their comparability. The alleged unreliability of original materials that form the basis for the neat tabular presentations of the *Uniform Crime Reports* is a common allegation among criminologists (Biderman, 1966; Cipes, 1963; Wolfgang, 1963). As far back as 1931, the National Commission on Law Observance and Enforcement (the Wickersham Commission) (1931:34) had commented caustically on "the unsystematic, often inaccurate, and more often incomplete statistics available for this country." Thirty-six years later, the President's Commission on Law Enforcement and Administration of Justice (1967:27) was no less appalled by the state of official statistics on crime. "If it is true, as commission surveys tend to indicate, that society has not yet found fully reliable methods for measuring the volume of crime," it was noted, "it is even more true that it has failed to find such methods for measuring the trend of crime." Particularly revealing was a compilation by the commission of instances in which changes in reporting procedures between 1959 and 1965 resulted in increases in reported crime in eleven major cities of between 26 and 202 percent.

Criticisms of reported criminal statistics, however, have not delved deeper than the official figures that appear in the *Uniform Crime Reports.* The present essay represents, to our knowledge, the first attempt to determine the credibility of raw materials from which the reported figures on crime are taken.

Instructions supplied to police departments by the Federal Bureau of Investigation request that an offense should be classified as forcible rape or attempted forcible rape if it involved actual or attempted sexual intercourse with a female forcibly and against her will. This definition excludes specifically cases of statutory rape, in which no force was employed and the victim was under the legal age of consent or otherwise was legally incapacitated from agreeing to participate in the act. Sodomy and incest offenses are also eliminated by definition from the forcible rape category.

The classification rules, therefore, are reasonably clear. It is another matter, however, to apply the rules carefully and uniformly around the nation, where the exigencies of daily police operations are not directed toward niceties of classification, since such activity holds out little promise for easing the work burden. Nor, for that matter, is the FBI able to exert any real suasion or provide much immediate guidance to an operating agency.

Beyond this, the offense of forcible rape is one whose commission is unusually involved in various kinds of spurious considerations. Victimization surveys (President's Commission, 1967:17) indicate that probably three and a half times as many offenses of forcible rape go unreported as come to police attention; and this figure may itself be an underestimation since respondents are apt to manifest the same close-mouthedness in the face of interviewers that led them in the first instance to keep to themselves the details of their experience. Finally, there exists considerable discretion for a law enforcement agency to interpret variantly the behavior of the victim, the offender, and the police officer himself before deciding whether or not the behavior should be classified as forcible rape, regarded as totally unfounded, or placed into another category of crime (see generally, Skolnick and Woodworth, 1967). The problem is not that such procedures are erratic. If they were, the similar approaches across the nation would at least make the data comparable. The difficulty is that individual departments develop localized methods of dealing with cases so that the kinds of acts reported as a given offense in one site refer to very different forms of behavior than those reported from another area.

THE BOSTON AND LOS ANGELES DATA

The truth of the preceding observations becomes strikingly evident the moment the ingredients of the police reports on forcible rape from Los Angeles and Boston are examined. A considerably broader definition of what constitutes forcible rape obviously prevails in Los Angeles as contrasted to Boston, and it is not unlikely that it is this definitional quirk which year after year serves to place Los Angeles far above the remainder of the nation's cities in its reported rate of forcible rape. Indeed, in Los Angeles virtually any instance in which a person appears to be seeking "sexual gratification"—to use the term favored by that city's detectives—is apt to be classified as a forcible rape.

Two cases illustrate this point. In the first, a twenty-five-year-old man persuaded two sixteen-year-old girls to accompany him into a public park. In the park, he proceeded, according to their statement, to tickle each of the girls on the stomach and knees for about five minutes. Subsequently, the girls complained to police. When police officers apprehended the man, he was asked, among other things: "Did you come in your pants?" His answer was: "Yes, but I didn't use my hands. I did it on my own." The "sexual gratification" motif of the crime, rather than any attempt or likely attempt at sexual intercourse, was apparently the rationale for its inclusion among the forcible rape cases reported from Los Angeles.

The second case, not dissimilar, involved a man who inched near two young girls on a busy suburban street, then pinched one of them on the bottom. A police officer, who had been watching the encounter, immediately arrested the man. In his statement, the offender indicated that he frequently engaged in this sort of activity. His main satisfaction from it, he said, derived from frightening the girls. His case was also listed under the heading of forcible rape.

Instances such as the foregoing never appear in the sample of forcible rapes in the files of the Boston Police Department, although we may assume that similar kinds of activity go on there. For their part, the Boston police include as forcible rape a number of cases in which very young females—girls of eight and nine—are molested in parks by equally immature boys. Sexual intercourse does not take place, and perhaps could not have taken place. Again, it seems likely that a number of such cases occur in Los Angeles, but the files on forcible rape there do not contain them, probably because they are classified under the more amorphous rubric of "delinquency."

The style and quality of police reports in Boston and Los Angeles in regard to forcible rape cases merit mention. The Boston materials, in general, tend to be much more terse and formal than their counterparts in Los Angeles—perhaps this constitutes a bit of testimony regarding the divergent cultures of the two cities themselves. Each Boston report is "respectfully submitted" by the investigator for the review of his superiors. The Boston police reports, too, reflecting perhaps the puritan tradition said to be immanent in the city, are notably laconic and vague about the details of what occurred between the victim and the alleged offender. Preliminary moves on the part of each are described, the setting is detailed. Then, according to the typical Boston report, the culprit fell upon his victim and "raped her."

In contrast, the Los Angeles documents tend to be in the nature of Dostoevskian endeavors, with a goodly amount of Mickey Spillane added. The verbal preliminaries of street encounters that end in actual or attempted rape are often detailed word for word. "I'm going to fuck you," is, for instance, a routine bit of pre-rape conversation. "This is for you, you God damn whore, you prostitute. I've heard about you," another offender is quoted as saying. Bras, capri pants, and other garments are often ripped asunder.

The detailed nature of the Los Angeles material offers the researcher opportunity to delve into the possible motivations involved in the rape cases and to obtain an inkling of the prior interaction and relationship between victim and offender. Officers describe with some precision the victim's condition at the time she is being interviewed, and they probe for inconsistencies and contradictions in the complainant's version of events. The officialese of the Boston reports, on the contrary, carries the impression that the nature of the events has been, perhaps rather summarily, pressed into a preordained formula.

For our purpose, neither the Los Angeles nor the Boston procedures offered much encouragement for sophisticated comparative study. It is patently obvious that what each department regards as the kind of case to be classified as forcible rape and forwarded to the *Uniform Crime Reports* for tabulation as such is far from equivalent. It is apparent, too, that even were the events included in the sample data comparable, the discrepant attention paid to various kinds of details of the offenses in Boston and Los Angeles makes item-by-item comparisons difficult along a number of seemingly fundamental dimensions.

The need for standardized police reporting methods for the entire nation seems so obvious to us, particularly after our sessions with the Boston and Los Angeles data, that the absence of such measures, given the nature of public and political concern about crime, appears almost incomprehensible.

THE PATTERNS OF RAPE

In regard to the materials with which we were working, we can only echo the lament that Barbara Wootton (1959:308–9) put on record after her overview of major criminological research of recent times; "Poor quality of our data is an obstacle to progress," she noted. "We are constantly obliged to use the materials that happen to be available as distinct from that which would ideally have been both relevant and adequate."

Our analysis was undertaken only after a considerable effort to render the materials more comparable by eliminating cases that seemed to fall far short of what most persons would reasonably regard as meeting the criteria provided by the FBI for classification as forcible rape. This procedure resulted in our discarding thirty reported forcible rapes from Los Angeles; to us, these cases seemed clearly to be at best mild instances of frottage or other kinds of nuisance behavior. We did not discard any cases from Boston, retaining even the two that involved juveniles. This outcome did not represent, however, a testament to the greater ability of the Boston police to follow FBI rules, but rather to their habit of rendering their reports in so bland a manner that it was difficult to find grounds on which to differ—or to agree.

The following items, among the many that we compared, demonstrated statistically significant differences in regard to forcible rape offenses in Los Angeles and Boston (see table 11.1):

1. More rape offenses were committed during weekends in Los Angeles than in Boston.
2. Rape offenses in Los Angeles were distributed with relative evenness over the twelve months of the year. In contrast, Boston showed a clear seasonal trend, the majority of rapes occurring between May and September, with peaks in May and August.
3. Rape offenses were much more likely to be committed by more than one person in Los Angeles than in Boston.
4. A higher proportion of offenders in Los Angeles than in Boston were black or Mexican-Americans, though this result was no more than a reflection of the differing distributions of ethnic groups within the two communities. In 1960, Los Angeles reported a black population of 13.5 percent compared to 9.8 percent in Boston, but the Mexican-Americans, although regarded in Los Angeles as a distinct group, are counted, as they should be,

Table 11.1. Patterns of Rape in Los Angeles and Boston.

	Los Angeles		*Boston*	
	Number	*Percent*	*Number*	*Percent*
Period of the Week During Which Rape Was Committed (N = 154)				
Weekday	50	46	30	65
Weekend	58	54	16	35
Total	108	100	46	100
$\chi^2 = 3.90$ Sig .05 df = 1				
Seasonal Distribution of Offenses (N = 154)				
January-April	37	34	10	22
May-August	35	33	26	57
September-December	36	33	10	22
Total	108	100	46	100
$\chi^2 = 7.84$ Sig .05 df = 2				
Accomplices to Rape (N = 154)				
No accomplice	58	54	33	72
Accomplice	50	46	13	28
Total	108	100	46	100
$\chi^2 = 4.3406$ Sig .05 df = 1				
Race of Offender (N = 151)				
White	26	24	17	39
Black	67	63	26	59
Other	14	13	1	2
Total	107	100	44	100
$\chi^2 = 5.98$ Sig .05 df = 2				
Relationship of Offender to Victim (N = 151)				
Stranger	60	56	39	91
Acquaintance	48	44	4	9
Total	108	100	43	100
$\chi^2 = 15.38$ Sig .05 df = 1				

as part of the "white" population by the Census Bureau, and their numbers are usually only roughly estimated by reference to surname tabulations by demographers.

5. Boston showed a significantly higher percentage of rape offenses in which the offender was a total stranger to the victim.

Variations in the ages of rape victims and, when known, or estimated, the ages of the offenders were rather similar in both cities. Thirty-five percent of the victims in Boston were under twenty-one years of age and 37 percent of the Los Angeles victims. However, 61 percent of the Boston victims were under thirty as compared to almost 75 percent of the Los Angeles victims. In regard to offenders, 74 percent of the Boston and 80 percent of the Los Angeles group were reported to be under thirty, although 30 percent of the Boston group compared to 20 percent of the Los Angeles group were under twenty. Thus, more young victims were in Los Angeles, and more young offenders in Boston. The age patterns of the two cities, it might be noted, are quite similar. The median age in Boston during the 1960 census was 32.9 and that in Los Angeles 33.2. Los Angeles had slightly more persons in the younger age brackets (30.5 percent under eighteen, compared to 28.7 percent in Boston), but not to an extent adequate to account for the discrepancies in the rape statistics. Boston had a slight edge in the number of potential rape victims, registering 52 percent of its population as female compared to 51.7 for Los Angeles.

The higher percentage of young rape victims in Los Angeles suggests that an explanation for the variations in rape rates might fruitfully be sought in sexual climates. Certainly, by American mythology younger women represent more desirable sexual objects, creatures whose possession is urged upon the adult male population insistently, especially in a site such as Los Angeles with its reputation for hospitality to starlets and nymphets. The disproportionately higher number of rapes occurring during the weekends in Los Angeles suggests further the possible relationship between the offense and the "party" climate, which might impel perceived implicit sexual promise coupled with explicit sexual denial. The seasonal variations add further testimony to the oft-noted relationship between warm weather, human proximity, and the commission of personal crimes. Be it short tempers or short skirts, correlates of hot temperatures, the summer months obviously create rape-eliciting conditions in Boston, while the more uniformly balmy climate in Los Angeles leads to a more even yearly distribution of rape offenders.

Finally, the considerably greater number of accomplice offenses in Los Angeles would seem to point to the social nature of the behavior, a product of group definitions of proper sexual performance rather than of individual deviations. In the same manner, the strikingly higher number of offenses involving "acquaintances" in Los Angeles would seem to add to the possibility that the west coast city possesses specific cultural characteristics that contribute to its high rape rate. Rape in Los Angeles is inflicted upon known persons, in relationships possessing rather more symbolic and interrelational content than those represented by the "stranger" rapes reported so much more often from Boston.

There were a number of general impressions derived from the data that could not be tested statistically because of the failure of the reports uniformly to take cognizance of the items. We gained the impression, however, that more victims in Boston than in Los Angeles received serious injuries during the course of the rape offenses.

In general, it appeared that in Boston rape was more likely to be committed by an offender who had broken into and entered an apartment and then confronted his victim or had seized his victim in some deserted street or alley. It would have been interesting to determine whether this first pattern, similar to that employed by the much-publicized Boston Strangler, also characterized the city's rape offenses in the period before the Strangler's activities were known. In Los Angeles, rape more often seemed to involve an automobile whose occupants sighted a female walking or waiting for public transportation and then either forcibly abducted her or offered her a ride and later committed the rape offense. In Los Angeles more than in Boston, it also was apt to be true that the offender and the victim had met and conversed either at a bar or at a party prior to any sexual involvement.

RESUME AND INTERPRETATION

What light, then, does the comparative material from Boston and Los Angeles shed on the offense of forcible rape as committed in two divergent settings?

Among other things, of course, it fulfills our expectation that the more permissive city, rather than the more restrictive city, reports the higher rape rate. Police policies and police efficiency and reporting irregularities may mitigate, however, some of the sharp distinctions between the Boston and Los Angeles rates, but it appears that they would not likely reverse the findings. It would be necessary, however, to translate the best figures available into age-specific rates, besides introducing other regularizing refinements, before they may be regarded as definitive materials, truly indicating the actual differences in the behavior they are supposed to reflect.

The other findings lead into deeper speculative waters, where the eddies are apt to be treacherous. We would suggest, mildly, that each of the discrete findings offers some hint that the cultural character—as well as the ecological nature—of Los Angeles might well play an important part in conditioning the rate of forcible rape. Such a statement does not, of course, preclude explanations that offer supplementary insight. Jane Jacobs (1961: 10–37), for example, in her discussion of the impact of the quality of city life on crime rates, has also singled out Boston and Los Angeles for comparison. She finds that neighborhoods such as the North End in Boston show extremely low crime rates because they are marked with a vivid, flowing street life, in the face of which surreptitious acts cannot readily take place. Los Angeles, she finds, encourages crime by its anonymity and its long stretches of sparsely settled territory.

The suggestions of Jacobs, as well as the views put forward earlier in this report, underline a number of pressing needs in regard to research about sex offenses. For one thing, the basic data must be improved immeasurably, so that not only identification items but also data responsive to particular hypotheses concerning rape can be fairly tested. From our viewpoint, we would particularly be interested in comparative studies between, for instance, climatically congruent cities such as Phoenix and Los Angeles, and ecologically similar settings such as Boston and, perhaps, San Francisco. It is only when such materials become available that we will be able to reach fully substantiated explanations of the relationship between social conditions and criminal offenses such as forcible rape.

REFERENCES

Amir, Menachem. 1971. *Patterns in Forcible Rape.* Chicago: University of Chicago Press.

Becker, Howard S. 1965. "Deviance and Deviates," *The Nation* 201:115–19

Biderman, Albert. 1966. "Social Indicators and Goals." Pp. 68–153 in Raymond A. Bauer, ed., *Social Indicators.* Cambridge, Massachusetts: MIT Press.

Cipes, Robert M. 1963. *The Crime War: The Manufactured Crusade.* New York: New American Library.

Federal Bureau of Investigation. 1968. *Uniform Crime Reports 1967.* Washington, D.C.: U.S. Government Printing Office.

Gaylin, Willard. 1970. *In the Service of Their Country: War Resistors in Prison.* New York: Viking.

Gillin, John L. 1946. *The Wisconsin Prisoner.* Madison, Wisconsin: University of Wisconsin Press.

Gunther, John. 1951. *Inside U.S.A.* New York: Harper & Brothers.

Guttmacher, Manfred S. 1951. *Sex Offenses.* New York: Norton.

——. 1960. *The Mind of the Murderer.* New York: Farrar, Straus & Giroux.

Hoffman, Martin. 1969. *The Gay World: Male Homosexuality and the Social Creation of Evil.* New York: Bantam.

Jacobs, Jane. 1961. *The Death and Life of Great American Cities.* New York: Random House.

Levin, Meyer. 1956. *Compulsion.* New York: Simon & Schuster.

LeVine, Robert A. 1959. "Gusii Sex Offenses: A Study in Social Control," *American Anthropologist* 61:965–90.

Licht, Hans. 1969. *Sexual Life in Ancient Greece.* Trans. by J.H. Freese. London: Panther Books.

Mead, Margaret. 1950. *Sex and Temperament in Three Primitive Societies.* New York: New American Library.

Merton, Robert K. 1957. *Social Theory and Social Structure,* rev. ed. Glencoe, Illinois: Free Press.

Montagu, Ashley. 1966. *The American Way of Life.* New York: Putnam.

National Commission on Law Observance and Enforcement. 1931. *Report on Criminal Statistics.* Washington, D.C.: U.S. Government Printing Office.

President's Commission on Law Enforcement and Administration of Justice. 1967. *The Challenge of Crime in a Free Society.* Washington, D.C.: U.S. Government Printing Office.

Skolnik, Jerome H. and J. Richard Woodworth. 1967. "Bureaucracy, Information and Social Control: A Study of a Morals Detail." Pp. 99–136 in David J. Bordua, ed., *The Police: Six Sociological Essays.* New York: Wiley.

Wolfgang, Marvin E. 1963. "Uniform Crime Reports: A Critical Appraisal," *University of Pennsylvania Law Review* 11:708–38.

Wootton, Barbara. 1959. *Social Science and Social Pathology.* New York: Macmillan.

12 Rape in New York City: A Study of Material in the Police Files and Its Meaning

DUNCAN CHAPPELL
AND SUSAN SINGER

FEW crimes of violence against the person in New York City give cause for more concern than forcible rape. While rates of commission for most index crimes are decreasing, forcible rapes have exhibited a marked and sustained rate of increase. In 1972, the number of forcible rapes reported to the police in New York City rose by nearly 36 percent (from 2,415 in 1971 to 3,271 in 1972) over the previous year,[1] while the clearance rates for forcible rape stayed at a steady 31 percent in both 1971 and 1972. With regard to the conviction rate, the city's Criminal Justice Coordinating Council (Office of the Mayor, 1972:93) reported that, "in Manhattan for the first six months of 1971 only one person received a felony rape sentence. Only 13 persons charged with felony rape were convicted on any charge."

These statistics are testimony to the almost complete immunity rapists in New York City have enjoyed from effective prosecution. In no recent year have more than 8 percent of rape arrests resulted in rape convictions. Past blame for this situation has been laid primarily upon the requirement under New York state law for every element of rape to be corroborated: the identity of an assailant, lack of consent, and penetration (see generally, Ludwig, 1970; Younger, 1971). In the absence of an independent witness to a rape, or the use of extreme force by an attacker, satisfaction of the corroboration requirements has been exceedingly difficult.

Following concerted criticism of the rape law and pressure for changes from, among others, feminist groups and the State District Attorneys Association, the New York state legislature in its 1972 session modified the corroboration requirements for rape. The new law, which itself has been harshly criticized (Oelsner, 1972; see also Pitler, 1973), in substance required that only the victim's testimony of the forcible, nonconsensual nature of the rape be corroborated. Corroboration of the victim's testimony of penetration or of the assailant's identity no longer had to be provided. The new law also eliminated an extension of the old corroboration requirement to "incidental" crimes like assault. Incidental crimes were now to be considered separately on their merits, even should the rape charge fail.

Despite modification of the corroboration requirement, however, feminist and other interested groups renewed their claims that the law still gave less weight to the testimony of rape victims than to other victims of violent crime. Under this renewed pressure the state legislature passed a new bill in 1974, eliminating the corroboration requirement.

While evidentiary requirements may be altered by the legislature, it is far more difficult for the legislature's mandates to affect actual police attitudes and practices. Given the expectations of the law revisions and the community anxiety about rape, it seems appropriate to examine the intrinsic qualities of the crime of forcible rape and to appraise contemporary investigative practice relating to forcible rape in New York City. It was decided to commence with data extracted from official police records.[2] The balance of this article reports the results of this survey.

The Data Source

A total of 704 complaints of forcible rape, or attempted rape, made to the police in New York City between February 1, 1970, and January 31, 1972, formed the core data source for this study.[3]

The methods adopted to obtain this sample of complaints deserve some description for they illustrate the dilemmas confronting researchers working with official police records, and particularly with records of a police force as large as that of New York City. To compile a city-wide sample of complaints in any crime category in New York City presents significant logistical problems. While the New York Police Department (N.Y.P.D.) maintains a massive central record bureau for conserving and distributing crime information, it is difficult to tap this data source on a crime-specific basis beyond a precinct level.[4] At the precinct level, and more recently at the divisional level, complaints of crime are kept according to *Uniform Crime Report* categories as well as in sequential order. But the only synthesis of this data derived from the seventy-five precincts and seventeen divisions of the N.Y.P.D. is a monthly crime analysis document prepared by the staff of the department's computer section. This document finds its ultimate resting place in the department's crime analysis section.

As might be imagined, monthly crime analysis documents of the weight and magnitude produced in the N.Y.P.D. rapidly come to occupy substantial physical space. The authors discovered that the cramped confines of the N.Y.P.D. Crime Analysis Section permitted the conserving of no more than two years' supply of these documents in dust-covered cartons. Each month as a new printout arrived, an old one went into the trash can.[5] At the time sampling began for this study, the record of February 1970, was the oldest survivor of this cycling process.

From the monthly computer printouts the authors identified

on a random basis a one-in-ten sample of all forcible rape complaints, and a one-in-three sample of all attempted rape complaints. A list of selected complaints was then forwarded to the department's central record section for pulling and copying of specific files.[6] These file copies were subsequently collated by staff members of the crime analysis section. During this collation process, all file references that might permit identification of rape victims were removed, a condition imposed upon the researchers by the department for gaining access to the rape files.

The N.Y.P.D., like most police forces around the country, currently uses one type of complaint form (called the U.F. 61) for the initial recording of information about all types of offenses. The file material obtained in this study included a copy of the U.F. 61 completed for each reported offense, together with any additional Complaint Report: Follow-Up Investigation sheets attached to the U.F. 61.[7] Follow-up investigation reports are completed by the detectives assigned to the case, while the U.F. 61 is normally filled out by a precinct officer verifying the initial complaint.

The U.F. 61 and allied documents used by the N.Y.P.D. seem designed to facilitate the gathering of general statistical data about all categories of crime rather than to assist with the task of investigating a particular type of offense, such as forcible rape. A substantial portion of the U.F. 61 is occupied by space to be used for recording details of property stolen in the course of a crime—information rarely relevant in rape. The U.F. 61 also contains many open-ended questions for completion by police officers, rather than comprehensive check lists that might be devoted to specific evidentiary factors required in a crime such as rape.

A relatively uniform style of crime reporting prevails, marked by a terseness and rightness of expression, and legal and police terminology that rarely lapse into the vernacular. An excerpt drawn from the initial and follow-up reports of a rape illustrates this point: [8]

CASE #1

Details as reported by complainant and/or initial investigating officer:

Ptl. R. reports that complainant states that at time and place of occurrence two male P-R did force her into an auto and then in the vicinity of the Brooklyn Bridge did rape her.

Details as reported by follow-up investigating officer:

1. The undersigned interviewed the complainant in this case but she could add no further information than that which she had previously reported.
2. The undersigned interviewed persons in the area of occurrence in an effort to obtain information that would assist in this investigation but this was without results.
3. Alarm No. __ to remain active.
4. In view of the above-stated facts, the assigned requests that this case be marked CLOSED pending any new developments at which time the prompt and proper POLICE action will be taken.

While the overall quality and quantity of data in the New York reports was found to be somewhat lacking, enough information was available to enable the authors to delineate the general pattern of rape in New York City. Such variables as time frame, location, victim-offender relationship, force and weapons used by the offender against the victim, modus operandi of the offender, and some characteristics of both victim and offender have been used to determine this pattern.

Where possible, comparative references have been made to the earlier studies of forcible rape made by Amir (1971) in Philadelphia and Chappell et al. (1971) in Boston and Los Angeles. Because both of these studies excluded both attempted rape and unfounded cases, comparisons will use only offenses regarded as established cases of rape in New York City.

CORRELATES OF RAPE OFFENSES

The Time Frame

Criminologists have long delighted in plotting seasonal and allied trends among different categories of crime. In the case of forcible rape, long-term, seasonally-adjusted rates in the United States show a well-established pattern, with the majority of rapes occurring in the warmer months between May and September (Federal Bureau of Investigation, 1972:26–27). Amir's Philadelphia findings and the Boston police records both exhibited trends akin to the national pattern. However, in New York City and Los Angeles, as table 12.1 demonstrates, no clear seasonal pattern emerges, complaints of forcible rape being quite evenly distributed among the months of the year.

Probably of greater practical significance for planning allocation of police manpower and resources are the patterns of rape determined by day and hour of occurrence. In New York City, Philadelphia, Boston, and Los Angeles, as table 12.1 illustrates, the peak period for rape is the weekend. However, the weekend trend is more marked in Philadelphia and Los Angeles than it is in the other two cities.

In table 12.2 an analysis has been made of rape complaints in New York City according to the three eight-hour police tours of duty. It will be noticed that the day shift has the lowest incidence of complaints. The peak period for offenses reported to the police is 8:00 P.M. to 2:00 A.M.

The Location

Of substantial importance in designing tactics and techniques aimed at the prevention of rape, including giving early warning advice to potential victims of sexual attacks, is a consideration of the locations of these attacks.

Regrettably, the N.Y.P.D. records of rape contain only meager details and descriptions of the place of initial meeting between a rapist and his victim and the place where a rape is actually committed. But some indication of the danger spots can be obtained from table 12.3. It shows that initial encounters between a rapist and his victim take place most frequently in an interior setting, like an apartment building. Where streets or allied external sites are the setting for initial encounters, table 12.3 suggest that they are likely to lead to a shifting of the crime event to an interior location.

Table 12.1. Comparison of Forcible Rape Complaints in New York City, Philadelphia, Boston, and Los Angeles.

	New York City		*Philadelphia*		*Boston*		*Los Angeles*	
	Number	*Percent*	*Number*	*Percent*	*Number*	*Percent*	*Number*	*Percent*
Seasonal Distribution[a]								
January-April	119	30.5	171	26.4	10	22	37	34
May-August	135	34.7	266	41.1	26	57	35	33
September-December	135	34.7	209	32.3	10	22	36	33
Total	389	100	646	100	46	101	108	100
Period of the Week								
Weekday	243	65.5	371	57.4	30	65	50	46
Weekend	128	34.5	275	42.5	16	35	58	54
Total	371[b]	100	646	100	46	100	108	100

[a]No information was available in 63 cases of completed rape, 14 cases of attempted rape, and 27 unfounded complaints.
[b]No information was available in 18 cases.

Table 12.2. Classification of Rape Complaints by New York City Police Tours of Duty.

	Rape		*Attempted Rape*		*Unfounded Complaints*	
	Number	*Percent*	*Number*	*Percent*	*Number*	*Percent*
24:00–07:59	144	39.6	86	36.5	22	30.9
08:00–15:59	55	15.1	57	24.2	16	22.5
16:00–23:59	159	43.8	92	39.1	31	43.6
Various	5	1.3	0	0.0	2	2.8
Total[a]	363	100.0	235	100.0	71	100.0

[a]No information was available in 26 cases of completed rape, 4 cases of attempted rape, and 5 unfounded complaints.

Table 12.3. Place of Initial Meeting Between Offender and Victim and Place of Occurrence of Offense: New York City.

	COMPLETED RAPE				*ATTEMPTED RAPE*				*UNFOUNDED COMPLAINTS*			
	Initial Meeting		*Actual Occurrence*		*Initial Meeting*		*Actual Occurrence*		*Initial Meeting*		*Actual Occurrence*	
	No.	*Pct.*	*No.*	*Pct.*	*No.*	*Pct.*	*No.*	*Pct.*	*No.*	*Pct.*	*No.*	*Pct.*
Apartment (pvt.)	128	39.3	178	46.5	64	28.4	73	30.7	18	36.7	30	40.5
Apartment bldg.	42	12.8	62	16.1	63	28.0	68	28.5	5	10.2	7	9.4
Private house	7	2.1	9	2.3	2	0.9	2	0.8	0	0.0	0	0.0
Hotel/motel	10	3.1	18	4.7	4	1.8	5	2.1	4	8.2	6	8.1
Commercial bldg.	15	4.6	5	1.3	10	4.4	9	3.7	2	4.0	2	2.7
Auto, taxi, etc.	10	3.0	39	10.1	5	2.2	17	7.1	1	2.0	7	9.4
Street	88	27.0	17	4.4	59	26.2	29	12.2	16	32.7	16	21.6
Vacant bldg.	3	0.9	8	2.1	0	0.0	3	1.3	0	0.0	2	2.7
Yard, path	8	2.4	24	6.2	6	2.6	16	6.7	0	0.0	2	2.7
Woods, park	12	3.6	18	4.6	9	4.0	12	5.0	2	4.0	2	2.7
Miscellaneous	3	0.9	5	1.3	3	1.3	4	1.6	1	2.0	0	0.0
Total	326	100	383	100	225	100	238	100	49	100	74	100

NOTE: For Initial Meeting, no information was available in 63 cases of completed rape, 14 cases of attempted rape, and 27 cases of unfounded complaints; for Actual Occurrence, no information was available in 6 cases of completed rape, 1 case of attempted rape, and 2 unfounded complaints.

Street Encounters

A traditional image of rape is probably one of women being plucked from the street or sidewalk and dragged into bushes or into an alley where the sexual violation occurs. In reality, the pattern of attacks in New York City suggests that women who are seized in a public place like a street, subway, or park will be forced by their assailant to some building to be raped. Two cases illustrate this modus operandi:

> CASE #2
> Complainant stated that she hailed a gypsy cab at (10:30 P.M.) 182nd St. and S. Blvd. After telling tale about having to stop for something, driver entered apartment in vicinity of M and T Street and returned with two other perpetrators. Grabbing complainant, they carried her to roof, where they removed her clothing and committed multiple acts of rape and sodomy upon complainant and forced her to commit multiple acts of sodomy upon them. After a period of three hours, perpetrators fled.

> CASE #3
> Complainant reports that at (11 P.M.) 73 St. and A. Avenue she exited from shop. Complainant was grabbed by two male Negroes. Walked complainant south to her place of residence with knife in her ribs. Then raped and assaulted complainant and removed property from her apartment (jewelry and money).

In his Philadelphia study, Amir (1971:140) discounted the "image of an offender lurking in the dark waiting for his victim. . . ." "Crime in the street evokes, among other things, images of rape. Reality does not consort with this myth," observed Amir. By contrast, New York City data tend to "consort with this myth." More than one-third of all *initial* encounters between rapists and their victims took place either on a public street or in a park or similar open space. Many public encounters seem to be associated as well with public transportation facilities, unsuspecting victims being seized at night while waiting for or traveling in a bus, cab, or subway. Others involve victims who accept a ride in a car from a stranger. While, then, the streets in themselves may not be the scene of most rapes, they certainly constitute important points of encounter for the rapist and his victim.

Interior Encounters

Attacks upon victims taking place in an internal location in New York City accounted for 73 percent of the sample. A majority of rapes within buildings occur in, or in close proximity to, apartment dwellings—a reflection, among other things, of the living patterns and environment of the city. Apartment dwellers in New York far outnumber the occupiers of private houses both generally and as rape victims.

The N.Y.P.D. rape complaints suggest that in private as well as public apartment buildings elevators and allied "interior public space" areas represent high-risk locations for rape. As the case below illustrates, rape victims often made initial contact with offenders in an apartment elevator or in a lobby, and then were forced to accompany their assailants to a more secluded spot:

> CASE #4
> Complainant states that as she entered her apartment building lobby perpetrators entered behind her and followed her into the elevator. As elevator ascended perpetrator #1 drew gun and stated "this is a stick up," whereupon complainant screamed and said perpetrator struck her with fist. When elevator reached 4th floor, perpetrators dragged complainant to the 4th floor stairway landing where again struck her about the body and face. Perpetrator #2 then ripped complainant's dress and removed her underpants and perpetrator #1 forced complainant to commit an act of sexual intercourse. Perpetrators then removed complainant's purse, credit cards, and $8 in cash.

It will be seen in table 12.3 that almost 47 percent of the completed rapes, and 31 percent of the attempted rapes, were committed inside individual apartment units. The proportion of similar attacks occurring inside apartments in public housing projects was only 18 percent. Better interior public space security in private housing complexes may account in part for this variation with enhanced surveillance of lobbies, elevators, and stairways, requiring offenders to adopt alternative tactics to gain access to victims.

The differences may also reflect variations in reporting and recording in regard to victims living in public and private housing. The latter group, perhaps, may be more willing to notify police of sexual attacks occurring in any location while the former group may mainly reserve its complaints for those interior public-space attacks which bear all the trappings of a stranger-to-stranger crime. The presence of an offender within the victim's apartment can be viewed as a potentially "compromising circumstance" by the police, influencing victim reporting behavior and police recording practice.

Other Offenses

A number of the rapes of victims within their apartments in the N.Y.P.D. sample bear the hallmark of opportunistic attacks. Thus, a burglar, upon finding an apartment to be occupied by a vulnerable victim, rapes as well as steals. Case #5 provides an illustration of such an event:

> CASE #5
> Complainant reports that she was awakened in her apartment at 5:00 A.M. by two perpetrators, M/N, one holding a gun. Forced complainant to remove clothes. Perpetrator #1 had sexual intercourse. Perpetrators then fled taking TV, clothes, cash. Entrance by jimmying front door. Burglary-rape.

Investigator's remarks make it clear that the police viewed the primary objective of the crime as burglary, with rape as an afterthought. But the sparseness of detail makes it very difficult to determine with confidence the proportion of cases in which rape was not the principal motivating factor of an offender.

In Philadelphia, Amir (1971:179) found that among the 646 cases in his sample, 26 (4 percent) involved an "explosive rape" of a victim after the commission of another felony by an offender (in almost all cases burglary or robbery). In a further 37 cases (6 percent) in Amir's sample, the "victim was robbed or her place was ransacked after the rape."

The authors' New York City sample contained a much larger proportion of felony-rapes, as they are termed by Amir. Of the 389 cases of rape in the sample, 30 (8 percent) seemed to involve instances of rape following the commission of some other felony. In a further 72 cases (19 percent), the victim of a rape was also the victim of a contemporaneous robbery or burglary, as in Cases #3 and #4.

The actual number of felony rapes committed in New York City is almost certainly far larger than even these official records suggest. Apart from unreported rapes involving the commission of additional felonies, the authors were told by a number of N.Y.P.D. detectives that quite frequently attempted rapes, and on occasion forcible rapes, accompanied by a contemporaneous robbery, were classified as robbery rather than rape. The motivation for making this classification appears to lie in the acknowledged difficulty of establishing a case of rape in New York City.

Although not included among the cases studied in the New York City sample, a number of rape victims also became the victims of homicide. These events were classified for police and statistical purposes as homicides rather than rapes. In 1972, 41 victims of sex crimes (mainly rape but including sodomy and allied offenses) in New York City were killed by their assailants. This figure was provided by the N.Y.P.D. Crime Analysis Section and represented 3 percent of the 1,466 homicides recorded in New York City in that year. While specific figures are not available, officers of the N.Y.P.D. Crime Analysis Section believe that homicidal rape has increased in recent years. In 1965, for example, an internal N.Y.P.D. statistical study showed that of the 632 homicides committed that year in New York City, only 4 involved victims of rape.[9] Since 1965, rapes have been grouped with other sex crimes in annual N.Y.P.D. statistical studies of homicide, barring any reliable analysis of this felony rape category.

The Victim

We have already commented upon the purging process applied by the N.Y.P.D. to prevent identification of rape victims by the authors. This precluded, among other things, analysis of factors like the victim's place and area of residence, and the distance between her residence and that of the offender. Nor has it been possible to undertake a comparative analysis of such basic issues as the age and race of victims and offenders. In fact, there is no provision made in the N.Y.P.D. crime complainant form (U.F. 61) for recording the victim's age and race.

In only 13 percent of the sample was it possible to identify the race of victims, and the age of victims could be obtained in only 24 percent of the sample. Reporting of the race of victims by police appeared to be haphazard; information about age seemed most likely to be noted when the victim was a child or teenager. Of the 93 cases, 76 involved victims under 20 years of age; 30 victims were under 15 years of age. Under New York State law, and the law of most other states, the victim's age can be a material element in determining the degree of rape. A male, for example, is guilty of first-degree rape in New York if he engages in sexual intercourse with a female who is less than 11 years old, and of second-degree rape if he has intercourse with a female less than 14 years old, though no force or compulsion may be used.

Admittedly, information about a victim's age, and particularly her race (Geis, 1965) can be viewed as sensitive data which should be collected and recorded only to satisfy compelling purposes. It is suggested that these purposes exist in the case of forcible rape. For instance, detailed knowledge of the age structure of rape victims in a metropolitan area like New York City can assist in identifying rape-prone categories of females toward whom specific prevention campaigns can be directed. Similarly, knowledge of the race of rape victims can be of substantial significance when assessing broader trends in this crime category. The relative incidence of inter- and intraracial sexual attacks seems to be an important indicator of the level of social antagonism or interaction between ethnic groups in the community.

Victim-Offender Relations

During the present study, the authors had many informal discussions with members of the N.Y.P.D. A prevailing attitude expressed by the police was that the majority of rapes in New York City involved couples who met initially in a bar or in a similar social setting, and who subsequently misinterpreted one an-

Table 12.4. Interpersonal Relationships Between Offender and Victim: New York City.

	Rape		*Attempted Rape*		*Unfounded*	
	Number	*Percent*	*Number*	*Percent*	*Number*	*Percent*
Stranger	225	71.7	155	79.1	17	38.6
Stranger, but seen before	20	6.4	11	5.6	3	6.8
Acquaintance	50	15.9	20	10.2	11	25.0
Neighbor	0	0.0	1	0.5	0	0.0
Close friend/boy friend	8	2.5	1	0.5	11	25.0
Family friend	1	0.3	1	0.5	1	2.3
Relative	10	3.2	7	3.6	1	2.3
Total[a]	314	100.0	196	100.0	44	100.0

[a]No information was available in 75 cases of completed rape, 43 cases of attempted rape, and 32 unfounded complaints.

other's sexual intentions. The ultimate outcome of such an episode was viewed by the police as an unjustified complaint of rape, when reality, in their eyes, suggested that the woman "merely" had been seduced. Another frequently expressed police opinion was that a significant proportion of New York City rapes involved complaints by irate mothers about daughters who found themselves to be pregnant. Seeking to avoid parental anger, the daughters, who had been cooperative in their liaison, would allege rape.

The findings of this present survey represent notable variation from the police-held norm. In table 12.4, adopting a classification evolved by Amir, we analyzed the relationships between victims and offenders in the New York City sample. It will be seen immediately that an overwhelming proportion of the victims and offenders were total strangers. The category classified as "acquaintance" contains, among others, members of the social meeting fraternity assumed by the police to predominate among rape cases in New York City. The category classified as "close friend or boyfriend" tends to accommodate most of the so-called "pregnant daughter" cases.

In table 12.5 a comparison is made between Amir's Philadelphia data and the New York City findings. In New York City there were far more stranger-upon-stranger attacks than in Philadelphia. It will also be noticed that neighbor-upon-neighbor attacks were apparently nonexistent in New York City, but accounted for almost 20 percent of Amir's victim-offender relationships.[10] The high proportion of stranger-upon-stranger attacks discovered in the New York City study is also out of accord with the results of a number of other research investigations of rape (see e.g., President's Commission, 1967:40; National Commission, 1969:25).

Table 12.5. Patterns of Rape in Philadelphia and New York City.

	Philadelphia		*New York City*	
	Number	*Percent*	*Number*	*Percent*
Interpersonal Relationships Between Offender and Victim				
Stranger	273	42.5	225	71.7
Stranger, but seen before	62	9.6	20	6.4
Acquaintance	93	14.5	50	15.9
Neighbor	125	19.5	0	0.0
Close friend/boy friend	39	6.1	8	2.5
Family friend	34	5.3	1	0.3
Relative	16	2.5	10	3.2
Total	642[a]	100	314[b]	100
Race of Offender[c]				
White	216	16.7	123	25.4
Black	1,066	82.5	285	59.0
Puerto Rican	10	0.7	74	15.3
Other	0	0.0	2	0.4
Total	1,292	100	484	100
Age of Offender				
Under 15 yrs.	47	3.6	10	2.8
15–19 yrs.	521	40.3	73	20.3
20–24 yrs.	332	25.6	101	28.2
25–29 yrs.	207	16.0	81	22.6
30–34 yrs.	98	7.7	48	13.4
35–39 yrs.	37	2.8	23	6.4
40–44 yrs.	21	1.6	12	3.3
45 yrs. and over	29	2.2	10	2.8
Total	1,292[d]	100	358	100

[a]In Amir (1971:237), the total is 646, but his category of "no information" (4 cases) was deleted to make categories comparable. Hence percentages here differ slightly from those presented by Amir.

[b]No information was available in 75 cases.

[c]See Amir (1971:44). These figures represent the actual number of identified offenders, rather than the number of cases. No information was available about 51 offenders in New York City.

[d]*Ibid.*, p. 52. No information was available about 177 offenders.

Within the time frame of fourteen years between the earliest and latest study, we may be experiencing a trend toward a steadily expanding proportion of stranger-upon-stranger attacks.

Another possible explanation for the large number of stranger-upon-stranger attacks included in the New York City sample may be the pervasive but largely submerged influence of the New York State corroboration law. Its stringency was said to produce the low conviction rate for rapists brought to trial. Conscious of this conviction rate, and the corroboration requirements, the N.Y.P.D. may have screened out at the reporting stage most of the rape complaints which might in any way contain "suspect" victim-offender relationships, placing on the official record sheet only those complaints viewed as "genuine" stranger-to-stranger crimes. A similar pattern may also have occurred among rape victims, many realizing the futility of reporting to the police anything but stranger-to-stranger crimes.

If this thesis is correct, it should be anticipated that following the liberalization and then the abolition of the corroboration law in New York, a considerable increase of nonstranger rapes would appear in official records as part of the overall increase in reporting of rape. However, it is not clear that these new laws have substantially changed police attitudes or practices so much that this will be reflected in official complaint reports.

Force, Weapons, and Injuries

In about one-third of the cases, the offender was known or believed to be armed, most frequently with a knife. Weapons were used in the overwhelming majority of cases to intimidate victims into submissiveness, rather than physically to incapacitate them. While in 10 cases mention was made in the files that a victim was stabbed or cut by an offender, and in 7 cases victims were struck by miscellaneous weapons like clubs, chairs, or bottles, no victim was reported shot.[11]

Despite the relatively small use of weapons by offenders, in an estimated 15 to 20 percent of the cases victims appeared to require some hospital treatment for physical injuries. These injuries resulted, in the main, from beatings applied by offenders to intimidate or subdue victims who offered resistance. It was not possible to assess the gravity of the injuries from data contained in the files.

In approximately two-thirds of all cases in the sample, some form of physical force was used by offenders during the course of an offense. This force normally amounted to rough physical handling—pushing, pulling, holding, or slapping—rather than more violent acts such as kicking or punching.

Investigation and Detection

With such a large proportion of stranger-to-stranger crimes in the sample of New York City rapes, it is not surprising to discover that the overall detection rate for forcible rape by the N.Y.P.D. is very low. Of the 388 forcible rapes, and 239 attempted rapes for which information was available, slightly more than one-third were cleared by arrest. In the balance of the cases the offender either remained unknown, or was identified as a suspect but not apprehended. In comparison, nationally in 1971 the FBI (1972:14) reported a solution rate of 55 percent in cases of forcible rape, a decrease of 3 percent from the previous year.

In the follow-up reports attached to the initial complaint forms, investigating officers noted in terse terms the reasons for failing to solve rapes. In 65 percent of rapes and 75 percent of attempted rapes, results of the investigation were simply termed "negative" or "inconclusive."

The sample data give the impression that when a rapist used or threatened substantial violence to a victim, or when an attack was believed to be one of a series of rapes by the same offender, police were more likely to view the situation as serious, meriting allocation of substantial manpower resources to an investigation. Lack of corroboration was mentioned by police in only six cases as the reason for failing to solve a rape. In cases that resulted in an arrest, however, the presence or absence of corroboration appeared to be a major factor affecting the *outcome of further proceedings* against an alleged offender.

Table 12.6. Time Interval Before Offense Reported to Police in New York City.

	Completed Rape			*Attempted Rape*			*Unfounded Complaints*		
	Number	*Percent*	*Cumulative Percent*	*Number*	*Percent*	*Cumulative Percent*	*Number*	*Percent*	*Cumulative Percent*
Less than 30 min. after	66	17.9	17.9	77	32.9	32.9	15	21.4	21.4
30 min.–under 1 hr.	44	11.8	29.7	37	15.8	48.7	12	17.1	38.5
1 hr.–under 2 hr.	37	10.0	39.7	43	18.3	67.0	9	12.9	51.4
2 hr.–under 4 hr.	72	19.4	59.1	32	13.7	80.7	8	11.4	62.8
4 hr.–under 24 hr.	93	25.2	84.3	34	14.5	95.2	21	30.0	92.8
1 day–less than 3 days	13	3.5	87.8	7	3.0	98.2	2	2.9	95.7
3 days–less than 1 week	12	3.2	91.0	2	0.9	99.1	0	0.0	95.7
1 week–less than 4 weeks	14	3.8	94.8	2	0.9	100.0	0	0.0	95.7
4 weeks–less than 6 months	17	4.6	99.4	0	0.0	—	1	1.4	97.1
6 months & after	2	0.5	100.0	0	0.0	—	2	2.9	100.0
Total[a]	370	100.0		234	100.0		70	100.0	

[a]No information was available in 19 cases of rape, 5 cases of attempted rape, and 6 unfounded complaints.

Table 12.7. Number of Cases with or Without Accomplices: Philadelphia/New York City/Boston/Los Angeles[a] *(Rape Only).*

	Philadelphia (Amir)		*New York*		*Boston (Chappell, et al.)*		*Los Angeles (Chappell, et al.)*	
	Number	*Percent*	*Number*	*Percent*	*Number*	*Percent*	*Number*	*Percent*
No Accomplice	370	57.3	298	76.6	33	72	58	54
Accomplice	276	42.7	91	23.4	13	28	50	46
Total	646	100.0	389	100.0	46	100	108	100

[a]See Amir (1971:200); Chappell et al. (1971:187).

Table 12.6 shows the time interval elapsing before cases included in the sample were reported. It will be seen that the overwhelming majority (80 percent) of attempted rapes were reported to the police within four hours. There were, however, greater delays in reporting forcible rapes, 15 percent remaining outstanding for twenty-four hours or more, and 9 percent beyond seventy-two hours. The possibility that some victims may suffer physical injury or shock following a completed sexual attack may explain these variations in reporting time. In addition, it is not uncommon for a woman who has been raped to go home to cleanse herself before reporting an offense to the police, even if she has received no injuries requiring immediate hospital treatment. This delay may not only lessen the chance of apprehending the offender, but also destroy physical evidence, such as semen, that could provide corroboration of the victim's story.

THE OFFENDERS

Single and Group Offenses

Slightly more than 75 percent of the rapes, and 85 percent of the attempts, were known or believed to involve a single offender. Generally, the New York City data revealed far fewer paired and multiple offender rapes than might have been anticipated from other studies. Table 12.7 compares rapes committed with or without accomplices in Philadelphia, New York City, Boston, and Los Angeles. Only Boston, it will be noticed, had a percentage of crimes without accomplices approaching that of New York City.

Age and Race

Table 12.5 also presents the data available in the New York City sample contrasted with the findings of Amir concerning the race of offenders. The different ethnic composition of the populations of New York City and Philadelphia is reflected in the much larger proportion of blacks involved in rapes in Philadelphia, and the appearance of a substantial number of Puerto Ricans among the New York City offenders. In both cities blacks are disproportionately represented in the rape statistics, although less so in New York City where one quarter of the rapes were known or believed to have been committed by whites.

It is also apparent from table 12.5 that a very different age structure exists among the New York City offender group. Overall, offenders in New York City tended to be significantly older than their counterparts in Philadelphia. Amir's peak age category for rape, 15 to 19, contains 40 percent of his offender group but only 20 percent of New York City offenders. In New York City almost 50 percent of the offenders were aged 25 or over compared with only 30 percent of offenders of Philadelphia.

Amir's finding concerning the relationship of age to group rape is supported by the New York City data. We have already remarked on the high proportion of rapes with no accomplices found among the New York City sample. An analysis of the age of offenders involved in single, paired, or multiple rapes confirmed that the older the offender, the less likely he was to be a participant in a group offense in New York City.

CONCLUSIONS

Disposition of Rape Cases and Deterrence

Little mention has been made up to this point of the disposition of the rape cases in the sample in which an offender was arrested. In fact, information on this topic simply was not recorded in the police files studied. Conversations with N.Y.P.D. detectives suggested that in the vast majority of cases, disposition consisted of dismissal of all charges against an offender, usually on the basis of lack of corroboration of the victim's story. Without exception, the police officers with whom the authors spoke were extremely pessimistic about the possibility of successfully prosecuting a rapist in New York City.

The very few rape disposition statistics available from any

source tend to support this gloomy police prognosis. Current clearance rates indicate that the chance of being apprehended for a reported rape in New York City is about one in three, while the chance of being convicted of rape, particularly rape in the first degree, remains slight. Under these circumstances, if theories of deterrence have any validity, it is probably not surprising that rape is increasing so dramatically in New York City. For the rapist who might consider the consequences, the odds of evading apprehension, and if apprehended, of being convicted, must appear particularly favorable.

Data Deficiencies and Crime Complaint Forms

It is particularly disturbing to note extensive informational deficiencies existing in police files. The specific data absent from these files are not only of interest to social scientists; they are also of direct interest and relevance to the criminal justice system. What is in fact missing in many cases from N.Y.P.D. rape files is evidence that may be crucial to the successful handling of cases by the prosecution and courts.

We are well aware that in many cases of rape, evidence of any type is at a minimum, and particularly evidence corroborating the victim's account of the crime. However, on the basis of our study of the police files, we are convinced that the lack of a well-designed crime complaint form for reporting forcible rapes, and other sexual offenses, substantially increases the likelihood that there will be a failure to collect data essential to the subsequent successful prosecution of the rapist.

Few crimes present such thorny problems for the proper exercise of police discretion as does forcible rape. In ensuring that the necessary elements of the offense are made out, a police officer is called upon to make difficult decisions of law and fact (cf., Comment, 1968). Often these decisions must be made under conditions of considerable tension and stress, the officer having to deal with a distraught and perhaps incoherent victim. Under the circumstances, it is not surprising that an officer who takes the victim's initial complaint may fail to observe, or ask about, very important evidentiary matters. If, as is probably frequently the case, the victim initially reports the crime by phone or personally to an officer who has little experience handling rape cases, the chances that evidential clues will be missed are increased.

In the authors' view, the development of a new police crime complaint form for reporting rape and allied sexual offenses should receive the highest priority.

Corroboration, Police, and Jurors

At the outset of this article we mentioned that past blame for the low level of rape convictions in New York City was placed primarily upon the requirement under New York State law for each element of rape to be corroborated. The legislative modification and subsequent elimination of this requirement in 1974 may well expand the range of rape cases capable of being brought to prosecution, but comparative experience in California suggests that modification of the corroboration requirements is unlikely, by itself, to increase substantially the conviction rate in rape cases, and with it the deterrent capacity of the criminal justice system.

In California, following the common law tradition, no special requirements of corroboration are demanded in sexual offenses like rape (Younger, 1971:264). In legal theory California's so-called noncorroboration law permits the conviction of an offender on the basis of unsupported testimony of a woman that she was raped. But as a highly experienced Los Angeles County Prosecutor (quoted in Stumbo, 1972) has commented: "Legal theory is not legal reality . . . and in California, just like anywhere else in this country, a woman who hopes to win a rape case better have plenty of corroboration."

The same prosecutor, offering an explanation of the low conviction rate for rapes in Los Angeles County (less than 10 percent), said: "It [the conviction rate] all depends on the attitudes of the jurors and the cops who handled the rape in the first place. Most of the time, both are inadequate. Jurors are usually 12 hung up people who won't convict in a rape case if they can avoid it. And the police usually don't have the time, manpower, or inclination to thoroughly investigate a rape before they dump it on us to prosecute."

These remarks are almost certainly very pertinent to the situation in New York City. Sloppy police work, including a failure to secure appropriate evidence from the victim at the initial reporting stage, or to obtain the willing cooperation of the victim, can make the subsequent prosecution of any apprehended offender a fruitless exercise, no matter what changes are effected in the law of rape. And even if the police and prosecution are able to construct a strong case, convincing a jury that a woman has been raped is an exceptionally difficult task. The general cynicism of the male dominated criminal justice system in regard to rape is apparently shared by jurors (Stumbo, 1972:1): "Unless her head is bashed in or she's ninety-five years old, or it's some other kind of extreme case, jurors just can't believe a woman was raped. There's a suspicion that it was her fault, that she led the guy on, or consented—consent is the hardest thing to disprove. It's just his word against hers."

The Treatment of the Rape Victim

Changing the attitudes of criminal justice agency personnel and jurors toward rape represents a formidable job, for many of these attitudes are probably also those held by the majority of the community. But an excellent point of commencement for any attempt at change is with the law enforcement officers who are responsible for the investigation of rape.

Probably no factor is more crucial to the outcome of rape proceedings than the way the victim is treated by the police. Women's groups believe that the present treatment of rape victims by police represents one of the major deterrents to reporting this crime and to eliciting the further cooperation of those victims who officially complain that they have been raped.

One of the most sensitive and difficult police tasks in dealing initially with rape victims is eliciting information about the event. The manner in which this information is obtained can have a profound influence on the subsequent attitude adopted by the victim toward the police and the prosecution. Take, for instance, the following description (Williams, 1972) given by a victim of a brutal rape, of her encounters with the sex squad of the Washington, D.C. Police Department:

> "It's like, for instance, I had to tell the same guy four times that yes, that was the rope they used to tie me up with, and well, I had to tell the same story to three or four different guys, and it was like they couldn't care less." And she poured out the major frustrations, like having to sign one statement, which she said was fully accurate, and then later, at headquarters, being interviewed for a second statement, which contained, naturally, inconsistencies from the first one, and she'd even pointed out some of the inconsistencies to the cop taking the second statement and he didn't even change it to accommodate her memory, and so now there are two conflicting statements, both signed by her, and she knows that if they should ever catch the two and bring them to trial, the defense would butcher her on the stand because of the statements.

Illustrations such as this indicate the need to institute new procedures for the handling of rape victims to encourage reporting of the crime and the prosecution of the rapist. In this context the formation, at the beginning of 1973, of the N.Y.P.D. Rape Investigation and Analysis Section (*Newsweek,* January 29, 1973:59) represents a most significant advance toward removing the image of the police who handle rape cases as cold and callous. Until the squad commenced its operations, the role of policewomen in dealing with victims of rape and other sexual attacks in New York City was minimal. However, in the end result, it may be the training rather than the sex of the police officer that is important. Ideally, the rape victim should have a choice of speaking to a male or female officer who is skilled in sensitive handling of the victim, competent management of evidence, and investigation that will lead to the successful prosecution of the rapist.

NOTES

1. These and other statistics relating to rape and allied crimes in New York City were supplied to the authors by the N.Y.P.D. Crime Analysis Section.

2. The authors were, in fact, the first researchers to seek access to a city-wide sample of police records in New York following the announcement in September 1971 of Commissioner Murphy's new open record policy for the N.Y.P.D. (*New York Times,* 1971). A description of the authors' pioneering experiences may perhaps assist those who follow in search of data from this source.

3. At the time sampling for this study commenced in June 1972, January was the latest month for which city-wide information was available. The reason for selecting February 1970 as the sampling starting point is discussed later in the text.

4. Until July 1971, investigation of rape complaints and almost all other types of crime complaints was the responsibility of precinct-based detectives. Following that date, the detective force of the N.Y.P.D. was involved in a major reorganization in which division-based detectives became responsible for crime investigations, including rape complaints. The crime record system reflects the organization of the detective force; records that were maintained on a crime-specific basis only at the precinct level are now at the divisional level.

5. It appears that the computer discs used to produce these crime analysis printouts are not stored in archives, but rather are put back into general circulation. Thus, with the destruction of these printouts, the opportunity to tap detailed city-wide historical crime information is irrevocably lost.

6. A small proportion of errors in the crime complaint numbers recorded on the computer printout sheets from which sampling took place resulted in a reduction in the total sample of files received by the authors from the central record section. This loss accounts for the "approximate" sample size referred to earlier in the text. It was decided that sufficient data were in hand to obviate electing replacements for the lost files.

7. These were the only documents kept in the central record section from which file copies were obtained. A number of checks made of rape complaint files at the precinct level suggested that little if any supplementary information could fruitfully be obtained from alternative sources. Rape victims' medical records, if they existed, were regarded as confidential documents and were not made available.

8. Names of people and other potential identification features have been deleted in these cases. Otherwise, the material is reproduced verbatim from the files with no stylistic or other alterations.

9. The crime analysis section prepares each year a statistical summary of homicide trends in New York City. This analysis is for restricted internal use in the N.Y.P.D. Unfortunately, no uniform system of classification and

presentation of data has been adopted by the section in preparing these summaries over the years. The result is that it is impossible to make anything but the most general comparisons in trends in homicide for any extended period of time.

10. The absence of such neighborly attacks may perhaps be accounted for in part by the removal from police files of the name and address of victims. Without this information any determination that an apprehended or suspected offender was a neighbor of the victim had to be based on other statements recorded in the police files. The fact no such statements were discovered by the authors, while perhaps surprising, may well be a comment on the overall weakness of neighborly interactions found among New Yorkers. Neighbors in Philadelphia may be viewed as strangers in New York!

11. Obviously, it should not be implied from these study findings that rape victims are immune from being shot or killed. During the period covered by the study, newspaper accounts of rape indicate that some rapists were quite prepared to use guns and other weapons to incapacitate victims and/or evade apprehension. Note,for instance, the following headlines: "Central Park Rapist Slays Man and Shoots Hold Up Accomplice," *New York Times,* September 9, 1971; "Woman Is Killed Fleeing a Rapist: Falls to Death at Mid-Town Hotel—Her Friend Raped," *New York Times,* October 1, 1971.

REFERENCES

Amir, Menachem. 1971. *Patterns in Forcible Rape.* Chicago: University of Chicago Press.

Chappell, Duncan, Gilbert Geis, Stephen Schafer, and Larry Siegel. 1971. "Forcible Rape: A Comparative Study of Offenses Known to the Police in Boston and Los Angeles." Pp. 169–190 in James Henslin, ed., *Studies in the Sociology of Sex.* New York: Appleton Century Crofts.

Comment. 1968. "Police Discretion and the Judgment That a Crime Has Been Committed—Rape in Philadelphia," *University of Pennsylvania Law Review* 117:277–321.

Federal Bureau of Investigation. 1972. *Uniform Crime Reports 1971.* Washington, D.C.: U.S. Government Printing Office.

Geis, Gilbert. 1965. "Statistics Concerning Race and Crime," *Crime and Delinquency* 11:142–50.

Ludwig, Frederick J. 1970. "The Case for Repeal of the Sex Corroboration Requirement in New York," *Brooklyn Law Review* 36:378–86.

National Commission on the Causes and Prevention of Violence. 1969. *Final Report to Establish Justice, to Insure Domestic Tranquility.* Washington, D.C.: U.S. Government Printing Office.

New York Times. 1971. "Police Here to Open 'Files and Men' to Academic Researchers," *New York Times,* 17 September, 47.

Oelsner, Lesley. 1972. "Law of Rape: Because Ladies Lie," *New York Times, News of the Week in Review* at 5, 14 May.

Office of the Mayor. 1972. *Criminal Justice Plan.* New York: City of New York.

Pitler, Robert M. 1973. "Existentialism and Corroboration of Sex Crimes in New York," *Syracuse Law Review* 24:1–37.

President's Commission on Law Enforcement and Administration of Justice. 1967. *The Challenge of Crime in a Free Society.* Washington, D.C.: U.S. Government Printing Office.

Stumbo, Bella. 1972. "Rape: Does Justice Turn Its Head?" *Los Angeles Times,* March 12, Section E:1.

Williams, Robert H. 1972. "On Sketching the Violent," *Washington Post,* August 13, Potomac at 10–11.

Younger, Irving. 1971. "The Requirement of Corroboration in Prosecutions for Sex Offenses in New York," *Fordham Law Review* 40:263–78.

13 The Hitchhike Victim of Rape: A Research Report

STEVE NELSON AND MENACHEM AMIR

HITCHHIKING has long been a popular mode of travel for certain groups, particularly young men and military personnel. Within the last few years, a change has occurred with regard to hitchhiking. It has been adopted by one aspect of the youth and hippie cultures.* The embracing of hitchhiking as a mode of transportation by the hippie movement accounts for the increase in the numbers

Reprinted with permission from Israel Drapkin and Emilio Viano, ed., *Victimology: A New Focus* (Lexington, Mass.: D. C. Heath, 1973), 5:47–64.

* The distinction between "youth"—mainly white, college, and of middle-class origin—and "hippie" cultures is acknowledged. It is, however, the fact that both groups are composed of persons of similar age and appearances that is of interest to us, rather than philosophical attitudes.

of persons observed hitchhiking and the fact that so many girls and young women solicit rides.

Sociologically, the act of ragged vagabondage manifested by hitchhiking represents the repudiation of some of the traditional middle-class values of American society. Among the rejected values are: the middle-class belief that success is equated with material achievement, especially ownership of an automobile; distrust of strangers; class, ethnic, and racial prejudices; and the traditional view regarding the proper role of women (see Berger, 1967; Davis, 1967).

The repudiation of the material aspects of American society is demonstrated by the voluntary adoption of a poverty life style illustrated by the act of hitchhiking, the manner of dress of most hitchhikers (see Yablonsky, 1968), and their dependency upon the charity of others. The observer sees them standing along the main arterials singly and in groups, appearing to have few resources, and wearing old, faded, and patched items of clothing which are obviously discards. In repudiating the material aspects of American society, the hitchhiker becomes dependent upon the charity of others for food, shelter, and transportation.

The hitchhiker of necessity must reject the xenophobic distrust of strangers. He is dependent upon strangers for obtaining rides and is unable to be too selective in choosing with whom he rides—especially if this is the only offer after standing several hours in one location. The hitchhiker, especially the hippie hitchhiker, is less able to discriminate in his associations by appearance and dress because his own appearance and clothing are expressions of the view that appearance alone is not a valid determinant of social worth.

The hippie also rejects the class and ethnic prejudices of society, especially those regarding lower classes and blacks. He does not view them as a threat and feels no trepidation in associating with them or accepting rides from them.

The fourth societal value challenged by hitchhikers is the view of the proper role of women in society. Society has traditionally held that it is improper for women to solicit contacts with strangers, and the morals of any woman doing so were suspect.

This view is being challenged by the hitchhiking female, who represents female equality, freedom, and full participation in social life, proven and partially enacted by hitchhiking.

Two psychological elements found in hitchhiking coincide with elements of the hippie character. These are a spirit of adventurousness and indifference, and the thrill of deliberately challenging a potentially dangerous situation (Adler, 1965).

Hitchhiking conveys a spirit of adventure and independence. As adolescents and youths become emotionally independent of the family, hitchhiking provides a means of asserting this independence, and at the same time fulfilling the desire for adventure and excitement (Hildebrand, 1963).

There is a certain element of danger present in hitchhiking. Subconsciously, many of those who hitchhike may be reacting to the thrill gained from deliberately challenging a potentially dangerous situation.

A third special psychological element applies to the female hitchhiker. The motorist may frequently misinterpret the girl's lack of fear and her assumed participation in a subculture which emphasizes, among other things, free choice of sexual partners and a liberal attitude toward sexual relationships. The beliefs and attitudes of the female hitchhiker outlined above, combined with the perceptions of these beliefs by certain groups in society, mainly working class, lower middle class, and blacks, may contribute to the victimization of the female hitchhiker. Two of these perceptions are that the hippie hitchhiker is outside the mainstream of society and thus beyond its protection; the second is that hippies believe in and are engaged in hedonistic behavioral patterns.

The different life style as well as statements by the politically radical, contribute to the belief that the hippie has rejected society. Once relegated to the position of societal outsider, attacks upon him can be easily justified. This view has often been expressed to the authors in interviewing offenders (see generally, Brown, 1969).

For certain groups, the hitchhiking woman presents an image of promiscuity. This image is conveyed by the solicitation of contact with strangers, her apparel, and also as a result of the popular folklore regarding the promiscuity of hippies. Thus, if to pick up a hitchhiker is a sign of chivalry, the hippie hitchhiker cannot be accorded the protection that the chivalrous behavior assumed. The female hitchhiker is assumed to be unchaste and contemptuous of the societal double standard of sexual conduct. A popular belief is that the hippie girl will easily agree, or succumb to sexual flirtation, exploitation, or sheer pressure.

These combinations of assumptions result in a high vulnerability for victimization. The assumptions made by certain groups in society provide the justification, while the act of hitchhiking provides the situational circumstances which make the victimization much more probable and, at the same time, a "safe" type of offense.

Among the situational elements are the following: the fact that the offense occurs between strangers, one of whom is transient; second, the offender is able to isolate the victim in the course of choosing the location for the offense; the third element is the fact that the offender is able to escape safely by auto following the attack. An additional element is that, as we discovered, many hippie women either refuse to report the offense to the police, or although they may report being attacked, they refuse to provide complete details of the incident or to take further interest in the case. Their lack of interest is attributed in part to distrust and dislike of the police (Sheehy, 1971), a fatalistic view of the offense, or possibly they may be reporting only in order to prove male exploitation and chauvinism (Griffin, 1971).

The final situational element is that the offender, if apprehended, is able to claim that the victim entered the vehicle willingly and agreed to have sexual intercourse with him, changed her mind, and then made the "false" charge of rape.

With the increase in the number of persons hitchhiking, police agencies have detected an increase in hitchhike-connected crime, especially rape and robbery. The chief of police of San Francisco stated in early 1970 that part of the city's crime increase was attributable to hitchhiking, and other law enforcement officials have made similar pronouncements. There has been, however, a paucity of specific data to support these allegations.

The purpose of this paper is to determine whether there is a correlation between hitchhiking and the increase in reported rapes which has occurred in Berkeley. In addition, we intend to investigate the characteristics of hitchhike rape (HHR) and to determine how HHR differs from other types of rape, i.e., rape occurring in residences or on the street. Included in our discussion of the characteristics of HHR will be a discussion of victimization and victim-precipitated offenses.

METHOD

We reviewed rape complaints made to the Berkeley Police Department from January 1964 through December 1970. Only data for the years 1968 through 1970 were utilized, however. This decision was based upon the paucity of offenses prior to 1968. In 1967, for instance, there were only twenty-five rapes reported to the police, only one of which was a hitchhike rape. Prior to 1967, there were no hitchhike rapes and only one attempt located.

For the purpose of this paper, hitchhike rapes are defined as follows: Rape which results from the voluntary acceptance by the victim of a ride from a person(s) who is a stranger to her. The contact must occur on the public street and result from the victim soliciting or the offender offering a ride.

We relied solely upon police data because of its availability and the fact that the police department is the only agency which collects data of this type. The data collected reflect only those offenses which occurred in the city of Berkeley and were reported to the Berkeley Police Department. Instances in which the victim was picked up in Berkeley and transported to another city are not reflected in the data. In three instances, some element of the rape occurred in Berkeley and these reports were classified as rape for Berkeley even though the offense culminated in another jurisdiction. In one instance, the victim and her boyfriend were kidnapped almost as soon as they entered the offenders' vehicle and the rape occurred somewhere on the freeway.

It is suspected that a substantial number of rapes are not reported. . . . With regard to HHR, probably less than one-third of the rapes committed are reported. In addition to embarrassment and hostility toward the police, two other elements may be considered. These are the fact that the victim is a transient passing through the community, and more importantly, guilt feelings arising from the fact that the attack occurred as a result of the victim's own foolhardiness.

The data will be presented in terms of the numbers and percentages of rapes studied. It was found that there were several instances in which the offenders in a pair or group rape were of different races, white and black. These offenses were arbitrarily categorized as white. It is recognized that this decision weights the findings in favor of blacks, especially with regard to HHR offenses. We found, however, that this did not alter the interracial patterns of our findings. . . .

During the past ten years, the population of Berkeley has remained more or less constant numerically, while undergoing a change in its character. Berkeley has become part of the larger urban community. The increase in reported rapes reflects both an urban crime problem and also the changing character of the population. According to the Berkeley Police Annual Report, the reported rapes rose 59 percent between 1968 and 1970. The number of reported rapes increased from fourteen in 1964 to sixty-two in 1970, an increase of more than 400 percent. The average ratio of HHR to total rape reports for the three years is 20 percent, a significant proportion of the total reported offenses.

The year 1969 presents a variation from the other two years studied, with 16 percent of the total rapes being HHR. A possible explanation is the period of civil turmoil from January through May 1969. This resulted in increased police patrols in the city, especially in the South Campus area, which is frequented by students and hippies. Table 13.1 provides a breakdown by types for rapes in Berkeley. The categorization of the three types of rapes is based upon location of the offense—residential, street attacks, and HHR offenses. We found that approximately 50 percent of reported offenses were residential in nature, that is, occurring within an occupied building. The balance were divided between street attacks and HHR. A trend has begun which indicates a de-

Table 13.1. Rape Reports by Location.

Year	*Residential*		*Street*		*HHR*		*Total*	
	Number	*Percent*	*Number*	*Percent*	*Number*	*Percent*	*Number*	*Percent*
1968	19	48.7	11	18.1	9	12.1	39	100
1969	34	53.1	20	31.3	10	15.6	64	100
1970	33	54.1	14	23.0	14	23.0	61	100
Total	86		45		33		164[a]	

[a]On one case there is no information.

Table 13.2. Race of Victim: Non-HHR and HHR.

Year	*White*				*Black*				*Total*[b]	
	Non-HHR		*HHR*		*Non-HHR*		*HHR*		*Non-HHR*	*HHR*
	Number	*Percent*	*Number*	*Percent*	*Number*	*Percent*	*Number*	*Percent*	*Number*	*Number*
1968	22	73.3	8	88.8	8	26.7	1	21.2	30	9
1969	43	76.1	10	100.0	11	23.9	0	0	54	10
1970	35	76.1	11	78.6	11	23.9	3	21.4	46	14
Total	100	76.9	29	88.0	30	23.1	4	12.1	130	33

[a]Includes one Oriental victim counted as white for statistical purposes.
[b]The total number is 163 since on two cases there was no information on the race variable.

crease in the percentage of street attacks. This is possibly because this type of attack provides the most hazard to the offender.

RACIAL PATTERNS

Most studies (see, e.g., Amir, 1971) reveal that rape usually is an intraracial, intraneighborhood phenomenon with the highest percentage of victims being black. This was not found to be the case in Berkeley, especially with regard to HHR offenses. We found that rape is interracial, and that most victims are white. Rape also does not appear to be an intraneighborhood offense.

The assumption that rape in Berkeley does not appear to be an intraneighborhood offense is given credence by the interracial aspects of the offense. These indicate that the offenders must of necessity leave their neighborhood of residence in order to locate their victims, usually in the areas frequented by students and hippies. The necessity of leaving the offender's neighborhood is even greater with regard to HHR. The victims can only be located along the main arterials and these are, for the most part, removed from black neighborhoods.

Table 13.2 indicates that most victims in Berkeley are white. Of all victims, 76 percent, excluding HHR, were white. For HHR the percentage of white victims increases to 88 percent. These patterns remain constant during the three years studied. The President's Commission on Law Enforcement and Administration of Justice (1967) reported that for offenses other than homicide, a black woman was eight times more likely to be a victim of assaultive offenses than a Caucasian woman. This was also found to be the case by Amir (1971) in his study on rape in Philadelphia. He found that of 646 victims, 80 percent were black. Our findings are reversed from these studies.

Several factors must be considered in explaining the disproportionate numbers of white victims in Berkeley. For residential and street rapes, two situations contribute to the fact that most victims are white. These are the heterogeneous living patterns of the community, with the proximity to Oakland with its predominant black population, and the proximity of the campus community to the Telegraph Avenue area, an area which attracts persons from all over the Bay Area and the country.

The heterogeneous living patterns in Berkeley are buttressed by the free mixing of all groups in the campus area and actually throughout the city. These arrangements offer security to the offender. In a segregated community, a black walking in a white area is immediately suspected; such is not the case in an integrated community.

Also, it was reported to one of the authors that in some sections of Oakland, and especially on weekends, young blacks plan to rape young white hippies for a "thrill" or as a way to have a good time. Some girls also reported that middle-aged white men, some dressed as executives, attempt forcefully to flirt with the hitchhiking girls, often voicing their prejudice that hippie girls are very promiscuous.

The high percentage of white HHR victims is explained for the most part by the fact that, in general, few black girls or women hitchhike. The black women do not, as a rule, participate in the hippie culture, and thus do not expose themselves to potential victimization. It is interesting to note that the black victims of HHR did not solicit a ride from the offender, but were walking along the street or waiting for a bus. The contact was initiated by the offender in three of the four instances in which the victim was black. These situations can be described more as pick-ups than as hitchhike offenses.

The fact that few black women hitchhike is not surprising if we bear in mind that black women are very conscious of the hazards to be encountered in the urban city as a result of having been raised in it. Their white sisters, on the other hand, are frequently from the suburbs or small towns where life is considerably safer.

A second significant variation from other studies on rape was found in the Berkeley study. Rape was found in other studies to be generally an intraracial offense, in which the black intrarace events are in absolute numbers and in proportion greater than

Table 13.3. Race of Victim and Offender, Non-HHR and HHR Offenses.

Offender	*Victim*					
	White		*Black*		*Total*	
	Number	*Percent*	*Number*	*Percent*	*Number*	*Percent*
Non-HHR Offenses						
White	21[a]	21.8	1	4.3	22	16.0
Black	75[b]	77.1	33	95.7	108	82.4
Unknown	1	1.2	0	0.0	1	1.8
Total	97	100	34	100	131	100
HHR Offenses						
White	8[a]	27.6	0	0.0	8	24
Black	21	72.4	4	100.0	25	72
Total	29	100.0	4	100.0	35	100

[a]There were four instances of pair rape, in which one offender was white and the other was black. These offenses were arbitrarily categorized as white. . . . If the four instances of mixed pair rape included in the HHR data were classified as black, the percentage of interracial rapes involving black offenders and white victims would increase from 72 percent to 86 percent.
[b]One Oriental counted under white category.

intrawhite and interrace events (Amir, 1971:43–45). This was found not to be the case in our study for those offenses in which the victim was white. The intraracial character of rape was found, however, to hold in those instances in which the victim was black. Tables 13.3 and 13.4 demonstrate our findings.

The racial aspect found in our study may be a significant factor in the reporting of offenses. It is possible that a higher proportion of interracial offenses are reported than intraracial offenses. This, however, is not verifiable. General societal attitudes toward interracial intercourse and the special case of hippie victims must be considered an important factor for the victim in reporting an attack.

AGE PATTERNS

Berkeley's large student and hippie populations make it unique with regard to many other communities. The population profile is skewed by a heavy concentration of young persons between 18 and 25 years of age. It was found that most rape victims, including victims of HHR, were between the ages of 15 and 24, with the bulk between 18 and 24. This is the age group to which the students and hippies belong. Sixty-four percent of all rape victims, excluding HHR, were between 15 and 24 years of age. By excluding those victims between 15 and 17, we find that 54 percent of the victims were between 18 and 24.

The large number of college-age rape victims is explained in part by the changes which have occurred in the living patterns of women attending college. During the last ten years, changes have occurred in the residency requirements for women students. Lock-out rules have been abolished as well as the requirement that women live in approved housing. The result has been that many women students have moved into apartments in the community. This increased freedom has led to increased victimization by making the women more accessible to potential offenders.

The evolution of Telegraph Avenue into a hippie center has served to attract persons from all over the Bay Area to watch and in many instances exploit the hippies. Many of those attracted are drawn by the desire to obtain narcotics and/or "free" sex. These individuals were, in many instances, responding to the myths regarding the hippies discussed in the introduction to this essay. This supposed promiscuity and inferior status in society of hippie women has resulted in certain groups viewing any woman in the campus area, especially if she is casually dressed, as "fair game."

The findings with regard to HHR are similar to those for non-HHR, except that a greater proportion of the victims (85 percent) was between 15 and 24 years of age. Among HHR victims, 45 percent were found to be between twenty and twenty-four. The explanations for HHR age patterns are similar to those presented for non-HHR offenses.

This age pattern is to be expected. The upper limit of 24 is explained by the fact that most women marry by the age of 24 or have become independent to the point where they are able to afford their own transportation. The lower limit is explained by the fact that most girls are still under parental constraints below that age. We would expect that the majority of the victims in the category 15 to 19 years would be 18 or 19 years old. This was found to be the case, with five of the nine victims either 18 or 19, that is, the age of college students.

An interesting variation was observed between non-HHR victims and HHR victims. It is the difference between the normal curve plotted for the white victims of the two categories. The non-HHR curve is more normal with a peak occurring between 20 and 24 years. The HHR curve also reaches a peak between 20 and 24 years, but declines rapidly from 24 to 30, with no victims older than 30.

The age patterns of HHR offenders were for the most part based upon victim estimates. Data on the age of non-HHR offenders were not obtained. It was found that the average age of the offender is approximately five years above the average age of the victim; 57 percent of the offenders were between 20 and 29 years of age.

The apparent older age of the offenders is explained by the fact that it is they who have greatest access to automobiles and are also sexually more experienced. The older males also have less opportunity for social contacts with women than do the younger males in school. As a result, they would be expected to rely more upon prostitutes or other casual contacts to satisfy their sexual desires. The equating of the hitchhikers with "loose women" contributes to their victimization.

Our findings also indicate that in Berkeley, black males become involved in rape at an earlier age than do their white brothers. In each instance in which the offender was less than 20 years of age, the rape was found to be a pair rape, that is, two or more offenders were responsible. This would lead to the assumption that in these instances, the offenders are not responding to any abnormal pathology, but view their victims as persons to be sexually exploited in the same manner as prostitutes.

THE VICTIM

Thus far, we have focused upon the racial and age patterns of HHR compared with non-HHR offenses. We found HHR to be an interracial offense and the ages of the victims to approximate the ages of the student population of the city. HHR was also found to be a significant factor in the increase in reported rapes in Berkeley. In the following discussion, HHR will be considered in terms of victimization, that is, those characteristics common to the victim of rape and the nature of their victimization.

Rape by its very nature implies a process of social interaction between victim and offender. In every instance of HHR, the initial contact began with a voluntary social involvement between a would-be victim and offender. Those instances in which the victim was kidnapped off the street were excluded from consideration. The voluntariness of the initial relationship is what makes HHR a unique type of rape.

The previous statement that the victims of HHR appear to be students or hippies is borne out by information obtained from police reports. We found that 57 percent of the victims were students attending schools, ranging from universities to art colleges. Another 30 percent can be described from the police reports as hippies. Sixty percent resided in Berkeley, an additional 24 percent resided in the Bay Area, and the remainder, 15 percent, were either from out of state or their place of residence was unknown.

Three generalizations based on collected data can be made regarding the victims of HHR. These are: the victim's deportment contributes to her victimization; the victims are generally submissive; and there appears to be a fatalism on their part regarding the hazards in hitchhiking.

The deportment of the victim is an important element in her victimization. In 82 percent of the rapes, the victim was hitchhiking by herself, thus removing herself from any possibility of assistance. In 60 percent of the events the victims initiated the contact which led to their being raped. The deportment, that is, hitchhiking by herself, soliciting a ride from strangers, and the manner of attire, may have conveyed to the offender an image of the hitchhiker as a person with "loose" morals. In this instance, it is more the impression others have than the self-image which is important.

One of the most frequent views regarding rape is that great

force is used to overcome the resistance of the victim to the event. This was not found to be the usual case by Amir (1971) in the Philadelphia study. Our findings were similar. We found that the usual attitude of most victims was submission rather than resistance. In only 15 percent of the HHRs did the victim resist the offender. The amount of force exerted by the offender was usually a minimum, sufficient however for the victim to be able to say that she had been forced against her will to have intercourse with the offender.

It was found in 75 percent of the HHR events that physical force or some type of weapon was involved. In 52 percent of the events physical force, usually consisting of slapping or arm twisting, was used. Although the amount of force varied, in none of the instances was the victim hospitalized.

An interesting observation regarding the victims of HHR is that an apparent fatalistic or casual attitude prevails regarding the risks encountered in hitchhiking. It was found in several instances that the victim was not disturbed about being raped and was making the report because she felt that it was the thing to do. One victim told the investigating officer, "Rape is one of the risks the hitchhiker must be willing to accept." Another victim informed the investigating officer that she had been in California for six months and during that time had been raped four times. Although most victims do not express such views, they all are aware of the hazards involved in hitchhiking.

THE OFFENDER

Data for the offenders are not as complete as that for victims of HHR. In only 30.3 percent of the reported offenses were the offenders arrested or identified. In five of the instances in which the offenders were identified, one or more of them had a prior criminal record. In only two of these five instances, however, did the prior criminal record involve sex offenses.

In most instances no pathological patterns, such as inflicting torture on the victim, can be discerned from the police reports.

There were, however, three events in which a marked pathology was apparent from the report. Two of these were rapes committed by white males. The first offender kidnapped his victim and then drove to an isolated area where he forced the victim to submit to an act of sodomy. The second offense involving a white male occurred when the offender picked up three 13-year-old girls from a bus stop late at night. He then forced two of the girls from the car and raped the third. He was apprehended shortly after the offense and subsequently committed suicide.

The third rape which has some indications of being pathological in nature involved an adult black male and occurred when a 14-year-old black girl was raped after being knocked unconscious as a result of jumping from the offender's vehicle in panic. The offender picked her up and drove her some distance where he raped her.

Gibbons (1968) identifies two types of rapists who resort to some measure of force in their relationships with women. The first is described as "the violent sex offender," a person who is mentally ill and may cause death or serious injury to the victim. The second type is the "aggressive rapist," a sexual offender who resorts to limited amounts of force in coercing the victim into sexual activity. Such similar classification is also suggested by Amir (1971). The implication regarding the aggressive rapist is that he is behaving in a subculturally approved manner. The aggressive rapist is believed to be lower class or lower middle class in social status. "Apparently," Gibbons (1968:385) notes, "the general disposition to employ force is most common in this social stratum, so aggressive rape is a manifestation of class-linked toleration of violence."

If, as Gibbons and Amir maintain, aggressive rape is class oriented, it would explain the large proportion of black offenders involved in HHR. The lower class background of most HHR offenders is further supported when a class breakdown of the white offenders is made. We found that 50 percent of the white offenders were described as Chicano. Most HHR offenders who tend to show aggressive behavior toward females are of lower-middle or lower class background.

The lack of a pathological motivation is further demonstrated in instances of pair and group rapes. Pair and group rapes accounted for 48 percent of the HHRs reported during the three years studied. From the nature of these kinds of rapes, some degree of normative support is assumed from peer groups. The nature of group rape lends credence to the opinion that pair or group rape is not pathological in nature.

THE OFFENSE

Hitchhike rape involves a voluntary social contact between victim and offender, frequently initiated by the victim herself. In order for rape to occur, there must be, in addition to a vulnerable victim, certain other favorable circumstances as defined by the offender. These are both physical and psychological in nature.

Among the physical are the following: ability to locate and select a victim; ability to move the crime scene to a safe location, ability to isolate and overcome victim's resistance, a safe escape. HHR conforms to all these criteria.

It is relatively easy for the offender to select a victim from among the many hitchhikers standing along the road. Once the victim has voluntarily entered the offender's vehicle, he is able to select a safe location for the attack and at the same time isolate the victim from help. Following the event, escape is easily accomplished, usually either by abandoning the victim at the scene of the offense, or by selecting some other isolated location to let her out of the car.

The psychological factors which contribute to HHR are concerned with the offender's perception of his victim. These perceptions also explain the class difference involved in HHR.

Amir's (1971) study found that rape occurred among relatively homogeneous groups within society, that is, that rape is an intraracial intraneighborhood offense. As indicated previously, this was not found in the present study. Our findings are not, however, incompatible with those of Amir (1971) in his Philadelphia study. It appears that rather than one homogeneous group to which both victim and offender belong, we have two distinct groups differentiated by race and social class. The social class difference is modified by the behavior of the victim.

Racial difference also provides the key to HHR. As stated above, the conduct of the victim in soliciting a ride from strangers is not the approved, middle-class behavior. There is little precedent in this country for women hitchhiking. We saw that the morals of the female hitchhiker are viewed by certain elements of society as similar to those of a tramp; as a hippie she may be considered an outcast, thus placing her outside the usual societal conventions against aggressive behavior directed toward white middle-class women.

CONCLUSION

The study has shown that HHR for the three-year period studied represents an average of 20 percent of the total reported rapes occurring in Berkeley. HHR is an interracial offense in which the victims were found to be white women of college age. The offenders are five to ten years older than the victims, and generally black.

An assumption can be made that if there were no hitchhiking females, a reduction in the total number of rapes in Berkeley would occur.

After consideration, we are not in favor of a law forbidding hitchhiking. Our primary reason is that it would place too great a strain on the police resources and it also violates the citizens' right of free choice of the mode of traveling. In addition, in contacts with hitchhikers, we found that most of them are well aware of the hazards, either as a result of warnings from parents, police officers, or from occasional newspaper reports.

HHR is interesting because it is a "victim-precipitated offense" (see generally Amir, 1967), in which the victim's behavior contributes to her victimization. For this reason it is unique. Further study should be done regarding the reasons that women place themselves in such vulnerable positions. A second area in which additional study should be initiated is concerned with the offender's perception of the victim. We suggested certain ideas concerning what we believed the perceptions to be. It would be worthwhile to verify these.

There are two other areas in which further study should be undertaken. The first is to attempt to determine the ratio of reported to unreported offenses. The second area is a comparative study between locales to determine the percentage of their rape offenses attributed to hitchhiking. The inquiries should include states which forbid hitchhiking as well as those with different social and demographic characteristics. A difficulty we encountered was that most police departments do not distinguish between categories of rape, except for statutory and nonstatutory rape.

REFERENCES

Adler, Nathan. 1968. "The Antinomian Personality: The Hippie Character Type," *Psychiatry* 3:325–38.

Amir, Menachem. 1967. "Victim Precipitated Rape," *Journal of Criminal Law, Criminology, and Police Science* 58:493–502.

——. 1971. *Patterns in Forcible Rape.* Chicago: University of Chicago Press.

Berger, Bennett M. 1967. "Hippie Morality: More Old Than Young," *Trans-Action* 5(December):19–27.

Brown, Michael E. 1969. "The Condemnation and Persecution of Hippies," *Trans-Action* 6(September):33–46.

Davis, Fred. 1967. "Why All of Us May Be Hippies Someday," *Trans-Action* 5(December):10–18.

Gibbons, Don C. 1968. *Society, Crime and Criminal Careers.* Englewood Cliffs, N.J.: Prentice-Hall.

Griffin, Susan. 1971. "Rape: The All-American Crime," *Ramparts* 10(September):26–36.

Hildebrand, James A. 1963. "Why Runaways Leave Home," *Journal of Criminal Law, Criminology and Police Science* 54:211–16.

President's Commission on Law Enforcement and Administration of Justice. 1967. *The Challenge of Crime in a Free Society.* Washington, D.C.: U.S. Government Printing Office.

Sheehy, Gail. 1971. "Nice Girls Don't Get into Trouble," *New York Magazine* 4(15 February):26–31.

Yablonsky, Lewis. 1968. *The Hippie Trip.* New York: Pegasus.

14 The Psychology of Rapists

MURRAY L. COHEN,
RALPH GAROFALO,
RICHARD B. BOUCHER,
AND
THEOHARIS SEGHORN

A series of papers by Sarafian (1963), Kozol et al. (1966), and Cohen and Kozol (1966) describe a Massachusetts law for "sexually dangerous persons" and a treatment center established by the law. Although the specific purpose of this paper is to present some observations on the psychological factors involved in rape, the clinical data are based on experiences with this law and the

Reprinted by permission of Grune and Stratton, Inc., and the authors, from *Seminars in Psychiatry* (August 1971), 3(6).

treatment center, and therefore a discussion of both will be profitable.

Special legislation concerning sexual offenders is frequently enacted as the result of a social outcry to a particularly brutal or heinous crime (Guttmacher, 1951). This was the case in Massachusetts in 1957. Six weeks following his release from prison, a child molester kidnapped two boys and sexually assaulted and murdered them. In immediate response to this crime, chapter 123A of the General Laws of Massachusetts was written into law as a method for preventing the premature release of a potentially dangerous person.

The 1957 law provided for a commitment for an indefinite period if necessary for the protection of the public. Sections of this statute were found unconstitutional, and the entire law was replaced by the present statute, chapter 646 of the Acts of 1958. This law ordered the creation of a treatment center and fashioned a new term, "sexually dangerous person." The psychiatric facility created within the Massachusetts Correctional Institution at Bridgewater in 1959 is staffed by psychiatrists, psychologists, social workers, and educational, occupational, and recreational therapists, who are responsible for the care, treatment, and rehabilitation of persons who come under the purview of the law.

The law provides for a truly indeterminate commitment—one day to life. Indeterminate-sentence laws usually have relatively narrow limits within a fixed minimum and maximum term. The basic legal consideration here is that the commitment is civil and not criminal. The offender is not given a fixed penalty for his crime, but rather the period of commitment is determined by his mental condition. His release occurs when the psychiatric staff judges that he will offer a minimal risk to the safety of the community.

Since enactment of this statute, a number of articles (Cotton, 1969; Gould and Hurwitz, 1965; McGarry and Cotton, 1969; Tenney, 1962) have appeared containing critical comments of the law and the treatment center. These criticisms discuss the legal, ethical, and scientific aspects of the legislation, but only those criticisms of interest to the mental health professional will be presented here. These include problems of treatment and diagnosis and limitations of the statute to "sexually dangerous" (thus not including those who may be aggressively dangerous in nonsexual ways).

Many papers critical of the law recognize the paradox that although the indeterminate civil commitment is for the purpose of treatment, many of those offenders most subject to the application of the statute do not appear treatable by current techniques. This is a valid and worrisome observation. In a recent study completed at the center, only 36 percent of the patients were found to be responsive to psychotherapy. This is supported by the finding that 35 percent of the patients committed during the first six years (the first half of the total period of the existence of the center) are still committed patients. However, society has clearly taken the position that it has the right to protect its members from harm. The objections to a life commitment on the grounds of treatability are valid only when it can be demonstrated that the intent and application by society of civil commitment is not treatment and rehabilitation, but simply preventive detention.

Section 1 of the statute defines a "sexually dangerous person" as "any person whose misconduct in sexual matters indicates a general lack of power to control his sexual impulses, as evidenced by repetitive or compulsive behavior and either violence or aggression by an adult against a victim under the age of sixteen years, and who as a result is likely to attack or otherwise inflict injury on the objects of his uncontrolled or uncontrollable desires." This section has been criticized for its vagueness and for its limitation to the sexually aggressive. It is pointed out that "sexually dangerous" is a social-legal concept and not a psychiatric entity. It is a term that refers not to etiology, current process, or immediate symptom, but to future behavior. The law imposes on the psychiatrist a relatively unfamiliar demand and a responsibility that it is not certain should be given to him, and one he is frequently loathe to accept.

The problems are clearly difficult ones. If "sexually dangerous" is going to be determined by the part of the section that refers to past behavior "as evidenced by repetitive or compulsive behavior'' then it is not necessary to have the psychiatrist make the determination and there will be no way for the evaluation of change and release. If the emphasis is to be on "is likely to attack" there is then a behavioral prediction problem, and social scientists, other than the psychiatrist, should clearly be involved by statutory action and not only in clinical actuality.

McGarry and Cotton (1969:298) criticize still another aspect of section 1, that aspect resulting from the exclusive features of the law "if such programs for the sexually dangerous are justified, it makes no sense to exclude the repetitively aggressive dangerous offender without sexual overtones.'' Holden (1969:29) questions this feature not only from logical, but also from legal considerations.

> [The sex offender law represents] a special way of dealing with a particular class of criminal offender and such class is exposed to greater deprivation of liberty with less procedural due process than is the case for other criminal offenders. If society's particular concern is for its own safety, it is difficult to see why sex offenders alone should be singled out for indeterminate detention.

It is certainly a meaningful question as to why there is this peculiar separation of sexually dangerous from other forms of socially dangerous persons. It is clear that the answer resides within sociocultural and not psychiatric data.

Despite these and other criticisms of the law, it has operated (with three amendments) since 1958, and over 2,000 sexual offenders have been given preliminary examinations since that time. There was sufficient question regarding 800 of these men that they were sent to the treatment center for intensive study for a sixty-day observation period. Of this latter group 240 men were found to be sexually dangerous as described in the law and were committed to the center.

It is quite apparent from the data gathered that the men seen under this statute are seriously sexually disturbed and represent a significant threat to society. Two of many findings demonstrate this. Unlike the general findings reported in the literature of 12 to 17 percent sexual offense recidivism, 62 percent of the total group screened had one or more prior convictions for a sexual offense. Of the group committed to the center, 73 percent had a prior record for a sexual crime. In 47 percent of the committed sexual offenders, force or violence was associated with the offense. This is quite different from the overall data on sexual crimes that indicates aggression is comparatively rare (Ellis and Brancale, 1956).

Thus the center sees a selective sample. It is precisely this selectivity that has given us the opportunity to observe characterological sexual pathology and features of character related to such pathology, without the distortions created by clinical cases showing sexual deviancy as the result of transient neurotic regressions, traumatic environmental stress, the so-called accidental sexual offense (not a deviancy), or the deviances that are better ascribed to cultural disapproval than to psychopathology. This is not the man in alcoholic stupor urinating in an alley and arrested for exhibiting himself; not the disappointed lover misunderstanding the glances of a young girl as a seductive invitation and arrested for accosting; it is not the man on a date sexually provoked and then denied whose anger triggers off a sudden uncharacteristic, explosive rape; nor is the sexual assault an expression of a subcultural double standard or masculine culture machismo.

The patient seen at the center shows serious defects in social relationships and social skills, lacunae in moral and ethical attitudes, impulse-control functions that are tenuous and break down under relatively normal life stresses, ego functions (judgment, reality testing, reasoning, etc.) that seem entirely intact until he is sexually or aggressively provoked and only then do the ego distortions appear, and major disturbances in his sexual development that leave him fixated at an infantile, primitive level or make him susceptible to sudden and precipitous regressions.

The following sections of this paper will be devoted to one group of such sexual offenders, the rapist. The data were obtained from extensive clinical study involving diagnostic and psychotherapeutic interviews and psychological tests. The elaboration, correction, and refinement of these clinical observations are the result of four research studies (Calmas, 1965; Cohen et al., 1969; Lopez, 1969; Seghorn, 1970).

THE RAPIST

It is readily apparent that there is no congruence between rape and any specific diagnostic category. It is true that classic neurotic symptoms are a rarity, but all types of character neuroses, character disorders, and more severe borderline and psychotic states are represented. It is equally clear that there are some specific characteristics present in rapists that differentiate them from other criminals and from other sexual offenders. In addition, there is evidence that clear, differentiated classes of rapists can be observed, and such differentiation has significant clinical and research utility.

Guttmacher and Weihofen (1952:116) have found discriminate classes among rapists and regard motivation as the basis for a classification.

> Forced rape . . . has several basic motivational patterns. There is the rapist whose assault is the explosive expression of a pent-up sexual impulse. Or it may occur in individuals with strong latent homosexual components. . . . These are the true sex offenders. Another type that is also sexual in origin, although not so manifestly so, is the sadistic rapist. . . . Many of these individuals have their deep-seated hatred focused particularly on women. Then there is the third type of rapist who, paradoxically is not primarily a sex offender. He is the aggressive, antisocial criminal who, like the soldier of a conquering army, is out to pillage and rob.

The authors refer to three types. However, it appears that four groups are described, and although they do not present them in such terms, the following more dynamic statements seem to reflect their findings: (1) rape motivated by sexual impulses whose intensity has become so great that whatever defensive or controlling factors were present were overwhelmed and the sexual desire is expressed; (2) rape that is not a breakdown of defense, but is itself a defense against strong homosexual wishes; (3) rape that is the expression not only of sexuality but this impulse combined with deep-seated hatred or aggressive feelings toward women; and (4) rape that does not so much express sexual or aggressive wishes but rather a more general predatory disposition.

In a prodigious statistical study based on interviews and data retrieved from case folders, Gebhard et al. (1965:196) describe two major categories of rapists. In their taxonomy this group is referred to as "heterosexual offenders versus adults." The two varieties of aggressive offenses include: "(1) those in which the aggression is a means to an end, and no more force is used than is necessary to achieve the end (coitus usually); (2) those in which violence is an end in itself or at least a secondary goal; in these cases the female is either subjected to more force than is necessary or she is mistreated after coitus or other direct sexual activity has ended."

The nature of the differentiation is the motive, dealt with this time in behavioral terms. The authors do go on to discuss seven additional varieties that have little or no relationship to the two major categories quoted above, but in some instances, at least, awareness of factors other than goal behavior is indicated.

Anyone who has worked with such sexual offenders will immediately recognize the types referred to in the two classifications. He will also recognize the superficiality of the descriptions that results from a lack of attention to other psychological characteristics. The act of rape clearly cannot be understood unidimensionally simply in terms of motivation or, in fact, in terms of any single factor.

No effort will be made here to resolve the issue of whether rape can best be understood in terms of discrete categories or a point on a linear continuum. The multidimensional nature of the factors involved and the clinical phenomena themselves make it extremely difficult to consider the differences simply in quantitative terms. On the other hand, when considered from a multifactor point of view, the clinical data do not fit securely into categories. The compromise adopted here is to present a set of clinical classes based on descriptive and dynamic characteristics with an appropriate caveat to the reader that a typology is not intended.

Descriptively, the act of rape involves both an aggressive and a sexual component. In any particular sexual assault the part played by these impulses can be quite different. The primary aim may be hostile and destructive so that the sexual behavior is in the service of an aggressive impulse. In other instances the sexual impulse is the dominating motive, and the aggressive aspects of the assault are primarily in the service of the sexual aim. In a third pattern the two impulses are less differentiated, and the relationship between them can best be described as sexual sadism.

We have also observed a number of rapists within whom neither sexual nor aggressive impulses played a dominant role in the act itself. This is the group that Guttmacher (1951) refers to as the aggressive antisocial criminal and Gebhard et al. (1965) refer to as the amoral delinquent. We agree that this group should not be considered primarily as sexually deviant persons.

The remainder of this paper will be concerned with only the first three patterns of rape, since there are no new findings to contribute to the understanding of the antisocial character disorder.

The discussion of the classification will be concerned with those factors that appear to differentiate the three classes of rapists. These include the descriptive features of the act itself, the interrelationship of the sexual and aggressive impulses and the developmental level of these impulses, ego interests and attitudes, defensive structure, unconscious fantasies that appear to be directly related to the sexual assault, and the mode of objective relations and the level of object ties. These factors can be conceptually considered as separate and distinct, but they do not exist as independent forces, states, or structures, and will not be treated separately.

CLINICAL CLASSIFICATION OF RAPE

Aggressive Aim

In this pattern the sexual assault is primarily an aggressive, destructive act. The sexual behavior is not the expression of a sexual wish but is in the service of the aggression, serving to humiliate, dirty, and defile the victim. The degree of violence varies from simple assault to brutal, vicious attacks resulting on occasion in the victim's death. The savagery of the act clearly denotes the aggressive intent. When aspects of sexuality are present, they, too, enter the service of aggression as seen in biting, cutting, or tearing of the genitals or breasts, rupture of the anus through violent insertion of some object, or in other sexually mutilating acts.

The women certainly appear to be the victims of the offender's destructive wishes, and he, in fact, describes his emotional state as anger. These women are always complete strangers. This anger that is experienced is clearly a displacement of intense rage on a substitute object. The source of this rage is most frequently the mother or her representatives in the present, the wife or girlfriend.

The rape occasionally occurs in the offender's automobile where the victim is brought either by physical force or by threat with a weapon. However, the rape occurs most frequently in the victim's home with entrance gained by some ruse, the offender representing himself as a delivery man, repairman, or someone looking for a false address.

The rape often occurs in a series, and they appear as isolated instances in an otherwise relatively normal social and psychiatric history. There is, however, a long history of difficulty in heterosexual object relations in conjunction with an active sexual life. Many of these men are married and those who are not are engaged or dating with regularity. There are, however, considerable difficulties in these relationships that are marked by episodic mutual irritation and, at times, violence. They tend to experience women negatively as hostile, demanding, ungiving, and unfaithful, and frequently for good reason. The women they select are in fact assertive, active, and independent who, by their manner and attitude, ask them to accept passive components of relationships that they find intolerable. Features of the oedipal situation are reenacted time and again in involvements with divorced or separated women who are themselves mothers or with girlfriends or wives who are sexually promiscuous and not infrequently pregnant through affairs with other men.

Most of these patients have an adequate occupational history showing not only stability of work, but high level skills and achievement with qualities of inventiveness and creativity. They are competitive but are able to enter into cooperative, sharing relationships with men, although here, too, the more active features are dominant, with the passive demands of such relationships leading to conflict and anxiety. The work they do is clearly masculine as defined by this culture—machinist, truck driver, plumber, etc.

They appear generally to have mastered the various developmental tasks of childhood and latency with no gross signs of disturbance appearing until adolescence. In this period there is an impairment in intellectual attainment and excessive, exaggerated masculine activity. With regard to the latter they become involved in street brawls, become preoccupied with high speed driving, enter aggressive sports, usually outside of formal organized high school activity, and are overzealous in physical contact. In a dramatic way there is an increase in partially controlled, socially acceptable (if not always socially approved and legally sanctioned), aggressive behavior.

In a striking number of such offenders, there is a history of prepubertal or postpubertal sexual traumata with older women, frequently the mother. These experiences appear to be directly associated not only with the generalized aggressive display, but also with the development of rape fantasies and with the rape itself. A brief clinical case will demonstrate this.

> Bill was seen at age 14½. He was a large, well-built young boy, physically much bigger than his peers. In the summer following his tenth birthday, an attractive, married, 20-year-old aunt took him into a picnic area, parked the car, and disrobed. He recalled being in a state of panic as she took his hands and placed them on her breasts and her genitals. He remembers that the feeling of fear was accompanied by excitement and sexual curiosity. That evening he lay awake until midnight at which time he arose, dressed, and walked to her house feeling once again both apprehensive and sexually excited. Although he knew she was home, she did not answer his knocking at the door, and, disappointed and angry, he went home. Following this, he found himself preoccupied with memories of the sexual experience. He became

> intensely aware of older women, mentally comparing their covered bodies with the memory of the nude body of his aunt. At this time he began to have sexually sadistic fantasies involving a female teacher and his mother. In the fantasy, he would steal into a house and find the teacher or his mother fully clothed. He would assault and undress them, make love to them, and then stab or shoot them. This fantasy, with little change in content, became a nightly masturbatory ritual at puberty, and at the age of 14½ he acted out the fantasy with a neighbor. She had offered him money to help her move furniture and as he followed her up the stairs to her home, which was relatively isolated, he had the thought that she was sexually provoking him. He became angry and when they entered the home he put his arm about her throat and throttled her until she lost consciousness. He undressed her and had intercourse with her during which he recalls giving vent to a steady stream of obscenities and feelings of increased anger. He wanted to stab and cut her but instead reached for a metal lamp and beat her until he thought he had killed her. Bill did not recapture the memory of the early sexual experience with his aunt until the third year of his therapy at which point there was a dream in which this aunt appears.

In nearly all of these patients there is body concern and a body narcissism. They are physically attractive and tend to be attentive to body health and hygiene. There are moderate obsessive features and clearly the explosive outbursts represent an anal-sadistic regression as a response to certain types of stress. They are capable, however, of finding socially acceptable outlets for this aggression under normal circumstances and similarly capable of aim-inhibited feelings of warmth, kindness, and love. The characteristic mode of relating, however, is in a cool, detached, overcontrolled manner. They are active, assertive, excessively counterdependent, and intolerant of the passive aspects required of true mutuality in relationships. True friendships are rare, because of their hyperalertness to narcissistic injury and, more important, because of the absence of depth and intensity in the formation of object ties. The ease with which feelings and concern for others can be withdrawn facilitates the release and expression of unneutralized aggression. What is noteworthy is the frequent reappearance of the concern with feelings of compassion and efforts to undo, or make some kind of restitution to the victim.

The full dynamic meaning of the compassion and remorse is not clear but it is evidently not understandable by a simple formula of guilt.

One observation may contribute to understanding this phenomenon and also help to clarify the intensity of the rage and its displacement. In this type of offender there is frequently a splitting of the ambivalent feelings toward mother. Their own mothers, and women in abstract, are overidealized as the sources of fulfillment of all infantile and narcissistic needs. Real women are unfaithful, untrustworthy, and depriving. In usual circumstances these two images are fused in their relationships with women, with the splitting occurring in situations of stress.

This splitting of the mother ambivalence is only one feature of the defensive structure that includes displacement and isolation as primary mechanisms. Counterphobic attitudes prevail to assist in the defense against castration fears, but it is the ineffectiveness of this defense that gives rise to the primitive aggression when a woman is the source of the castration anxiety. The inability of these patients to develop real devotion and loyalty makes them incapable of experiencing such traits in others, and this presents an appearance of paranoid mistrust. However, it does not have the quality of basic distrust, and the paranoid mechanisms are not seen as primary adaptive features, although they do come into play during the regressive episodes.

There is nothing noteworthy about perceptual or cognitive functioning or generally with the autonomous ego functions while such patients are in confinement. No gross impairments are present, nor is any specific pattern discernible. The average IQ of this group is somewhat higher than the other groups of rapists and is in fact higher than all other groups found to be sexually dangerous (pedophiles, incestors, etc.).

In additional comparisons with the other groups of rapists to be discussed, this group has the highest level of social and occupational adjustment, the most mature relationships with both men and women (although relations with the latter are less adequate); they are most responsive to treatment, can be released following the shortest commitment period, and the postparole adjustment is made with fewer difficulties and is most successful.

Within the center disciplinary action occasionally must be taken because of surly or unruly behavior toward security personnel or for fighting with another patient. Even when these offenders are not so involved, they frequently appear to be actively suppressing such behaviors and for the most part they are successful. They do not have an excessive disciplinary rate and among their peers, they are the most socially desirable patients.

Thus, what is seen during the confinement is quite different from the behavior immediately preceding their confinement and is quite at odds with the primitive, brutal acts of sexual violence that brought about the commitment. The data seem to be best understood in terms of a decompensation approaching psychotic proportions in men who have been able to deal with their intense rage toward women in relatively successful ways. The aggression itself appears to be both the result of a splitting of the mother ambivalence and also a defense against the experience of helplessness they feel in all object relationships, but with particular intensity with women.

Sexual Aim

A second pattern of characteristics that has been observed is quite different from the above. Here the act of rape is clearly motivated by sexual wishes, and the aggression is primarily in the service of this aim. The degree of aggressive behavior varies, but there is a relative absence of violence and the act lacks any of the characteristics of brutality.

The offense almost always takes place out of doors in isolated places such as darkened streets, a park, or wooded area. Most frequently the offender embraces the woman from behind, touching her breasts or genitals, holding on to her with some force but not to any excessive degree. If the victim should struggle and thus require more physical effort in order to be held, the offender will release her and flee. Thus, most of the offenders are charged with assault with intent to commit rape. At other times the victim is so frightened that she passively submits, and the rape takes place without any additional force. When the offender is apprehended, it is discovered that he has carried out such acts many times.

He is always very sexually aroused and fully aware of what he is doing, although at times he feels as if he were performing under a compulsion. The victim is always a stranger but not one that he comes upon by accident. She is usually someone he has seen while on a streetcar or bus and follows her off when she leaves.

It is not an impulsive act, however. This is a scene he has lived through many times in fantasy. It is a fantasy that is not only used in masturbation, but one that preoccupies him throughout his waking day and is composed in a relatively fixed pattern. In the fantasy, the woman he attacks first protests and then submits, more resignedly than willingly. During the sexual act, he performs with great skill, and she receives such intense pleasure that she falls in love with him and pleads with him to return. This differs from the not unusual adolescent fantasy in that he spends a large part of the evening hours traveling about the city searching for its fulfillment and in fact acts out the fantasy over and over again.

Rape is not always a feature of his sexual fantasies. When it is, the aggressive component of the fantasized assault, although somewhat erotic, never approaches a sadistic quality and is always secondary to the sexual aim. There is no evidence from the behavior, the conscious fantasy, or what we have learned of the unconscious dynamics of the act, that the aggression is eroticized to the degree seen in the third pattern of rape to be described below.

These sexual fantasies and the frequently impotent efforts at rape are not the only indicants of a disturbed sexual life. From early in adolescence he was acting out in perverted ways. Perversions involved partial aims, part objects, and substitute objects. Although he developed erotic feelings toward both boys and girls, there was a marked inhibition to any form of interpersonal sexuality. He was voyeuristic, fetishistic, and exhibitionistic, but a real heterosexuality existed only in fantasy, and homosexuality was intensely repressed. The repressive defenses against the latter were not entirely successful, and albeit no direct acting out of the homosexual feelings occurred, this was accomplished only by withdrawing and isolating himself from his male peers.

As he developed through adolescence, the guilt and shame that he felt regarding his perversions together with the need to defend by avoiding the homosexual wishes affected all peer relationships. The sense of loneliness increased, he became shy and increasingly inept and defective in social skills. The passive-feminine features of his personality became more dominant and were accompanied by intense feelings of impotency and inadequacy. Active masculinity was temporarily suspended for the passive gratifications offered by fantasy.

As such offenders approach the end of adolescence or enter young adult life, the passive solution gives added strength to the underlying homosexual feelings and a break through of such feelings becomes a real threat. The acts of rape occur at this time, but not only as a defense against the homosexual wish. They are also efforts at renewal, an adaptive effort to escape the implications of the passive-feminine resolution. The acts also serve to protest and deny the feelings of being an impotent castrate. They are also attempts to relieve the shame related to the pregenital perversions. (These offenders are able to describe the acts of rape in great detail including their thoughts and feelings and they do this in diagnostic interviews and early in the psychotherapy. In contrast, it is frequently many years of psychotherapy before the patient brings the material on the perversions into treatment.)

This type of rapist shows little or no antisocial behavior apart from the repetitive sexual offenses. He is, in fact, socially submissive and compliant. His friends and neighbors see him as a quiet, shy, "good boy," more lonely than most, but nonetheless quite normal. There is generally an absence of even a moderate amount of aggressive and assertive behavior. His approach to the tasks of life are tentative and have a phobic quality. This lack of assertiveness combines with a very negative self-esteem and a low level of aspiration, preventing him from making significant attainments in either educational or occupational areas. There is a stable employment history, but the level of work is far below his aptitude and potential abilities. Although intelligence varies across a wide range from dull normal to bright average and above among the rapists in this group, in no instance is the potential realized. Scholastic records show poor performance and frequently withdrawal from school prior to graduation. A brief description of one young man will illustrate some of these latter observations.

> Donald was first seen at age 17, following his commitment for a sexual assault. He had been walking home when he saw a young girl walking through a park. He came up from behind, placed his arms about her and threatened that he would hurt her if she resisted. She was 10 years old. He pushed her to the ground, undressed her, and attempted intercourse, but as he penetrated her, she cried that it hurt. He withdrew and ran away. He recalls feeling sexually excited and frightened that he might be caught and that he might not have an erection or might have a premature ejaculation.
>
> He was apprehended soon afterward and immediately confessed to an additional assault that had taken place a few weeks earlier. On this occasion, the victim had screamed despite the threats and Donald had run away.
>
> He had always felt that he was the unwanted member of his family and described himself as "lower than a snake under a rock." He had no friends, male or female. From ages 10 to 15, he was placed in special classes as the result of being classified as retarded. The Wechsler Adult Intelligence Scale administered at the center five years following his commitment showed a verbal IQ of 93, performance IQ of 107, and full Scale of 99, which is clearly not retardation. He describes the five years in special classes as "one long, unhappy nightmare."
>
> Less than two years before he committed the rape, he was convicted of being a voyeur, and since this was his first offense, the case was filed. Four months later he was again convicted of peeping and was sentenced to a training school for one year. One month following his release, he began his sexual assaults on girls.
>
> The defensive structures lead him to feel despised and anticipate rejection, and involve a type of denial leading to a naiveté that permits him to be victimized and used by others.
>
> A very particular family pattern was noted. This pattern included a weak father, not a passive-submissive man but one who found the demands of family responsibility too much and reneged in his role as father and husband. The mother tended to be very cold and ungiving, and an inconsistent, but harsh disciplinarian who infantilized her son by overwhelming control and suppression. Such mothers appear to be

preoccupied with sexual morality, and the most excessive repression occurred in response to any expression of erotic interest or pleasure.

Despite her coldness, the young boy was completely dependent upon his mother. By virtue of her restrictive and repressive behavior, he felt quite safe and protected not only from external dangers but from the threats of his own sexual wishes.

For the most part, these patients respond very well to group and individual psychotherapy and to planned programs of vocational, educational, and skill training, but the psychotherapeutic work requires a rather extended duration—of from four to six years.

Sex-Aggression Defusion

The third pattern of characteristics we have observed reveals the presence of a strong sadistic component. There appears to be no ability to experience sexual excitation without some degree of violence being present. The degree of sadism is quite variable with the extreme position seen in lust murders where excessive brutality and mutilation occur before, during, and even after the murder. This is relatively rare. The most usual behavioral pattern is forcible rape where violence is used to excite the offender, and after intercourse there is no further aggression. Such an offender is frequently impotent with women until there is resistance. To become sexually excited he will provoke in a teasing, playfully aggressive sexual manner, eliciting resistant or angry behavior from his partner. Her resistance arouses in him aggressive feelings that become, as his sexual play continues, more intense and autonomous. The arousal and maintenance of the sexual desire appears to be a direct function of this initially mild arousal of aggression. It should be noted that the affect of anger is not present.

In most patients in this group the sadistic quality of their sexuality is projected onto the victim. He sees her struggle and protestation not as a refusal but as a part of her own sexual excitation. "Women like to get roughed up, they enjoy a good fight." This belief is maintained even when the victim is literally fighting for her life and the offender has to injure her brutally to force her to submit to intercourse.

Although there is some neutralization or toning down of the aggression in relationships unrelated to sexual partners or to sexual situations, even here there are qualities of untamed aggression. Such an offender is assertive, overpowering, and somewhat hostile in all situations. Warmth and affection are completely absent. The most friendly meeting is punctuated by a touching and pushing so that any encounter with such persons is a bruising one. In less pathological cases this is the extroverted football player type who crushes other people in his narcissistic exuberance.

Such patients are usually married and in fact many have been married and divorced a number of times with, of course, never a sense of commitment to the marriage. The patient and often his wife are quite active in extramarital affairs. For the offender this constant search and seduction is essential for his sexual excitement, not as a defense against feelings of inadequacy, but to satisfy the aggressive component of his sexual wishes. Intercourse with his wife is described as physically relieving but unsatisfactory; not infrequently, he has difficulty in obtaining or maintaining an erection. Quite often feelings of revulsion follow connubial coitus. In some instances the patient is successful in having his wife play a masochistic role and he can obtain satisfaction with the aggression modulated within the fantasy. The wife permits herself to be tied up and verbally abused as she acts out a scene of being physically assaulted and raped by a stranger.

In many ways such men are similar to the psychopathic character. There is an extensive history of nonsexual, antisocial behavior, an absence of stable object ties, a lack of concern for others, difficulty in tolerating frustration, and poorly structured control functions. Most different, and most perplexing in view of the more primitive organization of their instinctual life, is the presence of industry and initiative in skill development, although this cannot be used for a socially successful occupational career. The psychopath obtains gratification in getting away with things, with getting by with active manipulation of others rather than with his own active efforts. Gratification is also obtained through active mastery and personal accomplishment. These patients will manipulate, demand, and exploit in order to gratify felt needs, but there is little or no gratification simply from the act of manipulation.

Developmentally there is an absence of the latency period. Sexual and aggressive behavior toward younger children, peers, and animals is prominent throughout the prepubertal years. Other indications of impulsive behavior and general lack of control, expressed in truancy, stealing, running away, and lying, are also present.

In comparison with the other types of rapists, patients in this group show the greatest degree of paranoid features, and under certain conditions these are of psychotic proportion. The world is perceived as a hostile place where one's survival is constantly under threat. Every human contact is made tentatively with mistrust and suspicion, experienced as a battle in which someone wins and someone loses. They cannot experience any sense of interpersonal mutuality.

Their entire life is tempestuous. Family life is marked by cruel and abusive behavior of the family members toward each other, except for the mother. Oddly enough she appears as the only member of the family with warm and compassionate feelings. Her major fault lies in her need to give that is so intense it takes on bizarre qualities and distorts her judgment of her children's behavior. She denies, rationalizes, and excuses the defective development of internal controls and actively supports a primitive oral demandingness.

The fathers of these patients were physically and psychologically cruel and sadistic not only in their own behavior, but would incite, support, and often demand physically aggressive behavior among the children.

> Frank is a 42-year-old divorced man who, since age 13, has spent a total of only five years out of prison. He was committed to the treatment center with a history of brutal sexual assaults on women; assaults that began shortly after his marriage at age 18, and that would occur while he was on parole from the previous offenses. In all, he has been found guilty of six separate sexual crimes.
>
> Only one of these offenses will be described, but it is quite typical. When he was 22 years old, five months after having been released

from prison where he had spent eighteen months for a sexual assault, he met a girl in a dance hall. He was married at the time, but almost from the time of the ceremony, he had been involved in one illicit affair after another.

He spent the evening dancing with the girl and then offered to drive her and her two girlfriends home. He drove one girl to her home, but when he reached the home of the second girl, he learned that both she and the girl he had spent the evening with planned to leave together. He sped away, drove outside of town to a small cemetery, parked the car and told the girls he wanted to have intercourse with them. The two girls jumped from the car but Frank was able to catch each of them and knock them to the ground. One girl fell on her stomach whereupon he leaped astride her pressing her face into the earth until she lost consciousness. Leaving her lying there for the moment, he turned to the other girl, throttled her until she too was in a semiconscious state. He then carried them back into the car, forced them to undress, lighting up the interior of the car so that he might watch. He then forced each girl to fellate him under both physical force and verbal threats that they would be killed. Following this he had intercourse with one of the girls. He sat for a while with the two girls, took some money from one, and then drove them home. The girls were in a hysterical condition when they arrived and a physician was immediately called. The police were notified, given a description of Frank and his car, and he was apprehended about one week later.

When Frank was interviewed, he expressed disbelief that the police were called immediately. He stated that he may have been rough with the girls, but he felt that they were quite agreeable to his advances. He had concluded that they only reported him when they saw him some nights later in a tavern. He was with his wife and therefore could not respond to their invitations to join him at their table. It was his conviction that the girls were angry out of jealousy and not because of his sexual assault.

Frank was the fourth of five children born into a very unstable and chaotic family. Only the patient's younger sister appears to be without physical or psychological stigmata. His two older brothers have criminal records that go back to early adolescence and a history of antisocial behavior in their prepubertal years. His older sister was born with a deformed hand. After some years of marriage her husband committed suicide. His father has a criminal history, and three half brothers, children of his father's from a previous marriage, all have extensive antisocial history with the oldest currently serving a life sentence for murder.

His father was an alcoholic and physically abusive to his family, especially to the patient. On one occasion he hung the patient by his tied hands in order to beat him. On still another occasion, he sat on the porch firing a rifle into the ground about Frank forcing him to ridicule himself in front of other family members. The father's criminal record included assault and rape of a young girl.

His mother was a very passive, compliant woman, who although completely unconcerned about the social or educational development of her children, was very nurturing and giving, in fact in excessive and unrealistic ways. She appeared oblivious to the social and psychological pathology in her family. Although she herself was not actively antisocial, her intense needs to mother resulted in either a denial or passive support of the psychopathy. For example, during one of Frank's imprisonments, she kept him supplied with contraband drugs.

The cruel and abusive treatment he received from his father was only a part of the violence that surrounded Frank through his early and late childhood. His mother states that as a baby he would frequently beat his head against a wall or hit himself on the head with objects. At the age of 7 he was in an automobile accident and suffered fractures of the right leg, right clavicle, right forearm, and pelvis. At age 16, he was caught in the blades of a manure spreader and received a fracture of his left leg and extensive damage to his penis and testicles.

His memory of his first sexual arousal has the same violent quality. He recalls being in a hayloft with one of his brothers and two or three of his cousins, one, a girl two years older. They were jumping up and down thrashing the hay, when he noted that as she jumped her dress rose above her waist. He became sexually aroused and jumped closer and closer to her until they bounced against each other and tumbled together into the hay. This vivid memory in many ways represents the quality of his sexuality.

Frank is of medium height, extremely stocky and muscular with a short thick neck. During his commitment at the center he was on disciplinary report, repeatedly having difficulties with both security personnel and fellow patients. These patients were seriously injured in separate altercations with him and each one under similar circumstances. They had gotten him angry in some face-to-face disagreement, but he waited until he could assault them from behind or take them by surprise. In a sociometric study, Frank scored as one of the least desirable men among the patients.

His voice was loud, raucous, and demanding. His needs were peremptory and his requests were orders. Certainly a prison is a paranoid community, and Frank has spent most of his adult life in correctional institutions. Nevertheless, his suspiciousness, lack of trust, unprovoked hostility, and the projection of this hostility reflect a characterological paranoid quality that is not simply institutional.

SUMMARY AND DISCUSSION

This paper organizes some clinical observations of sexually assaultive behavior and of the men who commit such acts. Although for purposes of exposition the data were organized into classes of rape, the heterogeneity among the patients who seem to represent types leaves no room for conviction regarding classification. However, it is obvious that character patterns exist. Paranoid features are predominant in the group Sex-Aggression, less so but still present in Aggressive Aim, and relatively absent in Sexual Aim. The primitive quality of the aggressive impulse shows the same pattern. Sexual perversions are far more common in Sexual Aim, with excessive defenses against homosexuality through exaggerated masculinity, predominant in Aggressive Aim. The level of object ties, the capacity to experience love, tenderness, and warmth, the ability to be kind and generous are clearly different among the three groups.

Their response to therapy, psychotherapy, and other rehabilitative procedures is different as is the progress of such therapy. We have had little success with the group of patients classified as Sex-Aggression. With the group Sexual Aim an alliance is established readily, but the passive, oral demanding quality of these patients makes movement slow and arduous. The primary difficulty with the Aggressive Aim group is the tendency to fall back to paranoid mechanisms wherein a negative therapeutic alliance develops and treatment is then broken. The relative absence of the capacity for warm and intimate object relationship does not permit the relationship to be sustained in the face of the regression.

We are planning a study that will evaluate the extramural adjustment of patients who have been released. On the basis of some data from an earlier study and from clinical impressions, the Sex-Aggressive group represents the greatest risk of maladaptive behavior. Although the numbers are small, they are still informative. Only six patients from this group have been released from the center. Two patients were released by court action with no parole or probation supervision prescribed and therefore there has been no follow-up with regard to social adjustment, but there is no evidence of any criminal acts. Of the remaining four, three have had their release revoked and the fourth is having serious difficulties in his second marriage of six months. The data for approximately thirty other rapists who have been released, although not broken down into subgroups and with no information on social adjustment, show that only one patient has committed another sexual assault.

The clinical classification presented here is based almost entirely on descriptive features, and the problems attendant on such a procedure are fully recognized. It has been our experience, however, in clinical and research activity that the classification has a utility not afforded by any other currently available.

The men who have been described in this paper are clearly dangerous. Even in those instances where the aggression is minimal, each of these men has placed himself in situations with women where there is a possible threat to the life of the victim. It is also clear that we are not able to determine without extensive clinical work when, if ever, this danger is at a minimum.

We are fully aware of the objections to special sex offender statutes. These objections are not only legal and moral, but also include the diagnostic, therapeutic, and predictive inadequacies of clinical science. Nevertheless, society has a right to be protected from such narcissistic violence. The life-long pathological relationships with women seen in these three groups of rapists give no reason to believe that a prison sentence will make them less dangerous.

REFERENCES

Calmas, Wilfred E. 1965. "Fantasies of the Mother-Son Relationship of the Rapist and the Pedophile." Ph.D. dissertation, Boston University.

Cohen, Murray L. and Harry L. Kozol. 1966. "Evaluation for Parole at a Sex Offender Treatment Center," *Federal Probation*, 30(September):50–55.

Cohen, Murray L., Theoharis Seghorn, and Wilfred E. Calmas. 1969. "Sociometric Study of Sex Offenders," *Journal of Abnormal Psychology* 71:249–55.

Cotton, Raymond D. 1969. "Civil Commitments from Prison: Abuse of Process or Protection of Society?" *Massachusetts Law Quarterly* 54:249–57.

Ellis, Albert and Ralph Brancale. 1956. *The Psychology of Sex Offenders.* Springfield, Illinois: Charles C Thomas.

Gebhard, Paul, John Gagnon, Wardell B. Pomeroy, and Cornelia Christenson. 1965. *Sex Offenders.* New York: Harper & Row.

Gould, Donald B. and Irving L. Hurwitz. 1965. "Out of Tune with the Times: the Massachusetts SDP Statute," *Boston University Law Review* 45:391–410.

Guttmacher, Manfred S. 1951. *Sex Offenses.* New York: Norton.

Guttmacher, Manfred S. and Henry Weihofen. 1952. *Psychiatry and the Law.* New York: Norton.

Holden, L. 1969. "Sex Psychopath Laws Generally, in Massachusetts, Specifically." Unpublished.

Kozol, Harry L., Murray L. Cohen, and Ralph Garofalo. 1966. "The Criminally Dangerous Sex Offender," *New England Journal of Medicine* 275:79–84.

Lopez, T. 1969. "Emotional Expression in the Adult Sex Offender." Ph.D. dissertation, Boston University.

McGarry, A. Louis and Raymond D. Cotton. 1969. "A Study in Civil Commitment: The Massachusetts Sexually Dangerous Persons Act," *Harvard Journal of Legislation* 6:263–306.

Sarafian, Robert A. 1963. "Treatment of the Criminally Dangerous Sex Offender," *Federal Probation,* 27(March):52–59.

Seghorn, Theoharis. 1970. "Adequacy in Ego Function in Rapists and Pedophiles." Ph.D. dissertation, Boston University.

Tenney, Charles W., Jr. 1962. "Sex, Sanity and Stupidity in Massachusetts," *Boston University Law Review* 42:1–31.

15 Rape Trauma Syndrome

ANN WOLBERT BURGESS AND
LYNDA LYTLE HOLMSTROM

THE literature on sexual offenses, including rape, is voluminous, but it has overlooked the victim. There is little information on the physical and psychological effects of rape, the therapeutic management of the victim, and the provisions for protection of the victim from further psychological insult.

In response to the problem of rape in the greater Boston area, the Victim Counseling Program was designed as a collaborative effort between Boston College School of Nursing and Boston City Hospital to provide a twenty-four-hour crisis intervention to rape victims and to study the problems the victim experiences as a result of being sexually assaulted.

The purpose of this paper is to report the immediate and long-term effects of rape as described by the victim.

Reprinted by permission from the *American Journal of Psychiatry* (1974), 131:981–86. Copyright © 1974, American Psychiatric Association.

METHOD

Study Population

The study population consisted of all persons who entered the emergency ward of Boston City Hospital during the one-year period July 20, 1972, through July 19, 1973, with the complaint of having been raped. The resulting sample was made up of 146 patients: 109 adult women, 34 female children, and 3 male children.

We divided these 146 patients into three main categories: (1) victims of forcible rape (either completed or attempted rape, usually the former), (2) victims in situations to which they were an accessory due to their inability to consent, and (3) victims of sexually stressful situations—sexual encounters to which they had initially consented but that went beyond their expectations and ability to control.

The rape trauma syndrome delineated in this paper was derived from an analysis of the symptoms of the 92 adult women in our sample who were victims of forcible rape. Future reports will analyze the problems of the other victims not directly included in this paper. Supplementary data were also gathered from 14 patients referred to the Victim Counseling Program by other agencies and from consultation calls from other clinicians working with rape victims.

A major research advantage in the location of the project at Boston City Hospital was the fact that it provided a heterogeneous sample of victims. Disparate social classes were included in the victim population. Ethnic groups included fairly equal numbers of black and white women, plus a smaller number of Oriental, Indian, and Spanish-speaking women. In regard to work status, the victims were career women, housewives, college students, and women on welfare. The age span was seventeen to seventy-three years; the group included single, married, divorced, separated, and widowed women as well as women living with men by consensual agreement (see table 15.1). A variety of occupations was represented, such as schoolteacher, business man-

Table 15.1. Distribution of Marital Status by Age (N = 92).

	Age				
Marital Status	*17–20*	*21–29*	*30–39*	*40–49*	*50–73*
Single	29	25	0	2	1
Married	2	1	2	2	0
Divorced, separated or widowed	2	6	7	2	2
Living with a man by consensual agreement	4	5	0	0	0

ager, researcher, assembly line worker, secretary, housekeeper, cocktail waitress, and health worker. There were victims with no children, women pregnant up to the eighth month, postpartum mothers, and women with anywhere from one to ten children. The women ranged in physical attractiveness from very pretty to very plain; they were dressed in styles ranging from high fashion to hippie clothes.

Interview Method

The counselors (the coauthors of this paper) were telephoned when a rape victim was admitted to the emergency department of Boston City Hospital; we arrived at the hospital within thirty minutes. We interviewed all the victims admitted during the one-year period regardless of time of day or night. Follow-up was conducted by use of telephone counseling or home visits. This method of study provided an 85 percent rate of direct follow-up. An additional 5 percent of the victims were followed indirectly through their families or reports by the police or other service agencies who knew them. Detailed notes of the interviews, telephone calls, and visits were then analyzed in terms of the symptoms reported as well as changes in thoughts, feelings, and behavior. We accompanied those victims who pressed charges to court and took detailed notes of all court proceedings and recorded the victims' reactions to this process (Burgess and Holmstrom, 1973; Burgess and Holmstrom, 1975). Contact with the families and other members of the victims' social network was part of the assessment and follow-up procedure.

MANIFESTATIONS OF RAPE TRAUMA SYNDROME

Rape trauma syndrome is the acute phase and long-term reorganization process that occurs as a result of forcible rape or attempted forcible rape. This syndrome of behavioral, somatic, and psychological reactions is an acute stress reaction to a life-threatening situation.

Forcible rape is defined in this paper as the carnal knowledge of a woman against her will. The important point is that rape is not primarily a sexual act. On the contrary, our data and those of researchers studying rapists suggest that rape is primarily an act of violence with sex as the weapon (Hayman and Lanza, 1971). Thus, it is not surprising that the victim experiences a syndrome with specific symptomatology as a result of the attack made upon her.

The syndrome is usually a two-phase reaction. The first is the acute phase. This is the period in which there is a great deal of disorganization in the woman's life style as a result of the rape. Physical symptoms are especially noticeable, and one prominent feeling noted is fear. The second phase begins when the woman begins to reorganize her life style. Although the time of onset varies from victim to victim, the second phase often begins about two to three weeks after the attack. Motor activity changes and nightmares and phobias are especially likely during this phase.

The medical regimen for the rape victim involves the prescription of antipregnancy and antivenereal disease medication after the physical and gynecological examination. The procedure usually includes prescribing 25 to 50 mg. of diethylstilbestrol a day for five days to protect against pregnancy and 4.8 million units of aqueous procaine penicillin intramuscularly to protect against venereal disease. Symptoms reported by the patient need to be distinguished as either side effects of the medication or conditions resulting from the sexual assault.

THE ACUTE PHASE: DISORGANIZATION

Impact Reactions

In the immediate hours following the rape, the woman may experience an extremely wide range of emotions. The impact of the rape may be so severe that feelings of shock or disbelief are expressed. When interviewed within a few hours of the rape, the women in this study mainly showed two emotional styles (Halleck, 1962): the expressed style, in which feelings of fear, anger, and anxiety were shown through such behavior as crying, sobbing, smiling, restlessness, and tenseness; and the controlled style, in which feelings were masked or hidden and a calm, composed, or subdued affect was seen. A fairly equal number of women showed each style.

Somatic Reactions

During the first several weeks following a rape many of the acute, somatic manifestations described below were evident.

1. Physical trauma. This included general soreness and bruising from the physical attack in various parts of the body such as the throat, neck, breasts, thighs, legs, and arms. Irritation and trauma to the throat were especially a problem for those women forced to have oral sex.

2. Skeletal muscle tension. Tension headaches and fatigue, as well as sleep pattern disturbances, were common symptoms. Women were either not able to sleep or would fall asleep only to wake and not be able to go back to sleep. Women who had been suddenly awakened from sleep by the assailant frequently found that they would wake each night at the time the attack had occurred. The victim might cry or scream out in her sleep. Victims also described experiencing a startle reaction—they became edgy and jumpy over minor incidents.

3. Gastrointestinal irritability. Women might complain of stomach pains. The appetite might be affected, and the victim might state she did not eat, food had no taste, or she felt nauseated from the antipregnancy medication. Victims described feeling nauseated just thinking of the rape.

4. Genitourinary disturbance. Gynecological symptoms such as a vaginal discharge, itching, a burning sensation on urination, and generalized pain were common. A number of women developed chronic vaginal infections following the rape. Rectal bleeding and pain were reported by women who had been forced to have anal sex.

Emotional Reactions

Victims expressed a wide gamut of feelings as they began to deal with the aftereffects of the rape. These feelings ranged from fear, humiliation, and embarrassment to anger, revenge, and self-blame. Fear of physical violence and death was the primary feeling described. Victims stated that it was not the rape that was so upsetting as much as the feeling that they would be killed as a result of the assault. One woman stated: "I am really mad. My life is disrupted; every part of it upset. And I have to be grateful I wasn't killed. I thought he would murder me."

Self-blame was another reaction women described—partly because of their socialization to the attitude of "blame the victim." For example, one young woman had entered her apartment building one afternoon after shopping. As she stopped to take her keys from her purse, she was assaulted in the hallway by a man who then forced his way into her apartment. She fought against him to the point of taking his knife and using it against him and in the process was quite severely beaten, bruised, and raped. Later she said: "I keep wondering maybe if I had done something different when I first saw him that it wouldn't have happened—neither he nor I would be in trouble. Maybe it was my fault. See, that's where I get when I think about it. My father always said whatever a man did to a woman, she provoked it."

Table 15.2. Severity of Symptoms during Reorganization Process by Age (N = 92).

	Age				
Severity of Symptoms[a]	*17–20*	*21–29*	*30–39*	*40–49*	*50–73*
No symptoms: no symptoms reported and symptoms denied when asked about a specific area	7	4	2	0	0
Mild symptoms: minor discomfort with the symptom reported; ability to talk about discomfort and feeling of control over symptom present	12	16	0	2	1
Moderate to severe symptoms: distressing symptoms such as phobic reactions described; ability to function but disturbance in life style present	12	5	1	1	2
Compounded symptoms: symptoms directly related to the rape plus reactivation of symptoms connected with a previously existing condition such as heavy drinking or drug use	7	5	3	3	0
No data available	0	5	4	0	0

[a]At time of telephone follow-up.

THE LONG-TERM PROCESS: REORGANIZATION

All victims in our sample experienced disorganization in their life style following the rape; their presence at the emergency ward of the hospital was testimony to that fact. Various factors affected their coping behavior regarding the trauma, i.e., ego strength, social network support, and the way people treated them as victims. This coping and reorganization process began at different times for the individual victims.

Victims did not all experience the same symptoms in the same sequence. What was consistent was that they did experience an acute phase of disorganization; many also experienced mild to moderate symptoms in the reorganization process, as table 15.2 indicates. Very few victims reported no symptoms. The number of victims over age thirty was small, but the data at least suggest that they might have been more prone to compounded reactions than the younger age groups.

Motor Activity

The long-term effects of the rape generally consisted of an increase in motor activity, especially through changing residence. The move, in order to ensure safety and to facilitate the victim's ability to function in a normal style, was very common. Forty-four of the 92 victims changed residences within a relatively short period of time after the rape. There was also a strong need to get away, and some women took trips to other states or countries.

Changing one's telephone number was a common reaction. It was often changed to an unlisted number. The woman might do this as a precautionary measure or as the result of threatening or obscene telephone calls. The victim was haunted by the fear that the assailant knew where she was and would come back for her.

Another common response was to turn for support to family members not normally seen daily: 48 women made special trips home, which often meant traveling to another city. In most cases, the victim told her parents what had happened, but occasionally the victim contacted her parents for support and did not explain why she was suddenly interested in talking with them or being with them. Twenty-five women turned to close friends for support. Thus 73 of the 92 women had some social network support to which they turned.

Nightmares

Dreams and nightmares could be very upsetting; 29 of the victims spontaneously described frightening dreams, as illustrated in the following statement:

> I had a terrifying nightmare and shook for two days. I was at work and there was this maniac killer in the store. He killed two of the salesgirls by slitting their throats. I'd gone to set the time clock and when I came back, the two girls were dead. I thought I was next. I had to go home. On the way I ran into the two girls I knew. We were walking along and we ran into the maniac killer and he was the man who attacked me—he looked like the man. One of the girls held back and said, "No—I'm staying here." I said I knew him and was going to fight him. At this point I woke with a terrible fear of impending doom and fright. I knew the knife part was real because it was the same knife the man held to my throat.

Women reported two types of dreams. One is similar to the above example where the victim wishes to do something but then wakes before acting. As time progressed, the second type occurred: the dream material changed somewhat, and frequently the victim reported mastery in the dream—being able to fight off the assailant. A young woman reported the following dream one month following her rape: "I had a knife and I was with the guy and I went to stab him and the knife bent. I did it again and he started bleeding and he died. Then I walked away laughing with the knife in my hand." This dream woke the victim up; she was crying so hard that her mother came in to see what was wrong. The girl stated that in her waking hours she never cries.

Traumatophobia

Sandor Rado (1948) coined the term traumatophobia to define the phobic reaction to a traumatic situation. We saw this phenomenon, which Rado described in war victims, in the rape victim. The phobia develops as a defensive reaction to the circumstances of the rape. The following were the most common phobic reactions within our sample.

Fear of indoors. This occurred in women who had been attacked while sleeping in their beds. As one victim stated, "I feel better outside. I can see what is coming. I feel trapped inside. My fear is being inside, not outside."

Fear of outdoors. This occurred in women who had been attacked outside of their homes. These women felt safe inside but would walk outside only when necessary. As one victim stated, "It is sheer terror for every step I take. I can't wait to get to the safety of my own place."

Fear of being alone. Almost all victims reported fears of being alone after the rape. Often the victim had been attacked while alone, when no one could come to her rescue. One victim said: "I can't stand being alone. I hear every little noise—the windows creaking. I am a bundle of nerves."

Fear of crowds. Many victims were quite apprehensive when they had to be in crowds or ride on public transportation. One 41-year-old victim said: "I'm still nervous from this, when people come too close—like when I have to go through the trolley station and the crowds are bad. When I am in crowds I get the bad thoughts. I will look over at a guy and if he looks really weird, I will hope something bad will happen to him."

Fear of people behind them. Some victims reported being fearful of people walking behind them. This was often common if the woman had been approached suddenly from behind. One victim said: "I can't stand to have someone behind me. When I feel someone is behind me, my heart starts pounding. Last week I turned on a guy that was walking in back of me and waited till he walked by. I just couldn't stand it."

Sexual fears. Many women experience a crisis in their sexual life as a result of the rape. Their normal sexual style has been disrupted. For the women who had no prior sexual activity, the incident was especially upsetting. For the victims who were sexually active, the fear increased when they were confronted by their husband or boyfriend with resuming sexual relations. One victim said: "My boyfriend thought it [the rape] might give me a negative feeling to sex and he wanted to be sure it didn't. That night as soon as we were back to the apartment he wanted to make love. I didn't want sex, especially that night. . . . He also admitted he wanted to know if he could make love to me or if he would be repulsed by me and unable to."

This victim and her boyfriend had considerable difficulty resuming many aspects of their relationship besides the sexual part. Many women were unable to resume a normal sexual style during the acute phase and persisted with the difficulty. One victim reported, five months after the assault, "There are times I get hysterical with my boyfriend. I don't want him near me; I get panicked. Sex is OK, but I still feel like screaming."

CLINICAL IMPLICATIONS

Management of Rape Trauma Syndrome

There are several basic assumptions underlying the model of crisis intervention that we used in counseling the rape victim.

1. The rape represented a crisis in that the woman's style of life was disrupted.
2. The victim was regarded as a normal woman who had been functioning adequately prior to the crisis situation.
3. Crisis counseling was the treatment model of choice to return the woman to her previous level of functioning as quickly as possible. The crisis counseling was issue-oriented treatment. Previous problems were not a priority for discussion; in no way was the counseling considered psychotherapy. When other issues of major concern that indicated another treatment model were identified by the victim, referrals were offered if the woman so requested.
4. We took an active role in initiating therapeutic contact as opposed to more traditional methods where the patient is expected to be the initiator. We went to the hospital to see the victim and then contacted her later by telephone.

Management of Compounded Reaction

There were some victims who had either a past or current history of physical, psychiatric, or social difficulties along with the rape trauma syndrome. A minority of the women in our sample were representative of this group. It became quite clear that these women needed more than crisis counseling. For this group, who were known to other therapists, physicians, or agencies, we assumed a secondary position. Support was provided for the rape incident, especially if the woman pressed charges against the assailant, but the counselor worked closely with the other agencies. It was noted that this group developed additional symptoms such as depression, psychotic behavior, psychosomatic disorders, suicidal behavior, and acting-out behavior associated with alcoholism, drug use, and sexual activity.

Management of Silent Rape Reaction

Since a significant proportion of women still do not report a rape, clinicians should be alert to a syndrome that we call the silent reaction to rape. This reaction occurs in the victim who has not told anyone of the rape, who has not settled her feelings and reactions on the issue, and who is carrying a tremendous psychological burden.

Evidence of such a syndrome became apparent to us as a result of life history data. A number of the women in our sample stated that they had been raped or molested at a previous time, often when they were children or adolescents. Often these women had not told anyone of the rape and had just kept the burden within themselves. The current rape reactivated their reaction to the prior experience. It became clear that because they had not talked about the previous rape, the syndrome had continued to develop, and these women had carried unresolved issues with them for years. They would talk as much of the previous rape as they did of the current situation.

A diagnosis of this syndrome should be considered when the clinician observes any of the following symptoms during an evaluative interview.

1. Increasing signs of anxiety as the interview progresses, such as long periods of silence, blocking of associations, minor stuttering, and physical distress.
2. The patient reports sudden marked irritability or actual avoidance of relationships with men or marked change in sexual behavior.

3. History of sudden onset of phobic reactions and fear of being alone, going outside, or being inside alone.
4. Persistent loss of self-confidence and self-esteem, an attitude of self-blame, paranoid feelings, or dreams of violence and/or nightmares.

Clinicians who suspect that the patient was raped in the past should be sure to include questions relevant to the woman's sexual behavior in the evaluation interview and to ask if anyone has ever attempted to assault her. Such questions may release considerable pent-up material relevant to forced sexual activity.

DISCUSSION

The crisis that results when a woman has been sexually assaulted is in the service of self-preservation. The victims in our sample felt that living was better than dying and that was the choice which had to be made. The victims' reactions to the impending threat to their lives is the nucleus around which an adaptive pattern may be noted.

The coping behavior of individuals to life-threatening situations has been documented in the work of such writers as Grinker and Spiegel (1945), Hamburg (1967); Kübler-Ross (1972); and Lindemann (1944). Kübler-Ross wrote of the process patients go through to come to terms with the fact of dying. Hamburg wrote of the resourcefulness of patients in facing catastrophic news and discussed a variety of implicit strategies by which patients face threats to life. This broad sequence of the acute phase, group support, and the long-run resolution described by these authors is compatible with the psychological work rape victims must do over time.

The majority of our rape victims were able to reorganize their life styles after the acute symptom phase, stay alert to possible threats to the life style, and focus upon protecting themselves from further insult. This latter action was difficult because the world was perceived as a traumatic environment after the assault. As one victim said, "On the exterior I am OK, but inside [I feel] every man is the rapist."

The rape victim was able to maintain a certain equilibrium. In no case did the victim show ego disintegration, bizarre behavior, or self-destructive behavior during the acute phase. As indicated, there were a few victims who did regress to a previous level of impaired functioning four to six weeks following the assault.

With the increasing reports of rape, this is not a private syndrome. It should be a societal concern, and its treatment should be a public charge. Professionals will be called upon increasingly to assist the rape victim in the acute and long-term reorganization process.

REFERENCES

Burgess, Ann W. and Lynda L. Holmstrom. 1973. "The Rape Victim in the Emergency Ward," *American Journal of Nursing* 73:1741–45.

——. 1975. "Rape: The Victim and the Criminal Justice System." In Israel Drapkin and Emilio Viano, eds., *Victimology*. Vol. III. *Crimes, Victims, and Justice,* pp. 21–30. Lexington, Mass.: Lexington Books.

Grinker, Roy R. and John P. Spiegel. 1945. *Men under Stress*. Philadelphia: Blakiston.

Halleck, Seymour L. 1962. "The Physician's Role in Management of Victims of Sex Offenders," *Journal of the American Medical Association* 180:273–78.

Hamburg, David A. 1967. "A Perspective on Coping Behavior," *Archives of General Psychiatry* 12:277–84.

Hayman, Charles R. and Charlene Lanza. 1971. "Sexual Assaults on Women and Girls," *American Journal of Obstetrics and Gynecology* 109:480–86.

Kübler-Ross, Elizabeth. 1972. "On Death and Dying," *Journal of the American Medical Association* 221:174–79.

Lindemann, Erich. 1944. "Symptomatology and Management of Acute Grief," *American Journal of Psychiatry* 101:141–48.

Rado, Sandor. 1949. "Pathodynamics and Treatment of Traumatic War Neurosis (Traumatophobia)," *Psychosomatic Medicine* 4:362–68.

16 Crisis Intervention with Victims of Rape

SANDRA SUTHERLAND
AND DONALD J. SCHERL

Mental health workers often feel unprepared or unable to help groups of individuals whose acute or chronic emotional problems are outside the boundaries of their professional skills. Rape victims represent one such group. However, professionals learn a series of generic skills and, as their knowledge and experience broaden, they should be able to refine these skills and relate them to an array of specific problems. This article describes specific skills that may be used by mental health workers to help victims of rape.

During 1966 and 1967, thirteen rape victims were seen in a setting similar to that in which a crisis intervention team might be located—a community mental health facility, for example. All the

Reprinted with permission of the National Association of Social Workers, from *Social Work* (January 1972), 17:37–42.

victims were young, unmarried adult females whose past histories were consistent with psychological health and achievement. Although length of contact with these patients varied, most were seen within forty-eight hours of the assault. Then it was possible to follow the majority of them during their acute reactions to the experience. As a result, the authors were able to identify a predictable pattern of responses common to these patients: (1) acute reaction, occurring immediately after the rape, and usually lasting for several days, (2) outward adjustment, and (3) integration and resolution of the experience. A series of specific mental health interventions was then designed to help the patients work through each phase as smoothly and completely as possible.

PHASE 1: ACUTE REACTION

Immediately following sexual assault, the victim's feelings include shock, disbelief, or dismay, followed by anxiety and fear. If she feels she did not invite the rape, i.e., she was not seductive or willingly compliant, she usually reports it to the police immediately or seeks medical attention. If neither of these steps is taken promptly, the worker should be alert to the possible diagnostic significance of her delay.

It is extremely important during Phase 1 for the worker to encourage the patient to talk about the assault. Often her relatives and friends try to dissuade her from thinking or talking about it in the mistaken belief that she will become more emotionally distressed. However, if others refuse to listen, the patient may conclude that they are embarrassed and ashamed and want to punish her for what has happened.

The worker must help the victim deal with the following issues during the acute phase: (1) medical attention, (2) legal matters and police contacts, (3) notification of family or friends, (4) current practical concerns, (5) clarification of factual information, (6) emotional responses, and (7) psychiatric consultation.

Medical attention

If the patient has not received medical attention when first seen by the mental health worker, arrangements for a physical examination should be made immediately to provide for the victim's health and any future medicolegal requirements. The examination should include tests for venereal disease and pregnancy. Since most pregnancy tests are negative until several weeks after conception, they are often postponed. However, they are valuable for legal purposes because they indicate whether the woman was already pregnant when the rape occurred.

The worker should know in advance which hospitals and clinics will accept rape victims and under what circumstances. Some will not treat such patients unless a police report has been filed; others are reluctant to become involved because of the time required for court appearances if the victim presses charges against her assailant.

Legal Services and Police Contacts

Although the patient may not currently plan to press charges or take any legal action, the worker should encourage her to discuss her situation with an attorney immediately. This step is important because her feelings and plans will fluctuate in the future. Unless the worker has had special legal training, he should not give the patient specific legal advice. He should, however, help her to locate competent legal services.

If the assault has not been reported to the police, the victim must decide whether she will do so and what role she wants the worker to take in that process. She should be aware that if she reports the rape, she can expect to have extensive contact with the police. For example, she will be asked to answer questions about the assault, locate where it occurred, and identify the assailant in a lineup. If she is anxious about reporting the assault to the police, it is appropriate for the worker to accompany her.

If the woman decides not to report the rape, she should be

aware of the possible consequences. In evaluating his own legal and moral obligations, the worker must remember that he has no proof, other than the alleged victim's statement, that a crime in fact occurred.

Notification of Family and/or Friends

The authors found that a rape victim's anxiety usually diminishes significantly after she has talked with a relative or friend about the assault. Thus the worker should help her decide who will be told (for example, parents, fiancé, friend, clergyman) and how this will be accomplished. After deciding whom she will notify, the woman has several alternatives: she can handle the notification herself, call or talk with the person in the worker's presence, or ask the worker to talk to the person while she is present. If none of these choices are possible, the worker can notify the relative or friend after discussing with the victim what she wants said.

As a general rule, the victim should do as much as possible herself. However, if she is unable to take any necessary step, she should be present when that step is handled for her. This will reduce her opportunities to misunderstand, distort, and fantasize about what the worker has said or done.

Current Practical Concerns

As part of meeting the victim's emotional needs, the worker should help her deal with current practical problems. For example, she should be prepared for possible publicity and the steps she can take to maintain her privacy. If the assault has already been publicized, she should know how to respond to possible questions. Other practical problems involve repair of windows, doors, and locks; money for the patient's immediate needs (if she has been robbed); and what she can do if she becomes frightened. By dealing with these details, the victim begins to detoxify the experience and temporarily sets it behind her. When this occurs, she enters Phase 2.

Clarification of Basic Information

It is important for the patient to understand the implications of what has happened to her. For example, one young woman who was unusually anxious during her initial interview with the social worker finally sobbed that she did not want to be pregnant. When the worker said it was impossible to tell at that point whether she was pregnant, the patient was astonished because she had thought all intercourse resulted in pregnancy. Although such serious misunderstandings are rare, the worker should be sure the victim's fund of information is adequate and accurate.

Emotional Responses

To respond appropriately to the issues that are psychologically relevant to the patient during Phase 1, the mental health worker must be willing to help her cope with both her feelings and reality. Thus an attitude of warmth, calmness, empathy, and firm consistency is likely to be most useful, that is the worker must be personally involved yet professionally objective. Because he must deal with the patient's emotional crisis as it manifests itself in both her behavior and affect, he would be as wrong to listen passively to her as he would be to guide her actively.

In the early part of the relationship, the worker may have to see the patient daily. Hours of his time may be spent on activities such as arranging for medical care, making a referral for legal services, helping the patient with police requirements, or just listening to her—all of which are valid uses of his time and energy. The worker will also want to formulate some tentative diagnostic impressions about why this person was assaulted at this specific time and place and assess the victim's strengths and limitations. These insights will help him understand the diagnostic meaning of the rape to the patient, which in turn will aid him in formulating a treatment plan.

Anticipatory guidance is an additional skill that is often useful in helping a rape victim not only to understand what she is currently experiencing, but to respond appropriately to the impact of later phases. Because a healthy single woman's emotional responses to rape are predictable, the worker should discuss them with her. The victim should be assured that her feelings are similar to those experienced by other women in her situation and that after several days or weeks, she will be able to return to her usual activities feeling less troubled (Phase 2). She should also realize that most women go through a third phase in which they feel depressed and mentally relive the experience. The worker should also give her the names of available mental health resources in case she needs further professional help during Phase 3.

Psychiatric Consultation

Although a psychiatrist should be consulted about each case, he will not need to be involved directly with the patient in most instances. However, when diagnostic, medicolegal, or clinical issues merit psychiatric evaluation or intervention, or the patient requests a psychiatric interview, he should become actively involved. For example, a psychiatrist would be helpful in evaluating the patient's current mental status or underlying pathology or in determining whether specific responses are normal or psychopathological.

PHASE 2: OUTWARD ADJUSTMENT

As the victim deals with practical problems, various psychological mechanisms such as denial or affect, suppression, and rationalization are called into play. She resumes her normal activities and appears to be adjusting to the assault. Her interest in seeking help and talking about her experience wanes rapidly. This response is healthy and should be encouraged, despite the fact that it represents an interim period of pseudoadjustment.

The worker's appropriate role in Phase 2 is one of support rather than challenge. Although he may be tempted to challenge the patient's defenses, such interference is unproductive and unsound. Final resolution and integration come later, after the patient has worked through the experience during Phase 3; thus her emotional reactions should be allowed to run their course.

Unless the woman requests specific help, there is relatively little for the worker to do during Phase 2. He should encourage the patient to keep her follow-up medical appointments. However, because she denies the emotional impact of the assault and feels it is best forgotten, she will often fail to keep these appointments.

During Phase 2, the worker may have additional opportunities to work with the patient's relatives or friends, who may want to talk with someone after helping the patient through the acute crisis. Often they feel that the woman has been ruined and may convey this to her so strongly that it becomes part of her self-image. They may be extremely angry with the patient, feeling that she was seductive, careless, or did not heed their warnings. In such situations, the worker can help these relatives or friends realistically evaluate the rape and their own reactions to it.

As in Phase 1, anticipatory guidance is important because most patients do not expect to experience further emotional reactions. The worker should describe the feelings that rape victims normally experience during Phase 3 and assure the patient that mental health resources will be available if she needs them.

Sometimes a rape victim will seek help for the first time during Phase 2, usually because a friend or relative generally is reluctant to involve herself in an intensive helping relationship at this time, and should not be criticized for her feelings. The worker can help her gain perspective about her current reaction by describing Phases 1 and 3 and can offer psychiatric services if she requests such help. It is also helpful if the worker talks with the relative or friend who urged the victim to seek help. The aim of such an interview is to counsel the person about the victim's current status and predictable future reactions and to give him an opportunity to discuss his own feelings.

PHASE 3: INTEGRATION

When Phase 3 begins, the patient usually feels depressed and wants to talk. She should again be reassured that such feelings are predictable and usually do not indicate serious emotional problems. Arrangements for counseling can appropriately be made at this time.

Frequently, a specific incident precipitates Phase 3, for example, the patient finds she is pregnant, receives a court summons, or sees a man who resembles her assailant. In such cases, the worker should direct his initial efforts toward helping the patient deal with the precipitating factor and discuss her feelings with her after the practical problem has been resolved. When there is no identifiable precipitant to Phase 3, the victim seeks help because she finds she is constantly thinking about the assault and wonders why.

In the third phase, two central issues must be worked through with the victim: her feelings about herself and her feelings about the assailant. Often she feels guilty, unclean, or damaged, and it is useless for the worker to reassure her until she has talked about these feelings. Although the worker may believe there was nothing the woman could have done to prevent the attack, he must be cautious about saying so. It is preferable for the victim to reach this conclusion (if it is an accurate one) on her own, guided by appropriate questions from the worker. Some patients need to go through a period of guilt and self-punishment as a first step toward integrating the experience. If the worker challenges their guilt prematurely, such patients often feel he does not understand and therefore cannot help them. If a patient does bear partial responsibility for the assault, she must be helped to understand her behavior before she can fully integrate the experience.

The victim's feelings of being dirty or despoiled may be more difficult to deal with. If she continues to be troubled by such feelings, a psychiatric consultation should be arranged to evaluate their origin and prognostic significance, and if necessary, psychiatric treatment should be initiated.

The second major issue to be resolved during Phase 3 concerns the victim's feelings about her assailant. Her initial feelings of anger—denied, suppressed, or rationalized during Phase 2—now reappear for resolution. Frequently, her anger toward the assailant is distorted into anger toward herself, which exacerbates the characteristic depression of this phase. Thus, it is important for the worker to permit the patient to express this anger.

The victim's depression, fear, and anxiety can be considered within normal limits if her depression is reactive, time limited, and nonpsychotic. Further careful evaluation is needed if her normal sleeping or eating patterns are disrupted, she suffers from generalized fears, or indulges in compulsive rituals.

The type of mental health services the patient needs during Phase 3 depends on her personality structure and how easily and completely she has experienced Phases 1 and 2. Although it may be necessary for the worker to see the patient frequently at the beginning of this phase to help her deal with specific problems or crises, this should be discouraged later in this phase. If such feelings persist, a psychiatric consultation is advisable.

Usually Phase 3 is relatively brief. After several weeks, most women have integrated the experience and it takes its appropriate place in the past. If the patient does not accomplish this within a reasonable period, her response is probably not within normal limits; i.e., the rape has created or rearoused feelings that the ego cannot handle without the development of symptoms at the psychotic, neurotic, or behavioral level. In such cases, the worker must evaluate the degree of stress involved in the experience and its aftermath and the ego's capacity to cope with stress of that magnitude.

Occasionally a rape victim seeks professional help for the first time during Phase 3. In such cases it is important for the worker to understand why the victim asked for help and what the specific reasons are for her emotional discomfort. In addition to the issues usually dealt with in Phase 3, it is helpful if the worker discusses with the patient her reactions to date and how she has dealt with them. If she can relive the shock, anxiety, and dismay of Phase 1 and be reassured that these reactions are normal and predictable, it will be easier for her to resolve the issues that normally arise during Phase 3 and integrate the total experience. All women seen during Phase 3 should be reassured about the continued availability of mental health resources.

CONCLUSION

As a result of their work with a number of young, unmarried adult victims of rape, the authors were able to delineate three predictable and sequential phases that apparently represent a normal cycle of emotional responses to sexual assault. Using this knowledge, the authors then developed a series of interventions to help these patients work through these phases successfully. The response patterns described provided only a general context in which to help such patients; the detailed contents for individual patients were as varied as their personalities, backgrounds, and experiences. Thus no one victim required each intervention as described.

Although rape victims represent a specific group, the generic skills to help them are included in the repertories of most mental health workers and are general enough to use with diverse groups of patients. In any treatment situation a meaningful conceptual framework must be developed to understand the patient's emotional reactions so that the necessary countermeasures can be applied.

One important question that remains unanswered is whether the information gathered by the authors has implications for the prevention of rape. For example, if a woman enters a socioeconomic or cultural area different from her own, she should anticipate how her presence will be interpreted by those who live there. By understanding her own behavior and how it is perceived by others, and by knowing how to avoid communicating inappropriate cues, it is possible that rape could sometimes be avoided. Although the sample size was not large enough to justify any broad generalizations, the information described in this article may have useful applications in preventing such crimes.

17 The Philadelphia Rape Victim Project

JOSEPH J. PETERS

ACCORDING to official reports, the incidence of rape is increasing in urban areas. Philadelphia police records showed 646 cases of forcible rape in 1960. In 1968, approximately 800 cases of alleged rape were brought to Philadelphia General Hospital (PGH) by the police for gynecological examination, and in 1972, 864. Although most rape victims are brought to PGH because of the reluctance of other city hospitals to treat such cases, 864 is a fraction of the rapes committed annually. Various authors (Amir, 1971; Massey et al., 1971) estimate that from 5 to 35 percent of forcible rape cases are reported to the police. While the 35 percent estimate seems more realistic to this author, how can anyone reliably estimate the number of unreported rapes?

Police and court statistics, generally obtained from sources such as the yearly *Uniform Crime Reports,* form the basis of so-

The research for this study was supported by the National Institute of Mental Health (Grant Number 21304).

ciological literature on the subject. While these studies offer data on matters such as the number of rapes reported, convictions obtained, charges dropped, and victim's relationship to the offender, they tend to view rape from the point of view of the legal process instead of from that of the individual victim. Although surveys based on questionnaries supplement these types of official records, their authors, such as Kinsey, et al. (1953) and Landis (1956), do not separate alleged rape from other sexual offenses. Consequently, their victim data are diluted by a wide range of sexual assaults such as exhibitionism and sodomy. An additional problem with these surveys is that the information is often gathered retrospectively, years after the assault. Amir's (1971) published information on forcible rape was gleaned from 1958 and 1960 Philadelphia police records. While interesting, it reflects the vicissitudes of official record keeping and the distortions of plea bargaining in the criminal justice system. Clinical studies of the victims and interviews with the family, police, and other participants in the postrape scene at the time of the incident can avoid some of these problems. The Philadelphia rape study is attempting this, as will be described in this article, which also provides some preliminary data.

A clinical study of women personally involved with alleged rape shows that the emotions are so intense that the responses of the victim, her family, and the community can be both irrational and insensitive. Certain practices of the police and court personnel in handling victims are abrasive and demeaning. Individual reactions within the criminal justice system are often highly subjective and appear to be differentially affected by variables such as race and socioeconomic status. A program organized to study rape victims should take these factors into consideration by including among its staff both males and females from various socioeconomic backgrounds and races, persons who are sensitive to the plight of the rape victim.

Another problem in studying rape victims lies in the sequence of emotional reactions to the rape. Although the initial shock of the rape experience is usually coupled with intense concern for the victim, a period of denial of emotional response by both victim and those close to her often follows. This serves to blunt the emotional shock of the trauma. Then, once the rapist is apprehended and convicted, the authorities' interest in the victim is ended. The subsequent emotional, biopsychological, and sociolegal effects that the experience might have on the victim's postrape adjustment and mental health are generally ignored. Although community resources are freely spent to convict and rehabilitate the offender, little is done for the victim.

PGH RAPE CENTER

The Philadelphia General Hospital Center for Rape Concern was established in 1970. The unit is staffed by an interdisciplinary team and is an outgrowth of a group psychotherapy program for probationed sex offenders initiated at PGH in 1955. The sex offender program was originally staffed by six certified psychiatrists. In 1966, the team was expanded to include research sociologists and psychologists as evaluators of program results. In the analysis of the sex offender program, the team became increasingly aware that the focus on offenders had resulted in inadequate concern for victims of sex crimes. The rape victim study was organized to remedy this defect. Its objectives are twofold: (1) to study the social and psychological effects of rape upon females and to correlate differential victim reactions with pre-rape personality, circumstances surrounding the rape, and support mechanisms from significant others, including community reaction and rehabilitative services; and (2) to study the effects of the criminal justice system on the victim.

PGH, a municipal hospital, is the logical location for this study since most of the reported cases of rape in the city are taken by the police to its emergency service. This practice results from the reluctance of private hospitals to handle rape cases because of possible entanglements with the criminal justice system and news agencies. Hospitals that cooperate with the police and report their findings run the risk of exposing their emergency service, laboratory, and record-keeping personnel to cross-examination during legal proceedings by the offender's attorney, whose objective is to discredit the evidence against his client.

When the victim is taken by the police to the PGH emergency service, medical and gynecological examinations record evidence of physical assault and vaginal penetration. The victim is treated prophylactically for venereal disease and pregnancy. During the first year of our program, we conducted an immediate psychiatric evaluation as part of this emergency-room examination, recording the victim's emotional state and reaction soon after the incident and collecting extensive social-psychological information. However, the chaos and pressure of other emergency-room problems dominated the information gathered. Rather than psychiatric data about rape-related reactions of the victim, we found more information about emergency room problems, such as the long wait before examination and the attitudes of attending staff and accompanying police. Therefore, we discontinued the emergency room evaluation, at the same time making efforts to do something about the victim's complaints regarding police and emergency-room personnel.

Information now is collected from the victim during a home visit by a social worker, made within forty-eight hours after the victim is examined in the emergency service. Originally, home visitors were of both sexes and various races. We still use both black and white social workers, but women only. We feel initial contact after being raped, particularly for the minors who constitute half our population, is less threatening if conducted by a woman social worker.

After an extensive social-psychological interview, the home visitor arranges for a staff psychiatrist to examine the victim. The psychiatrist attempts to assess the pre-rape personality for subsequent correlation with various aspects of the rape incident. The examination is used as a baseline from which to follow one-year post-rape adjustment in the following areas of the victim's life: personal, familial, social, vocational, medical, and psychological. The psychiatric interview is conducted at the hospital as soon after the initial home visit as possible, usually within one week. Subsequent interviews are arranged if, in the opinion of the examining psychiatrist, the victim is in need of additional counseling. However, the patient is free to reject the psychiatrist's judgment that a return visit is needed. For severely disturbed victims, where the opinion of the social worker is that they cannot come to the hospital, a staff psychiatrist is sent to the home to evaluate and make further recommendations for treatment.

The home visitor returns every three or four months for one year. Throughout this period she observes the victim's post-rape adjustment, offering aid in securing additional help if such is needed, and serves as a liaison for other recommended services.

At the onset of this project, the emergency-room personnel resisted the introduction of additional procedures for sexual assault cases. After overcoming this initial resistence, we found that they were relieved that physical care for pregnancy and venereal diseases are supplemented by psychiatric evaluation and home visitor follow-up. Nurses have been particularly cooperative. In the past, when they had referred victims for psychiatric treatment or to community mental health services, only 10 percent of the victims reported.

It is understandable that conventional referral usually fails. Not only have there been few experienced persons available to work with rape victims, but soon after the initial trauma, a massive denial, involving all parties, usually develops. The victim appears emotionally settled. The family is relieved to drop the charges. The police and courts, already overburdened and biased with a male viewpoint, are somewhat skeptical about the reliability of the victim's complaints and seem anxious to forget the matter. In fact, judicial practice requires that the judge, in his charge to the jury, mention the emotional state of the victim, influencing the perceived reliability of her testimony. In no other crime is this required of the judge. Community mental health services and even private psychiatric facilities do not want to become involved because they fail to appreciate the severity of the trauma to the rape victim, and they do not wish to become entangled in the criminal justice system. Those who do see the victim a few weeks after the offense often find little gross psychological reaction. This phenomenon is consistent with a report from Boston (Sutherland and Sherl, 1970) on thirteen cases of rape of women Vista workers between the ages of 18 and 24. The study reported that a period of denial and pseudo-adjustment developed a few weeks after the initial reaction of shock, anxiety, and dismay. No symptoms were evident during this time and conventional services were rejected. However, the authors report that a few weeks to months later, depression developed and that the cause of this postrape reaction frequently went unrecognized or was misdiagnosed because of the time lapse between the rape and the later emotional distress. Even the victim was unaware that her later problems were rape-related.

In the Philadelphia project, a home visit is attempted as soon as possible following initial contact, while anxiety and concern are at a peak and symptoms are not yet masked by denial and repression. In later visits over a period of a year, the home visitor monitors the victim's emotional state and thus is in a position to identify any delayed post-rape reaction and offer assistance in helping the victim to cope with it. For minors, a home visitor is sent during the evening or on weekends when the entire family is likely to be available. About half of the first attempted visits end in satisfactory contact.

PSYCHOLOGICAL EFFECTS OF CHILDHOOD RAPE

These contacts with the children and their families are especially important in order to spare the young victim future psychological problems that often may not appear until she becomes an adult. During twenty years of private psychiatric practice, the author has treated thirteen women who were victims of childhood rape and has had an opportunity to observe the consequences of failure to help the young victim at the time the incident occurs. Eleven were raped by people they knew, six by their own fathers. The offenders included an architect, a minister, and a judge. They were men the young girls trusted and even loved. While the psychological problems that caused the women to seek psychiatric help as adults were varied, the common denominator in all cases was the failure of the mother to give the child the support she needed at the time the offense occurred.

Only two of the thirteen victims were attacked by strangers. And although violence by a stranger is surely terrifying, at least it can be dealt with directly. Everyone can express rage at the offender and support the child. For the child, however, seduction or forcible rape by a respected authority figure is particularly disillusioning, and her difficulties are compounded when those surrounding the victim find it hard to accept that a loved one has perpetrated such a heinous offense. In their confusion, they withhold the support the child so desperately needs. It is imperative that the incident be dealt with as soon as possible in order to minimize psychic trauma, and there is no substitute for a mother's loving and consistent concern.

COURT STUDY

Our program also attempts to follow victims through court. A research lawyer and court observer try to ensure objectivity of evaluation by analyzing the procedure in court without previous contact with the victim. If the victim needs personal support in court, it is provided by the social work staff rather than the legal study staff. Ultimately, all information gathered by the legal staff will be compared with the victim's report of her response to the court experience.

T. Gibbens and Prince (1963) reported that in sexual offense cases involving children who came to court, the victims appeared to have a less satisfactory recovery than those who did not have to face the additional burden of court testimony. This reaction might be related to a more seriously disturbed family background or to the seriousness of the violation that gets to court rather than the court experience itself. Problems involved in trying to isolate the factor most disturbing to the victim who has to testify in court are illustrated by one of the cases in our study. A father charged with incestuous relations with his daughters, ages 9 and 16, was given a probationary sentence with the provision that he undergo psychiatric treatment. When he continued to engage his daughters in sexual relations, they reported this to their mother. She, in turn, notified the authorities, who instituted court proceedings that resulted in conviction and a five-to-ten-year prison sentence. The older daughter was called upon during the trial to identify a film her father had made of them during intercourse. As a result, she felt extremely guilty for contributing to her father's conviction and incarceration. Her mother, in contrast, felt the judge had been too lenient, and moved to reopen the case. What is most traumatic to the victim: her incestuous relations with her father; her court participation that helped to convict him; or her mother's willingness to expose her once more to continued court proceedings, including exposure to the sex film?

Not infrequently, the most disturbed victims and their families drop out of the lengthy court procedure. One victim visiting Philadelphia was raped by three men and their female accomplice. She was very disturbed and embarrassed at the preliminary hearing by the three attorneys defending the men. She then lost her appetite, could not sleep, and quit work. She and her mother refused to reappear in Philadelphia for the trial. In view of her traumatic response to the preliminary hearing, it appeared that she might be better off emotionally if she were to avoid the certain stress of the court trial. Following six months of intensive support by social and psychiatric staff, however, this victim recovered enough to withstand ten days of grueling trial by jury. Two of the males who were apprehended were found guilty. Without constant support during the trial by the PGH Center's staff, the victim could not have survived the ordeal of lengthy trial cross-examination by several defense attorneys.

POLICE REACTION

The initial response of the police to the alleged rape is particularly important because it determines whether the case will be introduced into the criminal justice process or dismissed as unfounded. Research in Philadelphia indicates that the decision of the police to give credence to a report of rape appears to be influenced by many factors. If violence and presumptive evidence of forcible rape are present and the offender is a stranger to the victim, there is a greater chance that the allegation will be taken seriously than if no physical harm is evident or if the offender is an acquaintance. There are also variations in police response that seem to reflect racial bias. If the victim is black and the offender is white, there appears to be less concern than if the combination is reversed. However, if the white victim is known to socialize with blacks, the police may be slow to respond to the victim's allegation of rape. In the minds of some law enforcement officials, association with blacks is tantamount to asking to be victimized. In the case of a 25-year-old white reporter who was forcibly raped when her apartment was broken into, for instance, credibility was high until the police found a poster of Eldridge Cleaver on the wall.

Nonresistance on the part of the victim also confounds the police determination of credibility. The victim frequently complains that the police discount her allegations and assume she actively participated in the sexual act because she reported lying passively at gun or knife point to avoid physical harm. This attitude is in contrast to nonsexual assaults, such as armed robbery or hijacking, where the victims invariably are advised against resistance to avoid the possibility of bodily harm.

The degree of emotional upset also appears to be an indicator of credibility for the police. One rape victim (Anonymous, 1969) has noted: "I told the policeman what happened. He was distant, seemed skeptical as he took notes, saying nothing to me that would indicate sympathy or concern. Perhaps it was the way I told my story . . . no tears . . . commenting on how skillful the intruder must have been to have climbed into my apartment in the first place . . . . The detective looked at me coolly and said, 'I still don't know exactly what he did do.' And then I realized that he hadn't believed a word." We frequently receive this same kind of complaint.

Police attitudes toward an alleged rape may often be affected by the victim's relationship to the offender. In one reported instance, a black victim reported that she had been raped by a male acquaintance. The police concluded that it could not be rape if the offender was not a stranger and they refused to question the man. The victim then told her fiancé and her brother about the offense. Later, the alleged rapist was found shot to death, and a gun owned by the fiancé was discovered at the scene. The fiancé is being held for murder and the victim's brother, whom the victim believes actually avenged her rape, is a fugitive. The rape victim has been admitted to a hospital for an acute psychotic reaction. She blames herself for her fiancé's incarceration, her brother's fugitive state, and the rapist's death.

The very young victim has special problems of credibility. Adults find it disturbing to accept the fact that another adult, usually known to the victim and perhaps a family member, can perpetrate such an act against a child. The problem is further complicated because legal codes fail to distinguish between acts such as rape, exhibitionism, and fondling, and employ general descriptions such as "corrupting the morals of a minor" and archaic terms like "sodomy." Because these anachronistic and imprecise legalisms also carry with them equally outdated punitive measures, police and court personnel are reluctant to subject alleged offenders to the possibility of harsh sentences for sexual molestation when those punishments were intended for forcible rape. A legal code that distinguishes between rape and lesser forms of sexual offenses and makes the punishment more realistically fit the crime might help to alleviate some of these problems.

ESTABLISHING CREDIBILITY

In studying the problem of victim credibility, the PGH rape center has tried to scale factors that might help determine the reliability of alleged rape reports. We finally chose five factors, scaled as follows, with 5 receiving the greatest weight: evidence of violent sexual assault, 5; evidence of nonsexual violence such as bruise marks around the neck, face, head and body and the condition of the clothing, 4; rape by a stranger, 3; an incident involving more than one offender, 2; if the victim is less than 16 years old and the offender is 10 or more years older than the victim, 1. While we remain skeptical about the value of the particular weights assigned, we hope that qualitative inclusion of these five factors may help toward establishing the credibility of alleged rape. The rape of highest credibility should have at least two factors and a rape of middle credibility at least one.

We have made an initial check of the applicability of this operational definition through a review of the records of the first 100 cases. Distributions reveal that 40 cases qualified for highest credibility, 48 middle credibility, and 22 low credibility.

DATA COLLECTED

We now present some of the data collected by the PGH social workers on 149 alleged victims during home visits. In this sample, adults (18 years and older) numbered 84 (56 percent), adolescents (13 to 17 years old) numbered 47 (32 percent), children (12 and under) numbered 15 (10 percent). Although the racial division for the total population was 21 percent white, 77 percent black, and 2 percent other, blacks comprised 95 percent of the adolescents. Adults and children were 69 percent and 67 percent black respectively.

In 95 cases (64 percent), there was only one offender per victim; in 54 cases (35 percent) there were two or more offenders. Of single offender cases, 82 (88 percent) were black and 9 (10 percent) were white. Of the 54 multiple offender incidents, the racial compositions were: all black offenders, 49 (91 percent), all white offenders 2 (4 percent), and two other. One incident involved offenders of two races.

In the single offender rapes, 22 percent were interracial, 3 percent white on black and 19 percent black on white. Interracial group rapes were 15 percent: 2 percent white on black victim, 11 percent black on white victim, and 2 percent (1 case) black and white on white victim. The total interracial incidents combining single and multiple offenders were 20 percent, somewhat higher than Amir's (1971) findings.

Concerning victim-offender relationships, adults were most

likely to be raped by strangers (80 percent), adolescents by a casual acquaintance (45 percent), friend (20 percent) or total stranger (25 percent). The majority of children were raped by a friend, extended family member, or acquaintance (9 of 15 cases)—the remaining 6 were raped by total strangers. There were only 3 incest cases reported, 2 involving adolescent victims and 1 an adult. No child victim incest cases were reported to the police in contrast to private practice experience where more than half the cases involved incest.

A total stranger was involved in 90 percent of the white victims and 51 percent of the black victims. This differential may reflect the fact that 40 percent of the black victims were adolescents. All nuclear and extended family cases involved blacks, which suggests that whites probably do not report intrafamily rapes to the police. These may be the cases which, years later, are found in a psychiatrist's office with emotional problems that are ultimately traced to childhood sexual experience.

Children and adolescents knew the name of their offender 70 percent of the time. For adults, 80 percent of the rapists were strangers.

Adults and children were judged by the social workers as not involved in precipitating their victimization in 90 percent of the rape cases. In contrast, adolescents were judged to lack discretion or to have complicity in over 40 percent of the cases. A separate credibility score, developed for use by home visitors, was lower for these adolescents. This probably parallels the police attitude and clinicians' impression that is frequently skeptical of rapes reported by adolescents. When parents allow the adolescent to go unsupervised and she is confronted by them for overstepping family norms such as staying out all night or becoming pregnant, she may claim rape. Clinicians regard the crisis as a family symptom rather than an exclusive problem of the victim or offender.

Of the 15 children, 10 (66 percent) told the social worker there were sexual acts other than penile-vaginal intercourse. In the adolescent sample, 39 percent, and in the adult sample, 19 percent, claimed no penile-vaginal intercourse. Because the police cannot classify these cases as rape, their annual rape totals are less than ours, which count all alleged rapes brought to the emergency room.

Intimidation by an object was reported in 78 cases, or one-half the sample. A knife was used in 52 percent of the cases, a gun in 30 percent. Those threatened with a knife or gun included 5 children, 9 adolescents, and 47 adults. Other objects such as a bottle, stick, or multiple items for threatening were reported by adults only (20 percent of the intimidated group).

Black victims more often reported intimidation with a gun; whites more often reported intimidation with a knife.

Prior sexual assaults were recorded for 33 percent of the children, 11 percent of the adolescents, and 8 percent of the adults. Prior nonsexual assaults were reported by 49 percent of the adolescents, 38 percent of the adults, and only 13 percent of the children. This finding suggests that sexual assaults of children may go unreported longer than nonsexual assaults (as incest seems to go unreported).

Victim's complaints of general physical distress from the rape is highest from adults, next from adolescents, and least from children. Whether these differences reflect the nonpenetration reported in 66 percent of the children or the phenomenon of withdrawal and noncomplaining in minors (adolescents and children) is yet undetermined. Perhaps the fact that the offender is more often known to them may spare the younger victim physical abuse.

There is a bimodal distribution on a scale of 0 (31 percent) to 4 (32 percent) concerning pain from the rape for the total sample. Adolescents report more pain than adults who, in turn, exceed children. But in all, the bimodal distribution persists.

Concern for venereal disease also reflects a bimodal distribution of 0 (42 percent) to 4 (24 percent). As expected, the concern is highest with adults, less with adolescents, and least with children. Whites predominate over blacks in fearing venereal disease.

Fear of pregnancy is again bimodally distributed in the total population 0 (55 percent) and 4 (23 percent). Adolescents are more fearful, followed by adults. This finding may reflect the adults' knowledge of contraceptives and abortion and the fact that children are unlikely to be as conscious of the possibility of pregnancy following rape. Further, fear of pregnancy may have precipitated the allegation of rape by the adolescent and/or her parent(s).

Pain from medical treatment is highest in adolescents, which may reflect reaction to the vaginal examination and penicillin shots to prevent venereal disease.

Fear of offender retaliation has a bimodal distribution at 0 (41 percent) and 4 (highest—25 percent). Adults report such a fear in 66 percent of the cases, adolescents in 53 percent and children in 33 percent. It is interesting to note that the greatest fear of offender retaliation is experienced by that part of the population (adults) most likely to be raped by strangers.

Fear of being raped again has the highest mean score for any type of fear the victim reports—60 percent of the sample recorded some fear. The level is high for all age groups. Five of the 10 children asked reported this fear (five were not asked for clinical reasons), 62 percent of the adolescents, and 66 percent of the adults. There is a strong racial division in this factor in that it was reported by 68 percent of the blacks compared to 42 percent of the whites.

Emotional distress was notable in half the cases while discussing the rape with the home visitor. Adults showed such distress 60 percent of the time, while 40 percent of the adolescents were so rated. Also, the more emotional distress shown, the more likely it is that the victim will appear on the high rape credibility score. (This observation parallels adult victims' complaints about police reponse to their allegations.)

In a separate category that records how withdrawn the victim acts, minors were rated more withdrawn than adults, which is consistent with observations from private psychiatric practice. Blacks were generally more withdrawn than whites.

Fear of negative familial reaction is highest in adults (10 percent). We had expected this in the adolescents (6.5 percent). Whites' concern in this area exceeds that of blacks (11 percent to 7 percent).

Finally, the criminal justice status of each case according to the victims' report to the home visitor reflects the following. After an average of twelve days, half the offenders have not been apprehended. Of the half who have been caught, 14 percent are awaiting preliminary hearing, 13 percent are awaiting trial, and for 5 percent the victims have not signed a statement. In 18 percent of the cases, charges have been dropped. The charges are most likely to be dropped for adolescents (35 percent). The offender is least likely to be apprehended for adults (60 percent) and children (40 percent). Adolescents (8 percent) most frequently have not filed a signed statement or are in the awaiting trial category (14 percent). The charges are dropped more by black (22 percent) than by white (10 percent) victims. The offender is not caught in 61 percent of the white victim cases and in 41 percent of the black victim cases.

We are currently correlating many of the factors being collected. Through cluster analysis, we hope to sift out information that can help guide social policy and change public attitudes toward victims of rape. Meanwhile, even before final data analysis, we have noticed many policy changes in the agencies with which we are undertaking this study. The police commissioner has opened a direct line of communication through which we can clarify victim complaints about police actions. Assistant district attorneys have come to discuss their problems in trying to prosecute a case and to solicit more reliable medical and gynecological information. We also advise attorneys to brief victims thoroughly prior to preliminary hearings and court trials so that they can understand their role in the prosecution's case. During sentencing conferences sponsored by the Philadelphia Crime Commission for Trial Judges, we have presented the goals of this study. Judges seem more protective, particularly when trying to spare children from unnecessary courtroom stress. Women volunteers are accompanying victims throughout their contact with the hospital, police, courts, and other agencies. These social changes seem to be developing prior to the conclusions of the data analysis (these changes will have to be taken into consideration as we review progressive segments of our information and when we compare past psychiatric hypotheses with those from the current study). The publicity that such a project attracts may have generated more victim reporting and thereby may account for much of the increase in our population, from an average of 50 cases a month during 1970 and 1971 to 70 cases a month during 1972, 82 cases a month in 1973, and over 100 cases a month in 1974.

CONCLUSIONS

Victims of rape have been subjected to an assault that is not only surrounded with aggression and hostility toward women, but is also complicated by peculiar cultural and personal attitudes toward sex. Immediate assistance and follow-up care can help the victim adjust to the rape and its aftereffects and prevent her further victimization by such prejudices. In an effort to guarantee the constitutional rights of the offender, the criminal justice system exposes the rape victim to skepticism and doubt. These attitudes may protect innocent men, but they also serve as a defense mechanism to spare decent men who are appalled that a fellow man can inflict such brazen and open indignities upon a woman or child. Whatever the source, they impose additional stress upon the victim.

The myths and taboos concerning rape are so deeply embedded in cultural attitudes that victims are forced to cope not only with the emotional problems attendant upon the rape experience itself, but also with the additional burden of irrational reactions of friends and relatives who are aware of the incident. Many of these people find it difficult to believe that the victim did not somehow elicit the rape through her own behavior. This is an area where education of the public is vitally needed in order to eliminate outmoded concepts about rape—concepts that owe their origin in part to the double standard applied to sexual practices in the past. A more realistic attitude on the part of society toward rape will go far in helping the victim adjust to the experience with minimal aftereffects.

Finally, it is our hope that through this program, humane and workable procedures can be established whereby the victim of rape can be assured of understanding and given all the help she needs in recovering from this most harrowing of experiences with the minimum of adverse aftereffects. Our program, which attempts to coordinate all aspects of the victim's postrape experience and needs—police and court system, emergency hospital treatment, home visits, and psychiatric evaluation and aftercare—can, we think, serve as a prototype for the treatment of rape victims in other communities. In this way, the woman who has been raped will no longer have to face the postrape ordeal alone, but will have the enlightened support of the community.

REFERENCES

Amir, Menachem. 1971. *Patterns in Forcible Rape.* Chicago: University of Chicago Press.

Anonymous. 1961. "I Was Raped," *Cosmopolitan* 167(July):34–8.

Gibbens, T. C. N. and Joyce Prince. 1963. *Child Victims of Sex Offences.* London: Institute for the Study and Treatment of Delinquency.

Kinsey, Alfred C., Wardell B. Pomeroy, Clyde E. Martin, and Paul Gebhard. 1953. *Sexual Behavior in the Human Female.* Philadelphia: Saunders.

Landis, Judson T. 1956. "Experiences of 500 Children with Adult Sexual Deviations," *Psychiatric Quarterly,* 30(Supplement):91–109.

Massey, Joe B., Celso-Ramon Garcia, and John P. Ernich, Jr. 1971. "Management of Sexually Assaulted Females," *Obstetrics and Gynecology* 38:29–35.

Sutherland, Sandra and Donald J. Scherl. 1970. "Patterns of Response among Rape Victims," *American Journal of Orthopsychiatry* 40:503–11.

18 A Selective Bibliography

FAITH FOGARTY

THE literature on forcible rape has proliferated at a staggering rate in the past several years making it difficult to keep abreast of all that is being published. However, at the same time, a good portion of the current literature on the subject is becoming repetitive and duplicates much of what has already been written, which is particularly true of articles found in popular magazines and some medical and legal journals. This is not to complain—the problem of rape cannot be overpublicized—but rather to explain why the present bibliography is selective and therefore not a complete representation of all literature on the subject of rape.

Whereas five years ago there was not much available in the way of a bibliography on rape as a separate subject, now such bibliographies are becoming quite common. Rape crisis centers across the country are compiling lists of literature and references relevant to their cause of aiding rape victims and seeking methods to prevent sexual assaults on women. Researchers involved in the study of rape have compiled extensive bibliographies covering all aspects of the crime. Two bibliographies in particular should be noted:

Chappell, D., G. Geis, and F. Fogarty. 1974. "Forcible Rape: Bibliography," *Journal of Criminal Law and Criminology* 65(June):248–63.

Walker, Marcia J., ed. 1975. "Toward the Prevention of Rape: A Bibliography" (partially annotated). Report No. 27, mimeographed. Center for Correctional Psychology, Department of Psychology, University of Alabama, University.

The present bibliography is divided into the following six categories representing the major areas of concern in treating the subject of rape:

1. Sociological and general perspectives
2. Legislative, prosecutive, and judicial aspects of rape
3. Police handling and investigative methods in cases of rape
4. Medical and medicolegal concerns in rape cases
5. Rape victims
6. Rapists

Although certain articles or books on rape may be germane to more than one specific category, no cross references are given in this bibliography. The reader is therefore advised to refer to more than one categorical section when seeking references on facets of rape that could be classified in more than one way.

In regard to rape in foreign countries, the literature written in English on rape in countries other than America and the British Commonwealth is somewhat sparse, and most of that which is written in foreign languages is either not known or not readily available here. Because only a few of the major citation sources used by researchers in America index foreign journals as a matter of course, the foreign literature on rape that is referenced at all in these sources is almost exclusively concerned with medical and medicolegal aspects of examining victims or treatment of sex offenders. Although some foreign articles are included here, this bibliography does not attempt to cover foreign material, since that coverage would be subjectively imbalanced and incomplete in scope.

The main, but not exclusive, sources of citations used in compiling this bibliography were: *Index Medicus, Index to Legal Periodicals, Abstracts in Criminology and Penology, Crime and Delinquency Abstracts, Abstracts on Police Science, Public Affairs Information Service, Sociological Abstracts*, and *Psychological Abstracts.*

SOCIOLOGICAL AND GENERAL PERSPECTIVES

Listed in this section are references to literature describing the phenomenon of forcible rape, its patterns, and the problems it poses in our society and in cultures different from ours. Surveys and comparative studies of rape are included along with more specific facets of the subject such as gang rape, alcohol involvement, and some interracial aspects of rape.

At the end of this section is a short list of published material on homosexual rape. This subject area began to receive attention in rape literature after corrections reform efforts revealed it as a prevalent problem in prisons.

Abbott, Daniel J. and James M. Calonico. 1973. "Black Man, White Woman—The Maintenance of a Myth: Rape and the Press in New Orleans." Mimeographed. Paper prepared in the Department of Sociology, Louisiana State University, Baton Rouge.

Amir, Menachem. 1967. "Alochol and Forcible Rape," *British Journal of Addiction* 62:219–32.

——. 1971. "Forcible Rape," *Sexual Behavior* 1(November):25–36.

——. 1971. *Patterns in Forcible Rape.* Chicago: University of Chicago Press.

Baltimore City Council Task Force on Rape. *Report.* February 1975.

Barber, R. N. 1969. "Prostitution and the Increasing Number of Convictions for Rape in Queensland," *Australian and New Zealand Journal of Criminology* 2(September):169–74.

Baughman, Laurence A. 1966. *Southern Rape Complex: Hundred Years of Psychosis.* Atlanta, Ga.: Pendulum Books.

Blanchard, W. H. 1959. "The Group Process in Gang Rape," *Journal of Social Psychology,* 49(May):259–66.

Boydell, C. L. and C. F. Grindstaff. 1974. "Public Opinion toward Legal Sanctions for Crimes of Violence," *Journal of Criminal Law and Criminology,* 65(March):113–16.

Brown, Julia S. 1952. "A Comparative Study of Deviations from Sexual Mores," *American Sociological Review,* 17(April):135–46.

Brownmiller, Susan. 1975. *Against Our Will: Men, Women and Rape.* New York: Simon & Schuster.

Center for Women Policy Studies. *Rape and Its Victims: A Report for Citizens, Health Facilities, and Criminal Justice Agencies.* By L. Brodyaga, M. Gates, S. Singer, R. Tucker, and R. White. Washington, D.C.: Law Enforcement Assistance Administration, April 1975.

Chriss, N.C. "Rape in Birmingham: Can a Black Be Acquitted?" *Nation,* December 28, 1970, pp. 690–91.

Clinch, Nancy G. and C. Schurr. 1973. "Rape," *Washingtonian Magazine,* 8(June):86–91, 120–24.

Cooper, H. H. A. 1973. "The Law Relating to Sexual Offenses in Peru," *American Journal of Comparative Law,* 21(Winter):86–123.

Csida, June B. and George Csida. 1974. *Rape: How to Avoid It and What to Do about It If You Can't.* Chatsworth, Calif.: Books for Better Living.

Curtis, L. August 1974. "Towards a Cultural Interpretation of Forcible Rape by American Blacks." Paper presented at the 8th World Sociology Congress, Toronto, Ont.

Davis, Angela. 1975. "Joanne Little: The Dialectics of Rape." *Ms* 3(June):74–77, 106–8.

District of Columbia [City Council], Public Safety Committee Task Force on Rape. "Report," July 9, 1973. Mimeographed.

Eidelberg, Ludwig. 1961. *The Dark Urge.* New York: Pyramid Books.

Feldman-Summers, Shirley and Karen Lindner. 1976. "Perceptions of Victims and Defendants in Criminal Assault Cases," *Criminal Justice and Behavior* 3(June):135–50.

Findlay, Barbara. 1974. "The Cultural Context of Rape," *Women Lawyers Journal* 60(Fall):199–206.

Gager, Nancy and Cathleen Schurr. 1976. *Sexual Assault: Confronting Rape in America.* New York: Grosset & Dunlap.

Geis, Gilbert. 1971. "Group Sexual Assaults," *Medical Aspects of Human Sexuality* 5(May):100–13.

Geis, Gilbert and Duncan Chappell. 1971. "Forcible Rape by Multiple Offenders," *Abstracts on Criminology and Penology* 11(July/August):431–36.

Giacinti, Thomas A. and Claus D. Tjaden. 1973. *Study of Rape Offenses Reported to the Denver Police Department, July 1970—June 1972.* Denver, Colo.: Denver Anti-Crime Council.

Ginsberg, G. 1973. "Effects on Men of Increased Sexual Freedom for Women," *Medical Aspects of Human Sexuality* 7(February):66–78.

Goldner, Norman S. 1972. "Rape as a Heinous but Understudied Offense," *Journal of Criminal Law, Criminology and Police Science* 63(September):402–7.

Hayman, C. R., moderator. 1972. "Roundtable: Rape and Its Consequences," *Medical Aspects of Human Sexuality* 6(February):12, 17, 21, 25–27, 31.

Hayman, C. R., C. Lanza, R. Fuentes, and K. Algor. 1972. "Rape in the District of Columbia," *American Journal of Obstetrics and Gynecology* 113(May):91–97.

Herschberger, Ruth. 1970. "Is Rape a Myth?" in *Adam's Rib,* pp. 15–27. New York: Harper & Row.

Hodgens, E. J., I. H. McFadyen, R. J. Failla, and F. M. Daly 1972. "The Offense of Rape in Victoria," *Australian and New Zealand Journal of Criminology* 5(December):225–40.

Horos, Carol V. 1974. *Rape.* New Canaan, Conn.: Tobey.

Karenga, M.R. 1975. "In Defense of Sister Joanne for Ourselves and History," *Black Scholar* 6(July):37–42.

Komiyama, K., I. Matsumoto, T. Doi, and K. Saito. 1970. "Behavior Patterns of Forcible Rape." Part I. "Situational Analysis of Criminals." Part II. "The Interpersonal Relationships of Offender and Victim," *Reports of the National Research Institute of Police Science* (Tokyo), 11(January):50–58, 59–72.

Kraus, J. 1972. "New South Wales: Trends in the Rates of Murder, Manslaughter, and Rape among Male Juveniles, 1956–1969," *Australian and New Zealand Journal of Criminology* 5(September):146–56.

Kutchinsky, Berl. 1973. "The Effect of Easy Availability of Pornography on the Incidence of Sex Crimes: The Danish Experience," *Journal of Social Issues* 29:163–81.

Lear, Martha Weinman. "The American Way of Rape," *Viva,* November 1974, pp. 43–45, 53, 110.

Lester, David. 1974. "Rape and Social Structure," *Psychological Reports,* 35(August):146.

Livneh, Ernst. 1967. "On Rape and the Sanctity of Matrimony," *Israel Law Review* 2(July):415–22.

MacDonald, John M. 1971. *Rape Offenders and Their Victims.* Springfield, Ill.: C. C. Thomas.

——. 1973. "False Accusations of Rape," *Medical Aspects of Human Sexuality* 7(May):170, 174–76, 181–84, 189–93.

——. "Group Rape [with commentaries by others]," *Medical Aspects of Human Sexuality,* 8 (February 1976): 58, 65–66, 68, 73, 78, 80–81.

Minturn, Leigh, Martin Grosse, and Santoah Haider. 1969. "Cultural Patterning of Sexual Beliefs and Behavior," *Ethnology,* 8(July):301–15.

Mintz, Betty. 1973. "Patterns in Forcible Rape: A Review-Essay," *Criminal Law Bulletin,* 9(October):703–10.

Miyazawa, Koichi. 1976. "Victimological Studies of Sexual Crimes in Japan," *Victimology* 1(Spring):107–29.

Murphy, Robert F. 1959. "Social Structure and Sex Antagonism," *Southwestern Journal of Anthropology,* 15:89–98.

National League of Cities–U.S. Conference of Mayors. *Rape.* Washington, D.C., April 1974.

Neville, D. G. 1957. "Rape in Early English Law," *Justice of the Peace and Local Government Review* (London), 121(April 13):223–25.

New South Wales, Bureau of Crime Statistics and Research. *Rape Offences.* Statistical Report 21, December 1974.

Ng, Allan Y. H. 1974. "The Pattern of Rape in Singapore," *Singapore Medical Journal* 15(March):49–50.

Prince George's County Council. "Report of the Task Force to Study the Treatment of the Victims of Sexual Assault." Mimeographed. Prince George's County, Md., March 1973.

Rada, Richard T. 1975. "Alcoholism and Forcible Rape," *American Journal of Psychiatry* 132(April):444–46.

Rasch, Wilfried. 1968. "Gewaltunzucht und Notzucht durch Gruppen jugendlicher Täter [Sexual Assault and Group Rape]," *Kriminalistik* (Hamburg), 22(February):57–60.

Robert, P., C. Pasturaud, A. Krementchousky and T. Lambert. 1970. "Jeunes Adultes Délinquants. Les Viols Collectifs" (Young Adult Delinquents. Group Rape), *Annuals Internationales de Criminologie* (Paris) 9:657–82.

Ruggiero, G. 1975. "Sexual Criminality in the Early Renaissance: Venice 1338–1358," *Journal of Social History,* 8(Summer):18–37.

Russell, Diana E. H. 1975. *The Politics of Rape: The Victim's Perspectives.* New York: Stein & Day.

Sagarin, Edward. 1975. "Forcible Rape and the Problem of the Rights of the Accused," *Intellect,* 103(May–June):515–20.

Schiff, A. F. 1972. "Rape," *Medical Aspects of Human Sexuality* 6(May):76–77, 81–82, 84.

——. 1973. "Rape in Foreign Countries," *Medical Trial Technique Quarterly,* 20(Summer):66–74.

——. 1973. "A Statistical Evaluation of Rape," *Forensic Science,* 2(August):339–49.

——. 1975. "An Unusual Case of Pseudo Rape," *Journal of Forensic Sciences* 20(October):637–42.

Schultz, LeRoy G., ed. 1975. *Rape Victimology.* Springfield, Ill.: C. C. Thomas.

Schwendinger, Julia R. and Herman Schwendinger. 1974. "Rape Myths: In Legal, Theoretical, and Everyday Practice," *Crime and Society: A Journal of Radical Criminology* 1(Spring/Summer):18–26.

Selkin, James. 1975. "Rape," *Psychology Today,* 8(January):71–76.

Shaffer, Helen B. 1972. "Crime of Rape," *Editorial Research Reports,* January 19, pp. 43–60.

Svalastoga, Kaare. 1962. "Rape and Social Structure," *Pacific Sociological Review* 5(Spring):48–53.

——. n.d. "Voldtaegtsforbrydelsen i Sociologisk Belysning" (The Crime of Rape in the Light of Sociology), *Nordisk Tiddskrift för Kriminalvidenskab* (Copenhägen) 49:309–23.

U.S. National Commission on the Causes and Prevention of Violence. *Commission Statement on Violent Crime: Homicide, Assault, Rape, and Robbery.* Washington, D.C., November 1969.

——. *Crimes of Violence.* Vols. 11 & 12. Prepared by D. J. Mulvihill, M. M. Tumin, and L. A. Curtis. Washington, D.C., 1969.

Viano, Emilio. 1974. "Rape and the Law in the United States: An Historical and Sociological Analysis," *International Journal of Criminology and Penology* 2(November 1):317–28.

Woods, G. D. 1969. "Some Aspects of Pack Rape in Sydney," *Australian and New Zealand Journal of Criminology* 2(June):105–19.

Wortis, Joseph. 1939. "Sex Taboos, Sex Offenders and the Law," *Journal of Orthopsychiatry* 9(July):554–64.

Homosexual Rape

Buffum, Peter C. 1972. *Homosexuality in Prisons.* Washington, D.C.: Department of Justice, National Institute of Law Enforcement and Criminal Justice.

Davis, Alan J. 1968. "Sexual Assaults in the Philadelphia Prison System and Sheriff's Vans," *Trans-action,* December, pp. 8–16.

Ibrahim, Azmy Ishak. 1974. "Deviant Sexual Behavior in Men's Prisons," *Crime and Delinquency* (January):38–44.

Kirkham, George L. 1971. "Homosexuality in Prison." In J. M. Henslin, ed., *Studies in Sociology of Sex,* pp. 325–350. New York: Appleton Century Crofts.

Roth, L. H. 1971. "Territoriality and Homosexuality in a Male Prison Population," *American Journal of Orthopsychiatry* 41(3):510–13.

Sagarin, Edward, and Donal E. J. MacNamara. 1973. "The Homosexual as a Crime Victim." In I. Drapkin and E. Viano, eds., *Victimology: A New Focus,* 5:73–85. Lexington, Mass.: Lexington Books.

Scacco, Anthony M. 1975. *Rape in Prison.* Springfield, Ill.: C. C. Thomas.

"Sexual Assaults and Forced Homosexual Relations in Prison: Cruel and Unusual Punishment." *Albany Law Review* 36(2):428–38, 1972.

Vedder, Clyde and P. King. 1965. *Problems of Homosexuality in Corrections.* Springfield, Ill.: C. C. Thomas.

Weiss, Carl and James Friar. 1975. *Terror in the Prisons: Homosexual Rape and Why Society Condones It.* Indianapolis: Bobbs-Merrill.

LEGISLATIVE, PROSECUTIVE, AND JUDICIAL ASPECTS OF RAPE

Blatant inequities found in our system of justice relating, in some cases, to rape offenders, but more often, to rape victims, have caused many states to scrutinize and revamp their rape statutes. In some states, such as New York, California and, in particular, Michigan, changes in the law have been made to help ease the rules of evidence, which in the past have made successful prosecution of rapists a near impossibility, and toward reducing the traumatizing and unfair treatment of rape victims in court.

The majority of references in this section of the bibliography pertain to literature regarding changes in the laws (particularly corroboration and resistance/consent standards), sentencing practices and penalties for rape, and impeachment of the victim's character and her credibility.

Aitken, Janet. 1974. "Rape Prosecutions," *Women Lawyers Journal* 60(Fall):192–98.

Babcock, B. A., A. E. Freedman, E. H. Norton, and S. C. Ross. 1975. "Rape," in *Sex Discrimination and the Law: Causes and Remedies* pp. 820–77. Boston: Little, Brown.

Bailey, F. Lee, and Henry B. Rothblatt. 1973. *Crimes of Violence: Rape and Other Sex Crimes.* Rochester, N.Y.: Lawyers Co-Operative Publishing Co.

Barber, Ross. 1974. "Judge and Jury Attitudes to Rape," *Australian and New Zealand Journal of Criminology* 7(September): 157–72.

Bedau, Hugo Adam. 1976. "Felony Murder Rape and the Mandatory Death Penalty: A Study in Discretionary Justice," *Suffolk University Law Review* 10(Spring): 495–520.

"Capital Punishment for Rape Constitutes Cruel and Unusual Punishment When No Life Is Taken or Endangered [*Ralph* v. *Warden*]," *Minnesota Law Review,* 56:95–110, November 1971.

Carney, Thomas P., Jr. 1971. "Presumption That Trial Judge Disregarded Incompetent Evidence in Reaching His Verdict Does Not Obtain Where an Objection to the Evidence Has Been Overruled," *Loyola University Law Journal* 2(Summer):420–35.

[Cautionary Instruction to the Jury]. "Criminal Law—Rape—Cautionary Instruction in Sex Offense Trial Relating Prosecutrix's Credibility to Nature of the Crime Charged Is No Longer Mandatory; Discretionary Use Is Disapproved. *People* v. *Rincon-Pineda,* 14 Cal. 3d 864, 538 P. 2d 247, 123 Cal. Rptr. 119(1975)," *Fordham Urban Law Journal* 4:419–30, Winter 1976.

Child, Barbara. 1975. "Ohio's New Rape Law: Does It Protect Complainant at the Expense of the Rights of the Accused?" *Akron Law Review* 9(Fall):337–59.

Cobb, Kenneth A. and Nancy R. Schauer. 1974. "Michigan's Criminal Sexual Assault Law," *University of Michigan Journal of Law Reform* 8(Fall):217–36.

Cohen, Sharon G. 1971. "The Eighth Amendment's Proscription of Cruel and Unusual Punishment Precludes Imposition of the Death Sentence for Rape When the Victim's Life Is Neither Taken nor Endangered [*Ralph* v. *Warden*]," *George Washington Law Review* 40(October): 161–72.

Collins, James W. 1976. "Constitutional Law—The Texas Equal Rights Amendment—A Rape Statute That Only Punishes Men Does Not Violate the Texas ERA. *Finley* v. *State,* 527 S.W. 2d 553 (Texas Crim. App. 1975)," *Texas Technical Law Review* 7(Spring):724–31.

"Complainant Credibility in Sexual Offense Cases: A Survey of Character Testimony and Psychiatric Experts," *Journal of Criminal Law and Criminology* 64:67–75, March 1973.

"Corroborating Charges of Rape," *Columbia Law Review* 67:1137–48, June 1967.

"Corroboration Held Necessary to Prove Sexual Abuse in the Third Degree Where Underlying Act is Rape," *New York University Law Review* 44(pt. 2):1025–33, November 1969.

"The Corroboration Rule and Crimes Accompanying a Rape," *University of Pennsylvania Law Review* 118(pt. 1):458–72, January 1970.

Dodson, Mildred B. 1975. "*People* v. *Rincon-Pineda* [(Cal.) 538 P.2d 247]: Rape Trials Depart the Seventeenth Century—Farewell to Lord Hale," *Tulsa Law Journal* 11:279–90.

Dworkin, Roger B. 1966. "The Resistance Standard in Rape Legislation," *Stanford Law Review,* 18(February):680–89.

Eisenberg, Robert L. 1976. "Abolishing Cautionary Instructions in Sex Offense Cases: *People* v. *Rincon-Pineda* [(Cal.) P. 2d 247]," *Criminal Law Bulletin* 12(January/February):58–72.

Eisenbud, Frederick. 1975. "Limitations on the Right to Introduce Evidence Pertaining to the Prior Sexual History of the Complaining Witness in Cases of Forcible Rape: Reflection of Reality or Denial of Due Process," *Hofstra Law Review* 3(Spring):403–26.

"Evidence—Admissibility—In a Trial for Rape, Prosecutrix May Not Be Cross-Examined as to Specific Acts of Prior Sexual Conduct with Men Other Than Defendant, Whether the Purpose of Such Cross-Examination Is to Establish Her Consent as an Affirmative Defense or to Impeach Her Credibility as a Witness. *Lynn* v. *State,* 231 Ga. 559, 203 S.E.2d 221 (1974)," *Georgia Law Review* 8:973–83, Summer 1974.

Florida Civil Liberties Union. *Rape: Selective Electrocution Based on Rape.* Miami [c. 1965].

"Forcible and Statutory Rape: An Exploration of the Operation and Objectives of the Consent Standard," *Yale Law Journal* 62:55–83, December 1952.

Giles, Linda E. 1976. "Admissibility of a Rape-Complainant's Previous Sexual Conduct: The Need for Legislative Reform," *New England Law Review* 11(Spring):497–507.

Gless, Alan G. 1975. "Nebraska's Corroboration Rule," *Nebraska Law Review* 54(1):93–110.

Green, Bernard, 1971. "Disposition of Juvenile Offenders: A Comment on *R.* v. *Turner* and *R.* v. *Haig,*" *Criminal Law Quarterly* (Toronto) 13(June):438–67.

Greenfield, D.E. 1967. "The Prompt Complaint' A Developing Rule of Evidence," *Criminal Law Quarterly* (Toronto) 9(March):286–97.

Grosman, B. 1963. "Drunkenness as a Defence to Rape," *Criminal Law Quarterly* (Toronto) 6(November):148–51.

Harris, Lucy Reed. 1976. "Towards a Consent Standard in the Law of Rape," *University of Chicago Law Review* 43(Spring):613–45.

Hooper, Anthony. 1968. "Fraud in Assault and Rape," *University of British Columbia Law Review* (Vancouver) 3(May):117–30.

Howard, Joseph C., Sr. August 1967. "Administration of Rape Cases in the City of Baltimore and the State of Maryland. Mimeographed, Baltimore: Monumental Bar Association.

"If She Consented Once, She Consented Again—A Legal Fallacy in Forcible Rape Cases," *Valparaiso University Law Review* 10(Fall):127–67, 1975.

Jarret, Tommy W. 1966. "Psychiatric Examination of Prosecutrix in Rape Case," *North Carolina Law Review* 45(December):234–40.

Koh, K.L. 1968. "Consent and Responsibility in Sexual Offences," *Criminal Law Review* (London), February, pp. 81–97; March, pp. 150–162.

Landau, Sybil. 1974. "The Victim as Defendant," *Trial* 10(July/August):19–22.

Le Bourdais, Isabel. 1966. *The Trial of Steven Truscott.* Toronto: McClelland & Stewart.

Leggett, S. 1973. "The Character of Complainants in Sexual Charges," *Chitty's Law Journal* (Windsor, Ont.) 21:132–35.

Ludwig, F. J. 1970. "The Case of Repeal of the Sex Corroboration Requirement in New York," *Brooklyn Law Review* 36(Spring):378–86.

Luginbill, D. H. 1975. "Repeal of the Corroboration Requirement: Will It Tip the Scales of Justice?" *Drake Law Review* 24:669–82.

McCann, Patrick F. D. 1968. "The Nature and Quality of the Act: A Re-Evaluation," *Ottawa Law Review* 3(Fall):340–48.

McDermott, Thomas E., III. 1975. "California Rape Evidence Reform: An Analysis of Senate Bill 1678," *Hastings Law Journal* 26(May): 1551–73.

Machtinger, S. J. 1949. "Psychiatric Testimony for the Impeachment of Witnesses in Sex Cases," *Journal of Criminal Law and Criminology* 39(March/April):750–54.

Maloney, Sharon. 1975. "Rape in Illinois: A Denial of Equal Protection," *John Marshall Journal of Practice and Procedure* 8(Spring):457–96.

Noland, William. 1973–1974. "Other Crimes Evidence to Prove Intent in Rape Cases," *Loyola Law Review* 19(Fall):751–58.

Oestreicher, David. 1971. "Prior Sexual Offenses against a Person Other Than the Prosecutrix," *Tulane Law Review* 46[pt. 1](December):336–43.

Partington, Donald H. 1965. "The Incidence of the Death Penalty for Rape in Virginia," *Washington and Lee Law Review* 22(Spring):43–75.

Pitler, Robert M. 1973. "'Existentialism' and Corroboration of Sex Crimes in New York: A New Attempt to Limit 'If Someone Didn't See It, It Didn't Happen,'" *Syracuse Law Review* 24:1–37.

Ploscowe, Morris. "Rape," in *Sex and the Law,* pp. 165–94. New York: Prentice-Hall, 1951; reprinted in Edward Sagarin and Donal E. J. MacNamara, eds., *Problems of Sex Behavior,* pp. 203–40. New York: T. Y. Crowell.

"Prosecution for Assault with Intent to Rape is Permissible Even after a Prior Acquittal for Rape, and a Present Intent to Rape in the Future Completes the Offense. *Douthit* v. *State,* 482 S.W.2d 155 (Tex. Crim. App. 1971)," *Texas Law Review,* 51:360–68, January 1973.

"Psychiatric Aid in Evaluating the Credibility of a Prosecuting Witness Charging Rape," *Indiana Law Journal* 26:98–103, Fall 1950.

"The Rape Corroboration Requirement: Repeal Not Reform," *Yale Law Journal* 81:1365–91, June 1972.

"Recent Statutory Developments in the Definition of Forcible Rape," *Virginia Law Review* 61:1500–43, November 1975.

Sasko, Helene, and Deborah Sesek. 1975. "Rape Reform Legislation: Is It the Solution?" *Cleveland State Law Review* 24(3):463–503.

Schiff, A. F. 1975. "The New Florida 'Rape' Law," *Journal of the Florida Medical Association* 62(September):40–42.

Schultz, LeRoy G. 1960. "Interviewing the Sex Offender's Victim," *Journal of Criminal Law, Criminology and Police Science* 50(January/February):448–52.

——. 1968. "The Victim-Offender Relationship," *Crime and Delinquency* 14:135–41.

Schwartz, Barry. 1968. "The Effect in Philadelphia of Pennsylvania's Increased Penalties for Rape and Attempted Rape," *Journal of Criminal Law, Criminology, and Police Science* 59(December):509–15.

Scott, I. R. 1975. "Conviction of Secondary Party for Rape Where Principal Acquitted [in *DPP* v. *Morgan* (England)]," *Law Quarterly Review* (London), 91(October):478–82.

Scutt, Jocelynne A. 1976. "Fraud and Consent in Rape: Comprehension of the Nature and Character of the Act and Its Moral Implications," *Criminal Law Quarterly* (Toronto) 18(May):312–24.

Smith, Cyril J. 1974. "History of Rape Laws," *Women Lawyers Journal,* 60(Fall):188–91, 207.

Smith, J. C. 1976. "The Heilbron Report," *Criminal Law Review* (London), February, pp. 97–106.

Sutherlin, Jerrilee. 1976. "Indiana's Rape Shield Law: Conflict with the Confrontation Clause?" *Indiana Law Review* 9(January):418–40.

U.S. Library of Congress, Congressional Research Service. *Rape: State and Federal Law.* By Charles Doyle. Washington, D.C., January 24, 1975.

Washburn, R. Bruce. 1975. "Rape Law: The Need for Reform," *New Mexico Law Review* 5(May):279–309.

Weddington, Sarah. 1975–1976. "Rape Law in Texas: H.B. 284 and the Road to Reform," *American Journal of Criminal Law* 4(1):1–14.

Welch, Deborah. 1976. "Criminal Procedure—Instruction to Jury That Rape Is Easy to Charge and Difficult to Disprove Is No Longer to Be Given. *State* v. *Feddersen,* 230 N.W.2d 510 (Iowa 1975)." *Texas Technical Law Review* 7(Spring):732–37.

Wesolowski, James J. 1976. "Indicia of Consent? A Proposal for Change to the Common Law Rule Admitting Evidence of a Rape Victim's Character for Chastity," *Loyola University Law Journal* 7(Winter):118–40.

Wolfgang, Marvin E. and Marc Riedel. 1975. "Rape, Race, and the Death Penalty in Georgia," *American Journal of Orthopsychiatry* 45(July): 658–68.

Younger, Irving. 1971. "The Requirement of Corroboration in Prosecutions for Sex Offenses in New York," *Fordham Law Review* 40(December):263–78.

POLICE HANDLING AND INVESTIGATIVE METHODS IN CASES OF RAPE

The investigative function of the police in cases of rape is crucial to the apprehension and prosecution of rapists. The apparent increase in the incidence of rape in recent years and the low rate of apprehension of offenders has made the public and some police departments aware of the need to improve police methods of handling rape cases. In some instances, this has resulted in various innovative, and hopefully more effective, procedures such as special rape investigation units and all-female rape squads. Although the police have been notorious for their insensitive, and sometimes hostile, treatment of rape victims, efforts are now being made in some police departments to sensitize the officers to the traumatic effects of rape on victims. It is thought that more sympathetic handling of rape victims will lead to better cooperation between them and the police.

These new attitudes are reflected in some of the literature cited in this section. Much of the other literature cited here deals with investigative methods and aids in apprehending rapists.

Astor, Gerald. 1974. *The Charge is Rape.* New York: Playboy Press.

Bard, Morton, and Katherine Ellison. 1974. "Crisis Intervention and Investigation of Forcible Rape," *Police Chief* 41(May):68–74.

Brown, William P. 1970. "Police-Victim Relationships in Sex Crime Investigations," *Police Chief* 37(January):20–24.

Chase, C., Jr. 1974. "Rape and Police Professionalism," *North Carolina Law Enforcement Journal* 24:67–72, 74–75.

Cottell, Louis C. 1974. "Rape: The Ultimate Invasion of Privacy," *FBI Law Enforcement Bulletin* 43(May):2–6.

Daley, R. 1972. "Rape," in *Target Blue,* pp. 154–60. New York: Delacorte.

Flammang, C. J. 1972. "Interviewing Child Victims of Sex Offenses," *Police,* 16(February):24–28.

Galton, Eric R. 1975. "Police Processing of Rape Complaints: A Case Study," *American Journal of Criminal Law* 4:15–30.

Griffin, Deborah. 1974. "A Self-Defense Program for Women: Be 'SAFE' from Rape," *FBI Law Enforcement Bulletin* 43(December):9–11.

International Association of Chiefs of Police. *Rape Investigation.* IACP Training Key #128. Washington, D.C., 1969.

Leppmann, Friedrich. 1941–1942. "Essential Differences between Sex Offenders," *Journal of Criminal Law and Criminology* 32:366–80.

Lichtenstein, Grace. "Rape Squad," *New York Times Magazine,* March 3, 1974, pp. 10–11, 61–65.

MacDonald, John M. 1969. "Rape," *Police* 13(March/April):42–46.

MacNamara, D. 1971. "Police and Sex: An Interview with a Criminologist," *Sexual Behavior,* 1(April):24–31.

Mant, A. Keith. 1964. "Three Cases of Multiple Rape," *Journal of the Forensic Science Society* (Harrowgate), 4(March):158–61.

O'Connell, L. 1974. *Dial 577-R-A-P-E.* New York: Putnam.

Peto, D. O. G. 1960. "The Taking of Statements from Victims and Witnesses of Sexual Offences," *Criminal Law Review* (London), 7(February):86–89.

"Police Discretion and the Judgment that a Crime Has Been Committed: Rape in Philadelphia," *University of Pennsylvania Law Review* 117:277–322, December 1968.

Putnam, Jerry D. and Denamac Fox. 1976. "A Program to Help the Victims of Crime," *Police Chief* 43(March):36–38.

Rife, Dwight W. 1940–1941. "Scientific Evidence in Rape Cases," *Journal of Criminal Law and Criminology* 31:232–35.

Shook, H. C. 1973. "Revitalized Methods Needed for Investigation of Rape Complaints," *Police Chief* 48(December):14–15.

Still, Agnes. 1975. "Police Enquiries in Sexual Offences," *Journal of the Forensic Science Society* (Harrowgate) 15(July):183–88.

Stratton, John. 1976. "Law Enforcement's Participation in Crisis Counseling for Rape Victims," *Police Chief* 43(March):46–49.

Svensson, Arne and Otto Wendel. 1965. *Techniques of Crime Scene Investigation,* 2d ed. Trans. by Jan Beck. New York: Elsevier.

Vitullo, Louis R. 1974. "Physical Evidence in Rape Cases," *Journal of Police Science and Administration* 2(June):160–63.

Williams, Robert H. "On Sketching the Violent," *Washington Post/Potomac,* August 13, 1972, pp. 10–11, 24–26.

MEDICAL AND MEDICOLEGAL CONCERNS IN RAPE CASES

A large proportion of material published on rape is concerned with medical and medicolegal matters. One of the reasons for this is the sometimes crucial importance of medical evidence and expert testimony in rape court cases. This is stressed in numerous medical journal articles, which are aimed mainly at doctors and provide guidelines for the best methods and procedures to be used for gathering proper and accurate medical evidence from victims. Other subjects covered in this section are: types of injuries sustained by rape victims, pregnancy and abortion following rape, and testing for sperms and seminal stains. Although some of the articles mentioned in this section deal with the medical treatment administered to sexually assaulted woman, more references on this subject can be found under RAPE VICTIMS, where the reader is referred particularly to the articles by Hayman et al.

Bassuk, E., R. Savitz, S. McCombie, and S. Pell. 1975. "Organizing a Rape Crisis Program in a General Hospital," *Journal of the American Medical Women's Association,* 30(December):486–90.

Bornstein, F. P. 1963. "Investigation of Rape: Medicolegal Problems," *Medical Trial Technique Quarterly,* Annual (March 1963), pp. 229–39.

Breen, J. L., E. Greenwald, and C.A. Gregori. 1972. "The Molested Young Female; Evaluation and Therapy of Alleged Rape," *Pediatric Clinics of North America* 19(August):717–25.

Capraro, Vincent J. 1967. "Sexual Assault of Female Children," *Annals of the New York Academy of Sciences* 142(May 10):817–19.

"Certification of Rape under the Colorado Abortion Statute," *University of Colorado Law Review* 42:121–28, 1970.

Chapman, M. G. 1969. "Postcoital Estrogens in Cases of Rape," *New England Journal of Medicine* 280(January 30):277.

Clark, J. H. and M. X. Zarrow. 1971. "Influence of Copulation on Time of Ovulation in Women," *American Journal of Obstetrics and Gynecology* 109(April 1):1083–85.

Cowan, Mary E. 1964. "Unusual Trace Evidence in a Case of Sexual Offense," *Acta Medicinae Legalis et Socialis* (Liège), 17(January/March):71–73.

Enos, W. F. and J. C. Beyer. 1974. "Standard Rape Investigation Form," *Virginia Medical Monthly,* 101(January):43–44.

Enos, W. F., J. C. Beyer, and G. T. Mann. 1972. "The Medical Examination of Cases of Rape," *Journal of Forensic Sciences* 17(January):50–56.

Eungprabhanth, V. 1974. "Finding of the Spermatozoa in the Vagina Related to Elapsed Time of Coitus," *Journal of Legal Medicine* 74:301–4.

Evrard, John R. 1971. "Rape: The Medical, Social, and Legal Implications," *American Journal of Obstetrics and Gynecology* 111(September 15):197–99.

Fisher, Russell S. 1949. "Acid Phosphatase Tests as Evidence of Rape," *New England Journal of Medicine,* 240[pt.2](May 5):738–39.

Graves, L. and J. Francisco. 1970. "Medicolegal Aspects of Rape," *Medical Aspects of Human Sexuality* 4(April):109–20.

Griffiths, P. D. and H. Lehmann. 1964. "Estimation of Creatine Phosphokinase as an Additional Method for Identification of Seminal Stains," *Medicine, Science and the Law* (London), 4(January):32–34.

Hartman, Robert. 1974. "Rape," *Illinois Medical Journal,* 145(June): 518–19.

Hayman, C.R. 1974. "Serological Tests for Syphilis in Rape Cases," *Journal of the American Medical Association,* 228:1227–28.

Hayman, C. R., C. Lanza, and E. C. Noel. 1973. "What to Do for Victims of Rape," *Medical Times* 101(June):47–51.

Helpern, Milton and Alexander Wiener. 1961. "Grouping of Semen in Cases of Rape," *Fertility and Sterility,* 12(November/December):551–53.

Kivela, Edgar W. 1964. "On Finding Spermatozoa in Suspected Seminal Stains," *Journal of Forensic Sciences* 9(January):138–39.

Louie, Steven. 1975. "Rape and Nursing Intervention: Locating Resources," *Imprint* 22(December):27, 32–33, 51.

McCombie, Sharon L., Ellen Bassuk, Roberta Savitz, and Susan Pell. 1976. "Development of a Medical Center Rape Crisis Intervention Program," *American Journal of Psychiatry* 133(April):418–21.

McGuire, L. S. and Michael Stern. 1976. "Survey of Incidence of and Physicians' Attitudes toward Sexual Assault," *Public Health Reports* 91(March/April):103–9.

Marcinkowski, T. and Z. Przybylski. 1966. "Seminal Stains: A Simple Device for Their Determination," *Journal of Forensic Medicine* (Johannesburg), 13(October/December):130–33.

Massey, J. B., C.-R. Garcia, and J. P. Emich, Jr. 1971. "Management of Sexually Assaulted Females," *Obstetrics and Gynecology* 38(July):29–36.

"Medical Testimony in a Criminal Rape Case, Showing the Direct and Cross-Examination of the Bacteriologist and Psychiatrists, and Including the Court's Instructions to the Jury," *Medical Trial Technique Quarterly,* Annual (March and June 1963), pp. 287–355.

Paul, David M. 1975. "The Medical Examination in Sexual Offences," *Medicine, Science and the Law* (London), 15(July):154–62.

Paulshock, B. and M. V. Andersen. 1970. "Estrogen Therapy after Rape?" *Annals of Internal Medicine* 72(June):961.

Ringrose, C. A. D. 1968. "Medical Assessment of the Sexually Assaulted Female," *Medical Trial Technique Quarterly,* Annual (December 1968), pp. 245–47.

Root, I., W. Ogden, and W. Scott. 1974. "The Medical Investigation of Alleged Rape," *Western Journal of Medicine,* 120(April):329–33.

Rupp, Joseph C. 1969. "Sperm Survival and Prostatic Acid Phosphatase Activity in Victims of Sexual Assault," *Journal of Forensic Sciences,* 14(April):177–82.

"Rx for Rape: The Listening Ear," *Emergency Medicine,* 7:240–63, February 1975.

Schiff, A. F. 1969. "Modification of the Berg Acid Phosphatase Test," *Journal of Forensic Sciences* 14(October):538–44.

Thomas, F. and W. Van Hecke. 1963. "The Demonstration of Recent Sexual Intercourse in the Male by the Lugol Method," *Medicine, Science and the Law* (London) 3(April):169–71.

RAPE VICTIMS

It is only in recent years that the plight of rape victims has been fully perceived and publicized. The rise in recognition of the rape victim's trauma as a legitimate and proper public concern parallels the emergence of the women's movement in this country.

Very little literature dated prior to the late sixties deals with victims of rape in a sympathetic manner; most of the material at that time showed an almost protective attitude toward accused rapists, who often have been portrayed as the innocent victims of vengeful, neurotic women. It is therefore not surprising that rape laws were devised in such a way as to make the prosecution's burden of proof inordinately heavy. (See under Legislative, Prosecutive, and Judicial Aspects of Rape for references to rape statutes.)

Credit must go to the women's movement, which espoused rape as one of its major causes, for wakening in society an awareness of the inequities meted out to rape victims and the insensitive, if not hostile, treatment they are given by officials in our justice system. The psychological trauma of rape victims and society's response—both positive and negative—are poignantly described in the literature cited in this section. The current movement seems to be toward an increasingly positive response to rape victims. Evidence of this is seen in the proliferation of rape crisis centers and the instituting of special hospital and police procedures for more sensitive handling of rape victims. (For more general material on rape and rape victims, see under Sociological and General Perspectives. Articles dealing with the court's concern with the credibility and character of the rape victim are cited under Legislative, Prosecutive, and Judicial Aspects of Rape.)

Bohmer, Carol, and Audrey Blumberg. "Twice Traumatized: The Rape Victim and the Court," *Judicature* 58(March):391–99.

Bond, J. 1975. "Self-Defense against Rape: The Joanne Little Case," *Black Scholar,* 6(March):29–31.

Boston Women's Book Collective. 1973. "Rape and Self-Defense." In *Our Bodies, Ourselves: A Book by and for Women,* pp. 92–97. New York: Simon & Schuster.

Burgess, Ann Wolbert and Lynda Lytle Holstrom. 1973. "The Rape Victim in the Emergency Ward," *American Journal of Nursing* 73(October):1741–45.

——. 1974. "Crisis Counseling Requests of Rape Victims," *Nursing Research,* 23(May/June):196–202.

——. 1974. *Rape: Victims of Crisis.* Bowie, Md.: Brady.

——. 1975. "Sexual Assault: Signs and Symptoms," *Journal of Emergency Nursing* (March/April), pp. 11–15.

——. 1975. "Sexual Trauma of Children and Adolescents," *Nursing Clinics of North America,* 10(September):551–63.

——. 1976. "Coping Behavior of the Rape Victim," *American Journal of Psychiatry* 133(April):413–18.

Curtis, Lynn. 1974. "Victim Precipitation and Violent Crime," *Social Problems,* 21(Spring):594–605.

De Francis, Vincent. 1971. "Protecting the Child Victim of Sex Crimes Committed by Adults," *Federal Probation* 35(September):15–20.

Devereux, George. 1957. "The Awarding of a Penis as Compensation for Rape: A Demonstration of the Clinical Relevance of the Psychoanalytic Study of Cultural Data," *International Journal of Psycho-Analysis,* 38(November/December):398–401.

Donadio, B. and M. A. White. 1974. "Seven Who Were Raped," *Nursing Outlook,* 22(April):245–47.

Factor, Morris. 1954. "A Woman's Psychological Reaction to Attempted Rape," *Psychoanalytic Quarterly* 23:243–44.

Gagnon, John. 1965. "Female Child Victims of Sex Offenses," *Social Problems* 13:176–92.

Georgia Department of Human Resources. *Rape and the Treatment of Rape Victims in Georgia: A Study by the Georgia Commission on the Status of Women.* Atlanta, 1974.

Gill, Sally. 1975. "Victims of Sexual Assault," *Imprint,* 22(December):24–26.

Greer, Germaine. 1973. "Seduction Is a Four-Letter Word," *Playboy,* January 1973, pp. 80, 82, 164, 178, 224, 226, 228.

Hardgrove, Grace. 1976. "An Interagency Service Network to Meet Needs of Rape Victims," *Social Casework,* 57(April):245–53.

Hartwig, Patricia A. and Georgette Bennett Sandler. 1975. "Rape Victims: Reasons, Responses, and Reforms," *Intellect,* 103:507–11.

Hayman, C. R. 1970. "Sexual Assaults on Women and Girls," *Annals of Internal Medicine* 72(February):277–78.

Hayman, C. R. and C. Lanza. 1971. "Sexual Assault on Women and Girls," *American Journal of Obstetrics and Gynecology* 109(February):480–86.

——. 1971. "Victimology of Sexual Assault," *Medical Aspects of Human Sexuality* 5(October):152, 157–161.

Hayman, C. R., C. Lanza, and R. Fuentes. 1969. "Sexual Assault on Women and Girls in the District of Columbia," *Southern Medical Journal* 62(October):1227–31.

Hayman, C. R., W. F. Stewart, F. R. Lewis, and M. Grant. 1968. "Sexual Assault on Women and Children in the District of Columbia," *Public Health Reports* 83(December):1021–23.

Hilberman, Elaine. 1976. *The Rape Victim.* Washington, D.C.: American Psychiatric Association.

Hogan, Walter L. 1974. "The Raped Child," *Medical Aspects of Human Sexuality,* 8(November):129–30.

Holmstrom, L. L. and A. W. Burgess. 1975. "Rape: The Victim and the Criminal Justice System," *International Journal of Criminology and Penology* 3(May):101–10.

"How They Help Rape Victims at the University of Chicago," *Resident and Staff Physicians* 32(August):31–32, 1973.

"How to Start a Rape Crisis Center." Mimeographed. Washington, D.C.: Rape Crisis Center, August 1972.

Jones, Cathaleene and Elliot Aronson. 1973. "Attribution of Fault to a Rape Victim as a Function of the Respectability of the Victim," *Journal of Personality and Social Psychology* 26(June):415–19.

Kalven, Harry, Jr. and Hans Zeisel. 1966. "Contributory Fault of the Victim," in *The American Jury,* pp. 249–57. Boston: Little, Brown.

Koupernik, C., P. M. Masciangelo, and S. Balestra-Beretta. 1972. "A Case of Heller's Dementia Following Sexual Assault in a Four-Year-Old Girl," *Child Psychiatry and Human Development* 2(Spring):134–44.

Lake, Alice. 1971. "Rape: The Unmentionable Crime," *Good Housekeeping,* November 1971, pp. 104–5, 188, 190, 194–96.

Lamborn, LeRoy L. 1976. "Compensation for the Child Conceived in Rape," *Victimology* 1(Spring):84–97.

Lear, Martha Weinman. 1972. "Q. If You Rape a Woman and Steal Her TV, What Can They Get You for in New York? A. Stealing Her TV." *New York Times Magazine,* January 30, pp. 11, 55, 60, 62, 63.

Lee, Betty. 1972. "Precautions against Rape," *Sexual Behavior,* 2(January):33–37.

Lewis, M., and P. M. Sarrel. 1969. "Some Psychological Aspects of Seduction, Incest, and Rape in Childhood," *Journal of the American Academy of Child Psychiatry* 8(October):606–19.

Lipton, G. L. and E. I. Roth. 1969. "Rape: A Complex Management Problem in the Pediatric Emergency Room," *Journal of Pediatrics* 75(November):859–66.

McCarthy, Colman. 1973. "In a Victim's Eye: The Aftermath of a Rape—A Refusal to Forget," *Washington Post/Potomac,* July 15, 1973, pp. 12, 13, 28.

McCombie, Sharon L. 1976. "Characteristics of Rape Victims Seen in Crisis Intervention," *Smith College Studies in Social Work* 46(March):137–58.

Medea, Andra and Kathleen Thompson. 1974. *Against Rape: A Survival Manual for Women. How to Avoid Entrapment and How to Cope with Rape Physically and Emotionally.* New York: Farrar, Straus & Giroux.

Meyer, Mary. 1974. "Rape: The Victim's Point of View," *Police Law Quarterly,* 3:38–44.

Nelson, Steve, and Menachem Amir. 1975. "The Hitchhike Victim of Rape: A Research Report." In I. Drapkin and E. Viano, eds., *Victimology,* 5:47–64. Lexington, Mass.: Lexington Books.

Notman, Malah T. and Carol C. Nadelson. 1976. "The Rape Victim: Psychodynamic Considerations," *American Journal of Psychiatry* 133(April):408–13.

Peters, J. J. 1973. "Child Rape: Defusing a Psychological Time Bomb," *Hospital Physician,* 9(February):46–49.

Roth, E. I. 1972. "Emergency Treatment of Raped Children," *Medical Aspects of Human Sexuality* 6(August):84–85, 89–91.

Roy, K. K. 1975. "Feelings and Attitudes of Raped Women of Bangladesh towards Military Personnel of Pakistan." In I. Drapkin and E. Viano, eds., *Victimology,* 5:65–72. Lexington, Mass.: Lexington Books.

Schultz, LeRoy G. 1973. "The Child Sex Victim: Social, Psychological and Legal Perspectives," *Child Welfare* 52(March):147–57.

Sebba, Leslie and Cahan Sorel. "Sex Offenses: The Genuine and the Doubted Victim." In I. Drapkin and E. Viano, eds., *Victimology,* 5:29–46. Lexington, Mass.: Lexington Books.

Selkin, James. "Rape," *Psychology Today,* January 1975, pp. 70–72, 74, 76.

Sheehy, Gail. "Nice Girls Don't Get into Trouble," *New York,* February 15, 1971, pp. 26–30.

Storaska, Frederick. 1975. *How to Say No to a Rapist—and Survive.* New York: Random House, 1975.

Sutherland, Sandra and Donald J. Scherl. 1970. "Patterns of Response among Victims of Rape," *American Journal of Orthopsychiatry* 40(April):503–11.

Symonds, Martin. 1976. "The Rape Victim: Psychological Patterns of Response," *American Journal of Psychoanalysis,* 36(Spring):27–34.

Weis, Kurt, and Sandra S. Borges. 1973. "Victimology and Rape: The Case of the Legitimate Victim," *Issues in Criminology* 8(Fall):71–115.

Weiss, E. H., N. Taub, and J. Rosenthal. 1972. "The Mental Health Committee: Report of the Subcommittee on the Problem of Rape in the District of Columbia," *Medical Annals of the District of Columbia* 41(November):703–4.

Werner, Arnold. 1972. "Rape: Interruption of the Therapeutic Process by External Stress," *Psychotherapy: Theory, Research and Practice* 9(Winter):349–51.

Williams, C. C. and R. A. Williams. 1973. "Rape: A Plea for Help in the Hospital Emergency Room," *Nursing Forum* 12:388–401.

Wilson, Cassandra and Noreen Connell. 1974. *Rape: The First Sourcebook for Women.* New York: New American Library.

Wood, Jim. 1976. *The Rape of Inez Garcia.* New York: Putnam.

Woods, Pamela Lakes. 1973. "The Victim in a Forcible Rape Case: A Feminist View," *American Criminal Law Review* 11(Winter):335–54.

RAPISTS

There appears to be such variability in the motivating circumstances and psychodynamics of men who rape that trying to devise a general typology to fit them all is difficult, if not impossible. Nevertheless, much of the literature cited in this section represents studies on sex offenders, including rapists, which attempt to find ways of categorizing them as to family history, education, age, psychological and, in some cases, biological makeup. The rest of the literature cited here is mainly concerned with therapeutic treatment of offenders, including the controversial use of castration. (For material written on the penalties for convicted rapists, see under Legislative, Prosecutive, and Judicial Aspects of Rape.)

Baker, D., M. A. Telfer, C. E. Richardson, and G. R. Clark. 1970. "Chromosome Errors in Men with Antisocial Behavior: Comparison of Selected Men with Klinefelter's Syndrome and XYZ Chromosome Pattern," *Journal of the American Medical Association* 214(November):869–78.

Beit-Hallahmi, B. 1971. "Motivation for Murder: The Case of G," *Corrective Psychiatry and Journal of Social Therapy* 17:25–30.

Brancale, R., A. Vuocolo, and W. E. Prendergast, Jr. 1971. "The New Jersey Program for Sex Offenders," *International Psychiatry Clinics* 8:145–64.

Bromberg, Walter and Elizabeth Coyle. 1974. "Rape: A Compulsion to Destroy," *Medical Insight* (April), pp. 21–22, 24–25.

Burgess, A. W. and L. L. Holmstrom. 1974. "The Rapist's View of Rape," in *Rape: Victims of Crisis,* pp. 21–34. Bowie, Md.: Brady.

Campbell, Horace E. 1967. "The Violent Sex Offender: A Consideration of Emasculation in Treatment," *Rocky Mountain Medical Journal* 64(June):40–43.

Cohen, M. and H. Kozol. 1966. "Evaluation for Parole at a Sex Offender Treatment Center," *Federal Probation* 30(March):50–55.

Cormier, B. M. and S. P. Simons. 1969. "The Problem of the Dangerous Sex Offender," *Canadian Psychiatric Association Journal* 14:329–35.

Costell, R. and I. Yalom. 1971. "Treatment of the Sex Offender: Institutional Group Therapy," *International Psychiatry Clinics* 8:119–44.

Denenberg, R. V. 1974. "Sex Offenders Treat Themselves," *Corrections Magazine,* 1:53–64.

De River, J. P. 1949. *The Sexual Criminal: A Psychoanalytical Study.* Springfield, Ill.: C. C. Thomas.

Dix, George E. 1975. "Determining the Continued Dangerousness of Psychologically Abnormal Sex Offenders," *Journal of Psychiatry and the Law* 3:327–44.

Ellis, Albert and Ralph Brancale. 1956. *The Psychology of Sex Offenders.* Springfield, Ill.: C. C. Thomas.

Evrard, Franklin H. 1971. "The Sex Offender," In *Successful Parole,* pp. 88–93. Springfield, Ill.: C. C. Thomas.

Falk, G. J. 1964. "The Public Image of the Sex Offender," *Mental Hygiene* 48(October):612–20.

Field, L. H. 1973. "Benperiodol in the Treatment of Sexual Offenders," *Medicine, Science and the Law* (London), 13(July):195–96.

Fisher, Gary and Ephraim Rivlin. 1971. "Psychological Needs of Rapists," *British Journal of Criminology* 11(April):182–85.

Gaensbauer, T. J. 1973. "Castration in Treatment of Sex Offenders: An Appraisal," *Rocky Mountain Medical Journal* 70(April):23–28.

Garrett, Thomas B. and Richard Wright. 1975. "Wives of Rapists and Incest Offenders," *Journal of Sex Research* 11(May):149–57.

Gebhard, Paul and John Gagnon 1964. "Male Sex Offenders against Very Young Children," *American Journal of Psychiatry* 121:576–79.

Gebhard, Paul, John Gagnon,. W. B. Pomeroy, and C. Christenson. 1965. *Sex Offenders: An Analysis of Types.* New York: Harper & Row.

Goldstein, M., H. Kant, L. Judd, C. Rice, and R. Green. 1971. "Experience with Pornography: Rapists, Pedophiles, Homosexuals, Transsexuals, and Controls," *Archives of Sexual Behavior* 1:1–15.

Halleck, Seymour. 1971. "Treatment of the Sex Offender: The Therapeutic Encounter," *International Psychiatry Clinics* 8:1–20.

Hartman, A. A. and R. C. Nicolay. 1966. "Sexually Deviant Behavior in Expectant Fathers," *Journal of Abnormal Psychology* 71(June):232–34.

Henn, Fritz A., Marijan Herjanic, and Robert H. Vanderpearl. 1976. "Forensic Psychiatry: Profiles of Two Types of Sex Offenders," *American Journal of Psychiatry,* 133(June):694–96.

Hitchens, E. W. 1972. "Denial: An Identified Theme in Marital Relationships of Sex Offenders," *Perspectives in Psychiatric Care* 10:152–59.

Howell, L. M. 1972–1973. "Clinical and Research Impressions Regarding Murder and Sexually Perverse Crimes," *Psychotherapy and Psychosomatics* 21:156–59.

Kant, H. S. 1971. "Exposure to Pornography and Sexual Behavior in Deviant and Normal Groups," *Correctional Psychiatry and Journal of Social Therapy,* 12:5–17.

Karacan, I., R. L. Williams, M. W. Guerrero, and P. J. Salis. 1974. "Nocturnal Penile Tumescence and Sleep of Convicted Rapists and Other Prisoners," *Archives of Sexual Behavior* 3(January):19–26.

Kercher, G. A. and C. E. Walker. 1973. "Reactions of Convicted Rapists to Sexually Explicit Stimuli," *Journal of Abnormal Psychology* 81(February):46–50.

Kerr, N. 1972. "Special Handling for Sex Offenders," *Perspectives in Psychiatric Care,* 10:160–62.

Kozol, Harry L. 1963. "The Medico-Legal Problem of Sexually Dangerous Persons," *Acta Medicinae Legalis et Socialis* (Liége), 16(April/June):125–28.

McCaldron, R. J. 1967. "Rape," *Canadian Journal of Corrections* 9(January):37–59.

MacDonald, G. J., R. Williams, and H. R. Nichols. 1968."Treatment of the Sex Offender." Mimeographed. Fort Steilacoom, Wash.: Western State Hospital.

MacDonald, J. M. 1973. "Castration for Rapists?" *Medical Aspects of Human Sexuality* 7:12, 17, 20, 25–27.

Manville, W. H. 1974. "Mind of the Rapist," *Cosmopolitan,* 176(January):74.

Marshall, W. L. and R. D. McKnight. 1975. "An Integrated Treatment Program for Sexual Offenders," *Canadian Psychiatric Association Journal,* 20(March):133–38.

Mohr, J. W. 1971. "Treatment of the Sex Offender: Evaluation of Treatment," *International Psychiatry Clinics* 8:227–42.

Oates, W. E. 1971. "Treatment of the Sex Offender: Religious Attitudes and Pastoral Counseling," *International Psychiatry Clinics* 8:41–52.

Orno, Anne Marie. 1965. "Social, Psychological and Surgical Treatment for Sexual and Chronic Criminals," *Canadian Journal of Corrections* 7(October):414–22.

Pacht, Asher and James E. Cowden. 1974. "An Exploratory Study of 500 Sex Offenders," *Criminal Justice and Behavior* 1:13–20.

Perdue, W. C. and D. Lester. 1972. "Personality Characteristics of Rapists." *Perceptual and Motor Skills* 35(October):514.

Peters, J. J., J. M. Pedigo, J. Steg, and J. J. McKenna. 1968. "Group Psychotherapy of the Sex Offender," *Federal Probation* 32(September):41–45.

Peters, J. J. and R. L. Sadoff. 1971. "Psychiatric Services for Sex Offenders on Probation," *Federal Probation* 35(September):32–37.

Polak, Paul. 1971. "Social Systems Intervention," *Archives of General Psychiatry,* 25(August):110–17.

Revitch, Eugene. 1965. "Sex Murder and the Potential Sex Murderer," *Diseases of the Nervous System* 26(October):640–48.

Rogers, Kenneth P. 1974. *For One Sweet Grape.* New York: Playboy Press.

Salerno, Marie. "Violence, Not Sex: What Rapists Really Want." *New York,* June 23, 1975, pp. 36–40.

Schultz, Terri. 1974. "Rapists," *Viva,* November 1974, pp. 46, 95, 104.

Serrill, Michael S. 1974. "Treating Sex Offenders in New Jersey: The ROARE Program," *Corrections Magazine* 1:12–24.

Shultz, Gladys Denny. 1965. *How Many More Victims? Society and the Sex Criminal.* Philadelphia: Lippincott.

Soothill, K. L., A. Jack, and T. C. N. Gibbens. 1976. "Rape: A 22-Year Cohort Study," *Medicine, Science and the Law* (London), 16(January):62–69.

Sturrup, G. K. 1971. "Treatment of the Sex Offender. Castration: The Total Treatment," *International Psychiatry Clinics* 8:175–96.

Sullivan, Peter. 1976. "Commitment of Sexual Psychopaths and the Requirements of Procedural Due Process," *Fordham Law Review* 44(April):923–49.

Takakuwa, M., Y. Matsumoto, and T. Sato. 1971. "A Psychological Study of Rape," *Bulletin of the Criminological Research Department* (Ministry of Justice, Japan), pp. 36–38.

Texas Department of Corrections, Division of Research. 1971. *The Sex Offender: A Statistical Report.* Research Report No. 6, prepared by J. E. Mabry et al., Huntsville.

Williams, Arthur Hyatt. 1965. "Rape-Murder." In Ralph Slovenko, ed., *Sexual Behavior and the Law* pp. 563–77. Springfield, Ill.: C. C. Thomas.

Willie, W. S. 1961. "Case Study of a Rapist: An Analysis of the Causation of Criminal Behavior," *Journal of Social Therapy* 7:10–22.

Wisconsin, Public Welfare Department. *Wisconsin's First Eleven Years of Experience with Its Sex Crimes Law, July, 1951 through June, 1963.* Statistical Bulletin C46. Madison, April 1965.

Index